AF605878

Livio Orazio Valentini

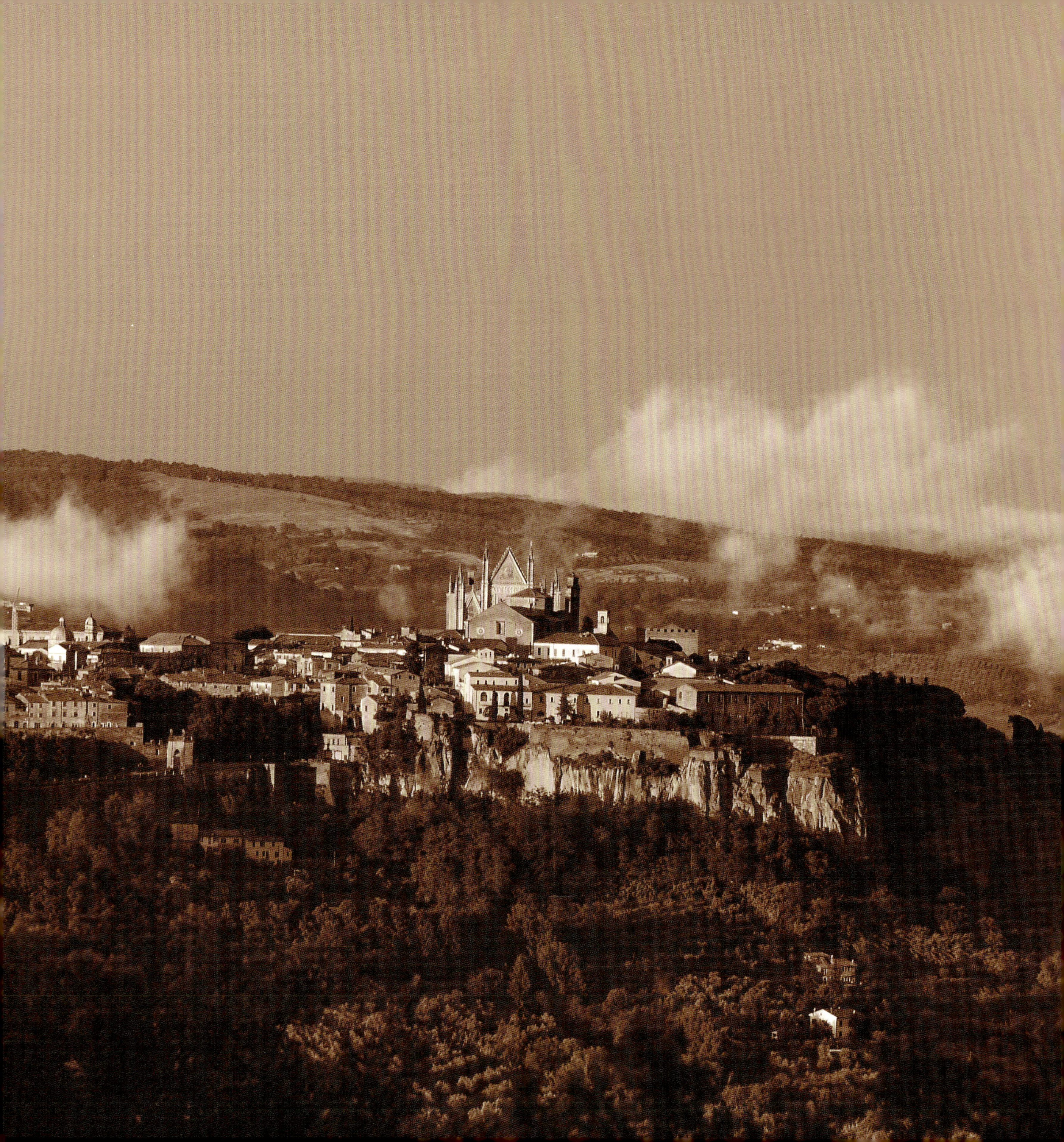

Livio Orazio Valentini

An Artist's Spiritual Odyssey

Robert E. Alexander *and* John A. Elliott

With Erika Pauli Bizzarri

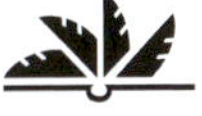

THE UNIVERSITY OF SOUTH CAROLINA PRESS

Publication is made possible in part by the generous support of Security Federal Bank.

Published by the University of South Carolina Press
Columbia, South Carolina 29208

www.sc.edu/uscpress

Manufactured in China

27 26 25 24 23 22 21 20 19 18 10 9 8 7 6 5 4 3 2 1

Library of Congress Cataloging-in-Publication Data can be found at http://catalog.loc.gov/.

ISBN: 978-1-61117-898-2 (cloth)
ISBN: 978-1-61117-899-9 (ebook)

To

Leslie, Lara and family,

and Rob and family

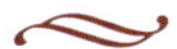

In memory of

Herschell and Savilla Elliott

Contents

Preface

In May 2003, Maestro Livio Orazio Valentini arrived at the Etherredge Center on the campus of the University of South Carolina Aiken (USCA) to unveil the painting *Galassia,* his galaxy for the new millennium. This highly original composition was the culminating achievement of a six-year relationship between Aiken and Orvieto, a hilltop town in the heart of Umbria where Valentini had lived since he was two years

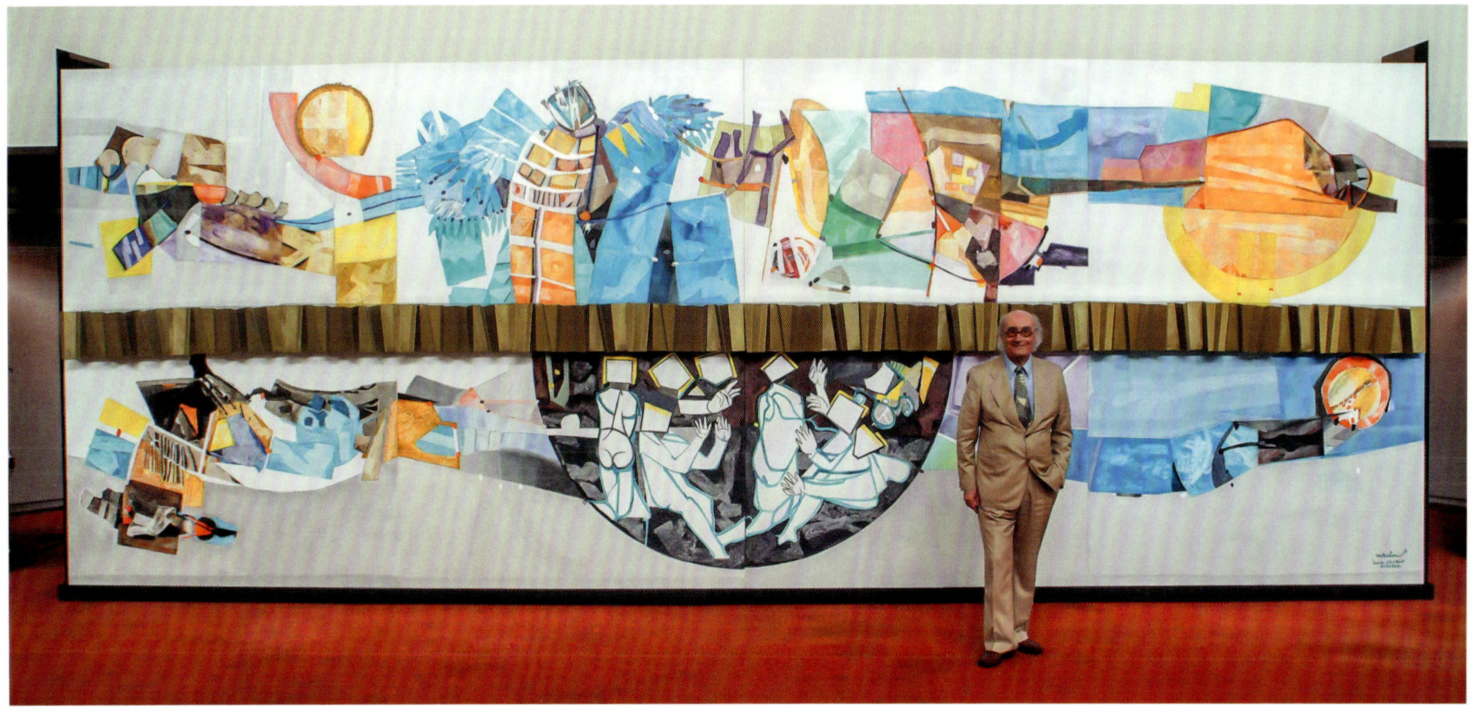

Livio Orazio Valentini with *Galassia* in the Etherredge Center Gallery. Photograph by Scott Webster.

old. *Galassia* was the capstone of the Maestro's painting career and a magnificent summary of his personal philosophy.

This book will serve as a memorial to Livio who passed away in July of 2008 at the age of eighty-seven. We will recount the Maestro's spiritual odyssey beginning with his confinement as a prisoner of war at Buchenwald and including the role he and his wife Flora played in founding the Istituto d'Arte in Orvieto. Our volume will also trace the course of Livio's life as an artist, from his early education to his time in Rome, the various periods in his art, his involvement in Aiken, and his subsequent career until his death. In his breathtaking imagery, Livio revealed his native heritage: a synthesis of Etruscan, medieval and Renaissance art, voiced in a post-modern style. Livio often spoke about the human condition through the metaphor of a caged bird. This gentle man taught all of us how compassion could overcome oppression, how art could bring cleansing, and hope could conquer fear. In the shadow of 9/11, Livio wrote that he hoped *Galassia* would "give us the chance to get in touch with the eternity in our

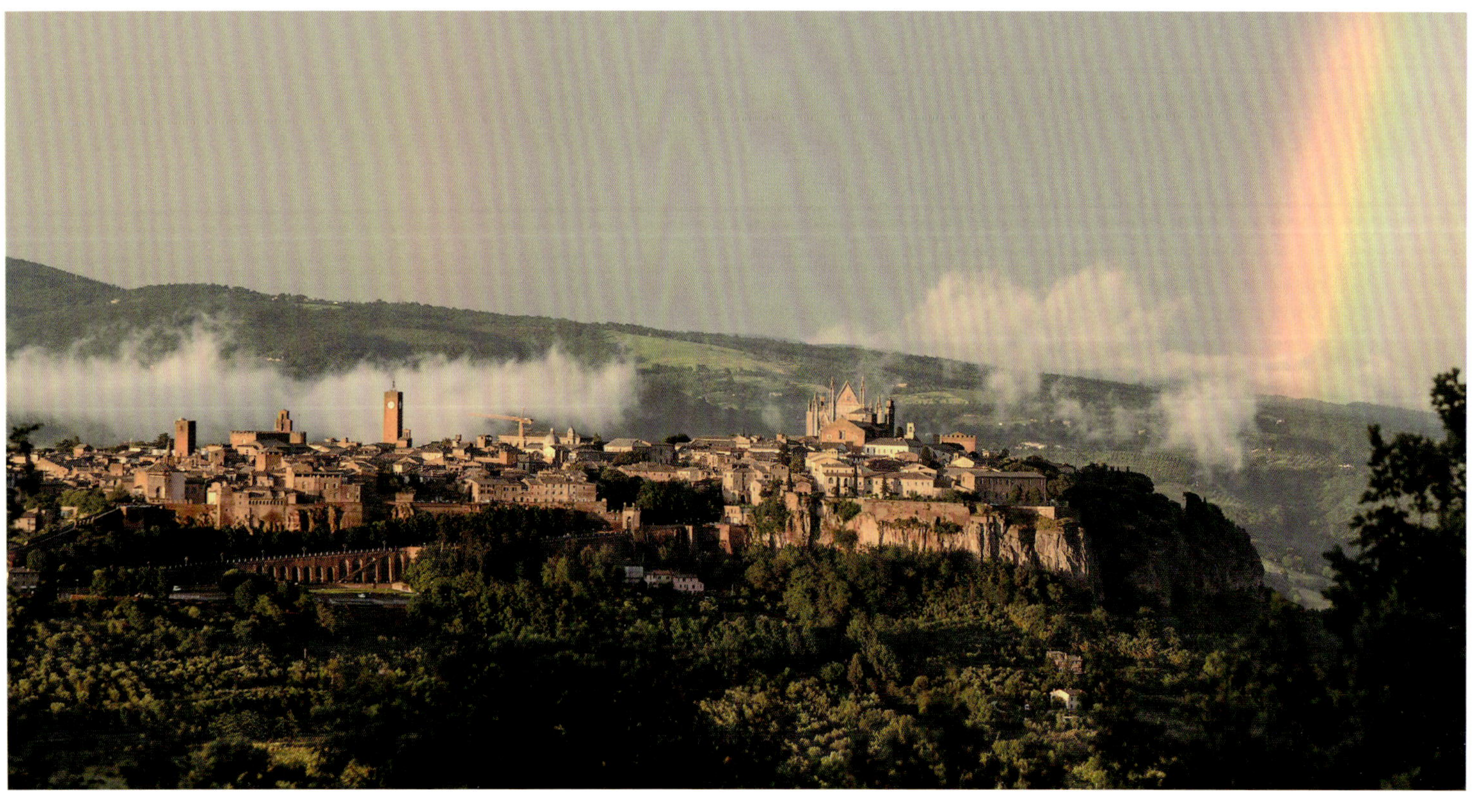

City of Orvieto, Italy. Photograph by Michael St. John.

deepest selves." May those who read our words come to appreciate our friend Livio, who suffered through war and returned to strive for peace. For USC Aiken and the citizens of our city, we remember Livio as our beloved friend, our Maestro for the millennium.

Livio's life and art were about his efforts to find freedom. The person who first suggested this explanation was Valeriano Venturi, a lawyer and Livio's friend. In an effort to understand Orvieto, he told us one had to go back to the thirteenth century when the society of the city and surrounding region was based on a lord and serf relationship. He traced the history through successive iterations of closed societies to the present. Throughout the centuries it continued to be a highly structured society and people were defined by their heritage and the circumstances of their birth. From Venturi's point of view, the ruling class of Orvieto was not open to outsiders rewriting their past to create a new future. Someone like Livio, who came from the small town of San Venanzo at the age of two, would always be seen as an outsider by the age-old Orvieto aristocracy.[1]

Orvieto, especially the old city on the hill, is virtually a museum housing centuries-old works by some of Italy's most famous artists. The daily experiences of the inhabitants of the town, rubbing shoulders with some marvelous examples of art ranging from the Middle Ages to the nineteenth century on every street corner, could be overwhelming to a young struggling artist, creating angst for the psyche and soul. As one of Livio's younger colleagues explained, "We grew up running around invaluable sculptures, hanging off them, using them to play hide and seek. They had no transformative value to us because they were everywhere."[2]

In addition, Livio lived through the horrific experience of the war and the concentration camp. Only those who can empathize with such degradation and horror can understand the impact it had on Livio's life. To all who knew Livio and his art, it is clear that these wartime memories were central to informing his passion for artistic self-expression and his quest for freedom. If one were to attempt to visually depict Livio's search for freedom, the best possible scenario might be a series of ever expanding ellipses growing from a single point that represents Orvieto. Each ellipse might portray a period in his art or some significant time in his life. The beginning of each would emanate from Orvieto and return as if drawn by gravity to the same point, always anticipating a new effort toward finding a sense of freedom. The ellipses represent Livio's attempts to escape the restraints of Orvieto or to cast off his memories or even his family in order to achieve his goal. In each ellipse he drives himself into a greater

Ellipses of Livio's art and career. Graphic by Michael Fowler.

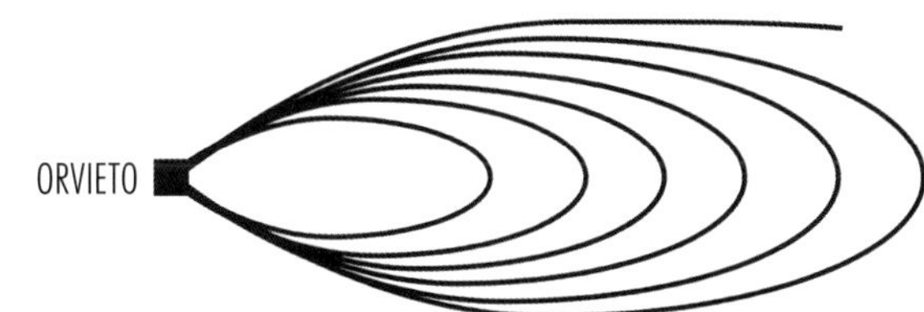

expanding orbit, breaking some of the traditions binding him to the past only to reach a point where his energy and desire are consumed and he thus returns to his origin, Orvieto. His ultimate goal is to break completely free and find that radical sense of freedom; to break the gravitational pull: of Orvieto, the traditions of art, the memories of war, and the controlling sense of family ties. There are those like Hannah Arendt, the renowned twentieth-century political theorist and German-Jewish exile who spent most of her American academic career at the University of Chicago, who believe the struggle between the desire for radical freedom and obedience to responsibility is part of the human condition and part of everyone's journey.[3]

To appreciate Livio's career one must understand that he delved into each work of art and infused the colors with his passion, endowing each work with a power only possible for one who sees the world in a special way. For Livio the struggle took on epic proportions and ruled his life, his art, and his daily existence.

Upon meeting Livio on campus, we became immersed in his art and his personality, particularly the spiritual message it conveyed: a plea of anguish that cried out for all of humanity to understand and embrace freedom as an essential element of what it means to be human. In our initial and many subsequent conversations, we found him to be a man with great sensitivity and vision. Because of his openness and clarity about his life-long pursuit of freedom, the temptation was to put him on a pedestal rather than think of him in mere human terms.

Years later and after his death, we still see these qualities in his life and his art but we have discovered not a saint but a man who had his foibles and weaknesses. One is reminded of the truism that people's strengths are also their weaknesses. Livio was a great artist who used his art to cry out against the injustices of the world and the inhumanity manifested in our day-to-day lives. In addition to his role as artist he was a father, grandfather, husband, teacher, friend, and citizen of the world. Livio constantly pursued beauty and freedom in whatever form he found it and color more than shape became his pathway in his search. He fulfilled his role as artist better than any of his other roles.

In addition to the illustrations in this book, we are providing a comprehensive offering of Livio's ceramics, paintings, and sculptures in the special USCA supplemental website valentini.usca.edu. Through the courtesy of the Valentini family, we are also able to provide an exhaustive selection of historic photographs of his family and friends. Included on this website is Alexander's final interview with Livio Valentini as well as our video entitled *Livio Orazio Valentini: A Maestro for the Millennium.*

Acknowledgments

We deeply appreciate all of the support, encouragement, and especially the endorsement this project has received from the Valentini family. Flora, Cristiana, Silvia, and Francesca have been very generous with their time and efforts to ensure that we have had access to the materials and information needed for us to tell Livio's story. Silvia in particular has gone above and beyond in getting us anything we have requested. To all of the family we express our deepest appreciation.

Our dear friend Erika Pauli Bizzarri has collaborated with us throughout the development of this book. Erika has been our chief translator as she was for Livio. She tirelessly served as our chief researcher in Italy and significantly contributed to the editing of the manuscript. In addition, Erika has been instrumental in orchestrating the photography taken throughout Italy. Her sons, Claudio Bizzarri, an archaeologist who specializes in the Etruscan period, and Lamberto Bizzarri, an IT specialist, contributed much to our understanding of the heritage of Orvieto.

The book would not have been possible were it not for George Custodi. His Italian roots and chance meeting with Livio became the hinge pin of this entire project. Had he not sought to make up his Rotary meeting, the Orvieto-Aiken connection would never have occurred. George played a central role in Livio's odyssey in Aiken. We wish to thank George for his wise counsel, encouragement, and enthusiastic support of our efforts.

From day one, Debra Murphy Livingston added steadfast encouragement as we undertook this project. Through the years she unfailingly served as a sounding board, drawing on her vast knowledge of Italian art and her extensive travel experiences.

Partners in Friendship (PIF), which George and Sandi Custodi, along with mayor Fred Cavanaugh and his wife, Lee, helped establish, was central to this story. We thank the PIF board and its current president Ernie Squarzini for their encouragement. Many members of the board served as escorts and hosted Livio during his time in Aiken.

Our deepest gratitude goes to Livio's Orvieto and Aiken friends who submitted to our interviews and willingly shared their perspectives on the man, his art, his spiritual journey, and his relationships with family and thus made the telling of his story possible. We especially appreciate Aldo Lo Presti's generous support on this project. During this same time he was writing his book entitled *Livio Orazio Valentini, il pittore di Orvieto.* He graciously shared original illustrations and invaluable information.

We owe a debt of gratitude to the administration of the University of South Carolina Aiken. In particular we want to thank chancellor Sandra Jordan, provost and executive vice chancellor for academic affairs Jeff Priest, chancellor emeritus Thomas Hallman, former vice chancellor Deidre Martin, executive assistant to the chancellor Sherri Jenik, and director of news and information Leslie Hull-Ryde.

Keith Pierce has been our steadfast ally for the myriad technical requirements of this project. He patiently supervised the entire production of the video, *Livio Orazio Valentini: A Maestro for the Millennium* and oversaw the complex kiosk project for the Etherredge Center. He has been a true and faithful partner in this enterprise.

Our friends in the USCA department of visual and performing arts deserve our warmest thanks as well. Michael Fowler, professor of graphic design, was our steady friend advising us on layouts and contributing the image of the ellipses in the preface. Ginny Southworth, professor of photography, offered valuable advice on the handling of copyrights. Most of all, Al Beyer, professor of art, was with us from day one. Al not only curated the original *Odissea* exhibit in the Etherredge Center but also shepherded Livio through the production of both *La Principessa* and most especially *Galassia.* We fondly remember Livio enjoying many a luncheon with Al, often conversing in French rather than Italian!

Jane Schumacher, former executive director of the Etherredge Center, was such a compassionate ally to Livio in the months he spent on our campus. She generously helped oversee his transportation and meals and was our most dependable resource on campus for arranging Livio's numerous lectures, workshops, and elaborate art receptions. Her daily kindness made Livio's stay with us a pleasure for all involved and she happily joined in our pilgrimage to Orvieto for the Mostra.

We also must acknowledge the newest of our fine arts friends, Jeremy Culler, professor of art history. Brand new to our campus, Jeremy has embraced this project with great enthusiasm. After our tenure, he plans to carry on further research for the permanent Valentini university collection with the idea of a retrospective exhibit and documentary.

To all our dear friends, we express our most earnest gratitude for sharing their bountiful talents and enduring support. The Etherredge Center and the USCA campus were transformed by the presence of our remarkable Livio. May future generations of students appreciate the magnificent Maestro and all he did to touch our lives as faculty and friends.

We appreciate the support we have received from the following photographers who have generously allowed us to use many of their photographs: Ron Williams, Thomas Gerish, Shelly Marshall Schmidt, Scott Webster, Giancarlo Pancaldi, Massimo Roncella, Marco Santopietro, Candace Bieneman, Nicola Boccini, Francesca Manetti, and Frank DiBona.

In particular Michael Andrew St. John, a new graduate from our fine arts program, served as our invaluable photographer of the many Valentini works collected in Aiken. Michael recently returned from Orvieto after participating in the archaeological dig. At the same time, having received the Valentini Scholarship from PIF, he worked seamlessly with Erika Bizzarri and Silvia Valentini to supplement our necessary illustrations. His technical expertise became a critical element as deadlines approached. Eleanor Prater advised us on graphic design issues and Emily Short graciously transcribed many of our interviews. Mary Claire Millies, Shannon Lynn Farrell, and Amy Westra provided us with invaluable staff assistance.

We are thankful for the support of the University of South Carolina Press and its staff members. Linda Fogle, assistant director for operations, became our guardian angel on this project.

Our deepest appreciation goes to Timothy Simmons, chairman of Security Federal Corporation, and J. Chris Verenes, CEO and chairman of Security Federal Bank, for the bank's substantial financial support of this project. Because of this support, all profits generated by this book will go to the Valentini Endowment in the USCA Partnership Foundation. The Valentini Endowment supports USCA students who spend time in Orvieto studying Valentini's life and art. It is a central element of the university's efforts to expand our understanding of Livio's contributions to our artistic heritage.

Our warmest personal thanks go to Leslie Alexander for her continuing support for this project, especially for the many hours spent reviewing the different versions of the manuscript and offering many helpful suggestions for improving it. She frequently drew on her personal friendship with Livio and his family to sharpen our insights. We alone bear responsibility for any errors, but we know there are fewer because of her diligence and generosity.

Chronology

DEC. 24, 1920 Livio born in San Venanzo (Terni). His parents are Alvise Valentini and Erminia Pacelli.

1921 Flora Bruno born in Arezzo. Her parents are Carmelo Bruno and Rina Coleschi.

1922 The Valentini family moves to Orvieto.

In grammar school, Maestro Nello Benini observes Livio's artistic talent.

C. 1935 Livio becomes apprentice to Michelangeli family in Orvieto.

1937 Livio marches in medieval costume in the Corteo Storico.

APRIL 1940 Livio called to arms in Sicily.

1940–1943 Livio's active duty in Greece and Albania.

1940 Flora's family leaves Arezzo for safety in the countryside.

1943–1945 Livio imprisoned in Germany (Berlin, Buchenwald).

1945 Livio escapes the concentration camp and at war's end, he returns to Orvieto, living with his parents. Flora returns to Arezzo as teacher at the Istituto Tecnico.

1945–1950: The Tonal Period

Livio begins his artistic activity after attempting various types of work. Attends evening school in artistic crafts under Professor Fernando Puppo. First contacts with Umbrian artists. He sells his first "professional" painting to Elio Custodi.

1947 Livio participates in the "Città di Orvieto" National Award.

1948 Livio participates in the "Accademia dei Filedoni" National Award in Perugia.

1950–1960: The Orvieto Informal Period

Livio's first public works:

Viterbo: SIP Society (telephone company).

Orvieto: Military Physical Education School.

Orvieto: Luca Signorelli Middle School.

Assisi: Galleria Permanente Sacra della Pro Civitate Christiana.

Rome: Oculistic clinic, "Figlie della Sapienza."

JULY 16, 1950 Holy Year Jubilee. As part of the celebration of the seven hundredth anniversary of the declaration of the solemn church feast day of Corpus Christi, the holy relic of Orvieto was taken to St. Peter's Basilica in Rome for the first time. Livio was commissioned to design a promotional brochure in honor of this event.

1951 Livio writes and illustrates a diary about his military experiences for his mother.

1954 Rome: Livio appears in "Il Camino" Group show with G. Dottori and A. Bruschettti.

La Spezia: VI "Golfo della Spezia" National Award.

SUMMER 1955 Livio meets Flora at beach resort of Follonica. He is creating ceramic tile and painted decorations for the Hotel Parrini. Flora is vacationing there.

JULY 2, 1957 Livio marries Flora in Church of San Damiano in Assisi. Friar Silvio Pellico conducted the ceremony. Witnesses were Manlio Bacosi and Ione Banchelli. Livio meets Father Ernesto Balducci in Florence. Livio exhibits at the Chiostro Nuovo.

1957 Orvieto: Retrospective Exhibition organized by the Istituto Storico Artistico Orvietano.

Terni: X "Città di Terni"Award.

1957 First daughter Cristiana born.

1960–1970: The Roman School period

1961 Second daughter Silvia born.

1962 Limited edition of the book *Impressioni.* Text by Benedetto Burli, woodcuts by Livio.

Foligno, Palazzo Trinci: Mostra d'Arte Sacra.

1963 Livio paints *The Massacre of Camorena.*

1964 Curates the first Exhibition of Umbrian Artists, "Premio Città di Orvieto."

1965 Curates the second Exhibition of Umbrian Artists, "Premio Città di Orvieto." Receives first prize at the "Maschera d'oro" National Exhibition in Rieti.

1966 Third daughter Francesca born.

1967 Livio sets up studio on Via Monte della Farina near Campo dei Fiori in Rome.

Perugia: XI Mostra d'Arte Sacra-Città di Castello, "Gabriotti" Award.

Participates in the VII Biennial of Sacred Art Bologna-Spoleto, Exhibition of Italian Masters.

Participates in the review of Umbrian artists in Spoleto.

1968–1970: The Pictorial cycle, "Germination"

1970–1980: The Cycle of the Birds

Portfolio of five silk screen prints published by "Arte Nuova Oggi" of Jesi in the series "Artisti contemporanei" (Essay by Ferruccio Masini: "The Parable of the Birds.")

1970–1979 Docent of drawing from life at the Istituto d'Arte of Orvieto.

1979 Livio leaves the Istituto d'Arte taking advantage of the privileges provided to war veterans.

1971 After his one-man show at the "Studium Parmense" he participates in research studies at the University of Parma on the meaning of expression: cycle curated by P. M. Toesca.

1973 Monograph *Livio Orazio Valentini pittore*, published by "Nuovi Quaderni di Parma."

1975 One-man show "Mostra Cantiere" in Sienes (Portugal) Exhibition at the Institute of Culture in Lisbon. Exhibition in the Gallery "Primero de Janeiro" in Oporto.

1976 Participates in the Exhibition of Figurative Art, Acquasparta. Participates in the IV Review of Visual and Contemporary Art in Umbria, "La Nuova oggettivita," Sangemini.

Illustrates the book of poetry *L'ira onesta* by A. C. Ponti (Umbria Editrice, Perugia).

Participates in "Gli artisti italiani per il Tribunale Russel e per la Lega dei Diritti dei Popoli, Palazzo dei Priori," Perugia.

1977: The etchings: Iconologies of the Cathedral of Orvieto

1978 Participates in the Festival of Two Worlds: "Artists for the Rights of Man" of Amnesty International.

Todi: Palazzo delle Pietre. Retrospective.

Orvieto: Palazzo dei Papi. Retrospective.

Contribution to Amnesty International on April 20th with "Report on Torture and Repression in the World," introduced by senator Luigi Anderlini. (Aldo Moro had been kidnapped the day before).

1979 Trip to Berlin. Visit to "the wall." Friendship with engineers Lipa and Serge Goldstein.

1980 Monograph, *Un muro, l'eccidio degli Uccelli* (A Wall, the Massacre of the Birds) with texts by Lipa and Serge Goldstein, Michele Greco, Gerardo Oreste, and a poem by Angelo Rossi.

1980–1991: The Signorelli period—The New Representation

1980 Nominated Accademico di merito at the Accademia di Belle Arti P. Vannucci di Perugia.

1982 Trip to Georgia (USA). Invited by the art historian Alan Graham-Collier to give a lecture at the University of Georgia.

1983 Creation of the *Monumento al 3 Reggimento Granatieri*, commissioned by the Associazione Nazionale dei Granatieri. The monument is located in Piazza Cahen in Orvieto.

1985 Trip to Nigeria upon invitation of the Italian firm Impresit. Graphic and pictorial activity inspired by Africa.

One-man show at the Rocca of San Gimignano with the patronage of the city and the "Cooperativa Nuovi Quaderni."

Participates with ten drawings in the book, *Orvieto: progetto per una città utopica*, by P. M. Toesca, A. Satolli, and L. O. Valentini.

1986 Opens a graphic art and ceramic workshop with his daughters who also had studied art.

Exhibition "Valentini and Signorelli's End of the World." Under the patronage of the city of Orvieto and the province of Terni as the opening event in the celebration for the seventh centennial of the Cathedral. Critical presentation by Dario Micacchi.

1988 Installation for "Strategie d'immagine" for Barilla at the "Cibus" of Parma.

Livio participates in the Arte Fiera in Bologna with ceramic sculpture, promoted by the region of Umbria.

1990: The Flight into the Quaternary

1990 Exhibition "Fuga nel Quaternario," Forte Spagnolo, L'Aquila, under the patronage of the Soprintendenza per i Beni Culturali dell' Abruzzo (Cultural Assets Bureau).

1991 Arte Fiera in Bologna, participates in the "Project at the computer" for the creation and realization of objects in ceramics organized by the Centro Ceramica Umbra.

1991 One-man show in the "Sala della Volta," of the city of Spello with the patronage of the Pro Loco and the city of Spello.

1992 Participates in the international Arte Fiera in Bologna, Salone Ceramica.

Exhibits in the Streker Exhibition Space in Freiburg (Germany).

Participates in "Ceramisti a Orvieto," in the Chiostro di San Giovanni in Orvieto.

Participates in the exhibition "Arte in Provincia," in Acquasparta, Arte Estate in Acquasparta.

1993 Participates in the international Arte Fiera in Bologna, presented by the Galleria Bora with works from the cycle "Fuga nel Quaternario."

1994 Retrospective exhibition "Works 1970–1993" in the Exhibition Center of the Province in Perugia, with the collaboration and patronage of the Accademia Belle Arti P. Vannucci of Perugia and the city of Orvieto.

Monographic catalog published by Guerra Edizioni, curated by M. Duranti and A. C. Ponti, with introduction by Enrico Crispolti and critique by Franca Calzavacca.

1994 City of Orvieto organizes the retrospective "Years 1970–1993" in the Palazzo del Popolo in Orvieto. The exhibition is presented by Massimo Duranti.

1995 Participates in "Etruriarte 6" in Venturina (Piombino); Livio is awarded first prize by the jury of gallery owners and publishers.

OCTOBER 1995 George Custodi meets Livio Valentini in Orvieto. Their new friendship will lead to the formation of Partners in Friendship (PIF).

1996 Participates in the "Materia plasmata" of sculptor ceramics in the Fortezza da Basso in Florence.

Invited to "Maestri della Ceramica" National Award of Vietri sul Mare.

Participates upon invitation of the jury, in the twenty-third Sulmona Award.

Presented by the Galleria Zammarchi of Milan, he participates in the international Art Fair in Barcelona (Spain), Ghent (Belgium), Turin, Milan.

One-man show at the Galleria Zammarchi of Milan.

Participates in the "Etruriarte 7" in Venturina (Piombino); awarded first prize for graphics by the jury of critics.

1997 Participates in the Arte Fiera of Bologna, presented by the Galleria Bora of Bologna and the Galleria Zammarchi of Milan.

In July participates in "Etruriarte 8" in Venturina, to maintain contacts with the Tuscan Maremma; in August he presents some of his latest works in a one-man show organized by the Rotary Club of Follonica.

FEBRUARY 1997 John Elliott begins correspondence with Livio through Erika Bizzarri.

MARCH 9, 1997 Elliott visits Livio and Flora at his studio in Orvieto. Soon after, a delegation from Partners in Friendship visits Orvieto.

1997 USCA and Partners in Friendship commit to sponsor one-man retrospective exhibit at the Etherredge Center. The exhibit is entitled *Odissea.*

NOVEMBER 4, 1997 Livio and translator Erika Bizzarri arrive in Aiken. Chancellor Bob Alexander meets Livio in the Etherredge Center.

NOVEMBER 10, 1997 Flora Valentini arrives in Aiken; she is joined by a delegation of fourteen dignitaries from Orvieto.

NOVEMBER 13, 1997 Grand gala for the *Odissea* exhibit held in the Etherredge Center. Livio presents the painting *Odissea* as a gift to the university.

NOVEMBER 19, 1997 Livio, Flora, and Erika leave the United States.

JULY 1999 Bob and Leslie Alexander visit Orvieto. Livio is offered position as artist in residence for USCA.

1999: The Aiken Period

OCTOBER 1, 1999 Livio arrives in Aiken.

OCTOBER–NOVEMBER 1999 Livio serves his first artist in residency term.

OCTOBER 30, 1999 The Maestro unveils the painting *La principessa nel sole in Aiken* as a commissioned work to the campus.

NOVEMBER 8, 1999 Livio returns to Italy.

AUGUST 26, 2000 Livio arrives in Aiken to begin his second artist in residency term. He does the majority of the work on his third painting, *Galassia,* an eight-panel painting/sculpture originally commissioned for the new Convocation Center.

OCTOBER 10, 2000 Livio returns to Italy.

Later Livio mails the bronze scale model for the sculptural frieze of *Galassia.*

APRIL 2001 Bob and Leslie Alexander, Liz and Rick Benton, and Bert and Linda Alexander visit Orvieto. Bob explored with Livio and his family the possibility of Bob and John developing a book about Livio and his work.

MAY 20, 2001 Livio returns to Aiken to complete work on *Galassia.*

MAY 2001 As part of the Piccolo Spoleto Festival, Livio's one-man exhibit "*Alter Ego*" is held at Charleston City Gallery.

JULY 29, 2001 Livio returns to Italy.

Galassia is not fully assembled with the frieze until after his departure.

MAY 1, 2003 Livio, Flora, their daughter Silvia, and Orvieto vice-mayor Stefano Mocio arrive in Aiken.

MAY 6, 2003 Gala to unveil *Galassia* in the Etherredge Center.

MAY 8, 2003 At the university graduation ceremony, Livio receives an Honorary Doctorate of Fine Arts from the university.

MAY 12, 2003 Ceremony is held at Pickens Salley house and Livio is granted honorary citizenship from the state. Senators Tommy Moore and John Drummond read proclamation that this is officially Livio Orazio Valentini day in South Carolina.

MAY 13, 2003 Alexander conducts final university interview with Livio in Ruth Patrick Education Center (with translation by Silvia Powledge).

MAY 14, 2003 Livio, Flora, and Silvia depart the United States.

MARCH 2004 A three person exhibit opens at the Cloister of San Giovanni in Orvieto. Exhibit features the work of Livio Orazio Valentini, Leslie J. Alexander, and Al Beyer. Bob and Leslie Alexander with son Rob, Al Beyer, John Elliott, Jane Schumacher, and Silvia Powledge attend the opening of the Mostra in Orvieto. Bob and John conduct a series of interviews with Livio and Flora at their apartment.

JUNE 9, 2004 The sculpture *Orvieto Città Unita,* Livio's final masterpiece, is dedicated in Orvieto.

APRIL 4–20, 2005 Bob Alexander, accompanied by George Custodi, visit Orvieto where Bob conducted a series of interviews with Livio, Flora, and Silvia and numerous friends of Livio's.

SUMMER 2006 Bob and Leslie Alexander travel to Orvieto. Bob and Erika accompany Livio on a sentimental visit to his birthplace, San Venanzo.

JULY 2, 2007 Livio and Flora celebrate their fiftieth wedding anniversary at the Duomo in Orvieto.

JULY 23, 2008 Livio Orazio Valentini passes away in Orvieto.

MAY 8, 2010 Cristiana, Silvia, and Francesca Valentini announce the formation of the Livio Orazio Valentini Association.

Introduction

THE ORIGINS OF Livio Valentini's relationship to Aiken are rooted in a conversation George Custodi had with Mayor Fred Cavanaugh in the spring of 1993. George suggested that Aiken was sophisticated enough to become involved in the Sister Cities program. Mayor Cavanaugh encouraged George to pursue the concept. That summer a small group of people met to endorse the idea. John Walker, Bill Weiss, and Rich Waugh from the Aiken Sunrise Rotary Club, June Murff of the Aiken Chamber of Commerce, and Steve Thompson and Frances Thomas of the city of Aiken agreed to work together to develop a Sister Cities relationship.

At the recommendation of this group, Aiken joined the official organization and made the required investment in dues and research to find the most appropriate partner. However, over a period of two years, none of the sister cities' suggestions matched the focus of Aiken's request. Eventually, the arrangement with Sister Cities was terminated and the committee agreed it would take time and patience to achieve their goal.[1]

In the interim, George and his family visited Orvieto in October of 1995 as part of his ongoing travel program to get reacquainted with his Italian heritage. George had left Italy at the age of eleven with his mother and stepfather, General William Berg. His birth father, an officer in the Italian Army, had been captured during World War II and spent several years in concentration camps. The family had been told that Lieutenant Custodi had been killed. Unaware of the real situation, George's mother married William Berg. Much later they discovered George's father had survived. His family's story is one of the many tragedies that are part of the fabric of war.[2]

George and his family stopped over in Orvieto to visit a distant cousin, Pia Custodi. One evening George, an active member of the Sunrise Rotary Club, searched for the

Orvieto Rotary Club which was scheduled to meet this particular night at the Ristorante Maurizio, across the piazza from the Duomo. He discovered from Gianfranco, a long-time waiter at the restaurant, that the Orvieto group was on a field trip in Spain. It seemed George would not be able to make up his Rotary meeting.

George said, "I told him there's got to be some Rotarian around here whom I can meet with because the rule of Rotary is even if you are out of town you should be able to make up the missed meeting. Gianfranco said 'there is one Rotarian who stayed behind, Livio Valentini.' Livio had been given the responsibility to come to the meeting place and take attendance. However, according to Gianfranco, Livio was not likely to show up." So he suggested George stop by Livio's art studio just around the corner on the Via Maitani. George walked to the studio and Livio invited him for a drink at the Hescanas Bar. This connection resulted in a lifelong friendship for Livio and George and was the genesis of the city-to-city friendship between Aiken and Orvieto.

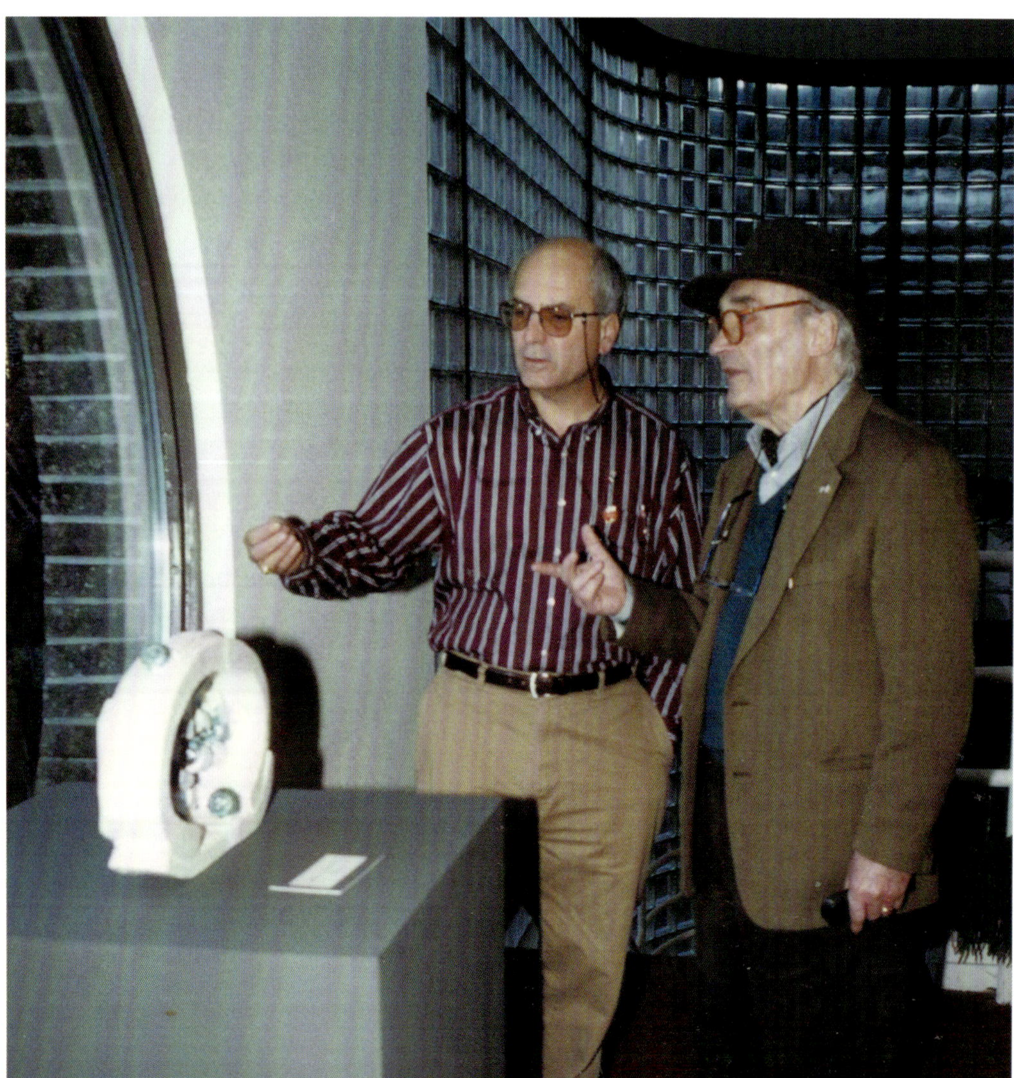

George Custodi and Livio Orazio Valentini in the Etherredge Center. Photograph by John Elliott.

George recalled, "We talked well into the late evening and we went from espresso to wine and I think we hit it off." George described his first impression of Livio as being a very open and friendly person. "He was about my father's age and he shared with me his World War II experiences. I saw him as a kind of father figure. My Italian father had died by then." They pledged to stay in touch. Livio promised he would contact Gaetano Toccafondi, president of the Orvieto Rotary, for the purpose of starting a relationship between the two communities. When George returned to South Carolina he talked to the Aiken Sunrise Rotary Club president John Walker. "I suggested we do a Rotary to Rotary exchange as a way of starting a long term relationship. We formed a committee that included me, John Walker, Art Lader, who was in charge of the high school German program, and Janet Morris, executive director of the Aiken Downtown Development Association. In addition, Mayor Cavanaugh appointed one of his staff to serve as a liaison with the committee. One thing led to another and soon we were forming a delegation to go to Orvieto to explore how the two communities could work together."[3]

In mid-March 1997, a delegation from Aiken under the leadership of Mayor Cavanaugh and his wife, Lee, and including members of Sunrise Rotary, faculty from the University of South Carolina Aiken, and several other citizens from Aiken, made the initial visit to Orvieto to establish a formal relationship. They were hosted by the city of Orvieto, Mayor Stefano Cimicchi, and the Rotary Club of Orvieto. The visit was a huge success and created a relationship that continues to this day. The Orvietani introduced our delegation to their Etruscan heritage and the culturally rich history of Umbria. The delegation was feted with wonderful foods and wines, especially the Orvieto Classico. The two cities signed formal agreements, which committed them to work toward exchanges, including artistic, cultural, educational, and tourist activities.

Orvieto immediately planned a reciprocal trip to Aiken. As part of this agreement, Orvieto requested we sponsor an art exhibit so their native son, Livio Valentini, could show his latest works. While Livio was well-known in the art circles of Europe, this was not the case in the United States.

The proposed exhibit of Valentini's art in Aiken raised numerous issues including the significant investment of time and money. The major stumbling block centered around which entity would be responsible for the various costs. The idea gained real momentum after John Elliott, at the request of the Aiken committee, spent time with Livio in his studio in Orvieto. According to George, "The idea of having Valentini come over with the delegation really took root when John Elliott got involved because he became very excited that we had connected with a significant Italian artist. John did some research and realized we had uncovered someone really important in Valentini. He deserves a lot of credit for being a driving force behind getting Valentini over here."[4]

Several members had asked John whether he thought Valentini's art was of the quality appropriate for an international exhibit. Based upon his review of Livio's catalogues, John felt certain this exhibit could be a great success. He had already planned to be in Italy over spring break codirecting an art history tour with Debra Murphy-Livingston for their combined group of students from the University of North Florida and USCA. When John asked if they might rewrite their itinerary to include a day visit to Orvieto, Debra immediately agreed. John then committed to give Partners in Friendship a professional face-to-face appraisal of Livio's work while visiting Orvieto.

John began correspondence with Erika Pauli Bizzarri. Often they communicated daily through e-mail. In February 1997 John wrote Erika to arrange to meet Livio on March 9 in his studio and then go to his gallery. He enclosed pictures of the Etherredge Center and said the insurance and shipping costs would have to be discussed.

Erika's involvement became a critical element in achieving our goal: to mount USCA's first international exhibit, with less than a year's notice, to finance, ship, and curate a major collection of paintings, lithographs, ceramic and bronze sculptures, with an accompanying catalogue and publicity poster both printed in Italy. The exhibit

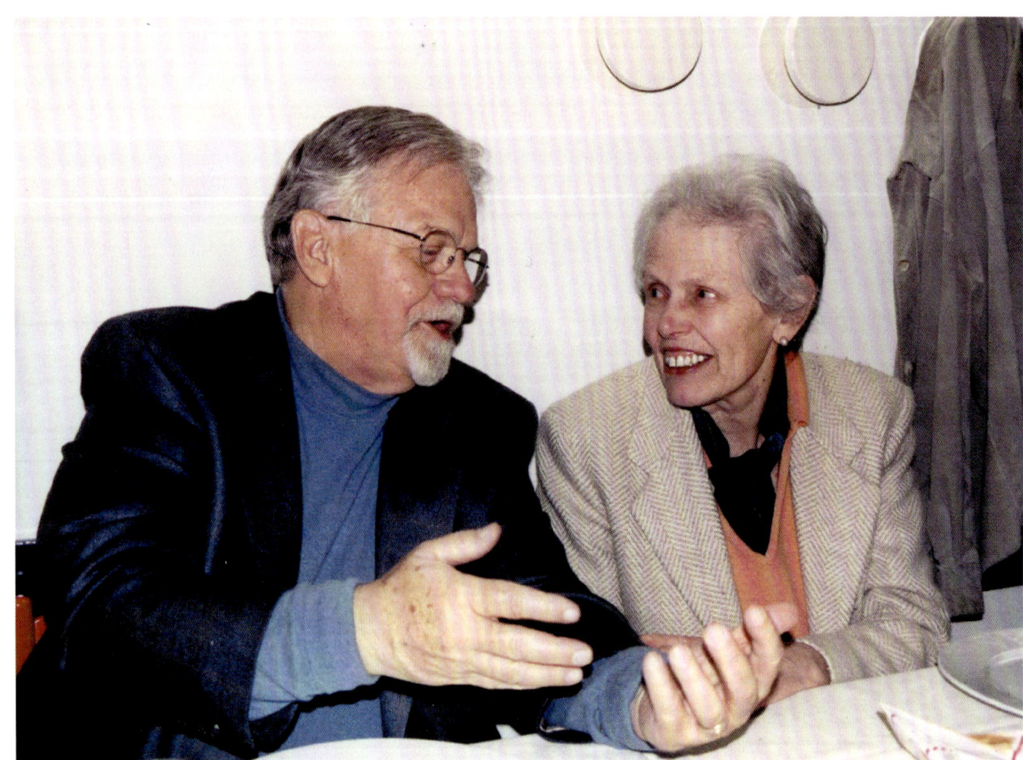

Robert Alexander and Erika Pauli Bizzarri. Photograph by Leslie Alexander.

would serve as a retrospective of the best of Valentini's decades of creativity. Working between George at Partners in Friendship and Al Beyer and John who curated the exhibit at USCA, Erika served as both Livio's translator and on-site coordinator, editing the catalogue as well as shepherding the preparation and shipping of the printed materials and Livio's art work.

On March 9, 1997, Erika met John in Piazza del Duomo while Debra and our students took a city tour. Erika led John to Livio's gallery located at Via Maitani. Having asked George what would be an appropriate gift for Valentini, he recommended Jim Beam whiskey and Livio seemed pleased when John arrived with it at the gallery. Because their time was limited, Livio hurried John and Erika through his collection, suggesting pieces he was considering for display in Aiken. John recalls trying to be conservative and advising against bringing some of the very large ceramic works since he feared both the expense and potential difficulties of transportation.

Erika recommended the university students take a tour of Orvieto Underground and visit the Faina Museum of Etruscan treasures. It was a Sunday so the Signorelli chapel in the Duomo didn't open until late afternoon.

John remembers meeting in the evening with Debra and their students as they gathered for a special dinner with the Valentinis. One of his fondest memories was walking arm in arm with Flora, Livio's wife, while Livio accompanied Debra to the restaurant. All along the way, Flora was pointing out the treasures of Orvieto; a facade from the fifteenth century, another from the sixteenth. She went on and on in her charming manner.

Erika had made reservations for the entire group at the Grotte del Funaro, a hollowed out Etruscan cavern where rope was produced in the Middle Ages. Over a delicious meal of regional specialities and Orvieto Classico, they toasted what would become a decade-long relationship with the Maestro and his family.

Once the decision was made to have a major exhibit of Valentini's work, the die was cast. *Odissea* (Odyssey) was the name Livio gave to his exhibit, which ultimately shaped the journey that Aiken would undertake with Orvieto as well as the one the university would participate in with the artist himself.

After resolving the major issues, USCA and Partners in Friendship agreed upon their responsibilities of sponsoring this enormous undertaking. At the university, our spring and summer were spent in preparation for the upcoming exhibit. Partners created a steering committee, which agreed to meet every Saturday morning in the Aiken Downtown Development Association (ADDA) conference room. Committees

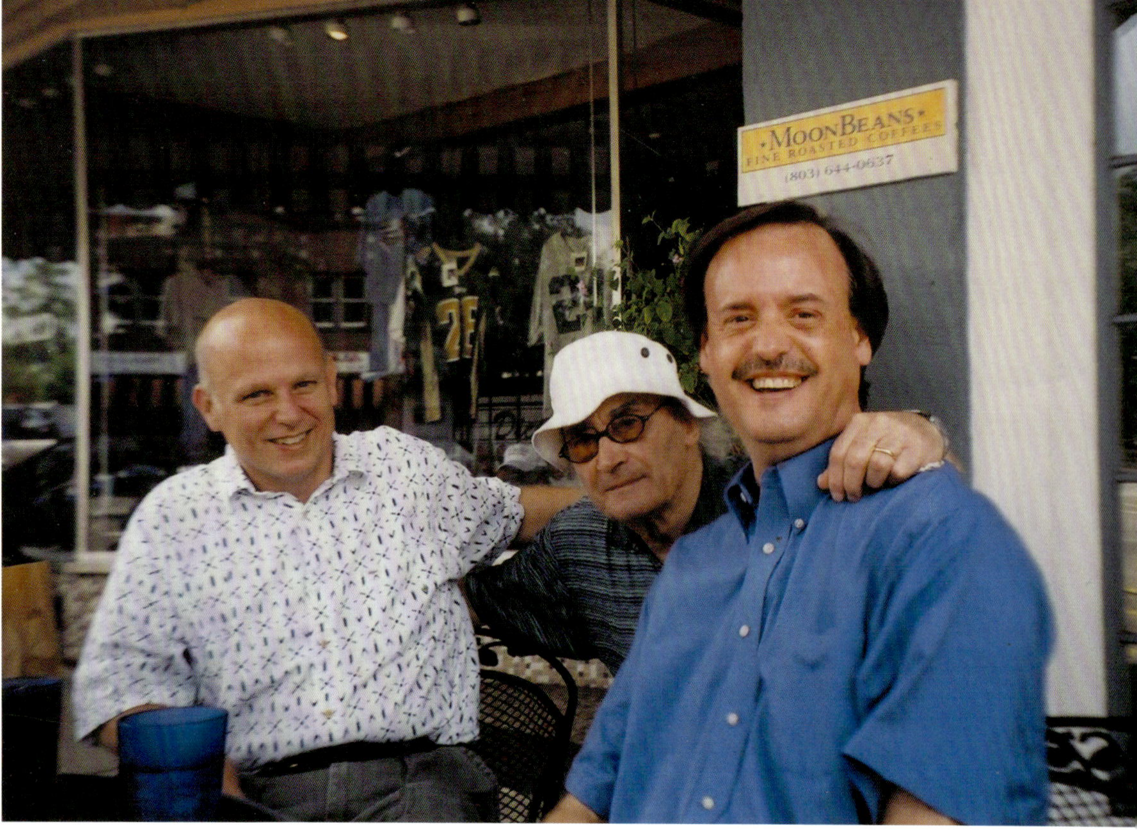

Professor Al Beyer, Livio Orazio Valentini, and John Elliott. Photograph by Bob Alexander.

were formed for art and culture, commerce and education, fundraising, publicity, and tourism as well as incorporating the partners' relationship with Orvieto. Downtown preparations coordinated by Janet Morris were underway for welcoming the delegation of fourteen dignitaries from Orvieto.

Al Beyer, professor of art at USCA, began designing and building a number of wooden kiosks, both large scale modular display cubes on which would hang framed works and smaller bases on which the sculptures would rest. Communication was sometimes spotty when we needed signatures or sketches for Livio's approval. John recalls sending international faxes for Livio to the Trattoria Etrusca and waiting for Erika to respond.

May was our deadline for the arrival of a series of prints, which Livio had agreed to make available to patrons in Aiken for the benefit of the partners. This led to our first experience with the international shipping situation. In Orvieto Livio had arranged for Fracassi International of Florence, Italy, to handle his shipments from Orvieto to the states. On our end, Emery Worldwide would handle materials once they reached the entry point in Charlotte. We had to quickly acquaint ourselves with Italian and American customs and the USCA finance office had to remember not to faint when a bill arrived citing a charge of millions . . . of lire.

Erika handled our written contributions to the catalogue while Livio supervised the photography of his works. That summer one thousand copies of the full color catalogue were delivered to the Etherredge Center.

The Italian delegation arrived on November 10, 1997. Lee Cavanaugh served as the chair of the host committee of the Orvieto delegation. The Orvietani participated in a number of business roundtables and work sessions on a variety of topics. In addition the delegation visited manufacturing facilities as well as schools and the thoroughbred horse operations for which Aiken is so famous. They met with city and county councils to familiarize themselves with local governments. The evenings were filled with social events in private homes and special dinners hosted by the city of Aiken and its citizens. The week was capped off with the opening of Livio's show on November 13, 1997, at the Etherredge Center, his first in the United States.

The first time Chancellor Alexander met Livio was in the gallery, standing in the midst of crates of art. Opened wooden boxes were scattered throughout the gallery amidst packing materials and display cases. Livio looked bewildered at the chaos surrounding him. Erika Pauli Bizzarri, his good friend and interpreter, accompanied him. John Elliott introduced them to Bob and that began the first of many conversations and a very special friendship. During their initial exchange, which involved sign language, awkward gesturing and "bambini" Italian translated by Erika, Bob and Livio developed the beginnings of their lasting relationship. It was to be spiritual in nature, one of the heart and soul. Bob was greatly moved by the depth of emotion and spiritual dimension reflected in Livio's art. As a result there was a non-verbal connection between the man, the art, and the viewer. Most striking were several pieces of art depicting birds impaled on barbed wire. As Livio subsequently explained, they were a metaphor for much of his journey through life.[5]

During a later interview, Livio reflected on this show, "At that moment I said to Erika . . . beyond the painting, it would be necessary for people to know me personally. They can see the paintings but they have to see me to see my soul. If they see my work but they don't believe in my personality, my spiritual conception, then it's as if they don't know anything. They have to know me also." Later in the same conversation as we explored further the concept of knowing the artist, we focused on the "presence of the barbed wire and impaled bird . . . and Livio's anguish." He responded:

> It is evident that people did not know me. . . . They did not know about the passion which surrounded me. I chose the birds because they gave me the possibility

> of expressing human freedom. If I had drawn men in chains it would have had less reality. The meaning was best expressed in tying up a bird or putting a bird in a cage. I preferred birds instead of using men. Men, who after this valiant war, this macabre war . . . , felt free because the war was finished. So I had these strong needs of representing freedom with the bird. It was very important for me as an artist to say what I thought with a special metaphor. Using birds was my metaphor.[6]

In a lecture at USCA, Alan Graham-Collier compared Livio's imagery of the birds to the repetitious studies of the French Impressionist Claude Monet. "When Monet would paint the facade of Rouen Cathedral over and over again it was to reveal the poetic and inspiring quality of the light playing on the great church, light as the phenomenon which evokes the spirit of hope, lends optimism to life." Graham-Collier explained, "When Valentini paints a bird strapped in bandages it is not to simply depict a bird in a rather unusual situation, but to present the bird as prisoner, express his compassion for a creature deprived of its natural and joyful way of life, the gift of flight. Yet more than this: the image of a bird incapable of escaping the gravitational pull of earth symbolizes the plight of the contemporary human spirit which Livio sees as also earthbound, unable to ascend and discover a transcendent home."[7]

Our effort to understand this spiritual man was a major impetus for writing this book. The man we met in 1997 and with whom we had a decade-long friendship was characterized by his search for freedom. He was deeply spiritual if not particularly religious. Maybe it is better to say he was not a pious man. During a lecture on one of his paintings of the Resurrection, Livio said, "I am a so-called Roman Catholic. I'm a lukewarm Catholic. . . . For this reason I have represented certain things with sensitivity. I call it the first resurrection that you gain in life, during life not after life, because you build your own resurrection. If you sow the seed, you will harvest your own resurrection. The other, after life, we don't know."[8] His spirituality was a core trait. He was constantly searching for the unknown that most human beings believe to be at the center of all existence. Daily he sought to unravel this great mystery of life, a search reflected in much of his work. To get to know Livio and to understand his art is to broaden one's understanding of life and become more fully engaged in one's search to peel back the secrets of the surrounding universe.

We discovered Livio was haunted by the anguish he experienced during the war in the death camps. His images of the birds impaled on barbed wire reflected the madness he witnessed being inflicted on his fellow comrades. The war experience became a focal subject in many of his most heralded works such as *The Massacre of Camorena*. This theme of war and man's inhumanity to man continued in his work in one form or another.

During one of our final interviews with Livio, he confirmed the central role the war and death camps had played in his life. More importantly he corroborated that Aiken had been the turning point of his art and his experiences with the community had resulted in significant healing for him. During those years immediately after the war he could never have imagined spending time at a place such as the University of South Carolina Aiken. "My time here helped me to recover myself humanly and spiritually. The people of Aiken welcomed me and helped me regenerate my artistic spirit. It brought happiness to that extraordinary element which is the imagination that drives my art." He expressed his deep gratitude to his friends in Aiken for helping him to recover a sense of meaning and professional significance. "I was given the possibility to enter the perfect happiness, like I always imagined in the extermination camps. This is a deep truth that always takes place in a situation between dream and reality."[9]

The drive to achieve freedom continued to be the dominating force in his art and his life until the very end. The better we came to know Livio over the years, the more we realized this was central to his existence. Many of his closest associates in Orvieto believed the motivation underlying his art, his personal relationships, and his family life was his longing for freedom.

While Livio was not well-known in the United States, he was very much appreciated among his peers and the corporate patrons of the arts in Europe, especially in Italy. As he spent more time with us at USCA we began to call him "*il piu grande artista del mondo*" ("the greatest artist in the world"). Of course his ego was most pleased with our game of elevating him to the heights of the ancient Roman gods. Whose would not be?

Some of his colleagues in Orvieto felt his success in art depended in part on a certain degree of naivety and innocence as a result of his rural background. This also explains his unique sense of color and the way he was able to maximize its impact. According to Livio, Pablo Picasso called him the "painter of the wine," describing him as "the Umbrian artist who mixed his paints with wine instead of water to produce some of the most unusual combinations of hues, values and tints in his paintings." Undeniably color and the way Livio used it became his pathway of expression in contemporary art.[10]

On one hand there was a sophistication and wit about Livio; on the other he could be tinged with innocence while spouting some inaccurate bits of historical data. The

Livio we came to know stood as a man and an artist who was before and above time. He sensed a truth that we all long to know and understand. He could convey this special knowledge through his paintings and sculptures in such a way as to connect with every person. He was at the same time humble and self-centered, flawed and yet pure as driven snow, both simple and complex. After all he was a prototypical Italian artist.

Livio's creative life is inexorably intertwined with the history, art, and people of Orvieto. To fully understand Livio's life and work one must see him in the context of his adopted city. "In . . . Orvieto modern life blends easily with the tranquil medieval surroundings of the city. That's why a lot of visitors easily fall in love with this city."[11] One of our unforgettable memories of Orvieto was the daily promenade of the citizens each evening along Corso Cavour and up to Piazza del Duomo. The Italian name for this activity is *passeggiata.* Older couples strolled arm in arm and stopped frequently to speak to their friends and neighbors. The younger population mimicked their parents and grandparents but more in the noisy style of teenagers who were full of energy and in a hurry to move on to something else. Nearly everyone strolled with apparent obliviousness to the history, statuary, and art surrounding them.

On Piazza del Duomo stands the Orvieto Cathedral with its Romanesque and Gothic architecture and with Luca Signorelli's famous *Last Judgment* in the San Brizio Chapel. Signorelli's frescoes are believed to have influenced Michelangelo's *Last Judgment* in Rome's Sistine Chapel and most certainly played a major role in the development of Livio's art. The Cathedral also houses the Corporal of Bolsena, a linen cloth on which the elements used in the celebration of the Eucharist are placed. It is said that during mass in Bolsena in 1263 when the German priest, Pietro da Praga, broke the host, drops of blood fell on the altar cloth. As a result of this miracle, Pope Urban IV declared the church feast day of Corpus Christi, celebrated every year in Orvieto with the pageantry and costumes that reflect the medieval and Renaissance periods to the delight of the tourists who contribute significantly to the city's economy.[12]

In his youth, Livio always took part in the Corpus Christi procession, frequently in the guise of a public notary. Earlier in the year at Pentecost, known as La Palombella, the descent of the Holy Spirit is symbolized by a dove sent down from the Church of San Francesco to the Cathedral of Orvieto. Clearly this imprisoned bird impressed itself in Livio's mind.

Today the Vatican continues to revere important holy days in the Roman Catholic calendar. Pope Benedict XVI dedicated the years 2013 and 2014 as an Extraordinary Eucharistic Jubilee, coinciding with the 750th anniversary of the Miracle of Bolsena.

The faithful who visited Orvieto and Bolsena were granted plenary indulgences with the forgiveness of temporal sins. The jubilee celebration began with the January 2013 opening of the Holy Door in the Orvieto Duomo and the Holy Door in the Church of Santa Christina in Bolsena. The jubilee continued until the Holy Doors were closed again in November 2014.[13]

For centuries, Orvieto was a place to be visited by Grand Tour travelers on their way to Rome. The city of Orvieto is situated equidistant from Rome and Florence on "a volcanic tufa plateau that rises 635 feet above the surrounding erosion valley at the junction of the Paglia and Chiani rivers in the province of Terni in Umbria." It has a population of approximately 24,000, including the small towns belonging to its district. "The plateau is riddled with man-made cavities: tunnels, galleries, cisterns, wells, quarries, and cellars" created throughout the ages, beginning with the Etruscans. The plateau has been inhabited continuously since at least the middle of the ninth century BCE. By 700 BCE a prosperous Etruscan town named Velzna had been established on the top of the plateau. It was on the main trade routes, the river and the salt road, and also had clay deposits.[14]

Velzna, one of the most powerful cities in the Etruscan league, played a significant role in resisting the expansion of Rome in its efforts to control the peninsula. The city was one of the last to hold out against the Romans. After a siege of two years, it surrendered and was razed by the Romans in 254 BCE. The remaining inhabitants were transferred to Volsinii Nuovo on Lake Bolsena, while the city on the cliff became known as Volsinii Veteres, a name given to it by the Romans when they first controlled the area. First century BCE Roman author, Valerius Maximus (*Facta et dicta memorabilia, IX, 9*) named Volsinii as one of the key cities of Etruria. He lists Volsinii, Perugia, and Arezzo as capital cities ("*Caput Etruriae*").

By the sixth century CE, the old city ("Urbs Vetus"), which later morphed into Orvieto, had become an important way station for the Gothic barbarians moving toward Rome. In 553 CE Belisarius, general of Justinian, the emperor of the West, once more laid siege to the town and drove out the Goths. In 596 CE Orvieto was occupied by the Lombard Agilulfo and had its own bishop.

The period of the Comune of Orvieto began in 1137 CE. Struggles for dominion of the area were continuous with Orvieto siding now with Siena, then with Florence against Siena. Papal influence increased in 1157 when a treaty between the Church and the Comune was signed. In 1212 battles between the Monaldeschi (the Guelphs or Papal faction) and the Filippeschi (the Ghibellines or Imperial faction) erupted. In his

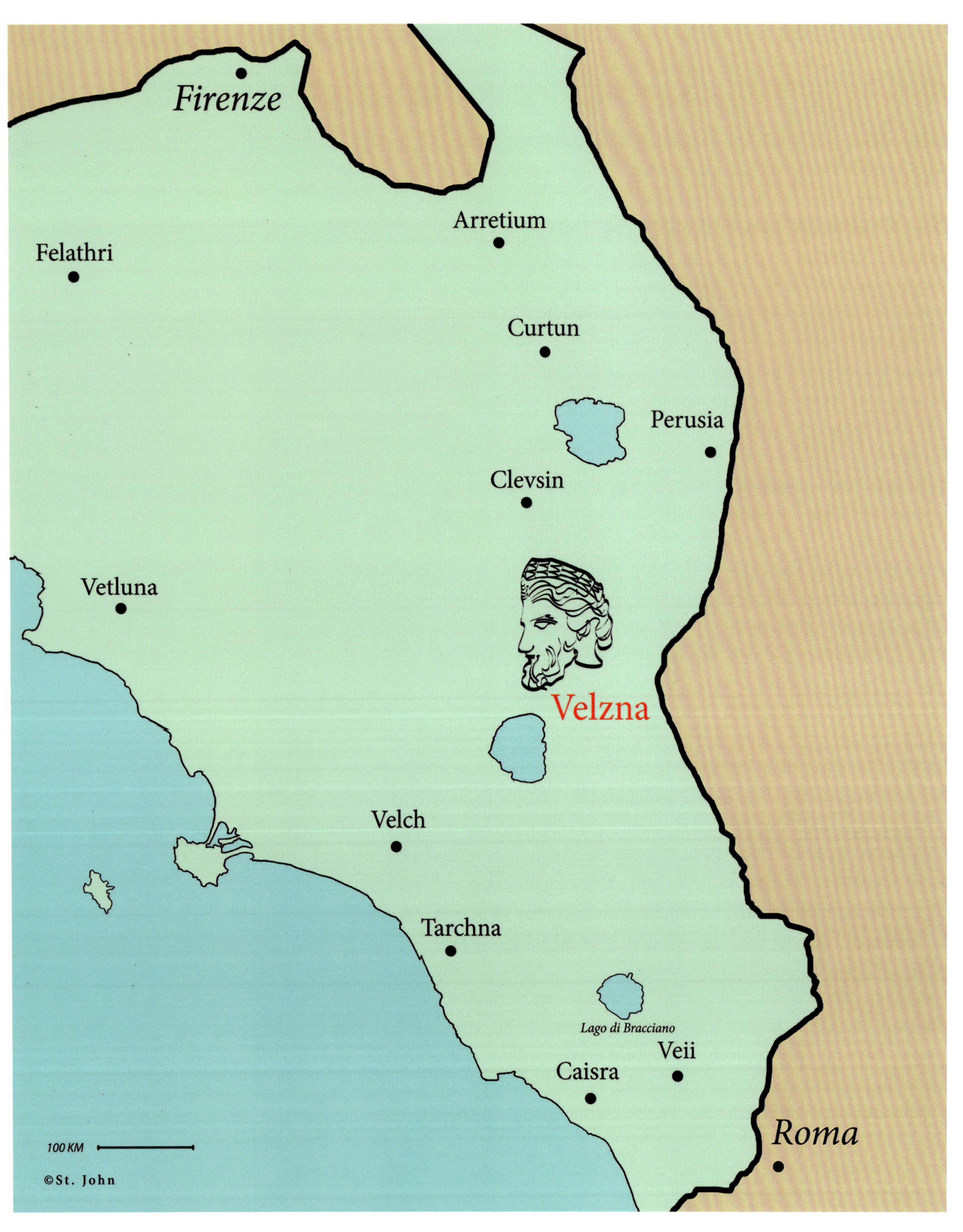

Map of Etruscan territories. Designed by Michael St. John.

Divine Comedy, Dante mentioned these feuds on a par with the Montagues and Capulets of Verona. In 1313 the Filippeschi were expelled. The Monaldeschi subsequently divided into four factions and warred against each other.

The city, with better air than Rome and more easily defendable, was favored by various popes, beginning with Adrian IV. In 1216 Innocent III proclaimed the Fourth Crusade from the Church of Sant'Andrea. In 1227 Gregory IX confirmed the Dominican Studium Generale in Orvieto, a school of theology where Thomas Aquinas subsequently taught. Boniface VIII, the pope who built the third and final papal palace, Palazzo Soliano, canonized Saint Louis in Orvieto in 1297. Gregory X received Edward I of England there on his return from the Crusades and Martin IV was consecrated pope there as well.[15]

The major tourist attraction, for which the Orvietani have their ancestors to thank, is the Cathedral (Duomo), dedicated to Our Lady of the Assumption. It is built on the highest point in town. "Orvieto's most striking sight is without a doubt the facade of its Duomo. The overall effect—with the sun glinting off the gold seventeenth- to nineteenth-century mosaics in the pointed arches, and the intricate Gothic stone detailing—has led some to call it a precious (or gaudy) gem and others to dub it as the world's largest triptych. It is to say the least, mesmerizing."[16] Pope Nicholas IV laid the first stone in 1290; some say to celebrate the Miracle of Bolsena. Work went on at a steady pace and by 1320 Lorenzo Maitani, the Sienese architect, sculptor, and engineer, had finished the sculpture on the facade depicting Genesis and the Last Judgment, something Livio would have grown up knowing.

Orvieto had its ups and downs. One of the first upheavals, the Black Plague, struck in 1348, decimating cities all over Europe. The Monaldeschi were by now lords of the area all the way to the Tyrrhenian Sea. But in 1354 the papal army, led by Cardinal Albornoz, "intervened with sufficient force to establish urban peace, under direct papal rule. Local institutions were allowed to survive, but Orvieto was absorbed as a fifth and northernmost province of the Papal States. Big new projects no longer came Orvieto's way, but the town still prospered as an agricultural center and a major producer of fine pottery."[17]

During the sack of Rome by the Holy Roman Emperor Charles V in 1527, Pope Clement VII took refuge in Orvieto, and it was during his residence there that he rejected Henry VIII's petition for divorce from Catherine of Aragon. This turned out be a "momentous decision in Western Civilization since it arguably started the Protestant

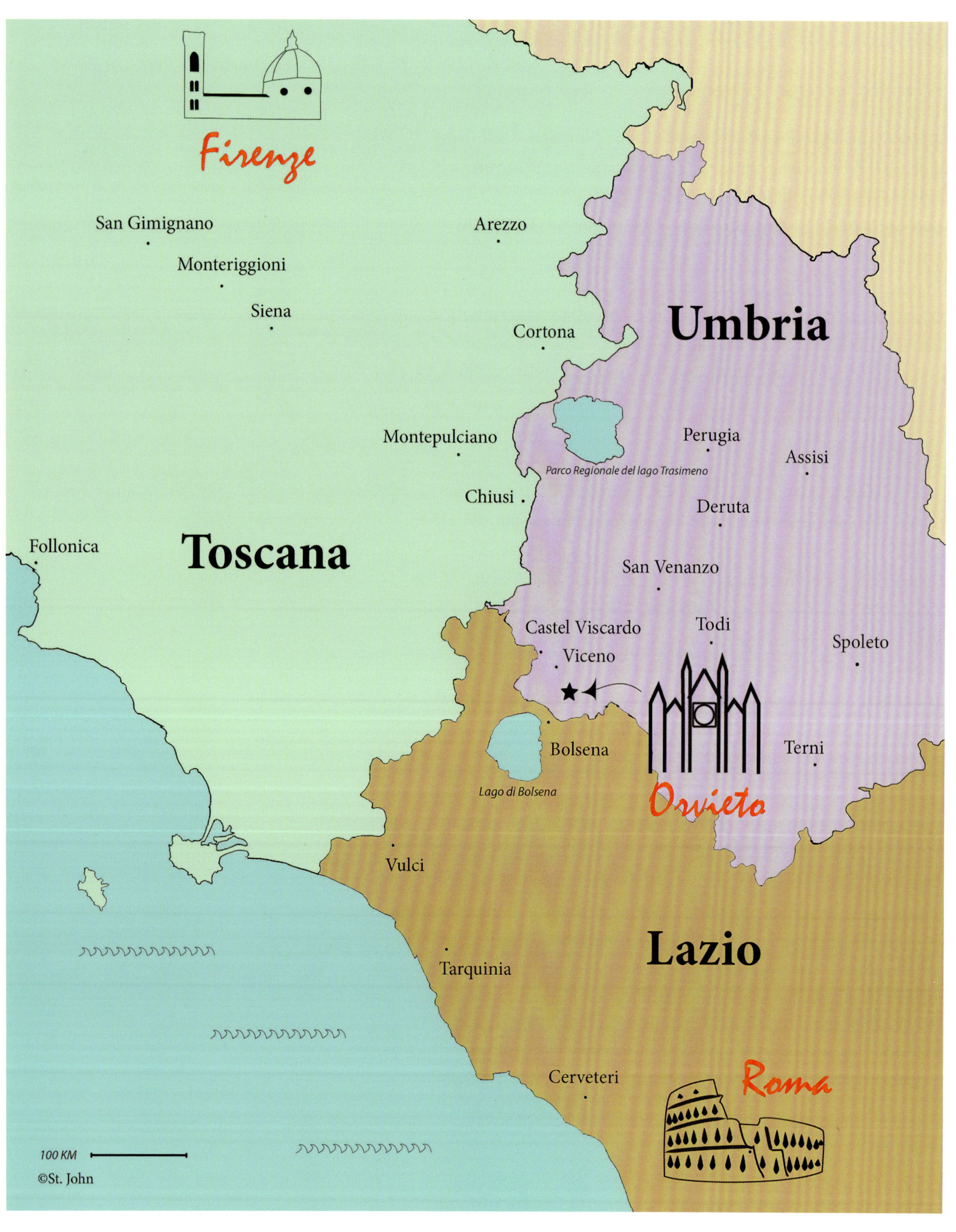

Map of Umbria, Tuscany, and Lazio. Designed by Michael St. John.

Reformation, at least on a state level."[18] And it was then that Orvieto's other claim to fame, St. Patrick's Well, was built to ensure a supply of water in case of siege.

Orvieto was annexed to the Kingdom of Italy in 1860, ten years before the Italian Unification, which later became the Italian Republic. Garibaldi, considered one of the fathers of Italy in his struggle for unification, is said to have toasted to Italy with Orvieto wine before leaving from Talamone. Prior to the Italian Unification, like most of the other cities and regions, Orvieto and the region of Umbria were divided politically with very different "historical traditions of government and law." A great sense of parochialism dominated what was to become modern Italy. Even under the efforts of Mussolini and Fascism, which imposed a highly centralized system of institutions and government, the regions still held onto their unique histories and traditions.[19]

In the twenty years immediately following World War II, the struggle of Italy to solve the economic, political, and cultural divisions within its borders was reflected in the conflicts going on in Orvieto. While multiple political parties existed, Italy was caught between two ideologies: "Communism, whose aim is a radical change in the existing social and political system, and Christian Democracy, which has as its goal a gradual modification of this system."[20]

The various political parties ranged on the political spectrum from the far left to the far right. Orvieto experienced a great deal of turmoil during this time, as did the rest of Italy. Some describe this as a period when Italy changed its governments as often as people change their underwear. The political history and the frequent changes in their government are best left to the Italians who are the masters of the game. Suffice it to say that Orvieto has had in recent years a very stable political environment by comparison to the whole of Italy. Throughout the time of the Aiken/Orvieto relationship, Orvieto had four mayors, all of whom, regardless of their political party, fostered a very positive relationship with Aiken's mayors and the larger partnership.

In the history of Orvieto, one story stands out above all the others: the story of how Orvieto was spared the fate so many other cites experienced during World War II. It was not bombed nor were any major battles fought in its streets. Orvieto was spared because of two military officers on opposite sides who decided that because of its magnificent cathedral and the architectural grandeur of the city they could not be party to the destruction of the treasures that made this city so special.

This is a story based on "a gentleman's agreement." On the Allied side was Major Richard Heseltine who "on June 14, 1944, . . . was the commander of the leading squadron of British tanks approaching Orvieto from Viterbo, another historic city that had not been spared as the Allies drove the Germans up the Italian peninsula, mile by bitterly fought mile." The local German commander of Orvieto was Lieutenant Colonel Alfred Lersen, who served under Field Marshall Albert Kesselring.

"Major Heseltine recalled that soon after making out Orvieto 'standing high on its island rock,' his forward troops reported seeing a Volkswagen staff car . . . with a big white flag fluttering out of the window." The young German officer inside was carrying a message, which he conveyed in "perfect English." The message was: "In consideration of the historic beauty of Orvieto, the German command proposes to the Allied command that they jointly declare Orvieto an open city." The major consulted with his superiors and the gentleman's agreement was concluded with the understanding that the ensuing battle would be fought thirteen miles south of the city.[21]

The highly decorated general, Field Marshall Albert Kesselring led the German command. He was credited with trying "to avoid the physical destruction of many important Italian cities, including Rome, Florence, Siena, and Orvieto." He pleaded the case for creating "open cities" so their architectural and historical treasures could be spared from the ravages of war. Orvieto was one of his successes.[22]

For half a century, the inhabitants of Orvieto considered themselves to have been lucky. But in 1994, Major Heseltine wrote the mayor, revealing the pact

> that was known only to a handful of people. After several unsuccessful later attempts to bring the two officers together for a reunion, the city did have a celebration. On April 28, 2004, mayor Stefano Cimicchi organized a ceremony in which the roles of the two officers who saved Orvieto were to be recognized. Major Heseltine, who was ninety years old at the time, shared the story with all those gathered. The last person to speak was Livio Orazio Valentini. "What made Orvieto unique was its art," he said, looking at Major Heseltine, a keen amateur painter. "Signorelli's pictures are unique. I believe that what happened here is that culture prevailed over people."[23]

In this remembrance, one of our recurring themes will be that of miracles. In so many ways, for a myriad of reasons, Orvieto can be considered a city of miracles. When countless Etruscan city centers disappeared, the victims of Roman aggression, Orvieto's residents persevered. In Orvieto the miracle of the Etruscans and Romans can be perceived in the fact that the city, even though besieged and conquered, continued to live in the sacred structures at the foot of the cliff. The Romans continued to come here, as did the defeated Etruscans. With the coming of Christianity, when most pagan centers were toppled, in Orvieto some sites were claimed for use by members of the new faith. One can trace a vertical historical stratigraphy in the medieval Church of San Pietro in Vetere, built on the remains of an early Christian church of the sixth century CE. Below that church, archaeologists have found evidence from both Imperial and Republican Rome constructed over an original Etruscan building.

All this is near where, according to popular tradition, the altar cloth of the Miracle of Bolsena was received. This Eucharistic miracle was one of various similar miracles that resulted in the *Bolla Transiturus,* the bull that established the feast day of Corpus Christi. Several decades after the Holy Corporal was moved to Orvieto, the Duomo was constructed. By this time Orvieto had become a bastion of safety for scholars and the pope himself. Orvieto attracted astonishing artists who decorated the structure with mosaic, bronze, stained glass, and fresco. Geniuses like Lorenzo Maitani (1275–1330) and Luca Signorelli (c. 1445–1523) became leading artists between the Gothic and Renaissance eras. Centuries later, when modern battle forces again approached the famed tufa plateau, two veteran warriors from opposing sides granted a miracle of intervention to spare the cathedral for another day.

When our friend Livio escaped death in the German concentration camps, he returned to his city of miracles and helped found an art academy, leading a modern renaissance to educate the next generation of young Orvietani. And when, all those years later, by the most fortunate of meetings, Livio encountered George, they forged another astonishing link, friend to friend, city to city, culture to culture, Italian to American. From this happiest of miracles arose a now decade-long international partnership.

Livio's coming to the university was the beginning of Aiken's cultural renaissance. The Etherredge Center was transformed into a new salon of the Medici with our university and civic leaders joining to support the *Gemelle nell'Amicizia,* Partners in Friendship. Can this union be considered anything but miraculous—the result of two Rotarians from different lands bonding over a cup of vino on an October night? Erika said one should add to this recipe, the university chancellor who had the wisdom to envision the far reach of international relationships for his city and especially for the students. His foresight led to commissions for original artworks that decorate our campus today. And finally came an art historian and Etruscan scholar given the gift of working daily face-to-face with an artist whose images blended the flavors of both ancient and modern Umbria. Through the establishment of these relationships, Livio's artistic universe unfolded, revealing a galaxy of brilliant dimension and exceptional spiritual depth.

With such an astonishing history of lucky happenstance, we look back fondly to the arrival of Livio and Flora at the Etherredge Center, speaking not a word of English but communicating with us all like old friends.

Livio started one of his early lectures with the following statement:

> I am Valentini and I come from Italy. I came to the University of South Carolina Aiken because I have many friends here and many people I know. I am a free man and I speak the only way I know how. I didn't read it in books because I have walked the road of experience to gain my knowledge. Experience is most often a more difficult road but I have found that one learns better when one learns that way. Learning by experience puts its roots in your cells and becomes a part of your DNA. Thus your experience becomes a part of your own being or person. It makes you who and what you are.[24]

CHAPTER ONE

Livio's Early Life

LIVIO WAS BORN INTO A WORLD of great uncertainty and political upheaval, shaped by war. His earliest years followed the end of the "Great War," World War I. Like the rest of Europe, Italy was reeling from high unemployment, large-scale strikes in the major factories, political unrest, and social convulsions. Even though Italy had fought on the winning side, the results were bittersweet. France and England had promised significant rewards, including major portions of the Ottoman Empire, for Italy's participation. While Italy did gain additional territory at the conclusion of the war, it was not nearly as much as had been promised. This major disappointment and the general economic conditions set the stage for Mussolini and his Fascist Party to convert Italy from a democratic monarchy to a totalitarian state. In general, people were open to Mussolini's promises of a better life and the creation of a new Roman Empire.

As a result of hyperinflation, unemployment, and social unrest in the early 1920s, many rural families were forced to relocate in an effort to find steady jobs and safe accommodations. The large estates could no longer afford the number of workers who had been required to operate these properties in the recent past. Additionally the owners were under political pressure to restructure and redistribute their lands. There was a struggle between communism and fascism for the soul of Italy. Life had become more difficult for the Italians who lived in small towns and rural areas.[1]

Livio's family experiences were typical of so many other rural Italians. He liked to tell how he was "born poor and curious. I was born on the 24th of December, so I disturbed my mother on Christmas day. I disturbed her but she was happy."[2] He was born in San Venanzo, a small mountain village in the Umbrian region of Italy just a few kilometers from Orvieto. Livio's parents lived and worked on the estate of Count

Claudio Faina. Their entire youth revolved around the small town and culture of this estate. They played together, worked together, grew up together, and were married in 1919 on the estate. The family lived in a small cottage, number fifteen, just beyond the manor house. They were an attractive young couple who lived a simple country life. Their first son, Livio, was born on the property and the family lived there until he was two years old.

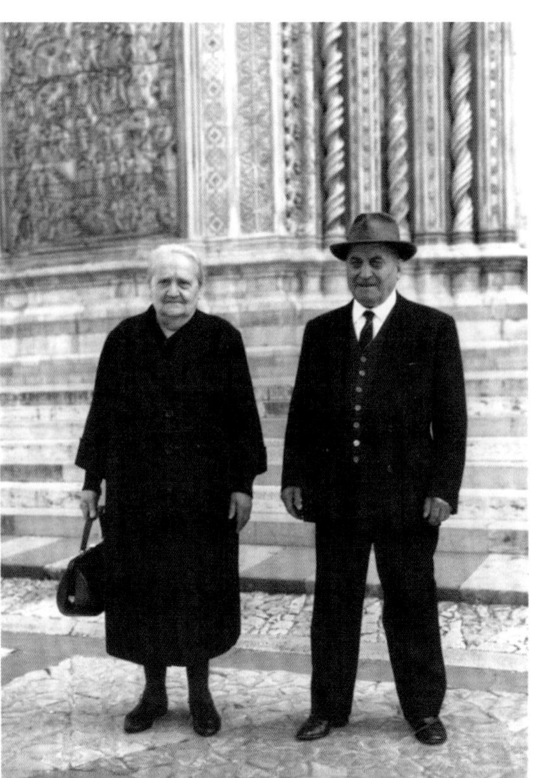

Livio's parents, Erminia Pacelli and Alvise Valentini. Photograph courtesy of the Valentini family.

Livio's mother, Erminia Pacelli (1893–1976), was the first of nine children. During her childhood years she worked in Count Faina's bakery with her parents. She had one of the most demanding jobs a young person on the estate could have. Bread and pasta were the staples for all Italian families. She was required to wake up before dawn and assist with preparations for baking. She began with the *lievito madre* (mother starter) that was kept from week to week and renewed each time. Bread was eaten with every meal while pasta was served at the midday and evening meals. In the bakery they made huge rough loaves of country bread with dark dough and a hard crust. She helped make a variety of pastas including *umbricelli,* a favorite in the Umbrian region. Bread was made daily because no preservatives were used.

In addition to her work in the bakery, she also played a major role in the care of her younger brothers and sisters. Until she was married, Erminia acted as a surrogate mother for her siblings. She was partially deaf as a result of an untreated childhood ear infection. This malady influenced her interactions for the remainder of her life.

Livio's father, Alvise Valentini (1890–1975), worked part-time on a seasonal basis at the count's estate. He labored in the fields helping to plant and harvest crops. He was a man of few words unless he had a story to tell and a man for whom the culture of food was important. He had an unusual aptitude for working with his hands and this skill would serve him well later in life. In pursuit of a better future and more secure life for his wife and son, he moved the family to Orvieto in 1922. Alvise's strength and practical intelligence won him a job with the railroad company. Over the years he worked his way up to become a train engineer. "Father drove a marvelous machine, a train. The train made a lot of smoke and Father was proud of that train. It was as if he owned it."

After they moved, Livio's mother no longer worked. He recalled, "Mother had plenty to do at home with me and my brother." His brother, Piero, was born in 1925, a sickly child who required much attention. Because of these health issues Piero became the major focus of Erminia's attention. While she doted on her second son, Livio was forced to become more self-sufficient. In some of his earliest photographs, he appears as a serious, dark-eyed boy, mature beyond his years. Although close, Livio and his brother seemed to live in completely different worlds.[3]

The transition from San Venanzo to Orvieto was a significant moment in Livio's early life. Most of his extended family remained behind in the village. He and his parents started their lives from scratch making new friends and learning to navigate their way around the town and its social structure. They were alone in this strange and new community. Livio remembered these early years of relocation and adjustment as a stressful time in the family's life.

Livio went to elementary school in Orvieto and felt he did not fit in easily with his fellow classmates. During our interview with him in his Orvieto living room, Livio indicated he did poorly in the more quantitative subjects like mathematics and science. He said he was distracted by his interest in drawing. Since he frequently had to repeat classes, he found himself surrounded by younger students, which became awkward and made school even less appealing. During this interview, Flora, always his advocate, said she would like to check the archives in the school to see why Livio was not promoted. She was convinced he had not been treated fairly.[4]

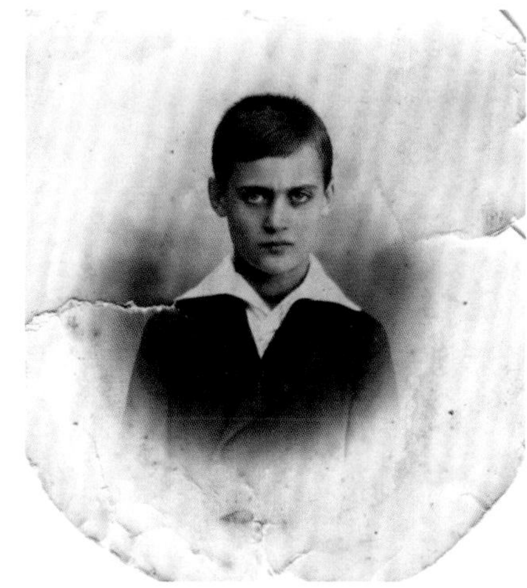

Livio at ten years old. Photograph courtesy of the Valentini family.

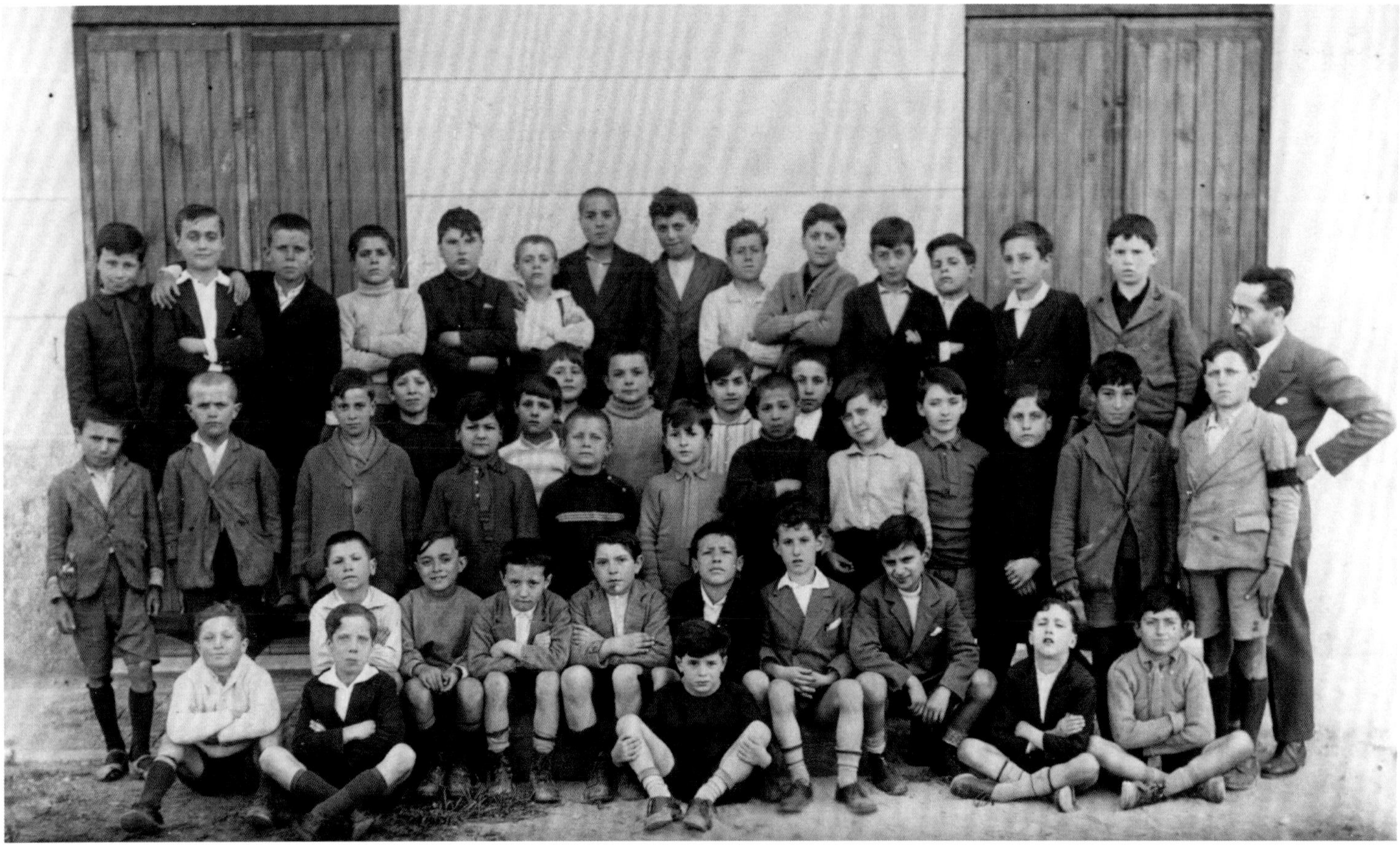

Livio's class in 1930 with art professor Nello Benini. Photograph courtesy of the Valentini family.

Art became Livio's alternative path. As a child, he was fascinated by drawing but could not afford private art lessons and had to "make do with the advice of his teacher." One of his earliest teachers, Maestro Nello Benini (1895–1958), did appreciate his artistic talent. Benini was also an etcher, painter, and illustrator of books.[5] He encouraged the boy to draw by telling him, "Livio, you draw good grapes." This was one of Livio's first affirmations related to his life's vocation. Because he came from a family of modest means, during Livio's formative years in painting, with only the encouragement of Benini, he was largely self-taught. When speaking to a group of young students in Aiken, Livio told the following tale:

> When I was a schoolboy my teacher, Maestro Benini, sent me to the blackboard and said "draw me a bunch of grapes." So I went to the huge blackboard and I made a little round thing for a grape. One of my classmates said "those are not grapes. Italian grapes are big." And so I drew huge grapes. Behold, the teacher pointed to me and said "that is how grapes are made!" So I already understood from my teacher to use my inner eye . . . and that a grape had an interior part and a surface part. Even in grammar school I understood intuitively that grapes were not just little tiny dots but rather they contained something, the pulp or meat. Grapes have this skin, this envelope around them. I knew it instinctively.[6]

Livio's fellow students thought he was a little strange. He was so committed to his art that he would often use money he had been given for chocolate to buy paints and brushes. Some of the older boys in school nicknamed him "Pittò," the diminutive of *Pittore* (painter). This was picked up by some of the village curmudgeons since even as a child Livio said that he wanted to be a painter when he grew up. He remembered playing with his friends in the streets and people calling out to him, "What are you going to paint today, Pittò?" When he was in his teens he felt the nickname was rather derogatory. Since money was scarce he took on all kinds of odd jobs so he could buy painting supplies. At the age of fifteen, he started working as an apprentice in the carpentry workshop of the Michelangeli family in Orvieto. Most of his teenage years were spent in this apprenticeship, refining his aesthetic skills and developing designs appealing to the modern eye. His work there would lead to one of his closest friendships and a life of collaboration with Gualverio Michelangeli. While Livio's parents did not understand his drive to become an artist, they certainly approved of his apprenticeship. It was not until he was eighteen that Livio painted his first canvas. When relatives in San

Venanzo, to whom he had given some of his landscapes, praised his work, he said it made him feel like he was becoming a real artist.[7]

When Mussolini assumed total power in 1922, he invaded much of northern Africa and established an Italian empire; hyperinflation was running rampant throughout all of Europe and Hitler and the Nazis controlled Germany. The political environment changed and by the mid-thirties Mussolini defied the League of Nations and expanded Italy's empire. Under his leadership Italy moved into an alliance with Germany. The Second World War began in 1939 as Germany conquered much of Europe and Italy was quickly drawn into the war, much to the chagrin of most of its population.[8]

Life quickly changed for Livio and many of his young friends as they were swept into the vortex of war. At twenty, in April of 1940, Livio was called up by the Italian army to serve in the infantry in Sicily. Livio felt that his poverty determined where he was assigned. He explained, "Those who came from poor families were sent to Sicily; those who came from rich families went to Viterbo." He was in Sicily for approximately eight months for basic training. He was shipped with his battalion to Albania in October of that year and soon found himself in combat. He was actively engaged in heavy fighting in Albania and Greece from 1940 into early 1943. When the Italians signed a peace treaty with the Allied Forces, his army battalion refused the demands of the Nazis to join in and continue the fight with Germany. A great debate raged throughout Italy as to whether they should sue for peace. Finally a treaty was signed and in July of 1943 Mussolini was removed from power and the German forces initiated a plan to disarm the Italian army and implement an occupation. The refusal of Livio's unit to fight with and for the Germans placed them in great peril. Several days before, on the Greek isle of Kefalonia, more than five thousand Italian troops had been slaughtered when they refused to fight for the Germans.[9]

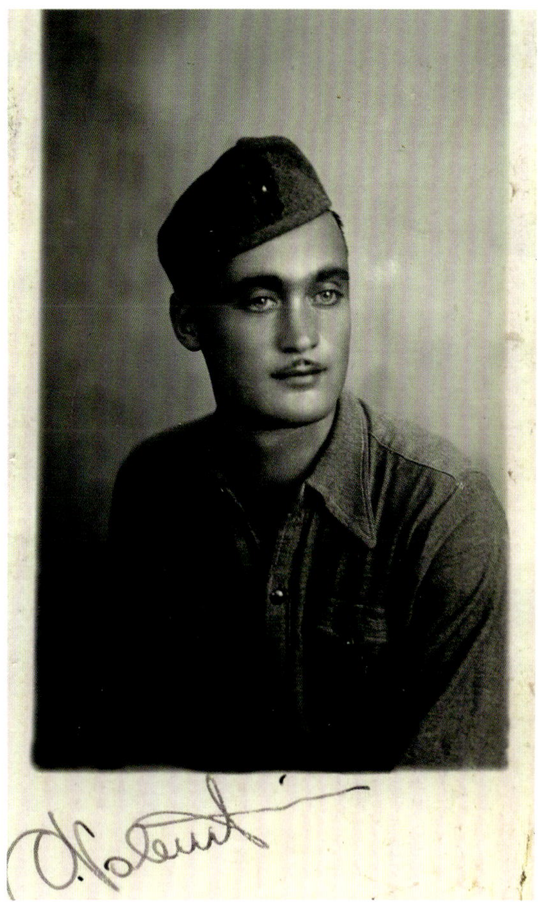

Livio in his military uniform, a photograph taken for his mother. Photograph courtesy of the Valentini family.

This act of defiance resulted in Livio's battalion being confined as prisoners of war from 1943 to 1945. Imprisoned for several months in Buchenwald, Livio and his fellow soldiers experienced the worst of the inhumanities people inflict on one another. He was transferred to Spandau and then to an area between Munich and Innsbruck. His final days in prison were in Berlin. During his time in the concentration camps he watched some of his closest friends die in front of Nazi firing squads. Only he and one other young man from Orvieto survived the "extermination camps," as Livio referred to these prisons.[10]

At the end of the war, Livio returned to Orvieto after escaping his imprisonment and traveling a tortuous and lonely journey through Germany and northern Italy where his life was frequently threatened. He faced the dangers of a population divided by the events of the war and the continuing struggles between the fascists and partisans, those suspected of supporting the Resistance. Skirmishes continued for several years after the war concluded, resulting in deeper schisms of the body politic. For years to come he would be haunted by these experiences just as Italy was torn by the struggle between the various political factions fighting for its soul.

At the end of the war he emerged from the camp weighing only sixty-five pounds. When he finally arrived home, just a skeleton of his former self, his mother and father were very concerned about his health and wellbeing. Even though food was scarce and rationing was still in effect, Erminia tried to fatten him up by cooking all of his favorite foods only to have Livio refuse to eat. He spent much of his time trying to learn how to live in the absence of war. Frequently he retreated to the countryside in an effort to shake the haunting memories of the death camps. He found comfort in returning to his earliest roots and visiting his relatives in San Venanzo.

Livio recalled:

> In the first few months, once I came back to normal life, I made a list of things I wanted to get rid of from my life. First, it's not necessary to eat. I'm talking about the meaning of nourishment itself. It's not necessary to exaggerate. I was trying to tell myself that I was not going to die of starvation. Other things can happen because you stop eating which are worse than starving. With hunger, feelings disappear; with hunger, love, affection and friendship disappear. You become like an animal. There's no relationship of any kind. You get isolated and realize recovery from hunger takes a long time. Because when you're truly hungry, you don't feel the need anymore. It becomes a flat line. That's the brutal thing.
>
> So you realize that life is very simple, it's extraordinary. Nothing is necessary; you just need to eat a little bit. I wasn't drinking coffee any longer. I wasn't eating any desserts. I wasn't eating anything superfluous; I eliminated everything. It was a style of life and it made me feel dignified. A man without wishes, without desires. These are the complications of existence.

He continued, "I imagine that lesson is not known by many people. This discipline, the keeping or conserving of your own ego, your own self. This feeling is almost unknown because man tends to enrich his needs, a rich man especially. A poor man does not have that many needs."[11]

CHAPTER TWO

Ricordi—Livio's Memoir

Like so many others who have known war, Livio bore the invisible scars that such horror imposes on the human psyche. For him they were manifested emotionally, philosophically, and artistically. Part of his healing process involved answering the many questions his parents asked him about his experiences. Erminia repeatedly queried him because she was unable to hear his responses. In an effort to satisfy her concerns, Livio wrote a memoir, *Ricordi*, about his time in the war. The best way to understand this experience is to read his own words as written in his memoir for his mother.

Translated by Erika Pauli Bizzarri

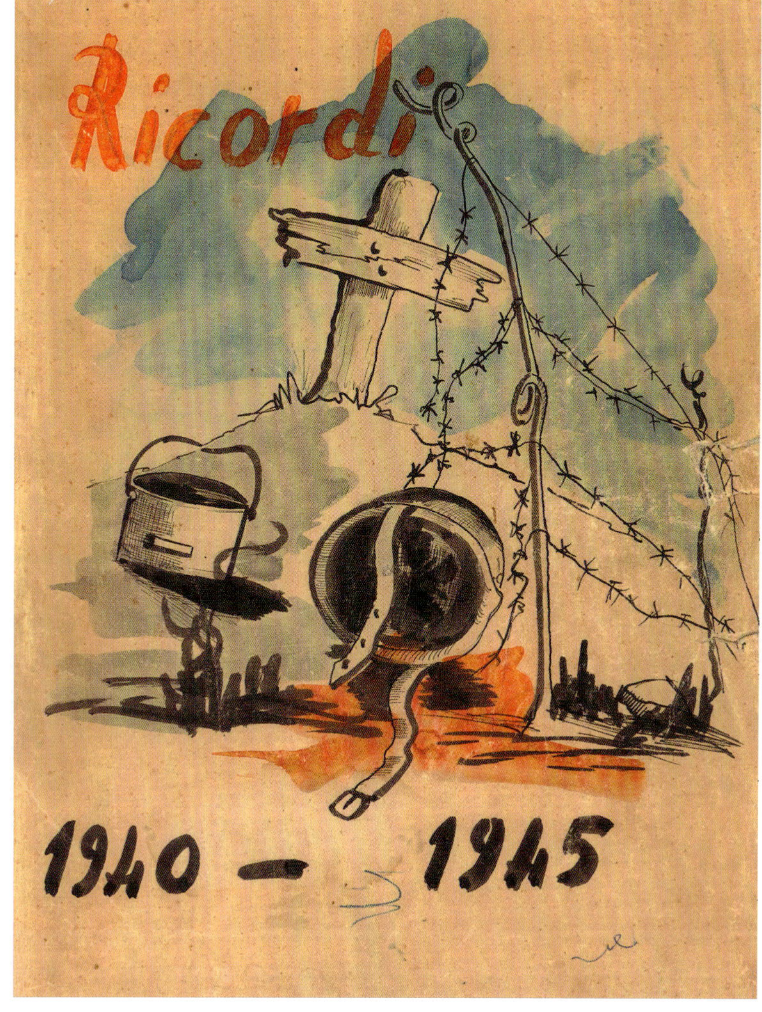

Memories

1940–1945

Orvieto January 1951

To my mother with love

Livio

This memoir was written by L. O. Valentini in 1951 for his mother, who was deaf and who had asked him where he had been all those years. The tale may seem rather naïve, elementary from a literary point of view, with no pretension of being literature. The sole purpose was to tell his mother what had happened and, perhaps at heart, to explain to himself an apparently absurd, but real story of the war adventure.

This is simply an account of the salient episodes and of my impressions during the war and in prison. I therefore ask those who read it not to be too harsh in their judgements for I have no literary pretensions.

January 6, 1951

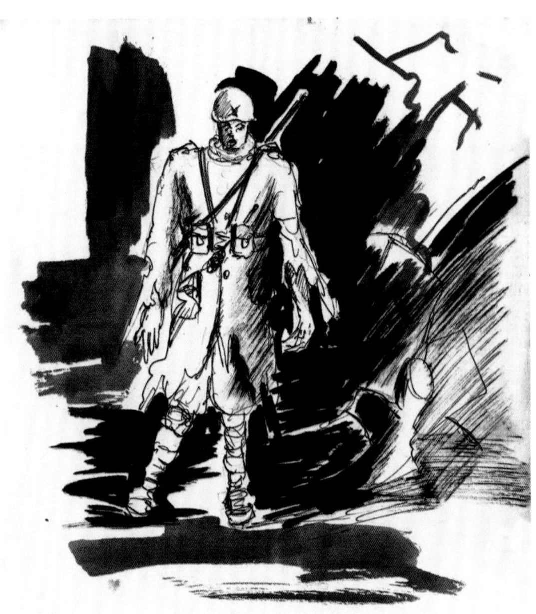

Self-portrait as soldier.

In April of 1940 I was sent to Sicily in the Infantry. About eight months passed and while I was disoriented by the new customs and habits I was also fascinated by this land with things that were new and strange to me: Etna with its plume of smoke, the black lava, the fertile hills with orange groves and prickly pears, the blue sea, the *faraglioni* or rocks of Taormina, the simple and good people who maintained the customs that characterize a personality that sometimes seemed strange to me.

In October of that year I embarked on a motor ship and left the island. My heart was heavy. From the deck the shores, the shores of my Native Land, became smaller and smaller, and I couldn't help but thinking: "Will I see her again?"

We touched on a new land, Albania, and my first impression was of the worst kind, an air of sadness and squalor, hostile people. Even that life-giving heavenly body, the sun, seemed absent, so black was the sky and so muddy the street. Durazzo was the first city I saw: narrow streets, crowded with people in their characteristic dress, their faces yellow from malaria, vendors of dry figs and fresh fruit. I saw a mosque and entered. I didn't know that one was supposed to remove one's shoes in a sign of respect. I had to leave at a run pursued by the unfriendly glances of the worshippers.

A few days later on a truck I found myself headed to the hinterland on my way to Corizza. The trip took a day, skirting the lake of Ocrida, its shores crowded with coots, and I had my first taste of that wild mountain land.

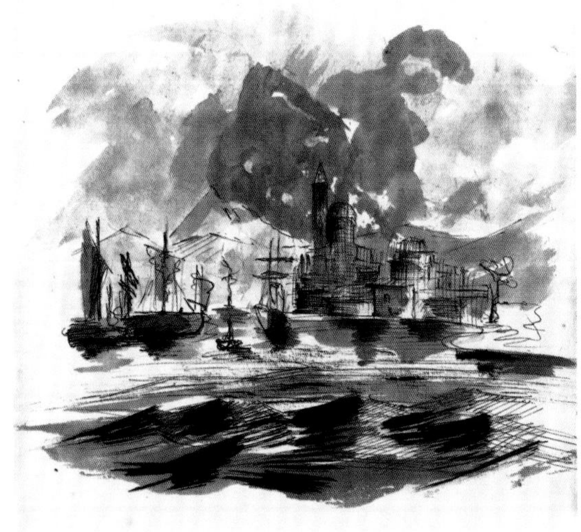

"We touched on a new land, Albania . . ."

In the meanwhile the war had broken out and I was getting closer [to the front]. I began to realize what war felt like: cannons firing in the distance, the coming and going of ambulances. I asked every soldier I met for news that sometimes reassured me, sometimes alarmed me. Enemy planes appeared in the sky and bombed the nearby airports. They were the Savoia-Marchetti planes Italy once sold to the Greek government and now it was hard to tell what nationality they were.

Winter was approaching, there was snow and it was cold, our battalion took up its position on a height in Darde. We stayed there several days while the front was coming closer. One night the order suddenly arrived to reach the front lines. We hurriedly equipped ourselves and began our approach. Our hearts were pounding and the silence was broken only by the sound of our steps.

We met three stretchers carrying wounded men. I approached them and naively asked what had happened. My question caught them by surprise and as was to be expected they told me to go to hell.

The battalion stopped in a clearing, we were told where to go, and were very close to the line of fire. We had been warned to be careful and everyone was quiet, hearts almost stopped beating. Every so often there was a volley of machine gun fire. With two other telegraph operators I was to reach a height further on used as an observatory. On the way we saw large holes in the ground left by artillery fire. Our artillerymen lying near their pieces pointed out the site. Once there and after consulting the map we set up our position.

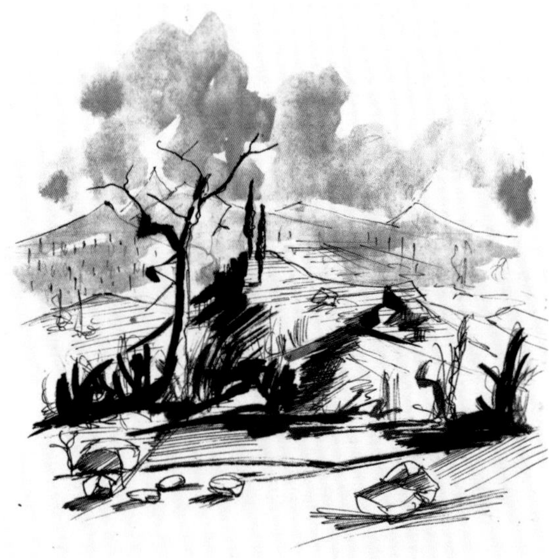

"With two other telegraph operators I was to reach a height further on used as an observatory."

At the first light of dawn artillery fire began on both sides. From our observation point we could follow all phases of battle. Our location however wasn't one of the best and we could see the "Parma" division gradually retreat from the great stage below and move closer. Naturally no matter what we couldn't leave our foxholes. Our comrades brought us our rations, consisting of a roll and a tin can, tossing them from a distance since they couldn't reach us. Once one of the cans fell too far away and we had to wait for night to go and get it. For water we had to crawl cautiously to a spring. Sometimes we found the Greeks there, and then we turned back making as little noise as possible.

The second day there, the "Parma" division withdrew and groups of panic-stricken soldiers were running in all directions. They passed by the place we were and we were worried and tried to stop them to see what was going on but they wouldn't stop. The enemy was right there below the rock outcrop and they were out of range of our machine gun since they were lower down. Only the use of hand-grenades stopped their advance. When things died down I heard enemy troops talking and a Greek soldier climbed up near us and called loudly: "Nicolaus!" I drew a blanket over my helmet afraid the moonlight might reveal me and I didn't fire to avoid worse trouble. The Greek passed near my hole and after setting off a few signal rockets went away.

The enemy had identified our position and the second day began to shell our small area and a projectile fell so close to the hole where I was sheltered that I was hit by a splinter in my hand and left leg. I noticed the wound on my hand that was bleeding right away and the following day I noticed the wound in my leg. Luckily they were not serious and I didn't worry about them, sure I couldn't have done anything about them anyway.

The morning of the third day the enemy artillery began a merciless pounding of Mount San Pietro, to our left where our battalion was. The gunfire was terrible without a pause; the mountain seemed to be burning. When the cannons quieted down we could hear the cries of our wounded. A few hours later our soldiers fled down the slopes of the mountain to the plain where the battalion commander led them back to their old positions, encouraging them with words and example.

That same evening I went to the command and on the way checked the telephone line that had been damaged. I can't tell you how terrible I felt when I saw that the battalion had been practically wiped out and hundreds of wounded lay on the ground. The white bandages stood out in the dark of night and everyone asked me for water but I could not help them.

After repairing the telephone line, I returned to my post cautiously for I knew the enemy was nearby. My buddies who were on the alert saw a shadow moving and not recognizing me, fired. It was a real miracle I didn't get killed and I threw myself to the ground behind a tree and shouted as loud as I could.

The rest of the night passed in great apprehension because we knew we were surrounded and that the rest of the battalion had left their positions. We were kept on tenterhooks and had our ears cocked for the slightest noise. What was to become of us?

The telephone rang around dawn and one of our men warned us to leave our position immediately and destroy everything. His voice was far, far away and urgent, we realized we had no time to lose. I detached the wires, grabbed the phone box by its leather strap and threw it down the slope. We destroyed the radio station and burned the documents in a hole, hiding the fire with a helmet and blankets. All this in a flash so we could get safely away as fast as possible and join the rest of our battalion.

We decided to walk apart from each other. It would take about half an hour in a terrain that was mostly flat, but with troughs here and there. I had been walking about five minutes when I saw a mule belonging to the enemy. The harness was not like ours and the animal too had different characteristics. The body was stubbier and the hoofs wider. There was a khaki coat on his saddlepack and I realized what was going on and was ready for anything. In a ditch I discovered a Greek soldier who thinking he was alone had dropped his pants and I'll let you guess the rest. I pointed my rifle at him and had to laugh at the tragicomic situation. I called my buddies and we made him follow us.

When we reached the place where the battalion command was, not a soul was around. Everything had been destroyed; even the food supplies had been abandoned in great haste. What to do?

We headed along a path trying to figure out where we were. Our prisoner in the meanwhile refused to walk, sure his comrades were near. Sometimes we even had to drag him along.

Before entering a mountain ravine, there was a burst of machine gun fire. We immediately threw ourselves to the ground just as we were ordered to stop. We abandoned the prisoner and fled into the ravine that was covered with dense vegetation where we could find shelter. We could hear the bullets whistle by and ran as fast as we could, for a while together, then separated.

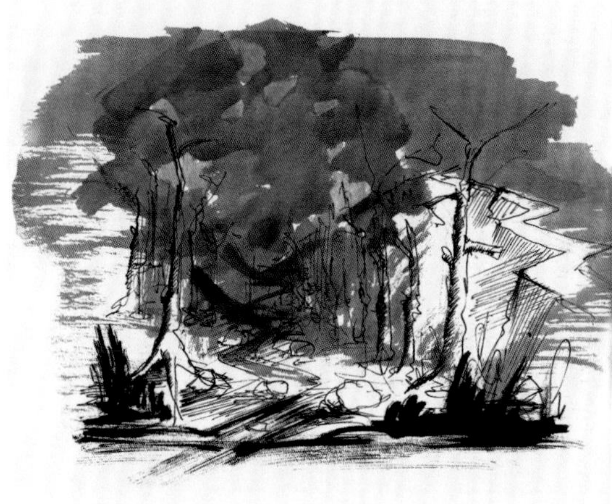

"I ran along the bottom of a valley between two hills where there was a brook."

I ran along the bottom of a valley between two hills, where there was a brook running zigzag so I wouldn't be hit. I threw away my equipment but kept the rifle. At least four men were following me and a burst of machine gun fire hit a rock near me and fragments of stone hit my mouth, teeth and under my chin.

I was bleeding and sweating and felt I was getting weaker. I had been running like that for more than a quarter of an hour. With a last burst of strength I climbed up the slope of the hill where I thought I would find the road. Finally at the top I found the road but it was occupied by Greek soldiers. Not far ahead in a curve I saw one of our tanks, shooting to keep them at bay, so I went back down the slope for a short distance moving over to where the tank was, my only hope for refuge. When I reached it I banged on the tank with the butt of my rifle.

Two soldiers opened the hatch and hoisted me in. I was bleeding so much from my mouth that they thought I was dead. They immediately applied first aid and since they had been ordered to withdraw they took me back to my unit where I was received with joy. I found out that many were missing, those who had returned didn't even have their rifles for they had left them behind in their flight. I was lucky because my wounds weren't serious.

We bivouacked on the top of a mountain where we felt safer and could get reorganized. But it was so steep and with such jagged rocks it was impossible to lie down without rolling off. We couldn't sleep and hung on to the rock but now and then a piece would come off and hit those who were lower down. We could hear them swearing and it was both funny and tragic.

I remember that that evening I filled my canteen with cognac and got plastered which made the situation even more difficult.

After a night and a day in that place, the front definitively broke up and we had to begin a long series of forced marches to get away from the enemy. We walked a whole night then stopped at dawn in a town to eat the last of our supplies. The mess consisted of pasta and beans. Hungry as we were as soon as it was cooked we couldn't wait and had eaten no more than a few spoonfuls when three or four cannon shots interrupted our party. We fell to earth, my mess tin flew in the air, it was a general scattering in all directions. One man was wounded and a mule was dead, the artillery had sighted us and shot right at the most crucial moment.

We had to start our march again on an empty stomach and without provisions. Besides this we were isolated and without means of communication. We were walking blindly hoping we were going in the right direction. We requisitioned some mules with Albanian drivers but on the third day after stealing some hand grenades from the boxes, they rebelled in a rugged mountain pass. In the commotion the mules fell into the ravines, and we had to carry what little material we saved on our backs to the top of a mountain almost three thousand meters high. There was a lot of snow and we couldn't stay there overnight because we weren't equipped for that temperature and had to go down the other slope.

After the snow, came a heavy rain that penetrated to the bone and lasted all night. Many soldiers fell to the ground exhausted by the long march. Because it was so intensely cold we had to keep active when we stopped and dug holes where we could take shelter from the bitterly cold air.

In the morning we continued our march. We had been marching for four days and were famished. In addition we were now thirsty and the soldiers drank the water that dripped down from their helmets. One of our planes appeared in the sky and threw down a folded map to tell us which way to go. The direction we were headed in was wrong and was taking us towards the border with Yugoslavia. I remember that immediately afterwards we crossed the woods with a great number of stuffed wolf heads, a local custom used to frighten off the other wolves.

The march continued and the hardships and hunger kept growing. We ate what we could find along the road: beets, roots, squash. We bartered our blankets and the few articles of clothes we still had with a few Albanians we met on the way for bread. The reconnaissance plane returned to tell us that planes would come to bring us food and blankets and we were ready so they could sight us. Words can't tell you what it was like to wait. After an hour three planes arrived, a bag of cans fell on a mule that died, other supplies ended up in ravines and we couldn't get at them. However it was really manna from the sky, since we hadn't eaten anything for five days!

We reached the mountain of Facia Kucit and camped waiting for the promised reinforcements. Since it was midwinter the front was not very active. During one of the minor engagements normally carried out, three prisoners were captured. Two of us were ordered to take them to the hinterland to the command headquarters. It would take three days of walking to reach it and we loaded up on cognac and supplies and started out.

It was a disaster because we got caught in a snowstorm in the mountains. A terrible wind was blowing that froze our breath and if it hadn't been for the cognac we would have been lost.

During a break the guide who had been sent with our group drank more than necessary, and fell to the ground despite the fact that we did all we could to get him to move. We had to keep jumping around all the time so we wouldn't freeze because the cold was really intense. Our guide remained immobile for a couple of hours. We shook him and to our horror realized he was dead. The cognac and his reaction to it had been fatal.

We buried him in the snow and made a cross on the tomb with branches so we could find the place later. The prisoners themselves took part in the painful episode. At this point it was up to us to orient ourselves since the man who had died knew these places well. We walked all night going down the mountain. A man saw us from the top of a peak and with gestures and shouts let us know we should wait for him. He was a captain of the Alpini who was to reach a height with his battery, but because of the ice he couldn't make it. So he himself was going to the regiment command to tell them the order could not be carried out and asked us to go with him. He was a handsome man of about forty, in poor condition and feverish. We told him what had happened and how long we had been in the front line without provisions.

After various vicissitudes too long to tell about here, we reached the command headquarters. I no longer had my shoes and after handing over the prisoners I sat down on some sacks of mule fodder waiting for a new pair.

After a day's rest we returned to our division. It was getting ready to move on and I felt ill at the thought of walking still more. I was dead tired and the soldiers of the division were just as tired. I had the advantage of having eaten well for a few days, while they had always been on rations.

As God wills, we started walking. They said the place was safe or at least on that side there was nothing to fear. At the end of the second day we moved into a valley with a small height on either side. There was no vegetation, nor a place to hide. We walked on the snow with the weapons on the mules and were not ready for an attack when volleys of machine gun fire suddenly arrived from the heights. We were already in the valley and realized too late that we had fallen into an ambush.

The colonel's horse at the head of the group was hit. There were documents in the saddlebags that many soldiers died in getting back. I was on the ground with two others. There was a sort of refuge about fifty meters away. The first of us fell under the

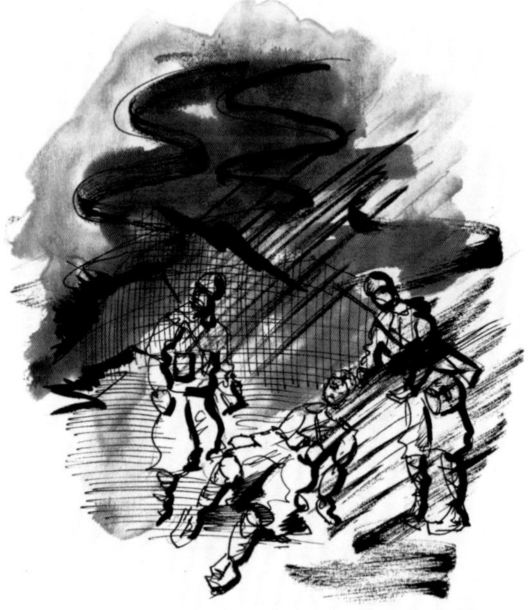

"Our guide remained immobile for a couple of hours."

machine gun fire, falling into a hole hidden in the snow and remained there where his foot stuck. The poor man tried to free himself, but in vain. I looked at him powerless. It was a question of a few seconds and then a burst of machine gun fire struck him full in the chest. I was wondering if I was to end up that way too, reached the wounded man just as he died, took the documents from his pockets and then also made a dash for it.

We mustered up and continued towards a safer place. Fifty men were missing. The battalion had been decimated after the battering it received. Everyone was tired, undernourished, and many had frostbite. The morale was very low and nerves were so edgy that hearing a shot was enough to throw the lines into confusion.

We passed the night gathered in a circle around the medical officer who tried to keep us moving so we would not freeze. It was not easy for we were exhausted and many froze their lower limbs.

The next day with three other soldiers I had to accompany one of our lieutenants who was charged with taking an important message to the third regiment which was not far off. When we arrived the colonel told us to remain with them. We weren't pleased at all for this was a new place, without friends and moreover we had heard that our battalion, which had been in the lines for four months, was going on leave.

We swore against this adverse destiny, we realized that the third regiment needed men and that was why they kept us, but we too had all the reasons in the world to wish for a bit of rest after all those vicissitudes. Our officer, a really understanding person and with good sense, told us not to worry and that he would make a request to the command and get us out of this situation. As for me I begged my buddies to keep calm, to keep together, and felt the responsibility not so much as a non-commissioned officer but as a man.

During the night though I realized that two of them had fled and I tried to go after them. I was alone in the middle of a deserted plain full of snow. The moon lit up the landscape. I will never forget that spectacle. The solitude so in harmony with my soul almost did me good. Every so often I stopped and called the fugitives. I returned empty handed but in a certain sense consoled and resigned. I had learned that only in moments of discomfort can one understand what some people we normally believe to be honest and loyal are really like.

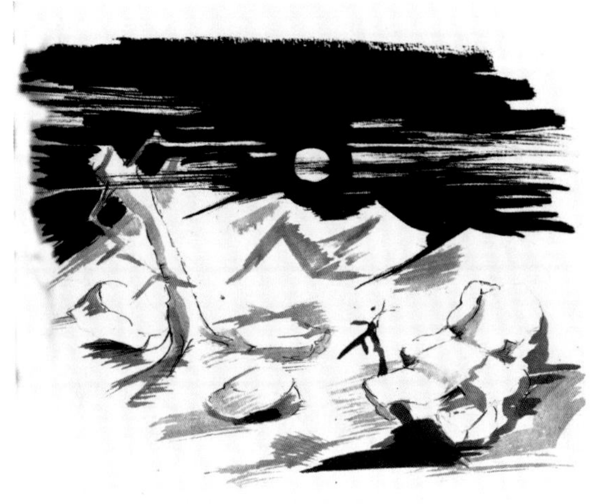

"The moon lit up the landscape. I will never forget that spectacle."

The other two were resigned like me, in the meanwhile we wrote a letter to the colonel asking him to send us back to our division. We barely managed, our eyes red and swollen from the snow and the smoke of the fires. We never got an answer.

The Greeks attacked the position and we were sent to the bottom of a valley which was the worst site. We felt that the end was near and the two comrades I had convinced to stay railed at me violently. It was my fault that they were in this predicament they might very well not live through. Depressed physically and morally as I was, it certainly didn't make me feel any better.

As luck would have it a tremendous thunderstorm broke out, and that's what saved us because the attack died down. We remained for a while huddled under a blanket while it poured, but suddenly we had the pleasant surprise of seeing our lieutenant calling us up to the top of the hill. Hope filled our hearts and we clambered to the top. There was mud everywhere and we sank in up to our belts but we already felt better.

The colonel was sending us back to our division and we could leave immediately. Imagine our joy!

Without waiting for anything we immediately set out but decided on a shortcut so we wouldn't have to pass in front of the command where we might be stopped again. We set off for a sharp ridge where we had to drag ourselves along straddling it for there was not enough room for our feet. We then reached the valley of the Devoli River. The course of this river is extremely winding and we had to cross it several times to shorten the distance.

We felt calmer and almost happy, but we were hungry. We found a squash, lighted a fire, cooked it and divided it into three equal parts. We walked for three days and nights, like in the fairy tales, before reaching our division that had moved considerably.

My shoes were worn out again, for those who don't know it snow and fire wear them out more than walking, so my big toes were sticking out. The road, if it can be called that, was made of rocks and pebbles and hunger made me imagine they were rolls and I kept stumbling over them with great pain.

At the end overcome by weariness and with my feet bleeding, I sat down on the ground. A mule with its driver went by and I asked him to let me mount the animal. He refused because the poor beast was suffering and undernourished but I just couldn't walk any more so I insisted.

The driver of the mule and my companions went on ahead. The mule walked slower than they did. It was dark and I couldn't see the road but at a certain point the animal stopped. There was no way of getting it to budge. I opened my eyes wide and realized that my feet were in the mud. Frightened, I realized we were in a swamp, a sort of quicksand of which there are many in Albania. The animal was sinking, what to do. I thought that a minute before we had been on solid ground so I gathered all my energies and jumped as far as I could in that direction. I was free.

Running I reached my group. It was horrible. Going back, the mule was no longer there. Sticking our bayonets into the mud we could feel the saddlepack the poor beast had on his back.

The road seemed endless, hunger and thirst gave us delusions and I mistook goat droppings for olives. It was only after having picked some up under a tree and was about to eat them that I realized my mistake.

From a height we finally saw the ordinance structures and even though we were exhausted we quickened our pace. There were some Italian civilian workers along the road and we asked them for bread. They had none and all of them looked at us with commiserating curiosity. We surely looked pretty awful after what we had gone through.

When we got to the tent of the officer on duty, we entered cautiously asking permission. Finally we could get some food into our stomachs. Behind the desk was a good looking junior grade lieutenant, and his shiny boots contrasted with our state. He looked at us for a moment speechless and then briskly told us to leave. He had not recognized our lieutenant as such because of the condition his clothing was in. Our officer took a step forward and gave him two resounding slaps, reproving him for his lack of comprehension. The second lieutenant excused himself saying he had not recognized him whereupon our officer added indignantly that you don't help human beings simply because they have bars.

We ate as you can imagine after three days of complete fasting and after a long period of hunger. I almost got ill after eating so much. The party lasted only a couple of days after which we left on a truck to reach our division, a few kilometres from Elbasan.

Of our whole division though, we found only twelve men. All the others, and there weren't many, were in the hospital recuperating. Joyfully we were reunited with our men. They all had on new clothing and were freshly shaved, but around their eyes there was still a halo of dirt that came down to the edge of their beard and that they hadn't succeeded in removing despite repeated washings.

We stayed in that encampment more than a week, eating well, sleeping all day, and getting ourselves cleaned up and in order, which we badly needed. The new conscripts arrived and I couldn't get on with them because they had a backward mentality and not having ever been in the war all they did was bluster around.

Then came the day when we had to leave for the front again. It was different from the first time when I had had a spirit of adventure and curiosity for the novelties we would encounter. Now with the past experience and the suffering I had been through, I did so with a heavy heart. I was tired and my body refused to take on other strains. But there was nothing I could do but leave.

On foot we reached a town that had not been completely abandoned. A few houses were still inhabited. It was winter and there was snow and those poor people had no other place to go. I was at the division command headquarters and since the front was practically at a standstill, except for an occasional insignificant skirmish in the environs, I found myself pretty well off.

We stayed there three weeks, but one evening the enemy identified the house where the headquarters was and destroyed it. I remember that at the time we were roasting a kid in a great fireplace. Everyone was gathered around, the whole squad and even the priest. The projectile fell right on the roast, with a deafening noise and we were all terribly frightened. Instead of putting on the helmet which I had set on the ground, I instinctively put on one of those enormous concave stones usually to be found in our kitchens and which serve as mortars for grinding rock salt. Luckily there were no wounded, except for the priest who had an abrasion on his head caused by a falling beam.

When things had calmed down I noticed people were looking at me and then I realized what I had on my head and that it was particularly heavy. My head flopped from one side to the other. Everyone laughed in contrast to the few terrible seconds of a minute before, but the roast had gone up in smoke!

One night we left again and were to replace the Ferrara division. Our battalion thus passed from the Ninth to the Tenth Army. In a zone where we were walking known as the Serpentina we were stopped and ordered to fall into line. The news immediately spread that the Duce was coming. Mussolini passed us in review. He paused in front of me and asked where I was from. When I told him Orvieto he said that the academy was there and pretty girls as well as good wine, then he looked at my shoes and observed that they were worn-out.

The Serpentina was the central zone of the front, where there were always terrible aerial battles. After a while our battalion returned to the Ninth Army. We didn't know that these shifts took place to prepare us for a great offensive. We were in the Val Tomorizza, the valley below Mount Tomori, the highest in Albania. The front was at a standstill, but one night we were suddenly ordered to move. It was April, the day before Easter. Our artillery began firing and that told us that something unusual was on foot.

We walked all night thinking how differently we would have spent the night before Easter at home. At dawn they stopped us. The valley was a great sea of fog and you couldn't see a thing. The company of "Arditi" was ordered to attack the enemy positions but it wasn't easy since the territory was rocky. Without the fog no one would have come back alive. We could hear great volleys of machine gun fire, then the "Arditi" returned to their former positions with a few losses. Crouched in our holes we thought of home, a chaplain brought us Communion there and that was how Easter day passed.

That evening we too were ordered to attack. We were worried about the danger lying in wait and we were well aware of it after what we had seen that morning. We walked cautiously and arrived at the enemy positions without anything having happened.

It was a pleasant surprise when we realized that the place was deserted because the enemy, for fear of being surrounded, had withdrawn. On dawn of Easter Monday we passed by the abandoned positions, with unexploded artillery shells scattered here and there and we had to walk most carefully. That time we were lucky.

The enemy continued to withdraw and we followed hard on their heels. We kept going without a break. We were exhausted and had all already eaten the reserves of food that had been calculated to last three days. Supplies were far behind because we were advancing so rapidly. So we were beastly hungry which made the march harder. At a certain point, overcome by weariness, I sat down at the edge of a slope. I felt my ears buzzing and I couldn't keep awake. Those who passed prodded me to continue marching, but I just couldn't. After an hour, I forced myself to get up and found myself alone. I then tried to overtake my comrades but they were further off than I thought.

Following mule tracks I had to be careful not to go on the wrong path and follow the Greeks, but luckily I knew that our animals had much smaller hoofs. I had to cross a stream, and because the footbridge was very narrow and because my legs wouldn't support me, fell in. That bath was really bad. I got real cold, with my uniform all wet I felt hampered and my movements were heavier than ever. But I had to walk. Never felt as lonely as then.

I met two mules with their drivers and joined them, putting my rifle on the saddle-pack and hung onto the tail. The animal was walking pretty fast and the road was all uphill and after a while I just couldn't do it any more. I sat down on the ground again to rest. After half an hour I started out when I realized that I had forgotten my rifle on the mule. Now what was I supposed to do? At this point I had lost them and I could do nothing but continue, unarmed. Luckily I met two other soldiers, lost like me, and they too were tired and famished. I felt better and almost stronger.

It wasn't an easy road. One steep slope after another and then still another. I just couldn't go on. In a lane we met a Coptic priest. I had never seen one before and was struck by the dignity of his dress. We stopped him and tried to get it across to him that we were hungry. It was not easy. Then we pointed to the bag he carried around his neck. He opened it and . . . miraculously, there was an enormous potato that he gave us then and there.

We couldn't wait to eat it. We made a fire and cooked our treasure under the ashes, divided it into three parts, all sweetness and light between us, and devoured it. In the meanwhile night was falling and we had to pass it where we were. Luckily we had our blankets.

The next morning we started off again. Suddenly a boar in flight ran into me from behind and threw me to the ground. If my companions had had their rifles ready, it would have been great. You can imagine our disappointment when we saw those hams run away. We were so hungry and just couldn't go any further that at a certain point we decided that if there was one more hill once we got to the top of the one we were climbing, we would just stop and wait for the good Lord to help us. As luck would have it when we reached the top we saw a town in the valley down below and the movement of soldiers.

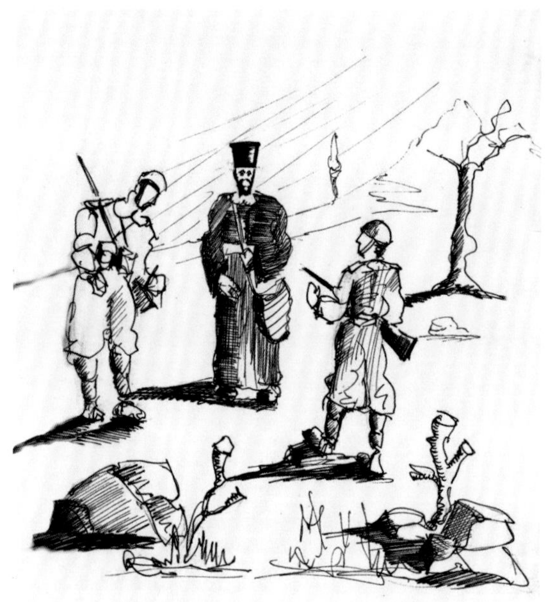

"In a lane we met a Coptic priest."

We ran down the slope and found our division camped there. Our captain was happy to see me but said he couldn't give me anything to eat until supplies arrived. While waiting he gave me a cigarette but after having smoked half I fainted. I was brought to by my captain slapping me and pouring cold water on me. As soon as I could walk I walked around the town and managed to pick up a string of dried figs that I ate then and there. But partly because I ate them so fast and partly because they were filthy, my intestines rebelled.

We stayed quite a while at Voskopoia, which is what the town was called. True, we slept on cement, but I could wash and eat. The war continued. There we weren't aware of it. One day the news arrived that hostilities had stopped. You can imagine how we jumped with joy, already thinking of going back home. There was a big party and we celebrated all day. But the news was false and we were devastated when we found our dreams had come to nothing. The day after came the official news that the war in Albania was really over. Nobody believed it and so there was no celebration.

We set out again, not knowing if they would send us home, which is what everyone hoped for. We were headed for Ponte Perati. The landscape was picturesque and we moved towards the Greek-Albanian border. In a large plain other divisions were camped, organizing themselves and resting. When I heard that one was the Cacciatori delle Alpi, I left my battalion to see if there was anyone from Orvieto. It was moving to meet people I knew. I greeted several of them. They were treated better than me and offered me things to eat that I was happy to accept, then I ran back to my division.

My battalion stayed there for a while, waiting for its destination. After the visit of a general I learned that we were going to Greece. This was the beginning of a march that lasted a whole month. It was already hot and we marched by night and camped during the day. In this way we arrived at Missolungi, a place hardly to be recommended and unwelcoming in all ways. We stayed there a few days before embarking for Patrasso. We had to be careful of mosquitoes and those on guard used unguents against insect bites, wore gloves and a net over their faces. One couldn't even light a candle without being submerged by a cloud of those nasty little beasts. Then we had to take pills of *italchina* and quinine was distributed in great quantities.

We embarked for the crossing and reached Patrasso which was deserted. As we marched, the band led the way. The inhabitants had all shut themselves in their houses. We pitched camp in a pine grove on a height. The first few days we went out in groups of six armed to the teeth. Gradually the city recovered its normal aspect and we began to see pretty Greek girls and everybody found his own girlfriend.

I was sent with others to the radio station in a castle near the sea. We had regal rooms and mine was magnificently furnished and even had an alcove. But I went to bed with my shoes on. In the morning we jumped out through the window and were on the shores of the ocean. Our girlfriends came to see us. Mine was the daughter of the manager of the provisions of the city, a sort of food administrator, and she always brought me delicious things to eat.

There were many Italian civilians in Patrasso and it almost felt like home. We adjusted easily. I remember that city with affection. I was sent to Megalopefco a few kilometres from Athens for a course of radiotelegraphy and almost every day I went to the capital. It did not live up to my expectations and the ancient monuments and a few other spots in the city were the only things that appealed to me: Piazza Psicalogna, Via Università, and the Royal Palace. I remember the guards in their skirts and slippers. After finishing the course of station master radio-telegrapher I returned to Patrasso and served as naval lookout. In the meanwhile the activities of the Greek partisans intensified. One episode of retaliation after another made round-up operations in grand style in the Peloponnesus necessary. Our division took part too. We were on the move for days, crossed many towns and in each one a census was taken in the town hall. The men who were found missing were considered partisans and therefore enemies so our troops burned their houses.

In one town we found munitions and were ordered to burn all the houses without mercy. A poor Greek whose wife was delirious with malarial fever begged us not to burn his house since he couldn't move the sick woman. I was moved to pity and asked the command to keep it and install the radio station there and he agreed. The owner was so grateful that he went to the chicken coop and wrung the necks of eight hens; then he broke open a sort of barrel full of cheeses and offered them to us. There were four of us and we left laden with gifts. We stopped when it was time to eat and cooked a chicken. But we weren't the only ones having a party because all the others were doing the same with the things they had taken. We returned to Patrasso happy and contented. That evening Badoglio signed the armistice. We all remember the date of September 8th. At first we celebrated at the news for the word armistice meant the end of the war. But then we realized that we were in real trouble. In the meanwhile the Greek civilians were leaving the cities with their household goods.

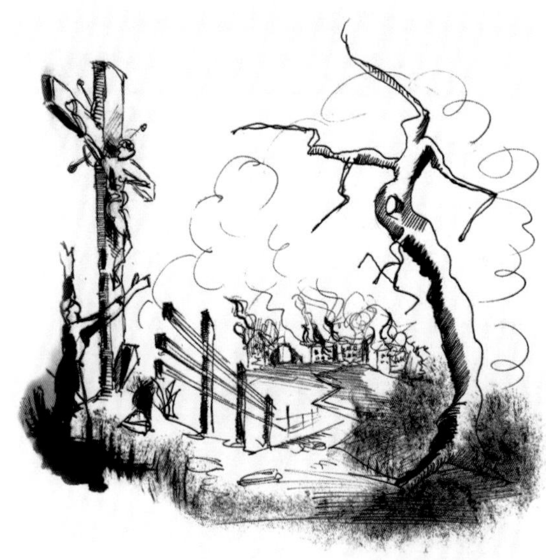

"... we ... were ordered to burn all the houses without mercy."

Next morning a telephone call was put through to the command, but the telephone line was down. There were two Germans, good friends of everyone in the barracks. When the occupying forces arrived with a tank and a truck full of soldiers, we didn't know what to do since we had no orders. Some wanted to shoot and some were against shooting. So the barracks were occupied without a shot as happened in many other cities.

The Germans rounded us all up. There were about five thousand soldiers from all the barracks of Patrasso and surroundings. We stayed there seven days and had nothing to eat except what some Greeks who took pity on us brought. One evening they called us together and it was said the Duce was to speak. There were loudspeakers and all around rows of machine guns to intimidate us. The voice speaking on the radio urging us to continue the war together with the Germans was not that of the Duce. We realized it was a trick to bring us to their side. The situation was serious because some of us wanted to rebel and the Germans would certainly have fired. One soldier was cool minded enough to climb on a pile of bricks and make a speech, telling us to keep calm. It was a daring act, but it worked and nothing happened.

We were taken to Athens on trucks and then on freight trains leaving for some unknown destination. When my turn came we climbed into an uncovered railroad wagon used for transporting coal. There were sixty of us packed in like sardines and it wasn't exactly happy. There was the vague hope that they would take us to Italy and even the most pessimistic had accepted this idea to console themselves. We had maps and could follow our itinerary. What a trip! It was a real cavalry and lasted all of fifteen days.

We passed by Salonika, entered Bulgaria passing via Sofia, crossed Yugoslavia via Belgrade and Zagabria, a small part of Hungary, Austria via Graz and Vienna, then Czechoslovakia via Prague and up through Germany to Berlin.

We were unrecognizable with our faces black from the coal dust. We slept one on top of the other like animals. When the wagons were closed at the borders with Germany, we couldn't even get off for water or anything else and it was a disaster but we managed as best we could.

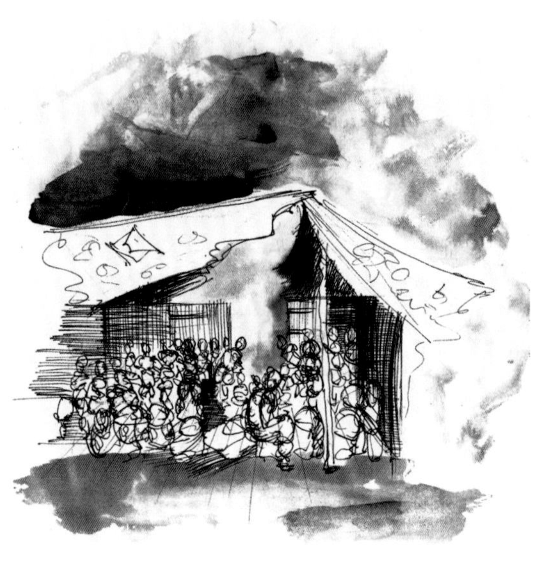

"... into an uncovered railroad wagon ..."

We had stretched canvas strips that served as roofing and which the wind blew away every so often. We had nothing to eat, but there was a cast iron stove in the middle of the wagon. It was not fastened and at every jerk or stop of the train, it bumped into one or the other of us so we decided to do without it despite the biting cold. The stovepipe was stuck into a hole that opened outside so it could serve as a urinal. One night by the light of a candle I saw that while one of my companions was using it, the tube leaked a few drops on the face of the man who was sleeping underneath.

Crossing Yugoslavia we were always hoping to return to Italy. It was absurd but we didn't want to convince ourselves. We anxiously awaited our arrival in Belgrade where we knew the railroad line split in two, for Italy and for Hungary. Our hearts were in our mouths, everything depended on what direction the train would take. I was already thinking of returning home, had been away three years, wondered how my mother was. I tried to imagine the meeting with my family and the joy of being in Orvieto again. We arrived in Belgrade and our hopes vanished. The train headed on to Hungary. What was to be our fate?

We arrived in Vienna with a bombing under way. After the danger was past, they made us get off with the excuse of seeing if there were weapons in our backpacks. When we got back on we found all the backpacks empty and the contents scattered here and there (the soldiers of the S.S. had plundered whatever they liked) and we had a hard time finding what was left. In one station they had momentarily removed the iron wires that closed the wagons. I tried to get off to get some water. A stationmaster yelled at me and I realised it wasn't allowed. I told him in German that I needed water. Seeing that I didn't give in, he gave me a kick in the behind. I felt my blood rise and was about to react when I saw a rifle aimed at me and had to calm down.

It had gotten terribly cold. I was dressed in khaki shorts and a shirt. The Germans in the stations looked at me with curiosity. In the towns we had gone through the civilians had thrown us things to eat but wanted clothing in exchange and I had sold everything. Not till the tenth day of our trip did the Germans decide to give us something to eat. It was a loaf of bread to divide among the sixty of us and we refused.

Conjectures were made as to what awaited us. Some said we would be sent to do farmwork, others we would have to work in the mines and that frightened us. In a small station called Buchenwald they had us get out. We were dead tired and were glad the trip was over. They took us to a vast concentration camp surrounded by triple barbed wire, with towers with floodlights and sirens. It looked like one of those well-organized prisons you see in American films.

"They took us to a vast concentration camp . . ."

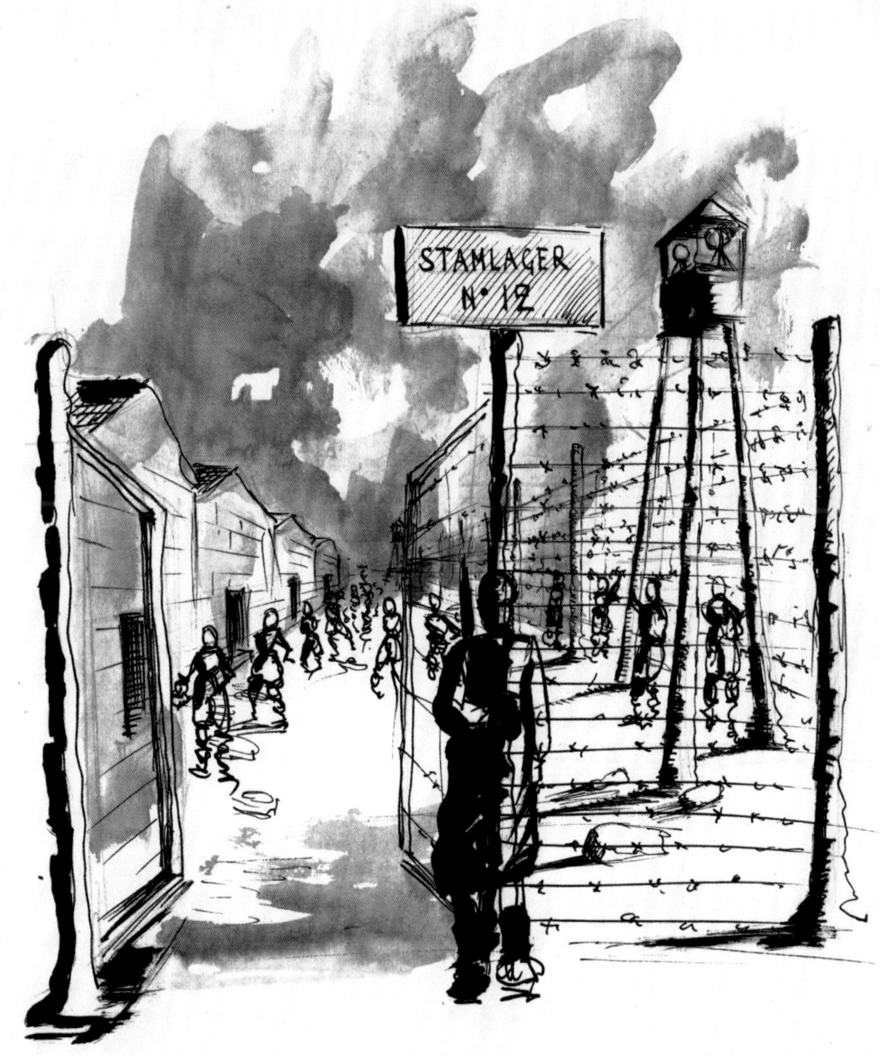

None of us had ever heard the name of Buchenwald and had no idea of the horrible place in which we were. The camp contained several thousand Italians. There was an area with sheds that served for the waiting period and we were lodged there. I stayed there fifteen days without doing anything. We were counted three times during the twenty-four-hour period and were always ready to be moved and admitted to the camp in which the lodgings were large tents. Trucks loaded with beetroot leaves arrived daily. The beetroot leaves were dumped into large ditches and washed there with jets of water so that the earth went to the bottom, after which they were taken out with big forks and boiled with a bit of salt. A bowl of that stuff was our soup. There was always half an inch of mud at the bottom. Together with a bit of bread and margarine this was the only meal of the day and for better or for worse. I finished it all I was so hungry. In the field there was a large ditch with a plank over it like a boardwalk that served as the toilet. At night it was lit by the floodlights and there was a sentinel. One night I had to get up to go there, the plank rocked and I fell in. I immediately fainted and came to under a jet of cold water that was washing me.

After a few days an epidemic of typhoid fever broke out and there was one death every day. We were all vaccinated and this delayed our admission to the final camp that took place after it had been washed and disinfected thoroughly. We could thus get to know the others. There were all nationalities: Serbians, Croatians, Russians, and also Princess Mafalda d'Assia. It had been a while that anyone had cigarettes. A few of us had managed to keep some and when we threw them across the barbed wire there was a fight to get them.

One day they photographed me with a number on my chest and took my fingerprints, just like in jail. They gave me an old Russian coat and wooden shoes and then set me on a train headed for Berlin. I was number 11.111.

After a short trip the train stopped in a part of the city called Tempelhof. I was lined up with other prisoners and we crossed through the streets of the city under guard to our new lodgings.

We were lodged fairly decently in a group of old buildings where there was also a small theatre. Many of us were assigned to work in the factories, others dug shelters and I was one of these. We had to get up at five in the morning and breakfast was handed out: tea and a loaf of bread to divide in seven. Often this brought about an argument. Hunger had banished any spirit of altruism and we were always afraid part of our ration, even a crumb, would be stolen.

We figured out a system that whoever divided the bread was to be the last to be served so that it would be in his interests to do it perfectly. After our group of seven became stable, we changed the distribution system. Once the bread was divided into equal parts, one member of the group turned around, another pointed to one of the pieces and asked him who was to get it and he answered with one of our names.

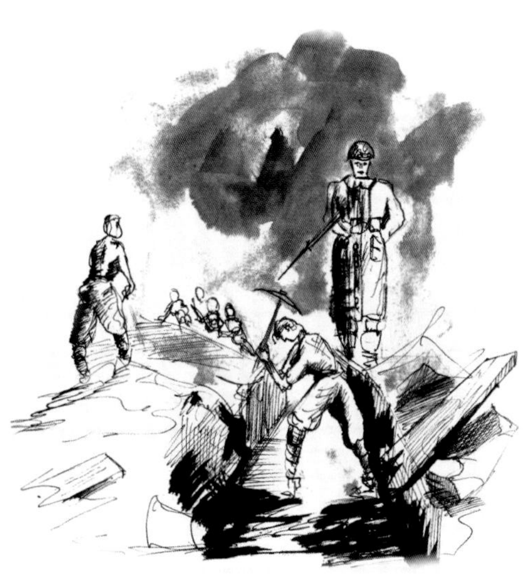

"We pickaxed all day till seven in the evening..."

After that they took us to work. We pickaxed all day till seven in the evening with a brief break at midday. The work could not be interrupted for any reason whatsoever. Before going to sleep they gave us a bowl of beetroot leaves, the only meal of the day. After a while we didn't even notice our hunger any more. We just couldn't shake off our exhaustion. Generally I took my morning piece of bread with me and ate it during the midday break. Once it was stolen from my coat pocket and partly out of anger and above all because I was so hungry, I felt sick and fainted. A German had pity on me and sent for some soup in a restaurant and that day I had a good meal.

Once we had to dig a shelter near a garden where there was a fine tree loaded with fruit that we kept looking at. The officer told us that he had counted the apples and if one was missing we would be severely punished. I was sure it was impossible to count them, since there were so many, so I decided then and there to steal one.

It wasn't easy. The tree was on the other side of a wire fence. If I managed to pick it, it would have fallen where I couldn't reach it. So I constructed a small basket of iron wire that I could attach to the end of a pole hoping to pick the apple that way. Since I could go near the fence to pick up the work tools, at the end of two days I had finished the basket.

At the first try I was so excited and fearful that the apple fell outside. On the second try I succeeded. When the shelter was done, the officer praised us because we had behaved well and said we should be rewarded and gave each of us an apple.

Normally I would have refused it, for my conscience wasn't really at ease since I had already taken one by myself. But I was so hungry that I ate it after having drunk the good coffee that the owner of the garden offered all of us.

For a few days I had to work with German soldiers. There were only two of us Italian prisoners and we were constantly humiliated, even by the kids in the street. We were accompanied to work by an old German soldier and one evening he got drunk and I had to accompany him back to his lodging. Along the street where we passed every day there was a large doorway with an enormous garbage bin and I always rummaged around in hopes of finding something to eat. Once as I was doing this I felt two apples fall on my head and glimpsed a woman who was shutting a window. It was strictly prohibited to feed the prisoners. Every day I went to work in a building where a good-hearted lady gave me a few pieces of bread and I had a good supply that I jealously guarded in my backpack. One day when I was hungry I found nothing there; my pantry had been plundered. The tram and buses had compartments for the prisoners. We were always packed in and there were all nationalities. Once a Russian gave me a large package and another Russian gave me a tiny one. I was curious to see what they contained and as soon as I was alone I opened them. In one there were boiled potatoes and in the other some salt.

Then the bombings began. We had to take shelter in a trench that was anything but safe. The alarm began at seven in the evening and ended around two in the morning. We shivered from cold and fright, and when we left we could see everything lit up like day by the great fires. We had to clear away the rubble and saw scenes of terror. If a prisoner was discovered taking something belonging to the people he was shot then and there.

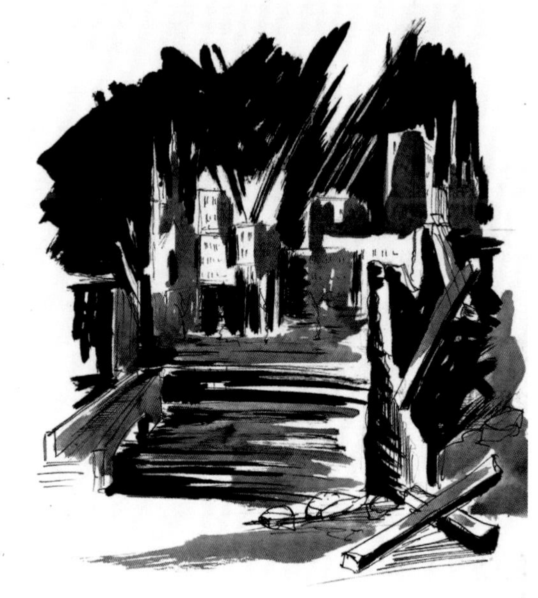

"... we could see everything lit up like day by the great fires."

I was transferred to a new camp in a peripheral area called Spandau. The lodgings were barracks near those of the French prisoners who got packages of supplies every week, and then barter began. I had nothing but what I was wearing but even so found a way to exchange it with others that were worse and in addition get something to eat. This trading went on at night and on the sly. I jumped from the window of my barracks and went into the other one where the French were. Once on my return I was discovered and the sentinel in the tower called halt while the nearby searchlight was turned on and the blinding light hit me. I realized I would be searched.

The German sergeant who reached me did not shoot but kicked me in my behind, breaking the crackers I had put in the back pocket of the jacket. At every kick I tried to cover the noise of the crackers being broken up with a sob.

Sometimes with a companion we had to help peel potatoes. We managed to keep some for ourselves and cooked them on the walls of the stove that was inside the barracks. The German who kept watch began to wonder how we got hold of the potatoes. He promised not to punish us if we told him how. Then we explained our system: we cut the potatoes in thin slices and then wrapped them to our legs under the cloth leggings that were part of our uniform. Nobody noticed that our calves were much larger than usual. The German laughed, surprised at our brilliant solution.

Our transferrals continued and we travelled all around Germany, lastly the area between Munich and Innsbruck. Finally they concentrated us in a camp near the latter. There were the usual sentinels and everything else. Things were coming to a head and one morning we realized to our great surprise that no one was controlling us. We didn't know what to do and if on the one hand we rejoiced on the other we were really worried. If we escaped they could capture us, if we stayed, we risked some kind of retaliation by the Germans who knew they were in trouble. I thought about it a while and decided for flight. Dressed as I was, with a torn Russian overcoat, I jumped the barbed wire at night and ran as fast as I could. I walked hoping to get closer to Italy, avoiding the railroad line and the more frequented roads. I continued in this way for a few days, and managed to join some Italian workers who were boarding a train that took me as far as Bolzano and shortened my road a great deal making it easier to get over the hardest part. In the meanwhile the war had ended.

By whatever means of transportation I found and partly on foot I arrived in Milan. I had no idea what was going on politically and found everything different from what I imagined. It was the day after Mussolini had been killed and in Piazza Loreto I saw a sight I couldn't understand. Armed people were milling restlessly around and you could have cut the atmosphere with a knife.

Since it wasn't possible for me to go to Orvieto right away, I thought I would write to some relatives of mine in Vercelli so I wouldn't take them by surprise, in particular since we hadn't been in touch for years. I managed to hitch a ride and by evening I was at their house. They received me warmly and took care of me, dressed me decently and I immediately felt a new man. But I couldn't wait to return home and immediately began the paperwork to have my regular documents.

One day I was calmly walking along the streets of Vercelli when a young arrogant man stopped me and said he had recognized me and that I'd better not bluster around like I used to. I still didn't know what was really going on politically and laughed and said I didn't know him. He slapped me a couple of times, other people approached and I was taken to the police station. My protests were in vain, and although I told them I had just come back from Germany no one believed me. They had mistaken me for someone else.

I was shut up in a cell with others who were there for political reasons. I resigned myself thinking that soon the mistake would be clarified. A day went by and my relatives looked for me. When they heard what had happened they did nothing to help me for they had been Fascists and were considered such and their intervention would have made things worse.

The second day I was in prison, they took me before a sort of court formed of partisans. They all looked pretty truculent with machine guns on the table. I was thinking that they would realize there was a mistake and would set me free, but I was mistaken.

They set me face to face with the person who accused me and he affirmed that I was the person, that he recognized me, as the Fascist who had cut his red tie in a sign of scorn some time before. I realized I was in real trouble. I denied it with all in my power but they didn't even listen and I was taken back to prison. I was in the hands of those hotheads and no one was going to help me.

I passed the night ranting and raving, about to have a nervous breakdown. Here I was finally in Italy, almost home, and adverse destiny had this sad trial for me. In the morning, since I hadn't calmed down, to satisfy me and for another face to face, the court called for another session. The man who accused me continued to say he was not mistaken and I said he was. No one listened to me so I had him ask me questions, to tell me how and when it had happened. When they told me the date, I remembered that that day I was in Milan, and told them so, happy to have found an alibi, for I remembered that I had the letter written to my relatives in my pocket. It had arrived after me and it was pure chance that I had kept it.

Triumphant I gave it to the judges. The contents as well as the date convinced them, but they still wanted to have a calligraphic examination to make sure I had written it. I filled pages and pages of paper and in the meanwhile my accuser kept looking at me and said that maybe, on second thought, I wasn't the person he meant. It was a real miracle that I didn't go after him!

As soon as I was free again, I said goodbye to my relatives, went to the first road-block and left with a truck that took me up to Modena and then hitched rides till I got to the station of Orvieto.

I can't tell you how excited I was when I saw the cliff of Orvieto. I walked towards the funicular that had started running again those days. Full of joy I hugged the ticket taker who was surprised at this sign of affection. When I told him I was returning from being in prison, he understood, but said he was sorry that he couldn't take me up since I had no money for a ticket.

Without thinking twice, I started walking up the *piagge* (slopes). I was tired, but what did that matter?

I was home.

And that was how that sad period so many were never able to tell about came to an end.

CHAPTER THREE

Livio's Life as Seen by Others

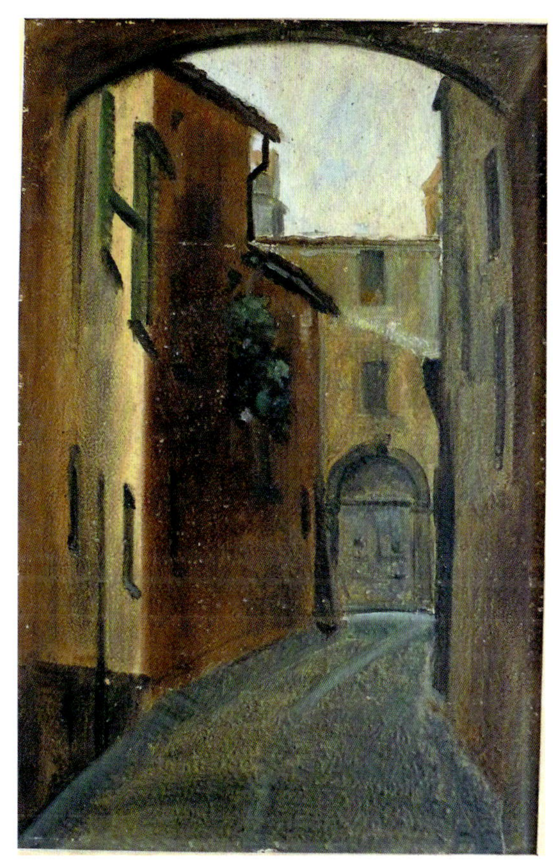

Professor Fernando Puppo, *Scorcio di un borgo* (Glimpse of a Village). Oil on canvas, 58 × 38.5 cm. Palazzo Coelli, Orvieto. Photograph courtesy of Fondazione Cassa di Risparmio di Orvieto.

Livio returned to Orvieto in 1945 and as a part of his healing process began evening drawing classes with Professor Fernando Puppo (1887–1962). At this time Valentini asked himself "how" to paint rather than "what" to paint. He first worked on the top floor of a *palazzo* on Via del Duomo n. 34, an attic used by the poet Angelo Rossi and frequented by the painter Eliseo Stella.[1]

Livio lived with his parents for two or three years while he struggled to establish himself as an artist. During that time, he said, "I did a lot of different things to make money and help the family." As he became more involved with Professor Puppo's classes, Livio started taking his art more seriously and worked as if he were a professional. While Livio sat on a street corner one day hoping to sell something, a man came by, lit a cigarette and watched Livio work on a painting. After he had extinguished his smoke, he said to Livio, "If you will put some more trees with green leaves on the branches in that painting I will buy it." Looking up, Livio said, "There are no trees with branches." The man responded, "There should be trees with branches and green leaves. If you could do that I will buy the painting." Livio was so desperate to make money he gladly complied with the request. After several more suggestions the gentleman indicated he was pleased and paid the asking price of thirty thousand lire, which according to Livio was not very much. However, he was delighted because he was now a "professional artist," having made his first sale.[2]

That work hung for years in the condominium of Pia Custodi, first cousin of George Custodi's father. The Custodi children called her "Zia" or "Aunt." Her husband, Elio, was the person who bought the painting from Livio. It is a very realistic scene of a man and a woman beaching two rowboats on a wide expanse of sand beneath a stand of palm trees. Across the water in the background is a typical Mediterranean village accented by a fogbank. The sunny afternoon draws one to the coast and evokes a sense of a romantic interlude. George and Bob spent several hours in March of 2006 sipping wine with Pia who was ninety-four at the time and discussing how her beloved husband gave the painting to her when they were first married.

Pia insisted on cooking the midday meal several times for George and Bob while they were in Orvieto. These were always feasts with a variety of regional dishes and lots of good local red wine. As we enjoyed her company, she would remind us her husband Elio had been "Mr. Orvieto" in his earlier years and she had won several glamour contests. She was still very lovely at the time of our visit, especially in spirit.[3] She celebrated her one hundredth birthday in January of 2012 and died in June of the same year. The painting, now called *Incontro sulla riva* (Meeting on the Shore), was bequeathed to George and his family.

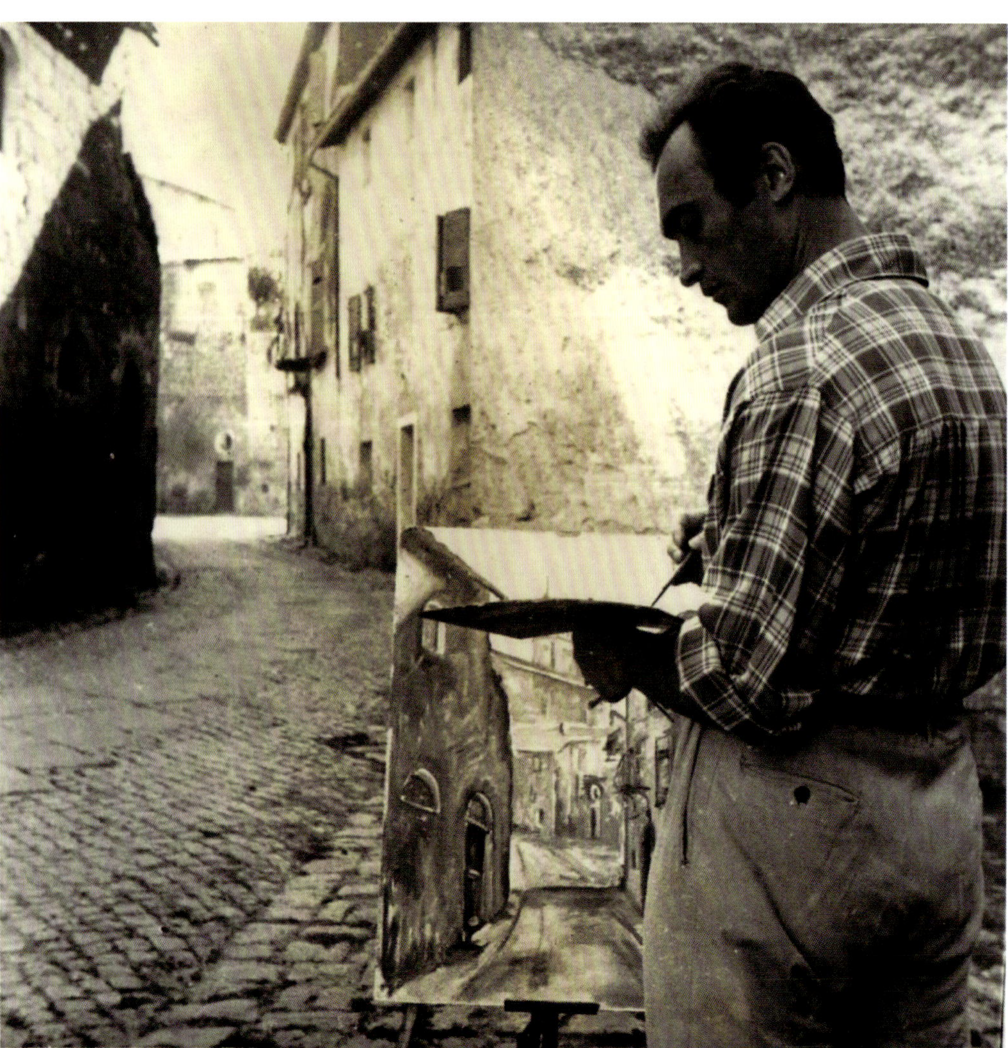

Livio Orazio Valentini paints near Santa Clara in Orvieto. Photograph courtesy of the Valentini family.

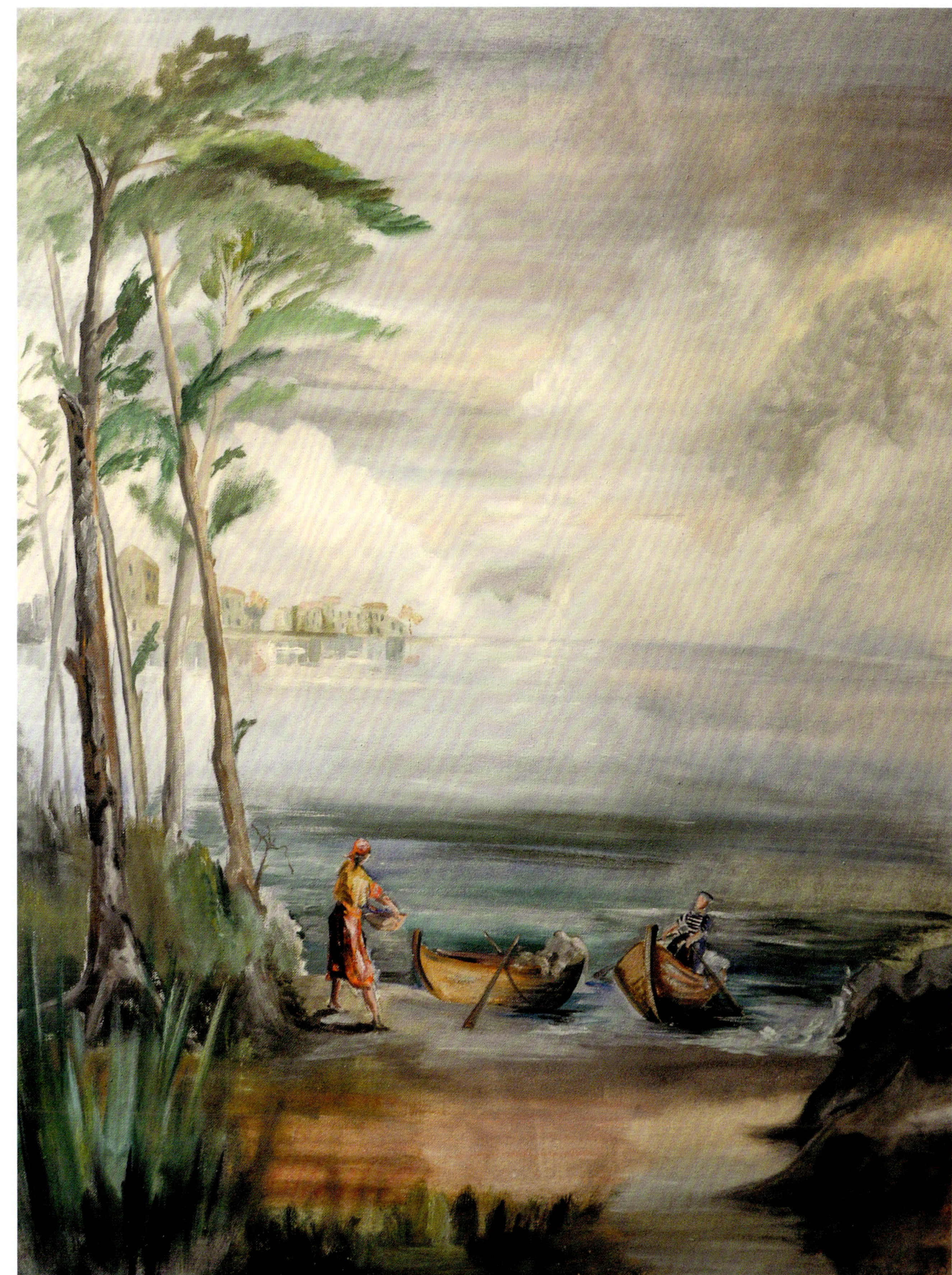

Livio's first professional painting, *Incontro sulla riva* (Meeting on the Shore), 1945. Oil, 119 × 152 cm. Collection of George and Sandi Custodi. Photograph by Michael St. John.

Over a period of several years, we had the opportunity to interview a number of Livio's friends in Orvieto. While the primary focus of our questions was about the man and his art, many of his friends ventured into more specific areas of his life. A recurring theme for several friends was their perspective on Livio's wife Flora's role in his development as an artist. Some wondered why his importance was not recognized earlier. Flora's dominance in his day-to-day life and the resulting limitations were certainly factors. Likewise, they credited Flora for her positive influence in the founding of the Istituto d'Arte and for providing financial stability for the family.

Livio worked with Puppo for several years refining his painting techniques and his use of color. Even though he was poor and outside the mainstream of Orvieto's cultural elite, Livio was fortunate to have several sponsors who would introduce him to their friends. As a young bachelor, war hero, and artist, he became very popular with the young ladies of Orvieto's party set.

"Livio found there were a lot of people who supported him as a man and an artist," said Torquato Terracina, then president of the Orvieto Foundation, Cassa di Risparmio. He had been a practicing architect and had known Livio professionally and personally since the 1950s. Terracina spoke of Elena Bonelli who "did a lot for Livio during his early time as an artist. She would bring him lunch and encourage him. Bonelli acted as his financial sponsor and she hosted special evenings when she invited guests for dinner and music. At these salons she introduced some of the wealthier people to Livio and his art."[4]

Elena Bonelli was a fine pianist. Her brother was an architect who wrote much about the Duomo. They were descended from the old families of Orvieto. However Livio eventually met the beautiful Flora Bruno and his relationship with Elena changed altogether. The carefree days of socializing came to an end when he met the love of his life.[5]

Flora was born in 1921 in the town of Arezzo to Rina Coleschi (1896–1973) and Carmelo Bruno (1883–1944). Flora was the second child of five siblings: two brothers, Carlo and Mario, and two sisters, Giuliana and Margherita. She described the early days of their childhood and time in the Arezzo elementary school as being family oriented. During the years the girls were in school "they were assiduously followed by their loving aunt Menchina, sister of their maternal grandfather," who was of Polish origin. The family environment was "serene and culturally stimulating."

Flora graduated from the Istituto Magistrale. In 1938 Carmelo and Mario moved to the Bruno family home in Lecce where her father devoted himself to their artisan workshop, specializing in making papier-mâché statues of sacred subjects. In the meantime Carlo completed his art studies and enlisted in the Italian navy and was assigned to Trieste. Giuliana and Flora enrolled at the university in Florence in 1939 where Flora began studying mathematics.

The bombing of Arezzo started in 1940. Like so many of the more affluent Italians, the Bruno family moved out into the countryside to escape the constant threat of war. They lived there for the duration of the fighting, but this move did not spare Flora's family from tragedy. Carlo left Trieste where he was serving in the navy and in 1942 joined the partisans in Tuscany. Margherita married in 1943 and moved with her husband to Liguria. On July 14, 1944, Carlo was killed in the massacre of San Polo in the outskirts of Arezzo, together with forty-eight others, including civilians and partisans gathered by the German troops from the Arezzo countryside. When the war ended, Flora returned home where she received the tragic news of her brother's death and learned that her father had also died from pneumonia. Her brother Mario remained with an uncle in Lecce until 1947 when Flora's mother was reunited with him. During that time, her mother sold her husband's house and settled his estate.[6]

Upon their return to Arezzo, Flora and Giuliana lived with their grandmother and an aunt until Giuliana married. Flora was able to get an annual post as a teacher in the Istituto Tecnico in Arezzo in 1945. She said it was the "type of teaching job that enabled her to return to the university in Florence," where she earned a degree in mathematics and received certification to teach. While studying for her degree, she worked as a governess with the family of the Ginori Princes in addition to giving private lessons. After receiving her degree in 1951, her first assignment was as a mathematics teacher in the lower school of the Istituto Tecnico in Gavorrano, followed by her second post in the middle school of Follonica, and her third post in the middle school of Cecina. She participated in the *Concorso,* a national competition for teachers, and was granted tenure. She taught mathematics for the remainder of her professional career.[7]

In a joint interview, Livio and Flora shared how they met in the beach town of Follonica in the summer of 1955. Livio was doing commissions for the Parrini family who owned the dance hall and hotel, painting "special panels which were used to cover the beach cabin doors during the dance parties." Flora had lost her lease for the house she lived in during the school year. Everyone in Italy was on vacation in July and it was impossible to find a regular cottage. She and her girlfriend wanted to spend their summer vacation at the beach so they rented a room in a hotel still under construction. Flora remembered, "We were dead tired. We had finally found a place to rest and just as we lay down, an orchestra began playing outside on the dance floor. Between one trumpet blast and another we managed to fall asleep. The next morning we went out for a brief walk, came back to relax and were about to take a nap when we heard the sound of clogs going back and forth in the corridor." Flora recalled that she threw open the window on the veranda and there stood Livio. He turned around with the brush in his hand and she began laughing. Livio reflected, "A beautiful young woman stuck out her head and told me to stop all of the noise." He assured her he was not the guilty party. This chance meeting was the beginning of their short courtship. Flora remembered their first encounter as "love at first sight when their eyes met." After a cautionary comment from Livio of "*calma, calma*," Flora said, "Maybe not love at first sight but curiosity."[8]

As Livio decorated the interior of the hotel he became very close friends with the Parrini family. Otello, the owner, remembered the first moments of the love story of Livio and Flora. According to Maurizio Parrini, the son and now owner of the hotel, his father believed he was responsible for their relationship. He said at the time, "We contributed to the genesis of their romance. We took part in their bantering because we saw Livio as very much in love. Father told him an artist should stay single because making love would dull his artistic abilities. Instead, Valentini's talents grew with his ever more beautiful masterpieces which to this day adorn our dining area and lobby."[9]

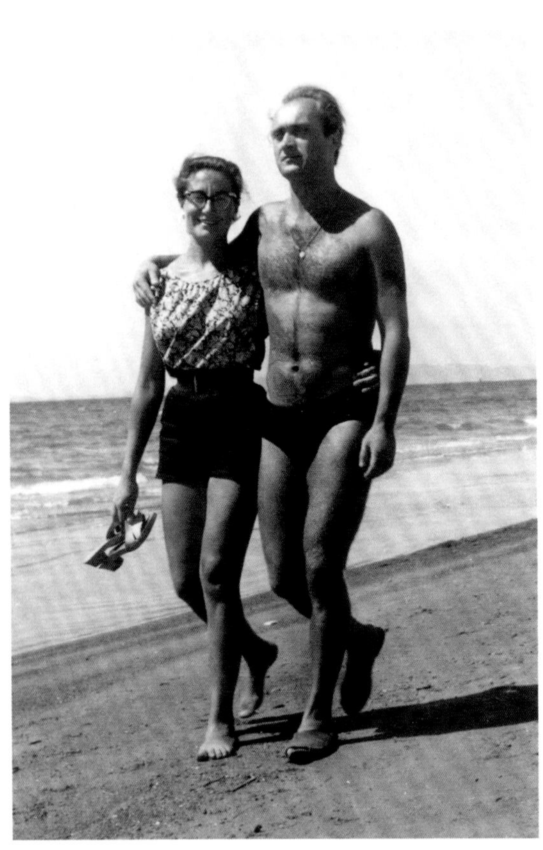

Livio and Flora at Follonica in 1956.
Photograph courtesy of the Valentini family.

Terracina, Livio's architect friend, owned a summerhouse in Follonica. The same summer when Livio and Flora met and had begun dating, Terracina organized a party. He invited a number of young people including Livio, a couple of Italian Olympic sailors and lots of girls. Terracina had a Citron convertible, which really appealed to the young ladies. They did not invite Flora but she found out about the party and became very mad at him and Livio.[10]

Livio and Flora did not see each other for a while; he was busy painting with a friend in the nearby countryside. She and her girlfriend left the beach for several weeks to take a special class. Eventually Livio and Flora began to date more seriously. One of their favorite pastimes was to go to the children's merry-go-round near the beach. Flora said her Follonica students thought it was wonderful to see her and her boyfriend riding on a merry-go-round. They would shout "*La Signorina Flora, la Signorina Flora*!"

The following fall, when Flora was living in Florence and teaching in nearby Cercina, Livio traveled to visit her. They met in the Boboli Gardens on these occasions and soon became engaged. In October of 1956 Flora became teacher of mathematics and science at the preparatory school in Orvieto. It was only a matter of time before their dating days were over and they were to be joined in matrimony. On July 2, 1957, they married in Assisi in the Church of San Damiano, which had previously been a convent. Franciscan friar Silvio Pellico performed the ceremony. The wedding party consisted of two witnesses: Livio's friend, the painter Manlio Bacosi, and Flora's friend Ione Banchelli, a teacher. Referring to a book written by the friar entitled *Le Mie Prigoni* (My Prisons) during our interview, Livio said, "We were off to a good start." In retrospect he seemed to be referring to their marriage as a type of imprisonment.[11]

However Flora said, "My family was pleased with my marriage to Livio. At the time he was fairly well known as an artist in that region. He eventually earned enough so that with my salary we lived comfortably." They settled in Orvieto in an attic apartment with barely enough room to include Livio's studio. Over the next nine years they had three daughters. Cristiana, the first, was born nine months after they were married. The next two daughters were Silvia, born in 1961, and Francesca, born in 1966. Livio had chosen the male forms of names for each of the children well before they were born because of his hopes for a son.

Livio and Flora continued to vacation in Follonica renting one of the small cabins on the beach. Flora recalled, "Follonica was the ideal place for the girls in the summer and for keeping the sailboat, especially since sailing was one of Livio's great passions as a young man."[12]

Some years later, a close friend related a story about Livio's daughters. A very successful vintner whose vineyards were outside of Orvieto came into town to do some banking and buy his weekly supplies. He encountered Livio and they began to discuss his art. During an extended conversation, he made it very clear he did not understand what Livio was trying to do with his paintings. He said that his grandchildren could do as well as what he had seen Livio do. He paused for a moment and said that Livio should make more daughters and paint fewer paintings. "You make beautiful daughters. The art I am not so sure about." This thought expressed the reactions of many who simply did not understand Livio and what he was doing with his art. However, Livio was fortunate enough to have a special group of friends who did understand who he was and what he was attempting to do.

During the early sixties, Livio surrounded himself with people who became his life-long friends and influenced his journey in significant ways. Benedetto Burli and Gualverio Michelangeli were Livio's closest friends. "They were three but

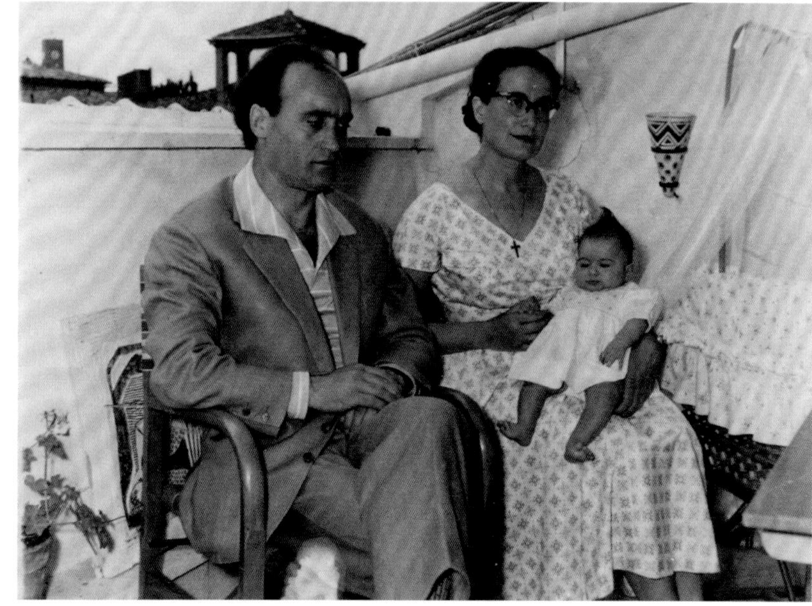

Livio and Flora Valentini with baby Cristiana on the terrace of their house in 1958. Photograph courtesy of the Valentini family.

one. You could not separate them," recounted Benedetto's wife Laura Boletta. Laura referred to them as the "three musketeers" who would spend most of their free time together sharing music, good local wines, and ideas. Benedetto taught philosophy in high school and authored several books. "The three of them got together, listened to jazz, and discussed philosophy, politics, and the arts." These were nearly always all-male evenings, usually at Benedetto's home. These extremely close friends authored a limited edition book, entitled *Impressioni,* published in 1962. Livio produced the illustrations in the form of woodcuts and Benedetto wrote the poetry. This volume led to Livio's exhibition at the Hotel Reale.

Laura recalled, "They were three soul mates who shared various creative interests and a closeness not often found among males. They shared a level of spirituality in their discussions of art and philosophy." They explored their deepest feelings and this helped sustain their friendship. According to Laura, these were happy times in all of their lives. Their wives only occasionally joined in the evenings until some jealously objected when they were excluded. As a part of the rhythm of life they drifted apart as their families grew in size and they assumed more responsibilities. Their evenings became fewer and fewer but the basic friendships remained for the rest of their lives. Laura believed these special friendships helped launch Livio's career.

In particular Laura spoke of the critical role Michelangeli played in Livio's early days as an artist. The Michelangeli family was involved in making furniture and accessory items for the home. With Livio, they introduced a series of unique designs featuring angels. These remain a major commercial success to this day. Livio worked for a number of years with the Michelangeli family designing furniture and others items they sold as he developed his own art. Nearly everyone interviewed indicated this relationship was a significant part of Livio's growth as an artist. He held several early exhibits in the space below the main retail store.[13]

Laura felt Flora's jealousy caused the relationship between Livio and Gualverio to change significantly. Livio stopped working for him when he started teaching at the Istituto d'Arte. Flora expressed her belief that Livio did not get the credit he deserved for many of the designs still being used by that family.

Starting in the late 1950s, Livio spent different intervals in Rome working with several other artists attempting to break into its art scene. According to Flora, Livio became acquainted with Monsignor Giovanni Fallani, president of the Pontifical Commission for the Sacred Arts in Italy. This relationship became very important because Fallani encouraged Livio to take part in shows in Rome. He urged Livio to experience the ambiance of Rome and associate with the artists there. In 1967 Livio moved his studio to Rome and worked in that environment for about one year. Livio believed this experience helped him become a better artist. Flora on the other hand "did not think it was very useful."[14]

Flora complained when Livio was in Rome with his fellow artists for weeks at a time. Sometimes he came home on the weekends or she went to see him. During his tenure in Rome, she entered a competition to become a principal. Flora remained in Orvieto with their very young children, teaching full-time to support the family. She remembered their house, which also served as his Orvieto studio, being quite small and depressing. According to Flora he would spend weeks on end in Rome painting and socializing.

Flora believed Livio did not need Rome. She commented, "He was doing okay by himself. He had friends in Perugia who were also painters. I began to take greater interest in what he was doing later, after the girls were older. . . . I really became interested in his work in the period when he met the art critic Michele Greco who became personally supportive of Livio. When Greco wanted to include Livio in an exhibit of Roman artists, they refused him. Perhaps because of jealousy, the artists in Rome did not accept him yet. It was a closed circle."[15]

Even while exploring Rome, Livio continued to exhibit his art in Orvieto. Giulio Montanucci, who owned an art gallery there from 1967 to 1988, curated numerous one-man shows for Livio. Montanucci, a leader of the Communist Party in Orvieto following the end of World War II, represented Livio during those twenty-one years. Bob interviewed him in the basement of a convent, the location of the archives for the Orvieto Communist Party. The walls were lined with shelves containing old brochures, pamphlets, and numerous posters. To sit in that venue was a strange experience, like being drawn into another world.

Surrounded by his treasured memories, Montanucci began to reflect:

> Livio always took the side of those who were suffering, of the helpless and of the poor. His imprisonment during the war was undoubtedly a major reason for the decisive choices in his drawings and paintings. Examples are: his processions, the expression of the suffering of humanity, his carts simply made, his birds in cages and the chained, trapped, or pierced birds. These paintings gave witness to the side Livio was on. As a man of peace, he could not understand the arrogance of the state acting against its people who lived in concert with their culture, customs and traditions.

> My meetings with Livio regarding the monstrous and horrible wars of those years led inevitably to the question, "Why does one man want to kill another man?" He often referred to the *bas-relief* by the artist Bruno Canova who was interned in a Nazi labor camp as a young man. The scene shows two men, one Austrian and one Italian during World War I killing each other with bayonets attached to their rifles. This was a statement of the futility of war especially in the form of hand to hand combat where you eviscerate your enemy up close and personal.

At times, Livio's art was controversial to those in the Comune, the political governing entity of Orvieto. Montanucci remembered:

> Often Livio was boycotted by people who should have appreciated him the most. The best example is *The Massacre of Camorena,* one of his most important political statements. I suggested it, Livio painted it. The struggle was among the Comune leadership as to how and where it would be hung. The painting was displayed originally in the town hall and then after a major reaction it was moved to the Palazzo dei Sette, the governor's room, where it still is today. It deserved to be hung in a place worthy of its political and moral influence. After all it had been a gift from Livio to the Comune. Livio had asked for nothing but the costs of the pigments. He suffered much abuse from some leaders who should have been his strongest supporters. One of the insults hurled at Livio during this controversial time was "*Pitto* (Painter), who in the hell made you go to Ursoline on vacation during the war? It didn't help humanity in the least!" Members of his family believe Ursoline was a snide reference to his Catholic schooling as well as time in the concentration camps.[16]

One leader who did support Livio was Vladimiro Giulietti, who at the time of our interview was ninety years old but very alert. During the war he served in the Italian navy. He was a leader in the Comune for twenty years, serving as vice mayor for fifteen years and mayor for five years. Along with Montanucci, he encouraged Livio to commemorate the massacre at Camorena. He wanted to hang the painting in the Comune but many disagreed. There was quite a controversy over the subject matter and what it represented. "Even though Livio's tendency was more to the left than to the right," according to Giulietti, "he never used his art to advocate a particular position."[17]

Several years later, Livio spoke directly to the issue of politics and art when interviewed by Alessandro Bosi for a chapter entitled "The philosophy of good sense of

Valentini." Bosi asked, "In a moment in which the artists are used to taking on political 'labels', you seem to be doing all you can to refuse them. Is this impression right? If it is, can you explain why?"
Livio responded:

> I am always a bit embarrassed when I follow the arguments between "advanced" ideologies, of which the many or too many subtleties always evade me. I have my clear ideas, which I have put together, unobtrusively, on the basis of my personal experience of the world. And some of the ideological positions have my intuitive and immediate assent. Don't ask me to explain in words. The most traumatizing observation is that when the ideologists talk together, they agree at the end on one single point. . . . Don't ask me to take part in this game. When discourses become too abstract I soon lose the gist.
>
> There was a time when I painted stone splitters and processions. Do you think I wouldn't have been jumped on by the ideologist? I worked almost at the same time on *The Massacre of Camorena* and a *Via Crucis* . . . both works proceeded in the same identical vein. I have no doubts, but if the ideologist questioned it, are you sure I would find the right words to demonstrate my coherence?[18]

As Livio's focus returned to Orvieto, efforts began to establish the Istituto d'Arte as part of the public education offerings in Orvieto. The then-mayor charged Vladimiro and Sergio Ercini with the task of securing funding for the Istituto. The city had to provide the buildings while the operational funds were the responsibility of the central government in Rome, which was controlled by Christian Democrats. Since Sergio was a Christian Democrat, he took the lead and was successful in securing the first budget because of the political influence Orvieto had in Rome. Interestingly, Junio Gatte, the first director of the Istituto d'Arte, came from Florence as a political appointee. Sergio Ercini had enough influence to ensure that Livio was called to teach. Giulietti believed Livio's teaching in the Istituto d'Arte prevented him from receiving as much recognition and commercial success as the quality of his work deserved. "He never achieved the number of sales that he should have."[19]

The second full-time director of the Istituto d'Arte, Donato Catamo, shared his memories when it first opened in 1970. The Istituto was a fusion of teaching both the arts and the classics in a public high school. The Orvieto community put pressure on the government officials to establish such an institution. A formal request was presented

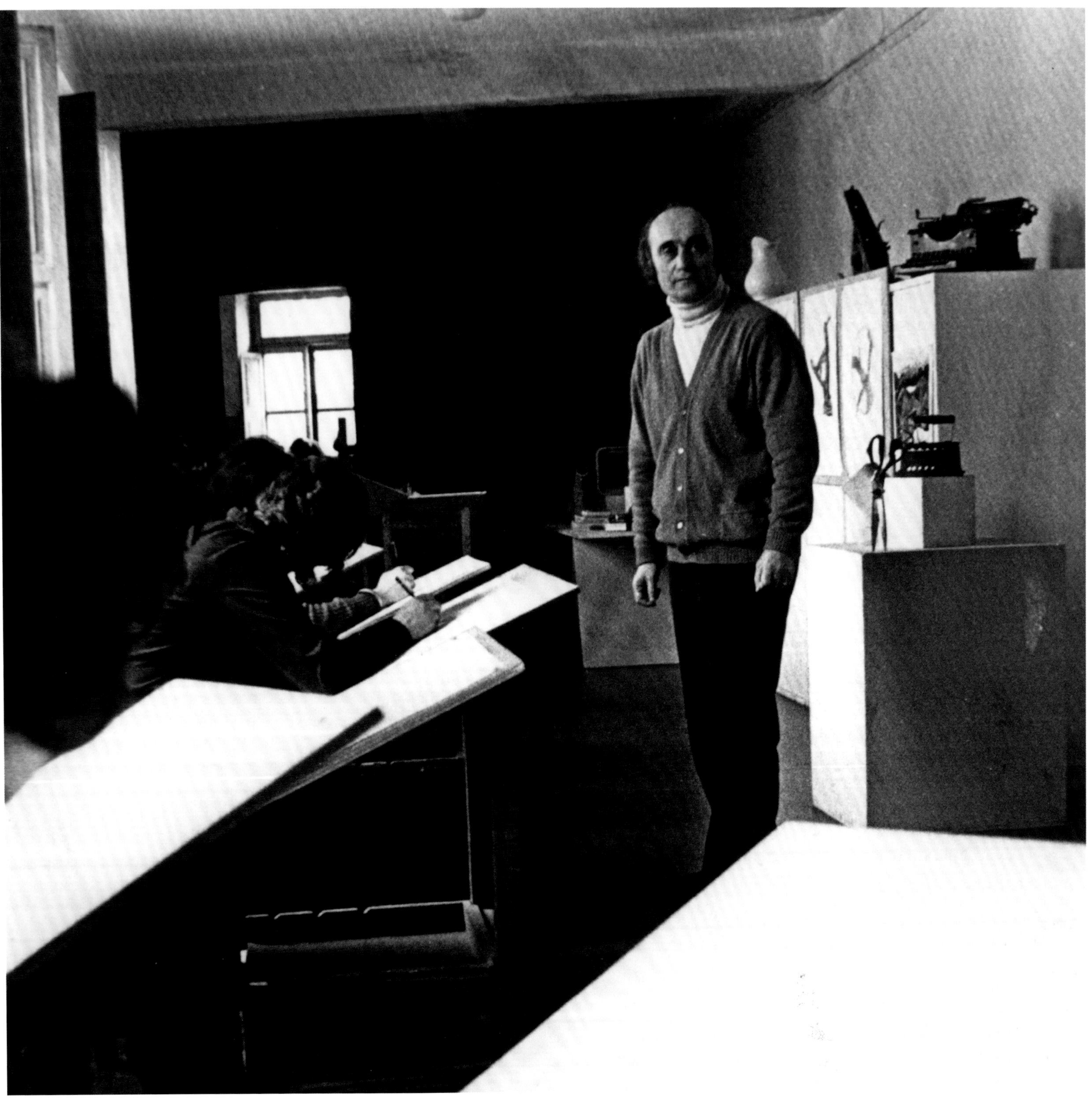

to the minister of education for art. Benedetto Borli, Giulietti, and Flora were commissioned to represent Orvieto in this matter. The Istituto opened in September with thirteen students. Catamo worked with Livio for nine of the ten years he taught there.

Because Livio had neither formal training nor a university degree and certification, he needed special dispensation by the Education Ministry in Rome in order to teach painting and ceramics. To receive such a special waiver, he had to prepare a folio of his work and take a series of tests both written and verbal before a committee in Rome. Initially the committee did not pass Livio but after some involvement by Flora and others using their influence, he was "approved and pronounced qualified to teach by the minister in Rome."[20]

According to Giulietti, "Flora's role was significant in getting the Istituto d'Arte approved. Several people believed she was motivated by her desire to keep Livio in Orvieto. She was not happy he was spending so much time in Rome. She became the primary lobbyist for the Istituto and was ever-present at the Comune meetings when the topic was discussed. She was determined Livio would teach at the Istituto full time."[21]

Flora felt that Livio, "should become a teacher based on his artistic merits. According to the law, artists who were well-known could teach in art schools." She explained there were courses not requiring a degree, but rather, certification, which prepared one to teach. With her encouragement, Livio took this series of courses offered in Perugia during the evenings. In the process he became a role model for other students. The final part of this certification was an exam with the Ministry of Art. "He presented his portfolio as a thesis on the egg and other things he had done at school. He discussed this work using the theme, the egg as a sign." Flora showed us the bound volume of these drawings using the egg as the point of departure. They all had the stamp of the principal of the school.

Traditionally the final part of the process was the oral examination. However this committee did not allow him to take the exam. He came home and told Flora they said he did not need the oral exam. She telephoned Rome to find out why. They replied he didn't have to take the exam because he didn't have his diploma from the art academy or a degree in architecture. She talked to the undersecretary of the Art Ministry and forcefully explained that "he had a right to take this exam and if the other professors, the examining committee, did not test him they should be penalized because they were wrong." Then she retained a lawyer who prepared the document threatening a suit if Livio was not allowed to take the exam immediately.

Livio in a classroom at Istituto d'Arte in 1970. Photograph courtesy of the Valentini family.

Flora went with Livio to the next meeting. After presenting Livio with a written declaration, the committee refused to administer the exam. Flora explained to them she had come on purpose and they had better listen to what she had to say. She told the committee she and Livio were prepared to take them to court. She told them she had talked to the undersecretary and he told her the committee had to allow him to be examined. Their response was "telephone Rome" so she did just that and the committee gave Livio his orals.

Flora was convinced the committee would get their revenge. She thought, "They'll take the feathers off him. Instead he came out smiling and everyone was happy. He had received the highest marks possible." Years later, remembering those days, Livio's comment was, "Good old Flora. If it hadn't been for Flora!"

Flora said, "Livio did not know how to fight back. You need a certain kind of character to survive in this world." Livio replied, "Flora and the professor came out of the room and he said he would like to have a wife who goes after things the way Flora does."[22]

Catamo continued, "Flora did a lot for the family financially and otherwise. She was the 'man of the family.' In one sense she left him alone and gave him the freedom to do his art. Otherwise she kept a tight rein on him and his activities as far as the family was concerned. She wanted to keep her man." Livio had the fortune or misfortune, depending on your point of view, to have an educated woman by his side who understood what he was trying to do.

According to Catamo, "Livio had his own ideas for his teaching. He worked very well with the other teachers. Typically he was the absent-minded artist to the extent he might forget where and when his classes met. When he started, Livio did not know anything about teaching or the responsibilities of the teacher. Flora and another professor helped with the basic issues involving faculty meetings and class schedules. Several of us on the faculty acted as buffers between him and Flora. Otherwise they would have driven each other mad."

Catamo recalled, "What made Livio so popular as a teacher was his naiveté, his sense of irony and his great relationships with students." He played soccer with them and the faculty on a regular basis. He encouraged students to come by his office in their spare time or in between classes. They felt they could discuss just about anything with him.[23] As an example of his relationship with students, Livio told the story about how he patted his oldest daughter Cristiana on the rear when she passed him in the hall one day and how she stopped and said, "Professor, you are not allowed to pat the girls on their bottoms. It is not permitted." And then he acted chastened and asked for her forgiveness.

At the height of his artistic career during his fifties and into his sixties, Livio continued teaching. Contrary to what some of Livio's friends thought, Catamo believed there was a positive relationship between his teaching and his painting:

> When you are teaching you are learning. This was a most important time for Livio's art. Some of his very best work was produced while he taught. He was able to give and receive. His colleagues at the Istituto gave Livio encouragement and suggestions for improving his techniques, especially in the areas of printing, photography and etching. For all of us it was a time of great intellectual and artistic exchange. It rivaled the time he had with his three very close friends. Teaching was an acknowledgement he was worth something; his work was affirmed, as well as his life as an artist. His family saw that he was valued and he became known as Maestro. This time in his life made a big difference to everyone.
>
> The experiences that were important for him as a painter were the war, his rural memory and his sense of color. Colors were strong in his paintings and he managed to get them to live together. He was very sophisticated in their use. He had great visual memory. His greens based on his rural heritage were exceptional. The colors he used were brilliant as they are in nature. They were more central to his work than shapes. Because of his visual memory he was able to put together colors that would harmonize. . . . Livio's rural background gave a naiveté and innocence to his work. He often used the expression "my humble origins."

There was an ongoing debate about Livio's understanding of the cultural significance of the art surrounding him. Catamo stated, "He did not have a strong cultural background. This allowed him to be original and not dependent on those who had gone before him. He tried to learn as much as he could but there is an old saying in Orvieto, 'an old donkey cannot learn new tricks.'" Clearly during his early years Livio was exposed to Orvieto's "encyclopedia" of art. If no other way than through the process of osmosis, he knew the past and its importance for understanding the present and living into the future. He was fond of saying he would never be bound by the conventions of time, a position undoubtedly shaped by his war experiences. Livio's thoughts were a little Greek. "His hand was guided by the mind rather than culture. The Greeks thought of the crafts and art together."[24]

"Livio was very generous and always protective of others no matter who they were," according to Catomo. As if to confirm this view of him, while we were sitting in his living room, Livio told the story of his friend, Orlando Tisato, a former priest who had come from Padua to Orvieto because he was in love with the patron St. Francis. Tisato had been a fifth grade student of Flora's and over the years had become a close friend of Livio's. As a grateful guest in the Valentini house, Tisato told them, "You are giving me paradise . . . Umbria, it's like being in paradise." Later Livio said he had been "shaped," literally "enlightened" by his friend's words and by the example he set as an accomplished painter.

Livio told the story of Tisato performing a dance representing his religious feelings about St. Francis. Tisato's art form was what today is known as performance art. He took off his shoes and shirt, as if he were St. Francis, and danced in front of the church like a whirling dervish. Sadly, the people laughed, because they didn't understand this fervent performance. Livio remembered the crowd throwing things at him and calling him crazy. So Livio spoke out vehemently, "I told them they should be ashamed for treating this man as an animal, for mistaking him for a street comedian." Livio defended him, "This is a humble man who loves the holy aspects of art and is expressing them in this dance as he does in his paintings."

Livio said, "I had never been madder at my fellow human beings for their insensitivity." In response, Tisato fell to his knees in front of Livio with a prayer of thanksgiving. Livio lifted him from the ground and embraced his close friend. Livio indicated that Tisato had taught him what life as an artist was about.[25]

Tisato was a driving force behind the 2005 documentary entitled, *L' Alfiere del Vento: a portrait of Livio Orazio Valentini.* The film was commissioned by the Comune of Orvieto in honor of Valentini's completion of his epic sculpture, *Orvieto Città Unita.*

According to Catamo, "Livio helped shape Orvieto with his naiveté and use of color. When one speaks of contemporary art and Orvieto one is speaking about Livio Orazio Valentini. Livio brought a wave of something new to Orvieto. He was a painter who did ceramics not a ceramicist who painted."[26]

Another friend of Livio's was Alberto Satolli, who studied in Rome and returned to Orvieto in the 1970s to practice architecture. He eventually taught with Livio at the Istituto d'Arte. Satolli designed the restoration of the interior of the Palazzo del Popolo and coordinated the project. He also designed the Palazzone Agriturismo, owned and operated by Livio's daughter Cristiana and her husband Giovanni Dubini.

For Satolli, "Much of Livio's work spoke of the spiritual dimensions of life" and he spent a great deal of time trying to understand Livio's art, especially his ceramics. He realized Livio was transforming two-dimensional art into three dimensions and was fascinated by Livio's use of iron and ceramics together. He felt that Livio transcended what most Umbrian artists were doing and especially liked his earliest figurative works inspired by Orvieto. Eventually he came to appreciate the birds even though they were more ideological. As Livio's work became more abstract, Alberto realized "the new direction was Livio's way of demonstrating growth and a deeper understanding of art. Livio returned to the figurative when he painted the Signorelli series. A ceramic Christ of Livio's was refused by the church hierarchy because of the way he decomposed the figure." Livio "did a number of small ceramic sculptures during that time. His designs were basic and simple but the simplicity was what made them so interesting." When Alberto was designing the restoration of the Palazzo del Popolo, he wanted Livio to create a large ceramic sculpture for the project but Livio refused. Soon thereafter Livio took a break from working in ceramics.

"When Livio returned to ceramics his form had become abstract." Satolli believed economics played a role in Livio's shift. "Flora pushed him to respond to the market. Flora was his public relations person as well as his manager. Sometimes when Livio was too forthright with a patron Flora attempted to smooth things over. While Livio did not always receive the local support his work deserved, the city did provide him with a new studio in recognition of his stature as an artist and his contributions to Orvieto's reputation in the arts. This was a very unusual act on the part of the Comune. Flora was instrumental in getting this recognition for him."[27]

Addressing the question of why Livio was not known by art collectors earlier, Catamo believed Livio's lack of a professional agent hampered his success. Catomo continued:

> The problem with agents is they want money. Livio did not have the financial resources to be aggressive in marketing his art. In addition, he did not want to be forced to pursue things he did not want to do. The continuous search for . . . freedom was critical for Livio. He was never conditioned by political views. In that sense he was free. He was not obligated to or aligned with any political party. So he refused the efforts of some agents who offered to help him with his marketing. Had he had a good agent, I am sure he would have been known much earlier.[28]

We have fond memories of interviewing the young ceramicist Marino Moretti, whose father, Luigi, taught with Livio at the Istituto d'Arte and for many years was his official photographer. On a chilly April morning Erika Bizzarri drove us several kilometers to the village of Viceno. Perched on the edge of the hill is the castle where Moretti and his family live and have his studio. We had to drive an extremely steep, curvy, and narrow street with absolutely no margin for error. The Morettis do not have to worry about uninvited guests. Moretti's father purchased the castle in complete ruin and restored it gradually over several decades. At one point it had been used as a grain storage facility, evidenced by the stain ringing the larger rooms at twelve to fifteen feet up on the wall. The rooms are huge and quite drafty most of the year but the family has managed to convert the castle into a very inviting home. Moretti's ceramic studio is a large room on the ground floor, dominated by a fireplace.

Moretti's family is one of the oldest in the Orvieto area with an important heritage in the ceramic arts. Both his grandfather and father were known for their fine collection of medieval pottery. As a child Moretti was surrounded by examples of Etruscan and medieval treasures. The family recently sold much of their collection to a major museum outside of Orvieto because the local institutions did not have the necessary resources.

In this magnificent setting of the castle and the context of his family's history, Moretti shared his perspective on Livio's work and life. While Marino was still in high school, he opened a studio in Orvieto across the street from Livio's old workshop. He and Livio had very few conversations at first. At times he felt they were just staring at each other somewhat antagonistically. It took years before they became friends. In one of their first exchanges, Livio commented on Moretti's busy school and work schedule. "That's why I don't see you out and about."

Over the years Moretti developed an appreciation for their differences. "I am a ceramicist. Livio was an artist who explored various fields in art. He used ceramics as one medium for his art. I always respected him as an artist. As I got to know Livio better he showed me a lot of his early work. We would talk about the technology of clay. Livio's discussions were always instructive for me. He was intuitive and experimented a great deal especially when he was using a potter's wheel in throwing the pots before they were fired." Livio was much more abstract in his ceramics than Moretti and was influenced more by the modern schools. "Livio's approach was the opposite of mine. He was a free spirit while I am a traditionalist who uses rules as my point of departure." Moretti was tied to form and shape when he was throwing a plate or vase while Livio was not.

Moretti became a commercial artist in 1993. He noted, "I was always in my studio by 9 AM while Livio was never in his studio before 10:30." As they became closer they had long discussions, particularly during the time when Livio was working on the Signorelli series. The routine developed as follows: Upon arrival at Moretti's studio, Livio opened the door and shouted out, "Good morning. Are you ready for the seminar?" The theme of their discussions was usually contemporary art. Livio constantly researched what he was doing. "Nearly every day he complained about how 'blind and deaf' Orvieto was to art and the artist. Contemporary art was not well supported in Orvieto."

When asked how Livio had influenced him, Moretti praised "his use of color during the 1980s and 1990s. He was absorbed with curiosity about the use of color and infected me with the same curiosity. Moreover, I appreciated Livio's transition from the figurative to the abstract." He felt that the artist always had to reinterpret what he had done before. "Using Signorelli as his reinterpretation, Livio went through several cycles from the figurative to the abstract." It always surprised Moretti that Livio could produce such large paintings, particularly the Signorelli canvases, in such a small studio. Moretti had great respect for the way Livio managed his studio.

Moretti acknowledged that not all of their conversations were about art. Frequently they stood outside during their breaks and admired the beautiful women who regularly passed by the studio. The two of them gossiped and told funny stories, never vulgar, but humorous and sarcastic about the politics and the politicians of the day. Livio was very sharp in his observations of the politicians. Occasionally Livio shared his war experiences. He loved to talk about what he and his special friends, the "three musketeers," had been doing.

Moretti mused about Livio's fortune as an artist:

> In art and life you can be very talented but you need luck. Maybe he did not have as much luck in the beginning. It is very difficult for an artist to be his own agent or have someone in his family act as his agent. Some are better managers than artists; they make money but not good art. Art has become more of an industry than an ideal. Certainly another factor was Livio's decision to remain in Orvieto. The city did not offer that many opportunities for Livio to develop his reputation as an artist. If he had continued his career in Rome however, he would have had more opportunities. Orvieto limited him but he was a big frog in a smaller pond.[29]

In a later discussion about his success as an artist, Livio expounded upon tensions between providing for his family and pursuing his career. Now, he began to better understand the need for money. Livio came to recognize his obligations and responsibilities.

While he realized the importance of the commercial side of art, he did not let that dominate his creative process. Livio fully embraced the centrality of providence in his artistic and commercial success.

Livio shared the following thoughts about this period in his life:

> So I decided to take a risk, decided to pay attention, I wasn't hurting anyone, I wasn't making anyone accept this, starting with my family. The joy and sadness were mine alone. When I went home in the evening, people could tell by looking at me that I was worried. They said, "what's the matter?" I said, "nothing." I said, "I'm not happy about one of my works," but that was not the truth. I was very happy about my work but I didn't have any money. I couldn't tell that to the whole world.
>
> The following day, I took something from the studio; I put it under my arm, a drawing, a painting, a sculpture, a little jewel I had made. And when I ran into my friends, I asked, "don't you need a drawing?" A street in Orvieto was like the Via Veneto in Rome. So many things, so many situations. Orvieto is a small town with narrow streets; it's not like Aiken. If somebody is on the other side of the street, you call out "excuse me!" So you realize your friend is right there. "Come stai? Bene, bene." You shake hands and you show the jewel. You start to play with it. "What's that?" "Oh, just a piece of jewelry that I made."
>
> They ask, "what are you doing with it?" "Oh, I don't know." "Are you selling it?" "Yes, I'm selling it." "How much is it?" "Just a little, because you're a friend, it's a special price." "I have to give a present to my wife but don't tell anybody." So he gave me the money, two hundred thousand lire, one hundred thousand lire, fifty thousand lire. So the circulation of the blood started all over again and little by little, became a feeling I called "providence." So everyday you think about the balance of life. I rely on providence, of which I have made a religion."
>
> So life went on; things started changing and you didn't need to run around with a painting under your arm. The others started coming to you and it became more interesting, more civilized. You knew that one person was interested in your painting so that was some kind of warranty. And life went on in your gestures, your habits and your routine. It was all part of your knowledge, part of your experience.
>
> You get enriched, you discover when you're doing a painting; you don't know how it will go or whom it will belong to. You look at it and ask yourself, "Perhaps this strange art is so complicated, who knows who will get interested in it? This painting is so cerebral, but who will respond to it?" The wallet is in a delicate position. First you

have your heart, but on top of it you have your wallet. It's a complicated exercise. There comes a miracle, providence, that thing that I was looking for, that complicated thing, that difficult thing, that hard-to-make thing; it had an order, for the money and for my heart.

In my experience, the process has matured. Selling art is not like selling a chair. Because the man who manufactures chairs knows they are necessary for people to sit down. The baker who makes bread knows it is necessary to eat. So it's really a question of giving and having . . . . Art has no rules for selling or buying. It can happen that nobody is interested in it. Or it can also happen that the artist wants to keep it for himself! So there's no commercial logic; there's an extraordinary difference between selling a work of art and selling a chair. Life goes on, strategies change, you create art, you sacrifice yourself, you work hard, you organize and you prepare shows.

Contemplating his growing success, Livio said:

People see your work, they look at you, critics speak about you. So your field of action gets bigger. There are more people who know you. People on TV speak about you. An important show or museum can consider you. No one can promise success. There is no established contract; no one can say what will happen to you. It's all providence.[30]

A work of art is full of humor, affection, knowledge and extraordinary people, so the meaning is always the same. Providence, adventure and passion surround the creative process. At this moment in Italy, I know in a house somewhere, in a gallery somewhere, in a museum somewhere, there are people looking at my work. This is a great feeling, a feeling that I cannot forget.[31]

Livio told the story of an acquaintance for whom he agreed to produce a number of paintings in return for a specified amount of money to be paid in advance. The deal was struck and Livio began painting. After several months passed and approximately half the paintings had been completed, Livio independently reevaluated the arrangement. He determined he had painted more than enough to meet the value he had been paid. Evidently the other person in the agreement came to the same conclusion since they never pursued the issue. One afternoon walking along the Corso Cavour with Erika, Bob met that gentleman in front of a small art gallery. When asked about the story, he said, "true, true." Then, when asked about his reaction, he laughed, shrugged his shoulders and said, "That's Livio!"

Marino Moretti said, "One can never accuse Livio of being superficial. He was a combination of the spiritual and cynical mixed with a healthy dose of sarcasm. He put everything into his work but did not always get the support he deserved which made it hard for him to have a sense of being appreciated. Only when he was truly satisfied with his work could he be happy."[32]

Another close friend, Don Marcello Pettinelli, reinforced Marino's evaluation of Livio. When we first met Monsignor Marcello, rector at Sant'Andrea, he was in his late seventies and still very active with his parish. He did not fit the stereotypical image of a priest. He rode a huge Harley motorcycle and made his own wine from his vineyards. When he entered the room his very presence seemed to suck the air out of it. His prominent and historic Orvietano family had extensive land holdings in the Umbrian region. An often-told story concerns his early days as a young priest at Sant'Angelo. Don Marcello had baked a leg of lamb for his Easter dinner and placed it in the window to cool while he said mass. He returned to discover the leg of lamb had been stolen by some of the local miscreants who afterwards went around Orvieto chanting "*Era bello quell' agnello, Don Marcello*" (That lamb was a beauty, Don Marcello). He let out a deep belly laugh every time he was reminded of that story.

We arranged to meet Don Marcello at Sant'Andrea, a place of both political and religious significance. In the middle ages it served as the seat of the Comune. The present-day church was built over the site of a sixth-century basilica. Don Marcello proudly showed us how the ancient tile mosaic floor revealed the outline of the original church. Beneath that level, Italian archaeologists discovered traces of what in Don Marcello's opinion had been an Etruscan temple of the sun god.

Later we joined Don Marcello for lunch at La Palomba, a family-owned restaurant on the Via Cipriano Manente, a small street that runs behind Sant'Andrea. While we visited with the owner, Giampiero Cinti, Don Marcello roared up on his motorcycle, jumped off and proudly produced three bottles of wine, two red and one white. He announced we would be drinking them with our lunch and if there was any left the restaurant staff could enjoy it. Our recollection is that the staff did not fare very well.

Don Marcello started ordering for all of us his favorite dish of *tagliatelle alla Don Marcello,* which obviously was named for him. Erika supplemented his order with vegetable plates and cheeses. In the meantime we drank his fine red wine and enjoyed a magnificent feast. Only when the Monsignor finished eating was he ready to talk.

He said he and Valentini were very close and had been for a long time since the first days when Livio began his studies with Puppo. Over the years they had many serious conversations and shared confidences with each other. He professed his deep respect for Livio.

The Monsignor related, "Livio never freed himself from his experience at Buchenwald. He seemed to be driven by it. Some thought that he was a revolutionary but he was not. He was just expressing himself and not so much against the government. This war experience and all its pain had to come out in some form. Art was the medium Livio chose. His use of birds reflected Livio's anguish. He wanted to bring things back into their right place and give them a sense of balance." He was worldly and at the same time spiritual. "When he was with people he could let go and show his humorous side. But there was something melancholic underneath all he did. He was not a happy person. He seemed always to be waiting for something, which explains much about him and his art. . . . Often we talked about very serious subjects and laughed about them. He questioned his own life and concluded the best he could do was to get on with it."

One of his constant questions was, "Why did all this happen? There was a deep sense of resignation in his work and in his conversations. Livio said, 'there is an answer but I cannot find it.' But he was never angry at God." As priest and friend, Don Marcello expounded, "Your own judgment is the only way you know someone. Each friend reveals himself from his own perspective. It is entirely subjective. You cannot free yourself from who you are in a relationship. Livio and I agreed on the basic values of what it means to be a human being."

In general Livio did not have a high opinion of priests. Bob remembers him frequently saying, "Priests have soft hands because they have never done an honest day's work." Such was not his opinion of Don Marcello Pettinelli. Livio held him in the highest regard and called him "a priest of the people."

According to the Monsignor, "In Orvieto you can have defects, people can gossip about you, but you are never alone. There is a caring that can only be found in a small town mentality. One of the major reasons Livio wanted to stay in Orvieto was because he was someone, even if he was never fully appreciated. He was accepted warts and all."[33]

After his exploration of the larger Italian art community and with considerable encouragement from Flora, Livio settled down to live and work in Orvieto. He reminisced about his children and grandchildren:

> So I still remember all my life, a lot of things just like a movie in front of my eyes. My daughters, three women, are all married and I have six grandchildren. My daughters

are Cristiana, Silvia, and Francesca. Cristiana married Giovanni Dubini and their children are Benedetta and Pietro. Silvia and her husband, Aldo Prosperini, also have two children, Giulia and Raffaelle. Francesca, the youngest is married to Carlo Papini and their children are Anna and Chiara. It is a very nice family.

One's family is not only the mother, father, children and grandchildren; it can also be a consortium, an active one, with a sense of unity. . . . My daughters studied graphic art and scenography at the Istituto d'Arte. They know about art. My wife, who is a mathematician, didn't care anything about art but has come to understand it. Mathematicians are hard headed; she finally understood the harmony between math and art.

Painting has another dimension besides color or design; it has a mathematical structure. It doesn't mean art becomes math but its structure and composition create a harmony with math. Each work has a mathematical relationship and an artist achieves this in a variety of ways. He uses his eyes, his imagination, but it's a mathematical work. To find the center requires the use of a yardstick. An artist has this ideal,

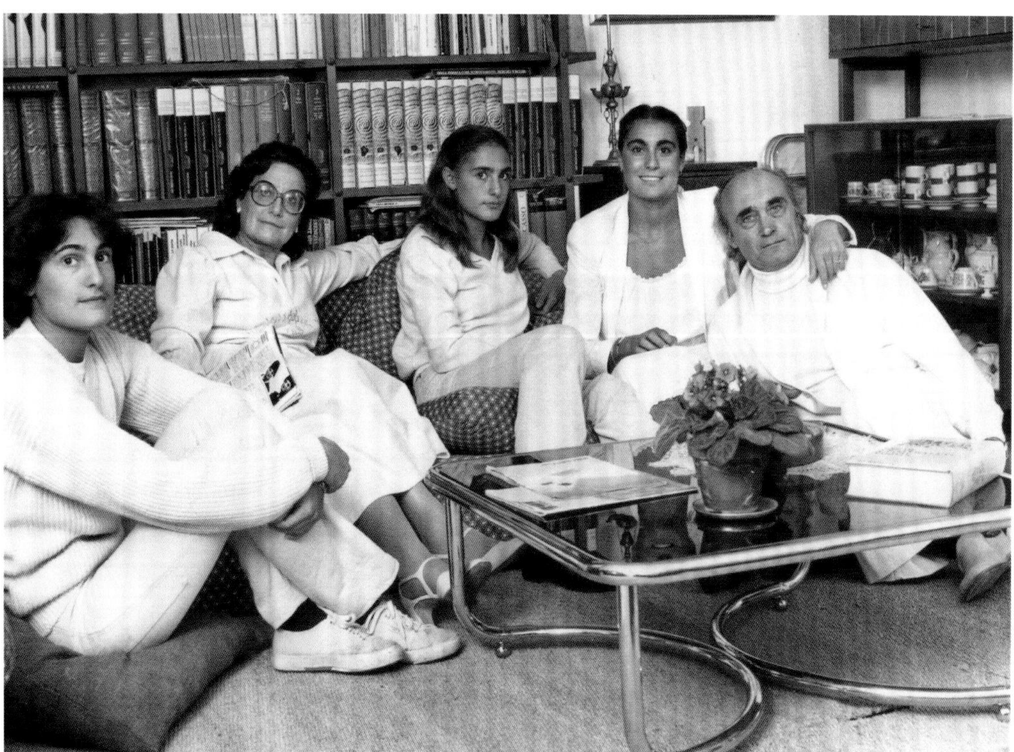

Valentini family at home in 1977. Photograph courtesy of the Valentini family.

> where all of the relationships in a painting become mathematical. So even my wife got interested in art. She came into my studio and said, "That won't work. No, you haven't got it yet." And sometimes she was even right. She said, "Here we need some white because we need light." So even though I was surprised about this, she did it and it functioned. So the family became a positive unit. My daughters were interested in everything related to organizing shows. There was this cohesion in our family.[34]

Despite the solidarity in his family around art, Livio shared, "My family doesn't know this. Sometimes I'm alone in my studio and I have big problems I need to solve . . . maybe an aesthetic problem, an existential problem, a money problem, a human problem. They don't understand this. An artist cannot link his problems to his family. The artist who has this practical discipline cannot turn against himself or get sad. An artist has to always look upwards. You always have to be optimistic because negativity is destructive."[35]

One could easily conclude Flora's role in his life and work was both a blessing and a major constraint. No one could have wished for a stronger ally than Flora when Livio was faced with bureaucrats determined to keep him from receiving certification to teach. Moreover, Flora played a key role by prodding the politicians to establish the Istituto d'Arte. Her personal mission was for Livio to have a place to "earn a living" in Orvieto and thus, minimize the need for him to travel at such a critical time in the young lives of his children. She pushed for him to be awarded commissions in various public buildings and schools. On the other hand, Flora discouraged Livio from pursuing artistic alliances with other artists in Rome and Florence where there was access to collectors and market makers. Numerous friends felt Livio might have received recognition and financial success with a professional manager. Instead, Flora assumed that role.

There is no doubt Flora wanted to control everything around her. Perhaps it was part of being a mathematician or just a family trait, but from first-hand experience we knew it to be real. During one of our last visits to Orvieto we spent the entire afternoon with Flora and Livio as well as dinner with them at Silvia's. The following day was busy scheduling interviews with Livio's friends. That afternoon we met the mayor, Stefano Mocio, who shared his views on Livio's contributions to Orvieto and we ended the evening dining at the Bizzarri's. The next morning we met Flora and she insisted we rearrange our schedule to join them at Silvia's. She also planned an excursion for us to see original sculptures from the Duomo collection in Sant'Agostino which is near the Church of San Giovenale. It was all we could do to maintain our own plans and convince her we had to finish the research we had come to do.

We have the greatest admiration for Flora and her many contributions to Livio's success. These two days became a metaphor for the role Flora played in Livio's life. Our minor experience with such a forceful and strong-willed woman demonstrated her dynamic and dominating role in her husband's and her family's lives.[36] Many agreed Flora's involvement limited the recognition Livio's art deserved. On the other hand, had Livio been married to a more submissive woman he might never have achieved what he did.

Clearly Livio was drawn to other people and frequently was absent from the family. This absence and Livio's interest in others created a tension in their relationship contributing to Flora's tendency to manage as much of her environment as she could. It was not that Livio did not adore his family, he did. Like many artists Livio lived for his art alone and while he loved his family, he was not a traditional family man.

In one of his early campus lectures Livio shared a poignant story, adding a new dimension to our understanding of his relationship with Flora. Describing the 1996 painting, *Laceration,* Livio remembered Flora's doctor ordering open-heart surgery. "I was worried. *Laceration* was made at the actual moment when Flora was undergoing the operation. I didn't want to represent what my wife was going through. I just wanted to paint because I was very nervous. But the image came out of the feeling I had at that moment. It was a miracle for me because it represented what was in my psyche. It became for me a statement of my most intimate expression." This painting was a central piece in the Odissea exhibit.[37]

In addition to Livio's memories, the time Bob spent with Silvia's family added to our understanding of Livio's art and of Flora's personality. Through the years, Bob's and Silvia's families became quite close. Bob met Silvia on his first trip to Orvieto in her father's studio. She had opened it for the tour buses that frequent Orvieto. Livio introduced her and explained that he had been asked to join the university as a visiting artist in residence. What started as a pleasant business relationship developed into a friendship both with her, her husband Aldo, and their children, Giulia and Raffaele. One summer Bob and Leslie hosted Giulia in Aiken and introduced her to other regions of the United States. She experienced the Midwest in Indianapolis, the new south in Atlanta, the mountains of North Carolina, the coast of South Carolina, and Charleston, our oldest city. Liz Benton took her to Washington, D.C., for a grand tour of the capital. Several

↞ *Laceration,* 1996. Mixed media on canvas, 130 × 109 cm. Collection of George and Sandi Custodi. Photograph by Michael St. John.

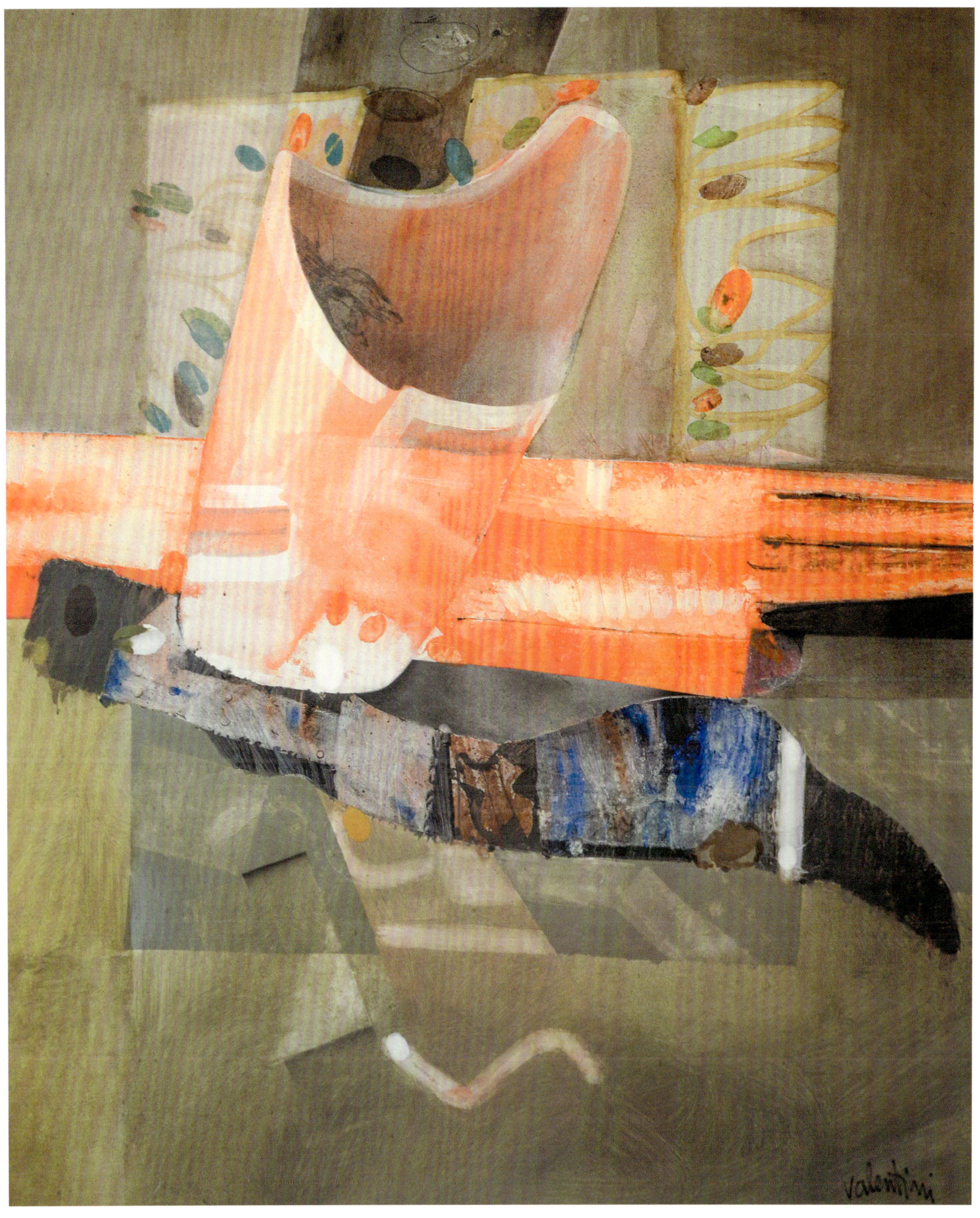

summers later, Silvia's son Raffaele came to spend the summer with Janet, Jack, and Michael Morris. Silvia joined Flora and Livio when they came to Aiken in May of 2003 for the unveiling and dedication of *Galassia*.[38]

Through these relationships we came to a better understanding of the Valentini family and Livio's constant quest for freedom. When Giulia visited Aiken she discussed her relationship with her grandparents. She was especially close to Aldo's mother, who showered her with a great deal of attention including weekly phone chats even while she was in Aiken. Giulia's relationship with her grandfather Livio was of a different nature. She found him to be more concerned with his art than his grandchildren. She admired his art and success but deeply regretted not being able to connect with him in a special granddaughter to grandfather way. She had her own aspirations in the arts and wanted to study architecture. Perhaps the problem was the result of Livio's need to concentrate on his art. One did wonder how much of these feelings were the typical ambiguity experienced by most teenagers toward their families.

On one of our last visits to Italy we included some interviews with Silvia's family. On a sunny March afternoon, we sat on the veranda at their home, sharing a glass of wine and discussing the family. Aldo said he had lost his father at an early age and though his mother had remarried and his stepfather had been good to them, he still searched for a father figure. Despite the fact he and Silvia had been married for twenty-six years, he never felt truly accepted. Instead of a father figure he would have settled for a friend. With Livio he got neither.[39]

The discussion then focused on Flora's tendency to supervise everyone in the family. Livio often told us Flora micromanaged his life. He admitted he had needed as much "help" as she gave him but perhaps not as much as she wanted to give him. She not only told him what he should do; she prevented whatever "silly things" he was tempted to do.

Control and his desire to escape was certainly a theme in our discussions as well as in his art. It was part of his search for freedom. Everyone we interviewed told similar stories validating this perspective on Flora. Numerous times Livio described feeling like a caged bird because of her guidance. In the 2005 documentary, Livio affectionately referred to his wife as the "retired Colonel." The story below seems to best illustrate their relationship.[40]

On the occasion of the joint art exhibit of Livio, Al Beyer, and Leslie Alexander in Orvieto, we hosted a dinner for friends who had traveled from Aiken and other parts of the United States. We dined at the Locanda Rosati, an Agriturismo owned by innkeepers Giampiero Rosati and his sister Alba. The inn is eight to ten kilometers from Orvieto. The trip from Orvieto to the inn is a story in and of itself. Snow and ice had blanketed the region the day before. We rode in cars and vans owned primarily by members of the Valentini, Prosperini, and Bizzarri families. We survived slipping and sliding our way through icy hills and curves. An apparent argument arose on our ride with Silvia driving Livio, Flora, and us in a typically small Italian car at a fast speed, especially considering the road conditions. At one point the conversation became so charged we were sure they were arguing whether they should stop and put us out on the side of the road. It was difficult to understand what blunder could have caused such a drastic reaction between Silvia and Flora. Actually, the two women were simply discussing Flora's difficulties with her glasses' prescription.

With snow and ice on the ground and the evening sky lit by a full moon, the entire area looked like a winter wonderland. Eventually we all arrived safely and were served some excellent local wines as we warmed ourselves around a huge fireplace. We were seated at a long rectangular table in no particular order. As fate would have it, this serendipitous arrangement contributed to our understanding of Livio and Flora's long relationship. Seated beside Livio was Frances Causey, a young friend of ours from New Mexico and a documentary film director of some renown. Seated next to Flora was Cathy Marreno, another young friend from Arizona who is a first-generation American of Italian heritage. Interestingly, Cathy purchased one of Livio's paintings from the show, which now hangs in her home near Tupac, Arizona. Her family still speaks Italian in her home so she was well equipped linguistically. Bob was seated between Livio and Flora. During the course of the meal he overheard Frances ask Livio the secret to his long marriage to Flora. Without missing a beat Livio puffed out his chest and with his characteristic grin said, "The ability to remember." Moments later as if choreographed, Cathy asked Flora in Italian what was the secret to her long marriage to Livio. After a considerable pause, Flora said, "The ability to forget." Both Cathy and Frances swore they had not heard the other's question; it had just come to them in the course of their conversations. Bob's placement gave him the perfect spot from which to hear and witness both conversations. These two responses, "the ability to remember" and "the ability to forget," seem to be an almost-perfect metaphor for the relationship Livio and Flora experienced throughout their marriage.[41]

On the occasion of their fiftieth wedding anniversary, Livio and Flora sent to their friends and family the following announcement with a full color abstract print that seemed to summarize their life together:

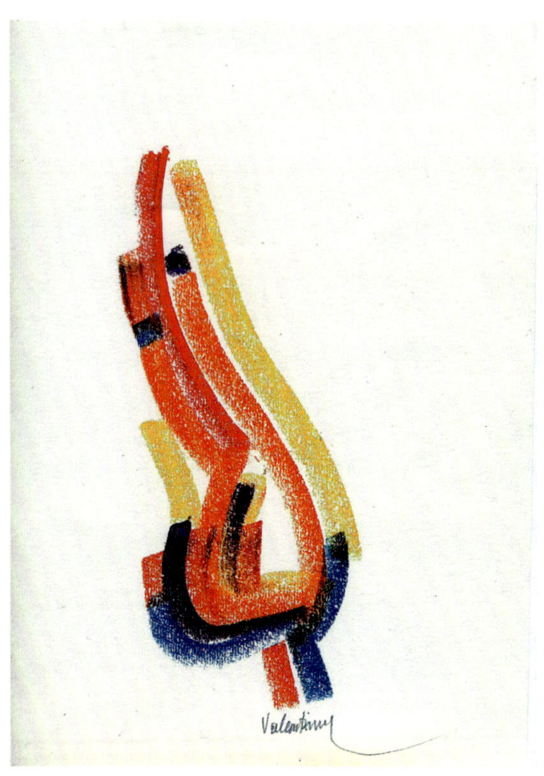

50th Anniversary announcement, 2007. Color print, 24 × 34 cm. Collection of John Elliott. Photo by Michael St. John.

Livio Orazio and Flora Valentini's Golden Wedding Anniversary

Assisi San Damiano 2 July 1957

Orvieto Cathedral 2 July 2007

Flora and Livio, together with their daughters, their husbands, grandchildren, siblings, relatives and dear friends, are happy to announce their Golden Wedding anniversary.

They were married in Assisi, in the church of San Damiano, with devout recollection and Franciscan simplicity, above all with faith in Divine Providence:

It was the beginning of a great adventure in work, art, in the will to express the best of oneself.

The days, the months, the years have passed and the house has been filled with paintings, sculpture, children and pupils, students, friends. We wonder whether so much time can really have passed, and whether so many things can really have happened, but the numbers tell us they have.

There's a secret and it's love for life.

"The love that moves the sun and the other stars" (*Paradiso,* XXXIII, line 145.)

CHAPTER FOUR

Periods of Valentini's Art

THROUGH OUR PRIVILEGED RELATIONSHIP with Livio, we developed a unique perspective of his imagery and emotions. We employed the method of *dietrologia,* an Italian term meaning the "science of discovering what is beneath the surface." With our goal of fostering an appreciation for and an understanding of Livio's art, we sifted through the layers to better understand his meaning. We worked like archaeologists excavating the stratification of deposits in the city of Orvieto, with its Etruscan, Roman, medieval and Renaissance roots.

With our use of artistic dietrologia, Livio's images became more easily understood, his influences more clear, and his motives more transparent. Only when one gains some knowledge of Livio's World War II experiences can his obsession with wounded and entrapped birds be comprehended. Only by knowing his deep appreciation for the Renaissance frescoes in the Duomo do the crystalline qualities in an angel's wings become more than just a color study. Only by knowing that for years as a maestro he taught the young people of Orvieto, do we recognize Livio's goals of illuminating the minds of our USCA scholars.

The dietrologia of appreciating a work by Valentini is like dining on an artichoke. One must peel away the layers to experience the flavors one at a time. A Valentini work of art is something to be savored, prepared to taste, with a lifetime of knowledge and the seasoning of a world of experience.

Livio's growth as a painter, sculptor, and printmaker can be evaluated through a series of art periods, which he sometimes called cycles. Simultaneously we should keep in mind those elliptical bands into which Livio's personal life seemed to fall as he searched for freedom. His success as an artist cannot be separated from the complexity of his home life. We have considered his education in Rome and the influence of his contemporaries, as well as the profound effect marriage and fatherhood had on his quest.

As we came to understand him, the Duomo, Livio's church, became another central character. As an artist he lovingly interpreted and reinterpreted the physical aspects of this Gothic structure: the facade shining with color and light, marble bas-reliefs, bronze creatures symbolizing the Evangelists, the gleaming mosaic of the Madonna and the marble and bronze *Maestà* of Mary and the Christ Child with angels. Within the Duomo are the all-important Signorelli frescoes, an influence he first quoted in his *Massacre of Camorena*.

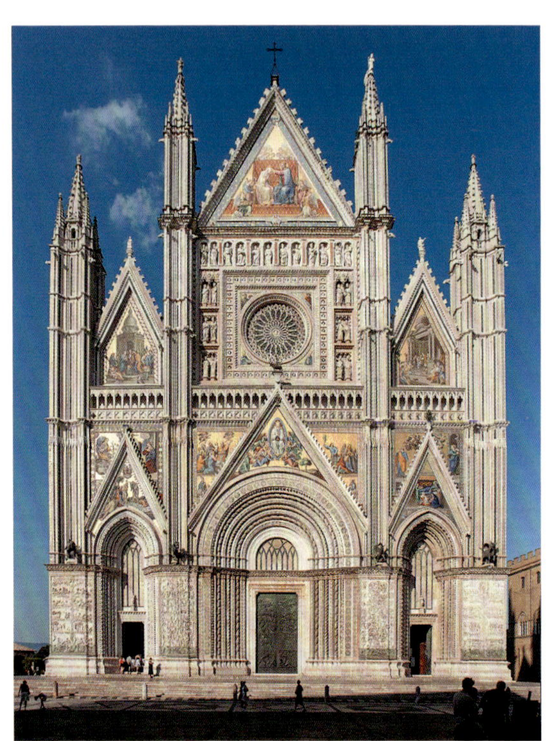

Façade of the Cathedral (Duomo) of Orvieto, dedicated to the Assumption of the Virgin Mary. Photograph by Hans Peter Schaefer.

The cathedral served as a spiritual and physical resource for Livio. Like the Carrara quarry from which Michelangelo harvested precious marbles, Valentini frequently returned to the Duomo for artistic inspiration and spiritual comfort. In later years, Livio said, "I love this cathedral so much because my studio is a few steps away." He and his daughters first established his studio on Via Maitani in 1986. Livio continued, "When I work, I take walks and I come up on this enormous space in the Cathedral and it seems to me I have the whole universe on top of me because of this phenomenon of imagination. It's like a wind of culture which blows around you."[1]

For the Valentini family, the Cathedral always held special significance. "I was able to request permission for Francesca to be married in the Signorelli chapel. The president of the commission said, 'Well, Valentini worked here, he revisited it and painted these scenes again.' It was very satisfying because Signorelli and many artists painted here. Because of my family's feelings, permission to use the Duomo was like a prize to me."[2]

The Tonal Period: 1945–1950

Livio resumed his artistic journey, safely back in Orvieto, the city of miracles where he had begun his training under Puppo. It was 1945 and Livio had just returned from the war and, as Massimo Duranti put it, felt "the need to cleanse himself of so much filth."[3]

Livio recalled, "As a young artist I needed to find an equilibrium, to find calm and peace, to find humanity again, to be part of the real world. I needed to overcome the war, to feel alive." He undertook a career in painting, living in the peaceful hill town. His fellow Umbrian artists nicknamed him "montanaro," a simple man from the mountains.[4]

Aldo Lo Presti has traced Livio's earliest exhibit to November 1945. He praises Livio's "vitality and strength of composition" coupled with "soft lines and soft colors."[5]

Due to a lack of appropriate gallery space, his first show was in Michelangeli's workshop on the Via Albani. The year 1946 brought further local displays of his work in association with the newly formed Istituto Storico Artistico Orvietano. In 1947, he entered three landscapes in the *VII Premio di Pittura Città di Orvieto* exhibit. Livio called his first "Tonal" works "naïve landscapes," representing his regional heritage.

Livio's acknowledged artistic debut was with five paintings in the same competition held the following year. In 1948, *Sotto la pioggia* (Under the Rain) won Livio an honorable mention in the Orvieto landscape section of the show. A steep angled view leads the eye along the city walls under an overcast sky. Contemporary photographs record Livio painting these canvases *en plein air.*

Livio's novice paintings reflect the guidance of Professor Fernando Puppo, whose landscapes are academic in nature with traditional perspective and naturalistic colors. Livio adopted Puppo's practice of oil painting on pressed board. Both Puppo and Valentini employed a subtle variation of shades and textures in nature. Some have called these Umbrian artists "*Maestri di Terra*" (Masters of the earth). Livio was counted among the "so-called Tonalists," whose work matured after World War II. Giuseppe Capogrossi (1900–1972) and Renato Guttuso (1912–1987) were also members of that movement and painted various Italian landscapes from beachfronts to quiet piazzas.[6] Livio explained, "By Tonal School we meant a stress on muted colors, although each artist was free to do what he wanted. It was like a note in music with one color by itself on a chord without any violent variations or changes."[7]

Hungry to meet other artists, both old and new, young Livio often took the train to the nearby city of Terni, a center for contemporary art. One local artist who strongly influenced Livio was Enrico Prampolini (1894–1956). An early proponent of Aero-painting, his bold landscapes focused on cosmic aerial views rather than traditional perspective.[8] Similarly, Gerardo Dottori (1884–1977) was one of the cofounders of Aero-painting and did studies of Umbrian scenery as well as sacred subjects.[9] James Soby and Alfred H. Barr described the style of this time as having "a love of freedom, with a perpetual revolt against the stale and conventional."[10]

Another artist who supported Livio's progress was Eliseo Stella, who eventually shared a studio with him on the Via del Duomo. Recently Lo Presti published a previously unknown Valentini composition, entitled *Cardatura della canapa* (Carding the Hemp), discovered on the reverse side of a Stella painting.[11] The fertile soil of Orvieto was perfect for the production of hemp. Here Livio portrays two laborers engaged in carding the fibers for manufacturing rope. A barefooted youth in a striped shirt and

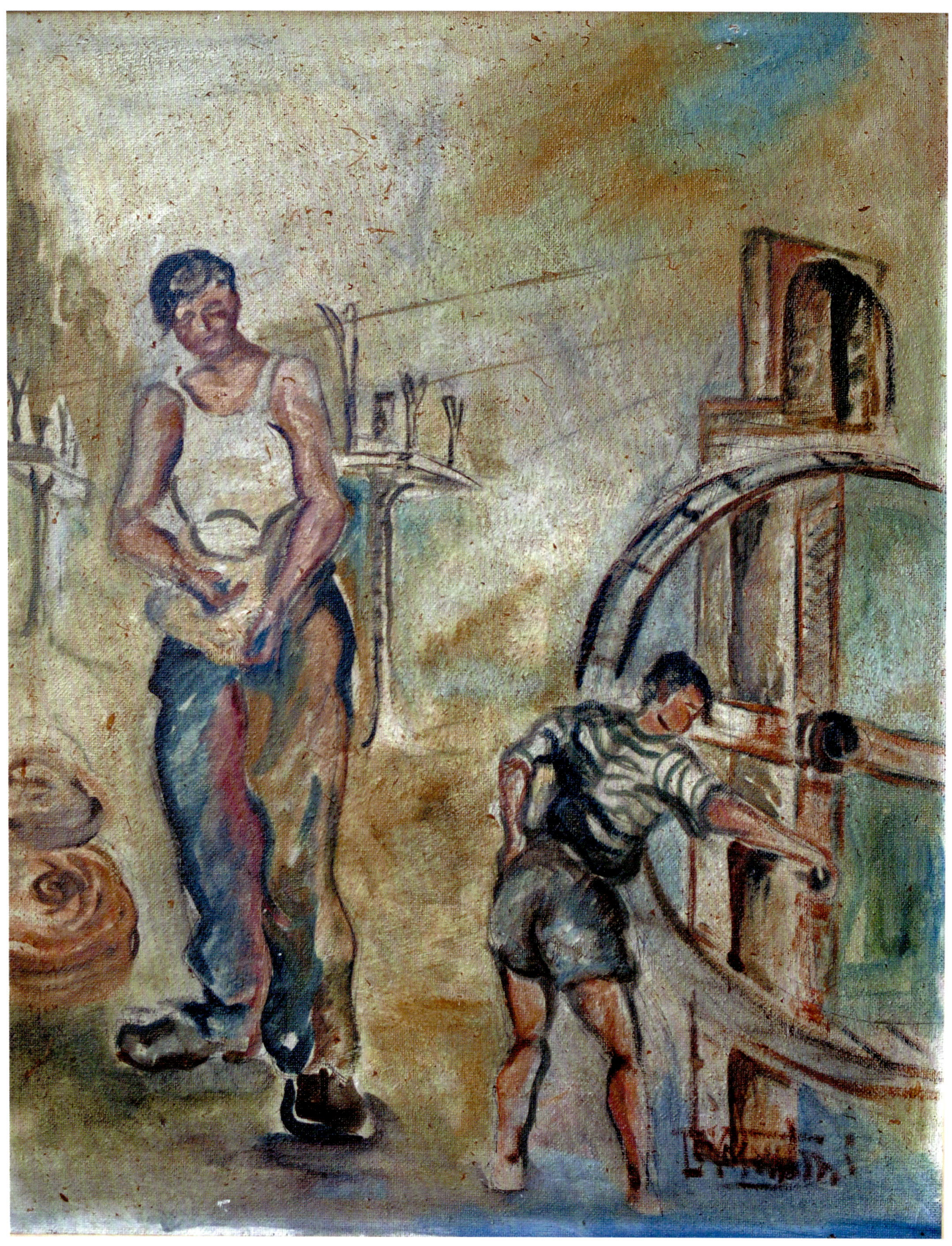

shorts leans into his job of cranking a huge wooden wheel by hand in order to twist the fibers hanging overhead into ropes. An older fellow, probably the father, stands with a hank of raw hemp wound about his waist while a finished rope lies coiled on the ground. Livio is showing an important industry in Orvieto, specifically in the area of town known as San Giovenale.

The street leading from Piazza della Repubblica to the Cava is called the Via Filippeschi but is known locally as Via del Cordone because workmen stretched out the ropes along this street.[12] A photograph shows young Livio painting in the piazzetta opposite the restaurant Grotte del Funaro with hemp rope stretched out to dry near the Church of San Giovenale. The Grotte, a rope-maker's grotto where we dined with Livio and Flora in 1997, has a collection of antiques used in this process, including just such a double wheel and a wooden hatchel for carding hemp. Significantly, Livio returned to this imagery numerous times in his later career.

The style of this painting is extremely naturalistic even if it is a bit primitive. Notice his attention to the workmen's musculature and rather sketchy perspective view of the wheel. Most apparent is the unique shading of color, in deep contrast to the vibrant hues which follow in Livio's future works. Overall, the tonal quality resembles the transparent washes of a watercolor rather than a conventional Italian oil painting.

From this same art period came *Incontro sulla riva* (Meeting on the Shore), Livio's first professional painting, the one purchased by Pia Custodi's husband, Elio. In this naturalistic landscape, Livio followed the rules of pure, conventional realism. Grey clouds hang over a Mediterranean beachfront where a pair of boats is perched. On the left we look over the shoulder of a woman in a red scarf and matching skirt. She carries a basket, perhaps for the yield of fresh fish. A sailor in a blue and white striped shirt is at the oars of the second craft. Livio captured the frothy foam tickling the edge of the seashore. The foreground acts as a frame for the center action. Tall grasses dissolve into a stand of palms bringing our attention to the distant background where we spy a group of village houses peeking through a fog bank across the simple harbor. In later paintings Livio revisited this same theme but abandoned the traditional academic style.[13]

The critic Dario Micacchi described Valentini as a painter who looked to the past to "bring dignity to an untidy present." His work focused on the Umbrian environment now that he was home again. This nostalgia for Orvieto separated him from more avant-garde Italians, "maintaining that painting should take inspiration from falling in love and from the figures, idioms, shapes, and colors and materials gathered in museums."[14]

Cardatura della canapa (Carding the Hemp), 1947. Oil on canvas, glued to wood, 58 × 73 cm. Collection of Daniela Borghini.

Exhibitions in Perugia, Rome, and Florence followed, with his work receiving national awards of merit. It was during this period that sweeping changes occurred in Italian art due to the arrival of influences from other parts of Europe and the United States. In 1948 the Biennial Exposition in Rome featured works by Marc Chagall, George Braque, and most importantly, Pablo Picasso, who would inspire many artists of Livio's generation.[15] In 1949 American collector Peggy Guggenheim arrived in Venice exposing Italy to the art of Jackson Pollock and abstract expressionism. Of particular significance for Livio was Giorgio de Chirico (1888–1978). Greek-born, his career in Italy began with metaphysical art in Florence which lead to a brief stay in Paris among the surrealists and then permanently to Rome where he met Valentini. As Dario Micacchi wrote, "Today everyone descends from the loins of Giorgio de Chirico."[16]

The Orvieto Informal Period: 1950–1960

Historic events occurring around Livio at this time affected his circumstances. The year 1950 marked an important moment in the history of Italy and the Roman Catholic Church. It was the Holy Year, celebrating the Jubilee on July 16th. Five hundred thousand pilgrims and citizens came to witness Pope Pius XII escort the Blessed Sacrament through St. Peter's Square. This event was of special importance to the residents of Orvieto because, for the first time ever, the holy relic of Orvieto was transported from the city for display in Rome as part of the ceremony of Corpus Christi. This was the Corporal, stained by the consecrated Host in the Miracle of Bolsena, which inspired Pope Urban IV to institute the Feast of Corpus Christi seven hundred years earlier and which, some say, led him to support the building of the Duomo in Orvieto.

To mark this 1950 celebration, Livio was commissioned to design the cover for a promotional brochure in honor of the Sacred Corporal, entitled *Lauda Sion* (Sing, Zion). When Pope Urban IV first established the Feast of Corpus Christi, he requested that St. Thomas Aquinas compose hymns for the event. *Lauda Sion* is one of the five hymns Aquinas composed in honor of the Blessed Sacrament.

On this cover, Livio created a stylized image of the magnificent *Reliquary of the Corporal,* designed to protect the sacred altar cloth. Today a modern reliquary holds the cloth since the original became too fragile to be carried through the streets. In Livio's drawing, the reliquary triptych morphs into the church facade in front of which gathers a procession of pilgrims. Behind the facade looms the huge dome of St. Peter's Basilica. Above, in the Gothic style letters of the title, Livio has inserted tiny representations of

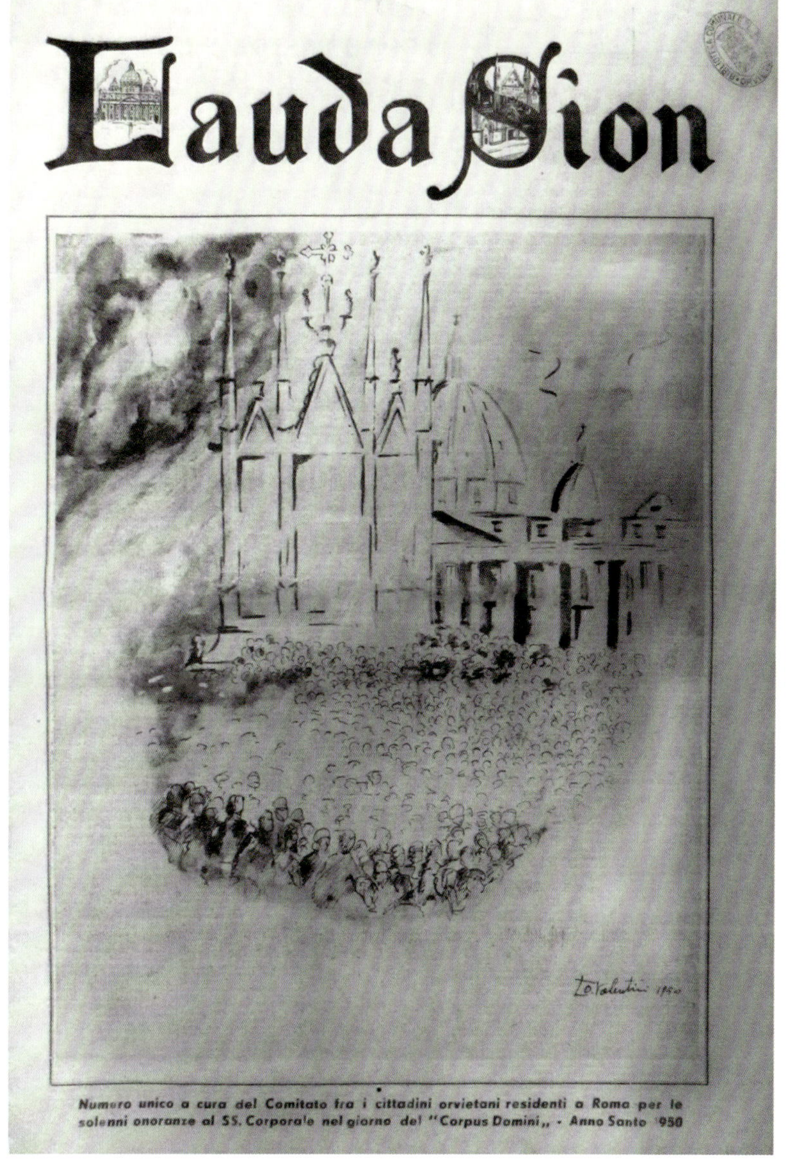

Lauda Sion (Sing, Zion). Printed cover, 30 × 44 cm. Collection of Biblioteca Pubblica, "Luigi Fumi," Orvieto. Photograph by Erika Bizzarri.

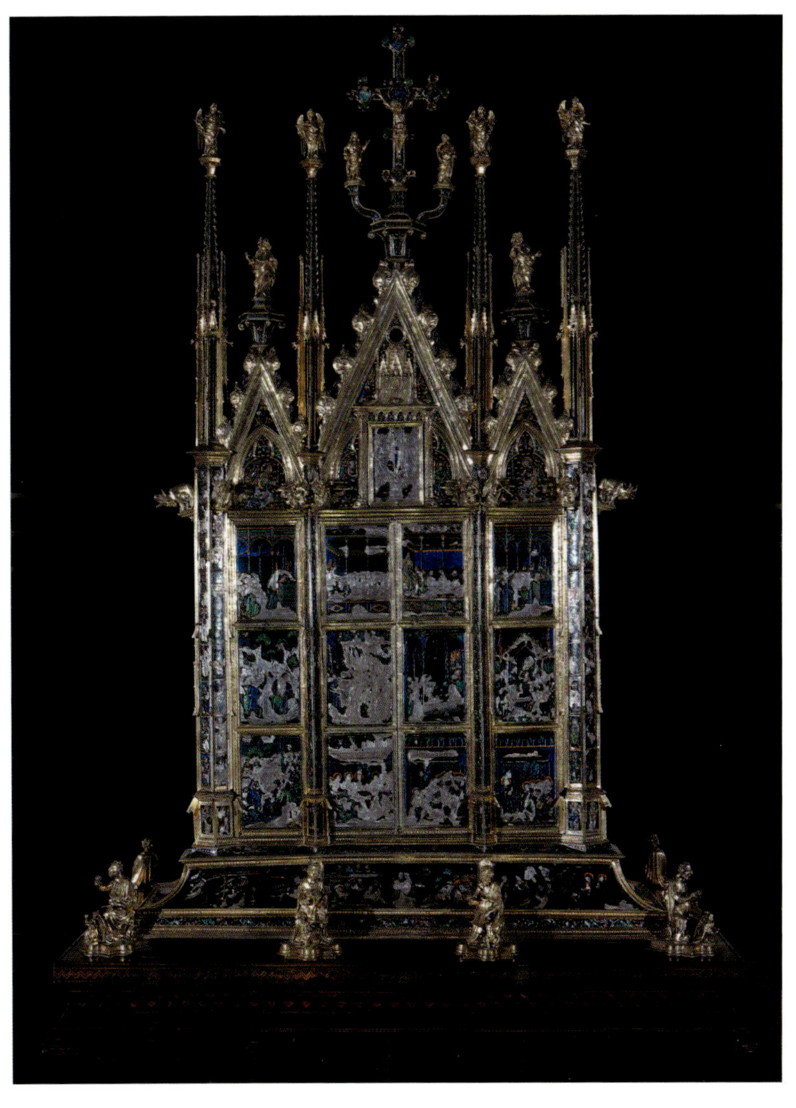

Reliquary of the Corporal (1337–1338). Collection of Museo dell'Opera del Duomo, Orvieto.

the two cities involved in this sacred exchange. St. Peter's is framed in the capital "L" of Lauda while the Duomo of Orvieto is enclosed in the curves of the capital "S" of Sion.

Why was Livio chosen to design the cover for this brochure? Perhaps it was because of his personal participation in the sacred processions, a part of the city's history. As noted above, Pope Urban IV ordered St. Thomas Aquinas to compose a special mass of the Blessed Sacrament to be performed annually in honor of the Miracle of Bolsena. St. Thomas Aquinas was teaching in Orvieto when he composed the hymns, including *Lauda Sion.* On June 19, 1264, Urban IV himself carried the Corporal through the streets of Orvieto in a solemn procession.[17]

Aldo Lo Presti recorded that in 1337 Orvieto began the annual festival of Corpus Domini (Corpus Christi) celebrated in May/June when the Sacred Corporal is born through the narrow streets of the city. Subsequently Orvieto added the Corteo Storico, an honorary medieval-style procession. Displaying dazzling banners with symbols of the history of the city, the parade winds from the Palazzo del Capitano del Popolo and up to the magnificent cathedral. Some four hundred performers in this procession wear ornate garments representing members of Orvieto's families of nobility and dignitaries from other cities, while others carry weapons signifying the city's military strength. Representatives of the Opera del Duomo carry great bundles of votive candles, traditional gifts from the Comune to the cathedral. More recently they have added an additional day of celebration to include the Corteo delle Dame e dei Popolani (Parade of the Ladies and Commoners).[18]

We theorize that Livio's participation in and fascination with such sacred processionals was one reason it became an important theme in his autobiographical artwork. A 1937 photograph records a youthful Livio in a chaperon cap and splendid costume, as part of the Corteo Storico. How did the teenage Livio become involved in this procession? It may be because the committee in charge of designing those historic outfits included Professor Puppo and Professor Benini, both of whom had been Livio's teachers. Imagine the civic pride the young artist felt in publicly honoring the heritage of arts in Umbria. In later years, a mature Livio assumed the role of public notary.

One of the early themes Livio explored as he developed his artistic identity was the religious procession. He painted *La Processione del Venerdi Santo* (The Procession on Good Friday). This oil painting represents the Via Crucis del Venerdi Santo, the Way of the Cross of Good Friday, a springtime candlelight procession through the historic center of town from the Church of San Giovenale to the Church of Sant'Andrea, perhaps because San Giovenale himself was considered among the first to bring Christianity to pagan Orvieto. In this traditional ceremony, a large illuminated cross and two smaller wooden crosses are born through the streets recreating the Passion of Christ.

Beginning about 1950 the Istituto del Drama Sacro chose Orvieto as the permanent home for the miracle plays performed on the steps of the Duomo. Before then, Assisi had been the center for such performances. In the Corteo Storico, standards painted by Gino Fritelli between 1922 and 1935 illustrate the history of Orvieto as a city of miracles. They depict the Mass of Bolsena, where the Miracle of the Host occurred, and the stories of Urban IV and St. Thomas Aquinas. According to reports, St. Thomas once heard the Crucifix speak to him, saying, "You have written well of Me, Thomas. What would you desire as a reward?" Thomas broke into tears, as he replied, "Nothing, Lord. I'm doing it all for you." Some believe this is the Crucifix that hangs today in the Church of San Domenico in Orvieto.[19]

Another miracle traditionally associated with this region is the healing of St. Bonaventure as a child by St. Francis. It was St. Bonaventure who was asked by Thomas what books of science he had studied, since Bonaventure was considered the most learned among his contemporaries. Bonaventure pointed to the Crucifix saying, "This is the source of all my knowledge. I study only Jesus Christ and Him crucified."[20]

In 1959, Livio created a trio of paintings on this subject. First was *San Bonaventura at La Verna.* It was Bonaventure who established a sanctuary and later a church at La Verna where St. Francis received the stigmata. Second was *San Bonaventura and the Reconstruction of the Church of San Francesco in Orvieto.* St. Bonaventure enlarged the old church where inside now hangs a wooden crucifix attributed to Lorenzo Maitani. In his third painting, *San Bonaventura Preaches at Assisi,* Livio introduced the saint surrounded by followers, some in medieval dress, standing with heads bowed and hands clasped in prayer.

In 1961 using a very similar style with figures arranged vertically in a city square, Livio created *Umbrian Procession,* in which ranks of marchers appear beneath the panoply of brightly colored banners. One participant carries the monstrance while a small boy bears the holy cross. Above them looms the largest of the images, a huge Christ suspended from the cross. Livio adopted an overall stylistic manner for this series. Might he have been influenced by the Byzantine mosaics of the emperor and empress from Ravenna with flattened figures and glistening costumes encrusted in gold?

In a later series of illustrations for the book *Orvieto: progetto per una città utopica,* Livio revisited these processions. A group gathers before the Duomo bearing the patterned standards. In another scene, Livio shows men reclining beneath the *umbraculum.*

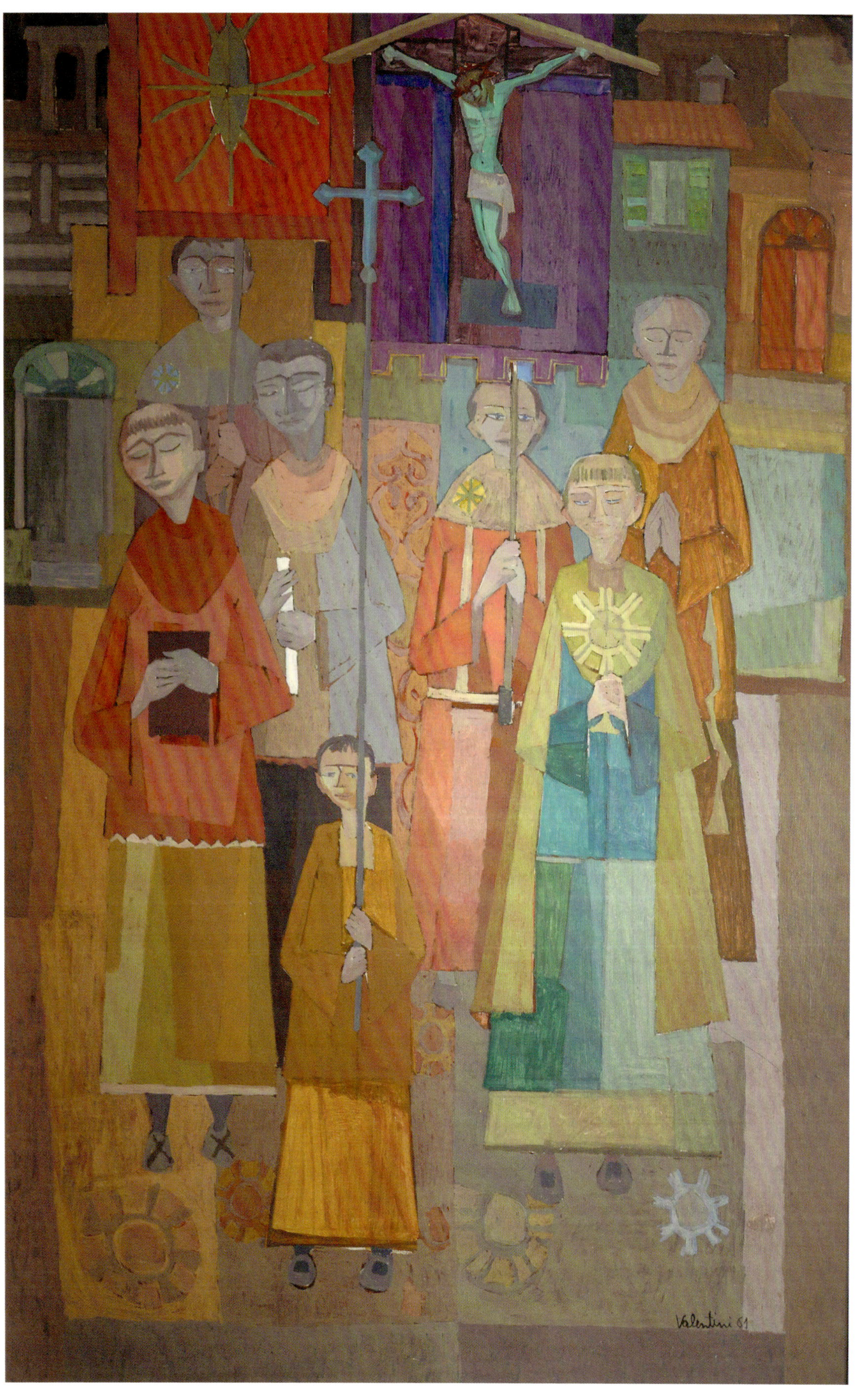

Umbrian Procession, 1961. 120 × 90 cm. Collection of the Valentini family. Photograph by Michael St. John.

Also known as the *ombrellino,* this red and gold striped umbrella is a historic piece of the papal regalia, once used on a daily basis to provide shade for the Pope. Traditionally the scalloped edges of the umbraculum are decorated with symbols of the cathedral and of various pontiffs associated with Orvieto.

It is easy to understand how meaningful these historic processions were for the people in this hilltop community. Toesca notes that in ancient Greece performing the tragic dramas served a purpose both sacred and at the same time political. As in the medieval mystery plays, these civic presentations allowed Umbrian citizens like Livio to publicly renew their sense of religious passion as well as their artistic heritage.[21]

Unquestionably, not every work by Livio during this period is necessarily so serious in nature. In 1950, Livio created an amusing illustration for a printed postcard, a novelty that synthesized all the most famous landmarks in Orvieto. Printed on the card is the short poem:

> The flask was knocking back Orvieto, all delicious,
> Portentous marvel.
> Old Orvieto, what is the matter?
> A gigantic hangover creates the most grotesque dance
> After these hostile times, towers, churches, and bell towers make the most
> perfect bow to the dear little flask.[22]

In a style which seems almost surreal, a wine flask casts a long shadow along the Corso Cavour while above it, drunken versions of the Torre del Moro, the Torre di Maurizio, and the tower of the Church of San Giovenale stagger and sway above the Church of St. Andrew with its crenelated campanile.

On center stage rises the facade of the Duomo, apparently untouched by inebriation. Also included is the Papal Palace, home to the Museo dell'Opera del Duomo, and an angled view of the Pozzo di San Patrizio. Although this is certainly a curious take on the architectural gems in Orvieto, at the same time it shows a pride of place always evident in Livio's work.

For Livio to have undertaken such an experimental approach to representing Orvieto should come as no surprise. Salvador Dali famously distorted his native Catalonia. In particular, Livio's lengthy archways and deep shadows remind us of the work of Giorgio de Chirico, whose influence Livio acknowledged.[23]

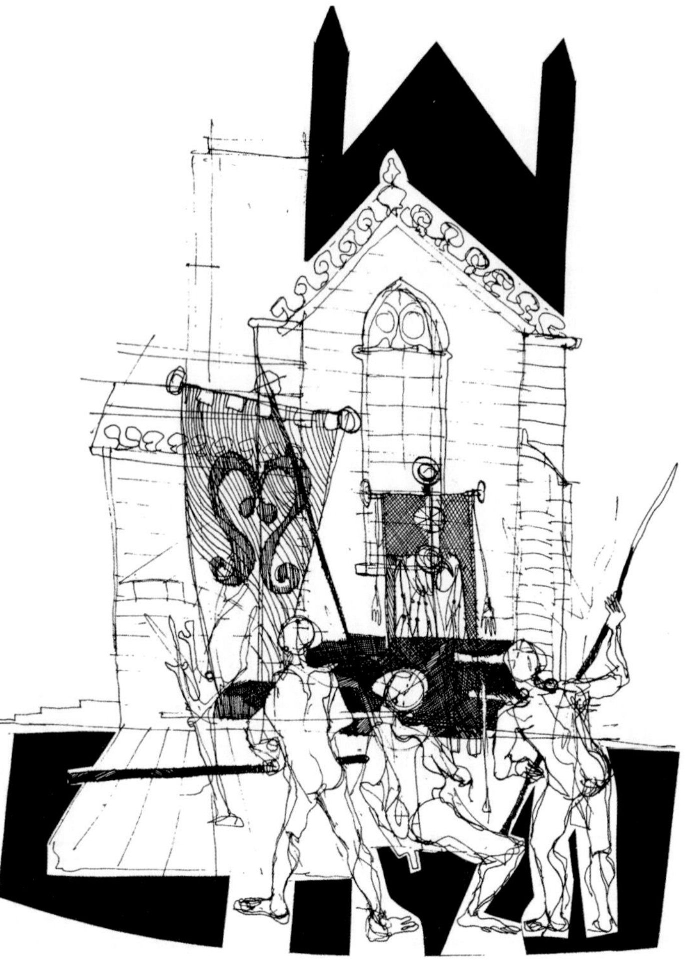

Men with standards in front of the Duomo. Print from *Utopica.*

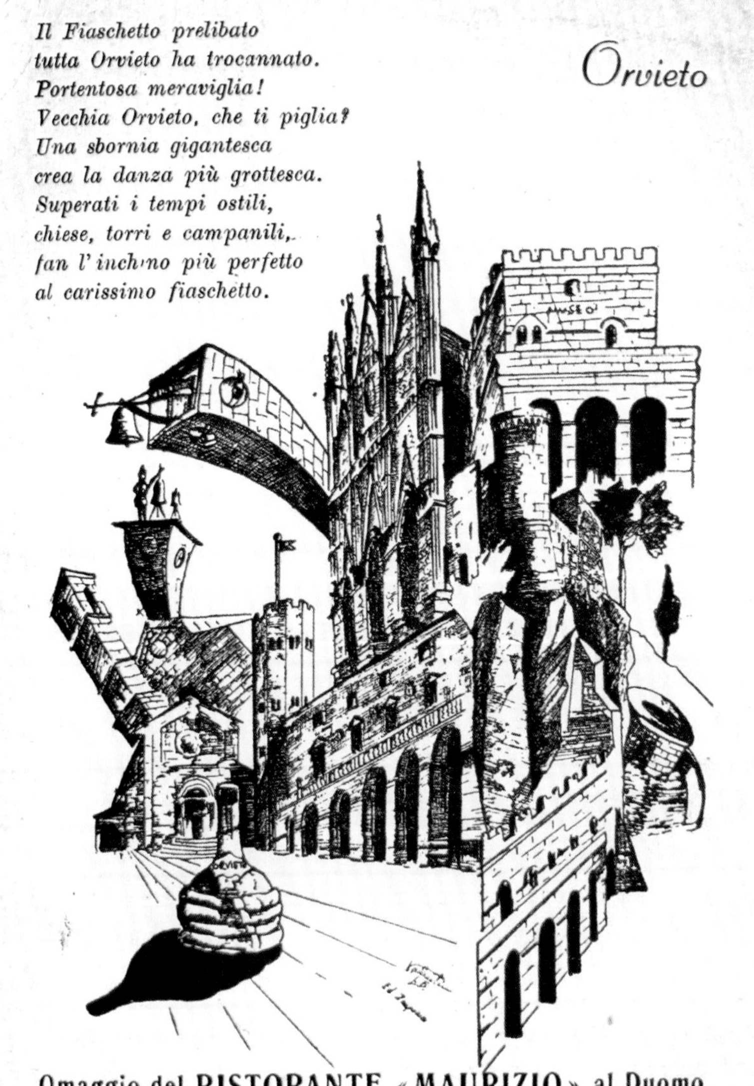

Sintesi di Orvieto (Synthesis of Orvieto), ca. 1950. Printed postcard. Collection of Dr. Franco Pietrantozzi. Photograph by Erika Bizzarri.

In the 1950s Livio struck up a friendship with fellow Umbrian Gerardo Dottori, by then seventy years old, and Alessandro Bruschetti (1910–1980), with whom he shared an appreciation for the natural environment of hills, lakes, and rivers. In 1954 Livio displayed his work in Rome for the first time with his friends in the gallery, Il Camino. The style of Valentini's work during this period has been termed "informal Orvietano." This personal realization of themes satisfied his artistic growth as well as the needs of new patrons.[24]

Very significantly in Rome Valentini came to know Renato Guttuso, who had befriended Pablo Picasso in the 1940s. As a member of the *Fronte nuovo delle arti* group, Guttuso's career spanned from paintings of Sicilian peasants to religious themes with a tendency toward daring expressionism. Of course Picasso (1881–1973) had found world renown through his introduction of cubism and perhaps it was Guttuso who helped Livio develop some of those same tendencies. The story goes that Guttuso carried a reproduction of Picasso's *Guernica* in his pocket and "called it his Communist Party membership card."[25] As a result of these new relationships in Rome, Livio's Orvieto Informal period debuted new color experiments and flattened cubic spaces.

One such example, dating to 1958, is in the collection of Erika Bizzarri. Livio captures the wave-like hills surrounding the city. Only a few shrubs dot the landscape while Livio concentrates on the deep perspective of shadows caressing the rising mountains. The Maestro has become very adept at varying the direction and intensity of hatch marks representing the depth of field. The tiniest trace of a building, perhaps a church, rests high on a center plain, the only indication of inhabitation.

Paesaggio con carretti (Landscape with Carts), from 1955, sets the scene nestled in the hills of Umbria, with gabled rooftops beyond a clearing where two- and four-wheeled carts stand ready for the next morning's market. In *Paesaggio con carousel,* Livio reveals a countryside merry-go-round, painted not in some garish circus shades but with muted tones and flattened forms. Livio said, "This is one of my works from the 50s, when I was just coming out of the war." He was searching for balance in his civilian life. Perhaps we should not be surprised these landscapes lack inhabitants. Where are the children who should be exploring this lonely playground?[26]

Like Guttuso, Livio's gentle countrymen became his next subject, with people at their everyday labor, laying pavement stones, or bringing livestock to market. One of these early paintings seems particularly important, *Venditore di uccelli* (Bird Seller). In the town square a sad-faced fellow displays four yellow birds in a splendid cage. He seems dressed for some public performance in a turquoise tunic, matching transparent

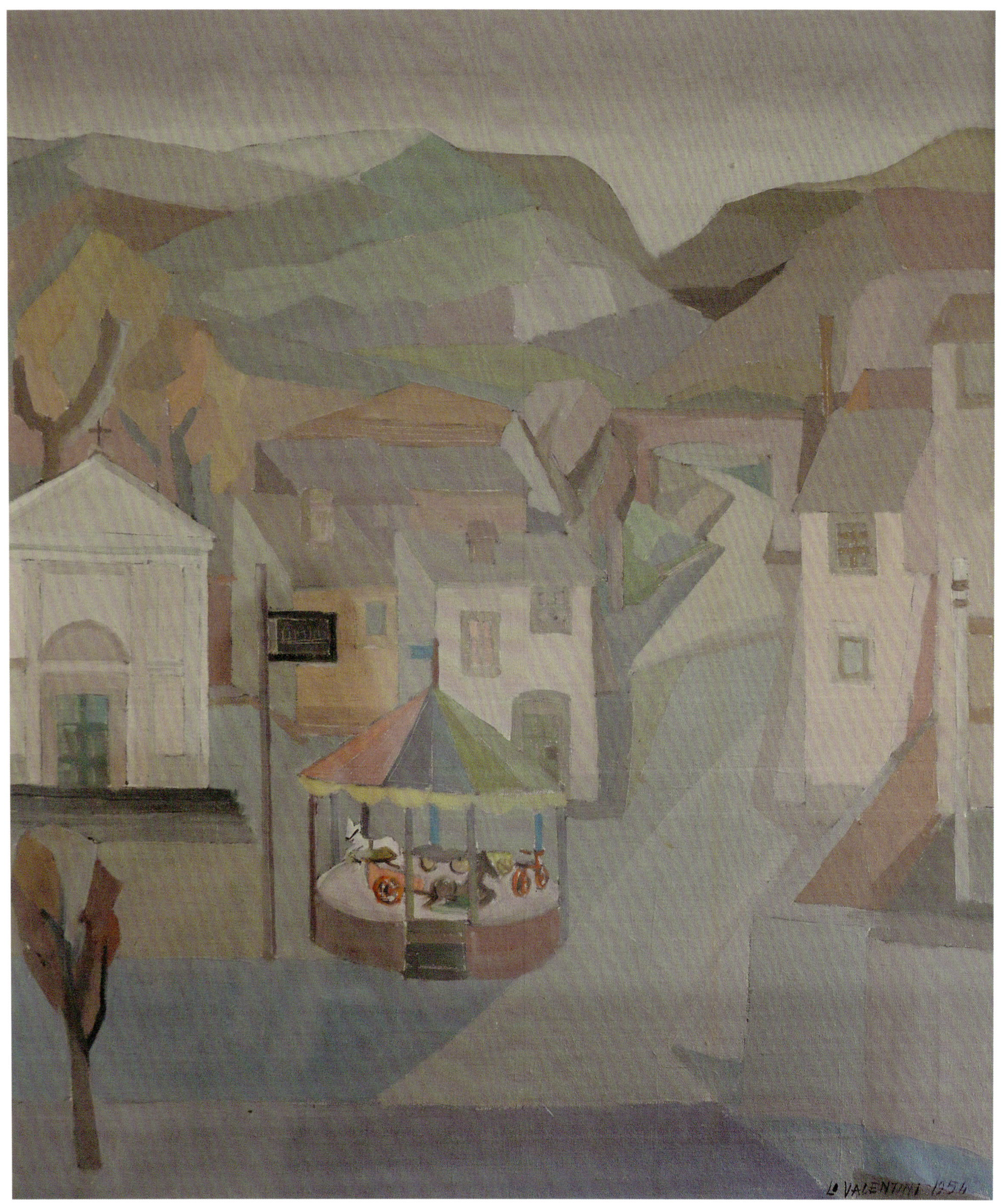
L. VALENTINI 1954

harem trousers, and slippers. The eight-sided cage is adorned with ruby-toned finials. One is reminded of the flames flickering over the heads of the Apostles when the dove of the Palombella appears.

In another example, *Venditori di uccelli* (Bird Sellers), a group of locals, a woman and two men with multiple cages, gather below an overhanging clock. Clearly the bird market is a popular spot in Orvieto. It all seems innocent enough with decorative birds calmly perched in ornamental cages. But might this be the origin of something deeper in Livio's artistic consciousness? Did the sight of these trapped birds spark what became Livio's decade-long obsession?

Speaking of this painting, Livio mentioned the moment "when an artist can become aware of what he has to do, to make his experiences concrete, to be useful to society." Livio said, "I started to express myself, making some real figures that unify the image of a metaphor, alluding first to violence and to being in prison." Later, we explore in detail his best-known metaphor in the Cycle of the Birds.[27]

As discussed in chapter 3, 1955 saw Livio spending time along the western coastline of Italy, in the beachside resort town of Follonica. One evening Livio met and became fast friends with Otello Parrini, who operated a restaurant and dance hall. Otello hired Livio to paint decorations for his establishment. Maurizio Parrini, son of Otello, remembered when Livio stayed with the family and was given a workshop in the cellar below the restaurant.

As previously cited, this hotel is where Livio and Flora began their courtship. In our research we discovered that many of the original works Livio created are still on display at the Hotel Parrini. According to Maurizio, Livio decorated the "entrance with painted and fired tiles, at the time quite innovative because he was the only one capable of doing them." Today when one enters the hotel, the first impression is of a stylized underwater world, realized in painted tiles running across the front of the reception desk. At left a blue octopus spreads his tentacles among bright yellow bubbles in a bed of sea coral. One can see Livio's new cubist tendencies in the way the background is divided into overlapping areas of color. The center of the frieze reveals three striped fish floating above a vivid pink lobster. The sequence ends on the right with what appears to be a stylized angelfish.

Although these works are all figural in nature, most intriguing is the first instances of Livio's abstracted forms, which dominate his later works. In art history ancient Minoan ceramicists created a decoration known as marine style in which the empty spaces around a sea creature are filled in with floating, hard to identify objects. In the

⇝ *Paesaggio con carousel* (Landscape with Carousel), 1955. Approximately 90 × 100 cm. Collection of the Valentini family. Photograph by Michael St. John.

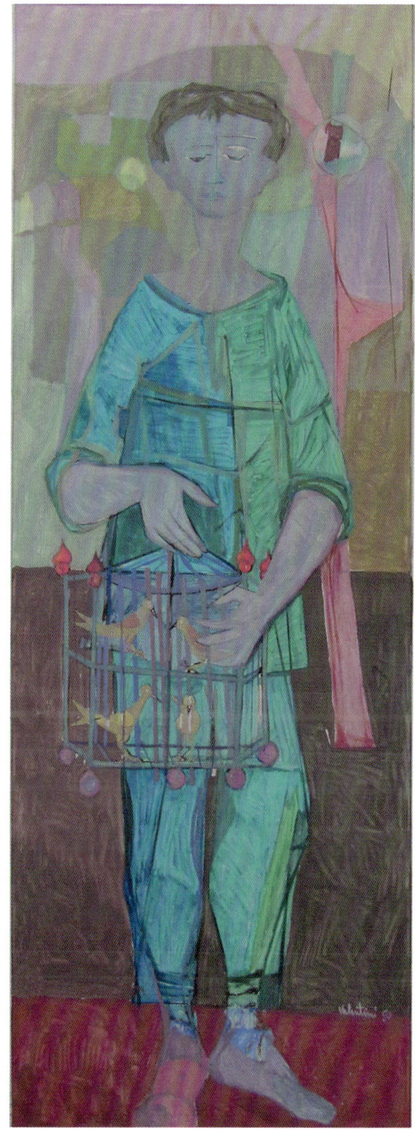

Venditore di uccelli (Bird Seller), 1962. Oil on canvas, 120 × 70 cm. Collection of Maria Crespi, Orvieto.

same way Livio injects odd little designs among the seaweed and bubbles. Tiny spheres pop up randomly in a shape that elsewhere could be interpreted as a shining star or a wheel-like snowflake. In later works by Livio those same stars appear, for example in a 1960 ceramic frieze created for a building on Via Angelo in Orvieto.

An abundance of those wheel-shaped stars decorates a polychrome tile piece on the Casa Colale in Orvieto. Oddly positioned above the second-story windows, a majestic woman rests on a great throne beneath a radiant sun. A great cloak stretches across her midsection where she cradles a bundle of the identical floral wheels. Livio's daughter Silvia conjectured that she might represent "prosperity and best wishes for the house and family."[28] We believe she might be interpreted as a goddess of nature blessed by the stars to her left and sun to her right. Close observation reveals a leafy halo on her head, with tendrils adorning the edges of her throne and a rug beneath her feet. All these handsome organic patterns mirror the abundance of Mediterranean life. Dare we compare her to Flora, Roman goddess of spring with a lap full of flowers in Botticelli's *Primavera,* or even go so far as to suggest she might honor her namesake, Livio's new bride?

Similarly one older photo of the facade of the Hotel Parrini shows a sunny yellow tile frieze running full length above the restaurant entrance. It too features sea life, shells, and the same starbursts scattered along the ocean floor. This original ceramic currently has been removed from the facade and placed in storage.

A visit to the hotel dining room today reveals two more examples of Livio's Orvieto Informal style. In both long vertical scenes, the same sort of villagers we first met in *Bird Sellers* now display the fruit of the sea. In the first a man and woman smile while they cradle a leggy squid in their oversized hands. Behind them on the shore is a charming boat with a sky-blue sail. Remember Livio and Flora summered at Follonica and enjoyed sailing with their daughters.

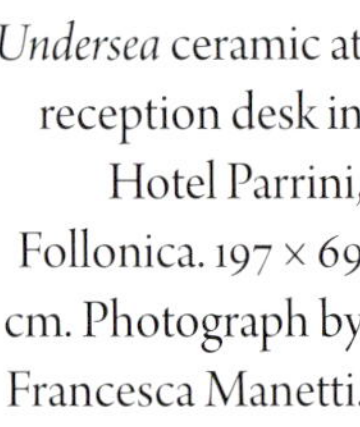

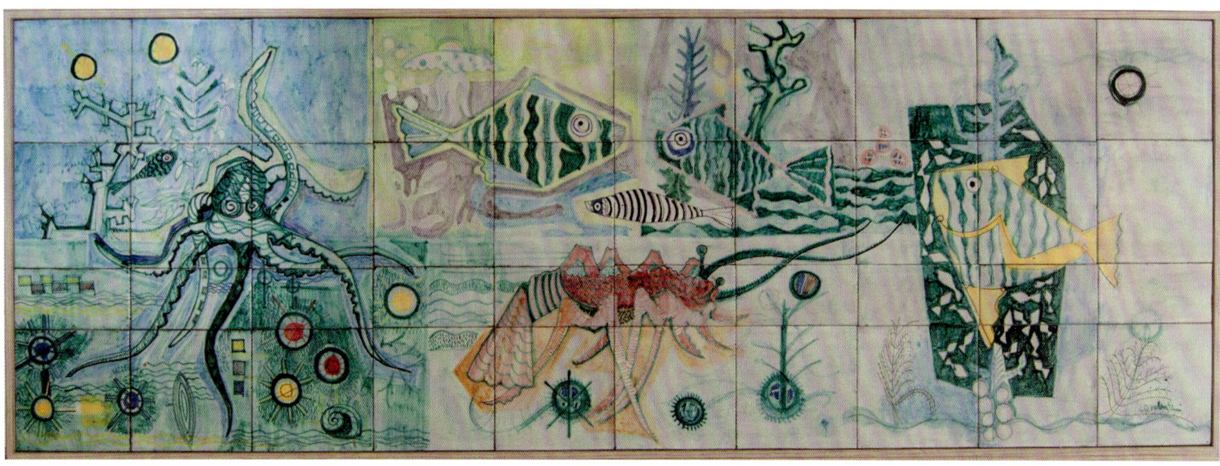

Undersea ceramic at reception desk in Hotel Parrini, Follonica. 197 × 69 cm. Photograph by Francesca Manetti.

In the other seaside vignette, another pair brandish common marine symbols; he holds a great serpentine eel while she wields a trident, the ancient symbol of Poseidon, over her shoulder. In each scene an alien looking, blue-tinged plant sprouts up in the foreground.

In 1957 Livio created a ceramic wall for the *Palazzo Lazzarini* in Orvieto, the historic location for the Istituto d'Arte. Here two fisherboys sit in a colorful village displaying the results of their day in the sun. Each holds a striped fish and one boy holds a tiny crab. In the forefront of the scene other creepy crawlies from nature appear: a serpent, a turtle, and a snail. Once again, most curiously, the landscape features weird flowering foliage resembling something from the world of Dr. Seuss.

Elsewhere in the hotel the Parrini family has framed at least eleven original panels Livio painted to decorate the beach cabins. It is easy to appreciate the relaxed environment captured in these bright hues and imaginative compositions. The pink cabins appear in the background of one of the panels. On the shore an empty craft appears, like some sort of floating deck chair and stool but equipped with oars to glide through the waves. Next to it stands an orange collie dog, perhaps waiting for his master.

Our next example shows a menacing spidery beast adrift among fierce fishes baring their sharp teeth. Notice how these spooky critters float along as a bubbly current spirals around a candy-colored mountain in the distance.

In the next cabin panel a somber woman rests on the shore while holding a bouquet of flowers, perhaps intended for a pair of angular vases at her side. Over her shoulder we see the fishing nets hung up to dry. In another panel a dark-haired fellow is pulling his nets from the sea. Apparently his luck has been good based upon the basket of fresh fish. The sails on his craft are all tied up, while in the next example a barefoot boy struggles with the rudder and the sails

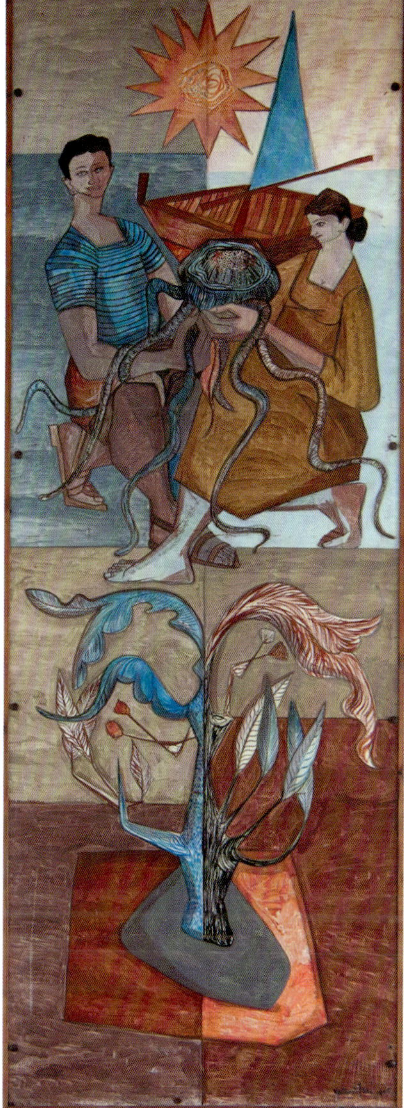

Couple Holding Squid, Hotel Parrini, Follonica. Acrylic on wood, 63 × 125 cm. Photograph by Francesca Manetti.

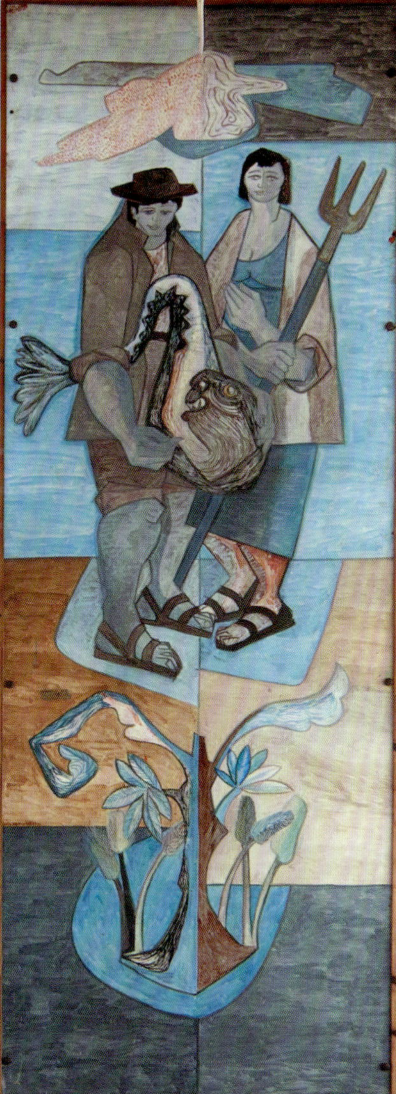

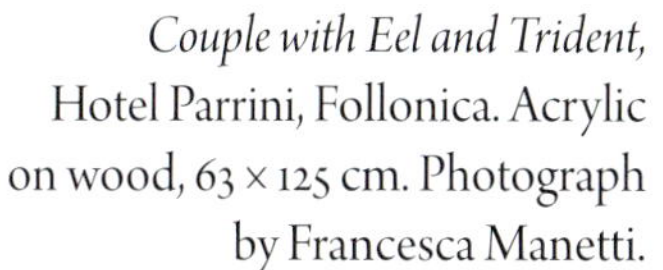

Couple with Eel and Trident, Hotel Parrini, Follonica. Acrylic on wood, 63 × 125 cm. Photograph by Francesca Manetti.

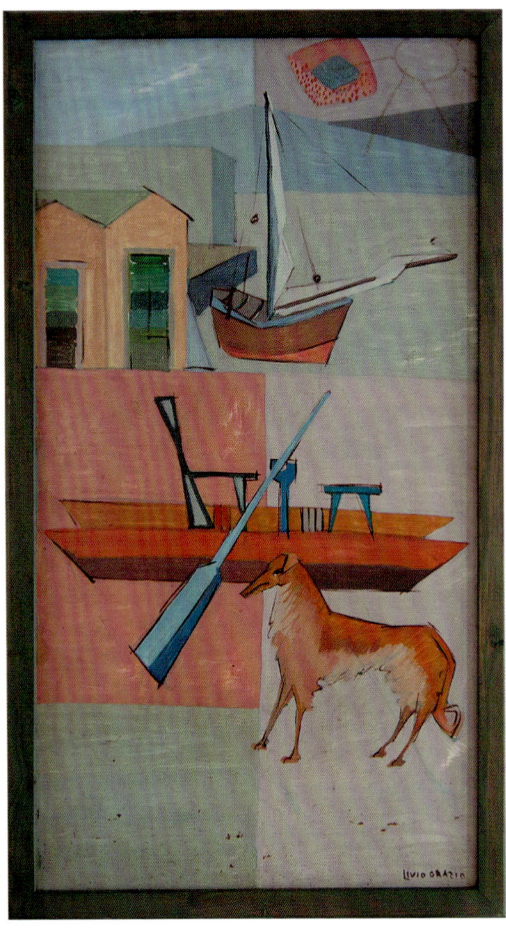

Collie Dog and Rowboat, Hotel Parrini, Follonica. Acrylic on wood, 63 × 125 cm. Photograph by Francesca Manetti.

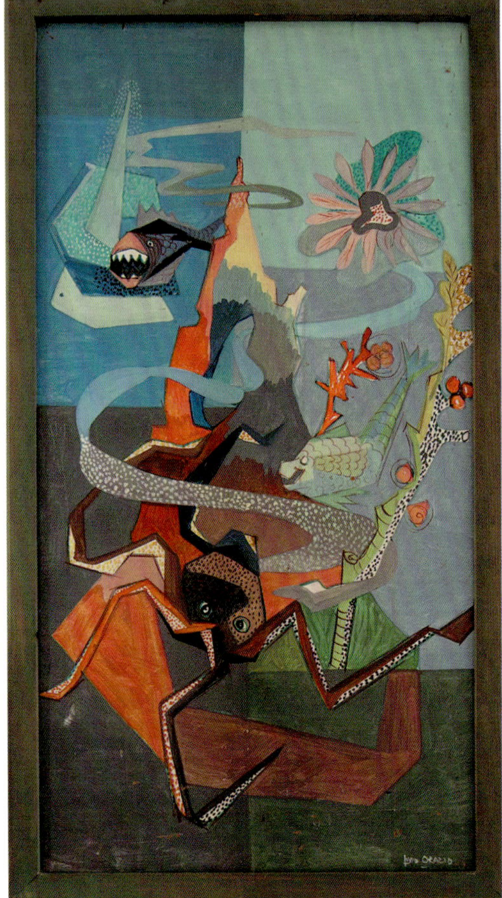

Sea Spider, Hotel Parrini, Follonica. Acrylic on wood, 63 × 125 cm. Photograph by Francesca Manetti.

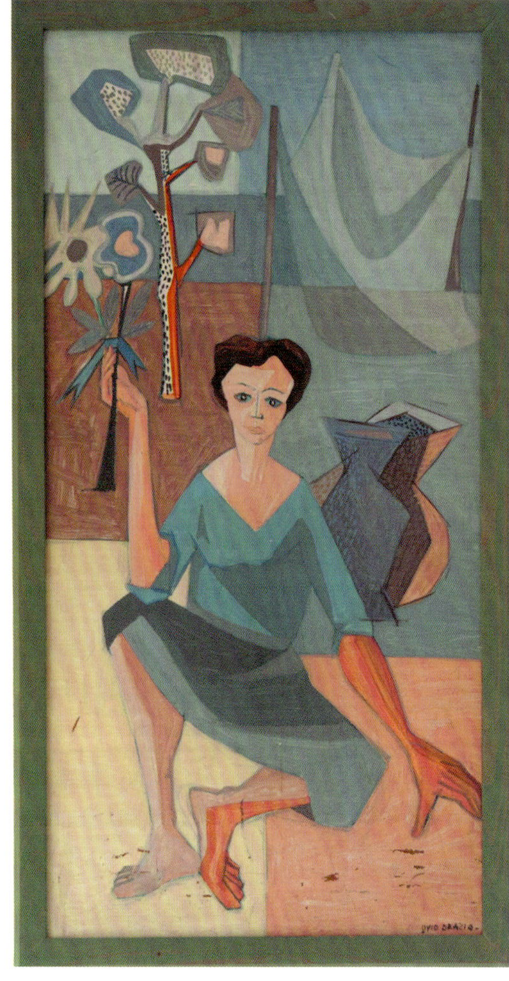

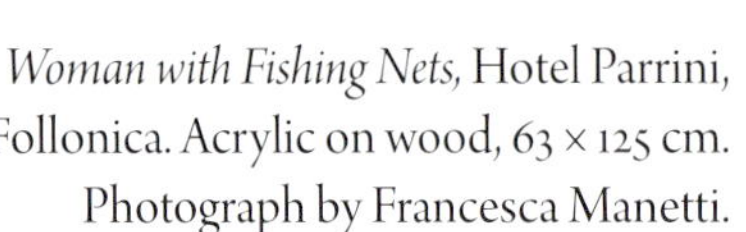

Woman with Fishing Nets, Hotel Parrini, Follonica. Acrylic on wood, 63 × 125 cm. Photograph by Francesca Manetti.

completely unfurled overhead. Livio nicely complements the young sailor's striped shirt with the vertical ribs inside his boat.

Another panel introduces us to the most experimental of Livio's figures. All of the characters in this series feature unique proportions, large gesturing hands and rather huge feet, either barefooted or in sandals. Their earthy peasant bodies remind us of the style Picasso favored in his Roman period. In this example, an orange-skinned beauty works on her ultimate Mediterranean tan under a radiant sun. Her startling skin tones and exotic, shadowed body make one wonder if Livio has briefly fallen under the influence of Henri Matisse (1869–1954). It is also worthwhile to remind ourselves that this is the time period when Livio met Flora. Contemporary photographs show them walking on just such a shoreline in splendidly chic Italian swimsuits, a most striking couple indeed.

The next two panels share a view of the boating life the Valentini family enjoyed so much. One scene shows three sailboats lined up in front of a distant village. Notice how carefully Livio has studied the rigging of the sails and the polka-dotted oars perched in one craft. Then, resembling some refugee from a Disney cartoon, a blue-feathered sea bird on stalky legs crosses the scene very near our point of view. A similarly silly bird with wings the color of Easter eggs appears in the next example. Beside him, a deeply tanned youth with a shock of blonde hair and a blue-striped sailor shirt carries a basket of recently caught fish. No wonder the bird is following him so closely!

In the next example, a scarlet long-necked bird pecks at the ground. We get a peek at one of the beach cabins with a brightly striped window shade blowing in the breeze. Two cotton ball trees support the fishing nets stretched between them, resembling a tempting hammock, and a pair of blue

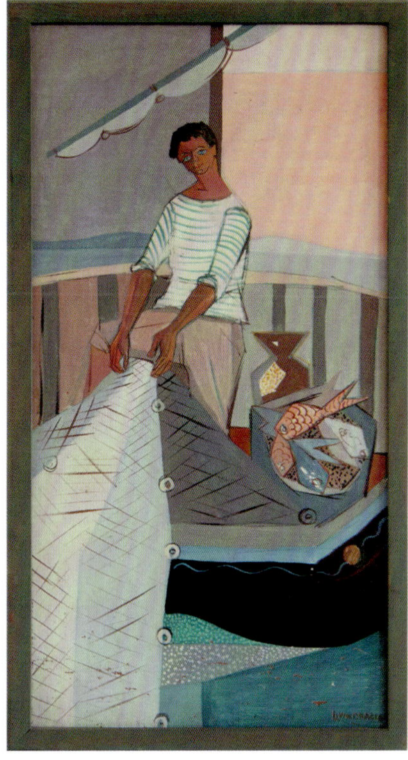

Man with Nets, Hotel Parrini, Follonica. Acrylic on wood, 63 × 125 cm. Photograph by Francesca Manetti.

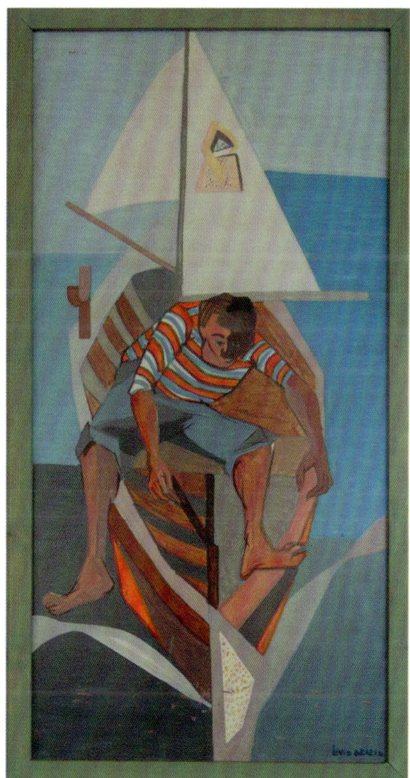

Boy at the Rudder of His Boat, Hotel Parrini, Follonica. Acrylic on wood, 63 × 125 cm. Photograph by Francesca Manetti.

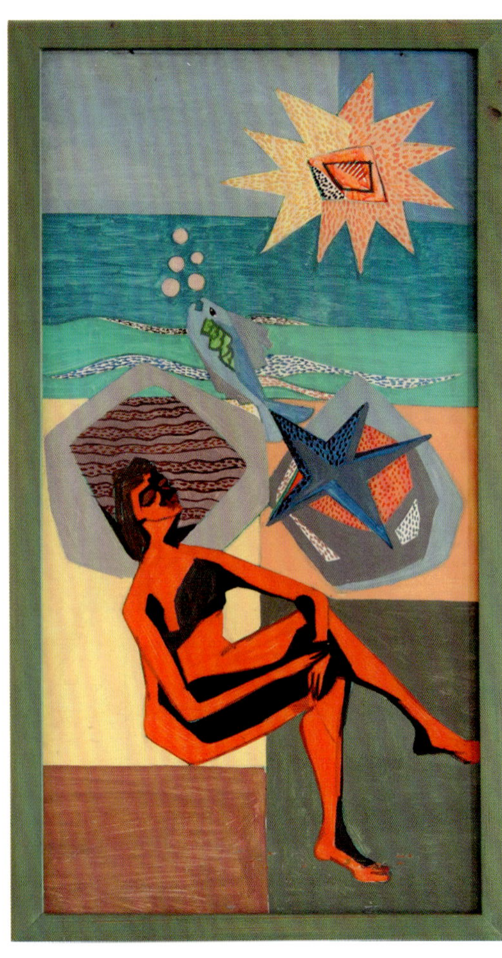

Tanned Beauty, Hotel Parrini, Follonica. Acrylic on wood, 63 × 125 cm. Photograph by Francesca Manetti.

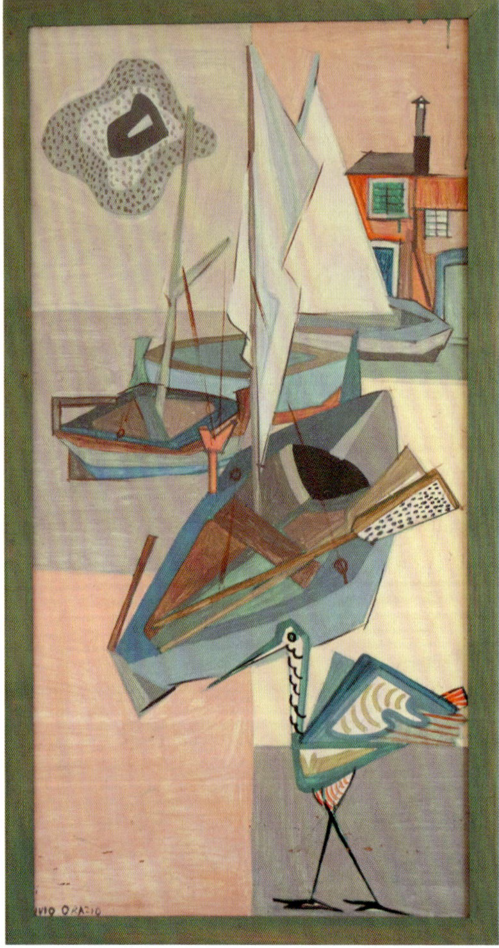

Three Sailboats, Hotel Parrini, Follonica. Acrylic on wood, 63 × 125 cm. Photograph by Francesca Manetti.

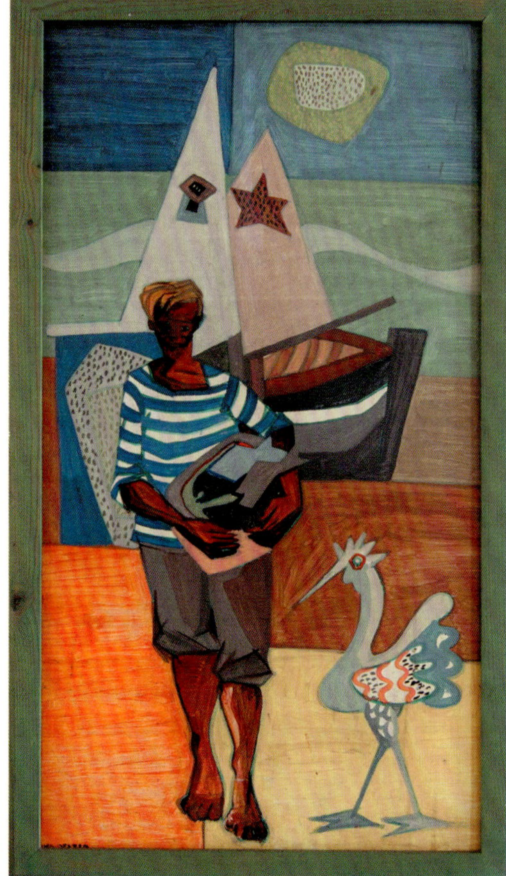

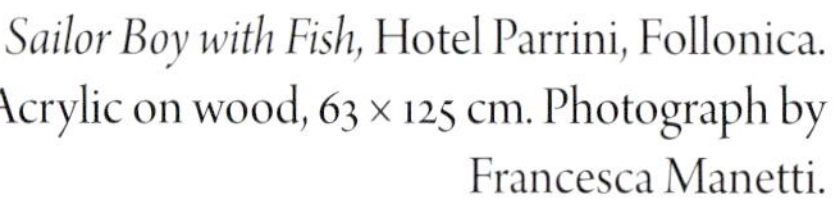

Sailor Boy with Fish, Hotel Parrini, Follonica. Acrylic on wood, 63 × 125 cm. Photograph by Francesca Manetti.

oars leans against one tree. In the center a sailboat painted the colors of the Italian flag cuts across the horizon.

In another panel a pair of stocky boys is building another sailing craft. Overhead hang the crisscrossed beams of a construction crane while beyond an aqua-colored cruise ship hovers near the shore.

Here a young woman balances her basket of mollusks on her hip while gently touching the antenna of an enormous pink lobster. There is something especially striking about the beautiful lass wearing a vibrantly striped shawl and huge sun hat shadowing her doe eyes. In contrast to the casual garb of this young woman, our next beach resident seems positively regal. Looking rather bored, she lounges on a wooden seat whose carved legs seem almost animated. She is very glamorous in an off the shoulder gown, an elaborate woven hat (or is it a crown?) and clasping a multicolored umbrella to shield her from the blazing sun. To finish the scene, a deflated flotation device hangs from her throne. This object with its animal head and spotted hide resembles some sort of sacrifice set up to honor this queen of the sand.

Appearing even more dramatically, and quite incongruously, the costumed character of the Harlequin dances on the beach beside a four-pronged anchor and a white and yellow boat. In his wide-brimmed hat, black mask, and patchwork colored suit, this merry prankster cuts quite a surprising figure—one who will recur in the near future. Just behind him a red rowboat sports the name "Fernanda." Aren't we curious about the identity of the namesake of this craft? Valentini signed all these paintings simply "Livio Orazio," the name Maurizio remembers his family calling him.

In addition to the numerous painted cabin doors, Livio created two panoramic friezes that currently hang in the hotel bar. The first is perhaps his most mature

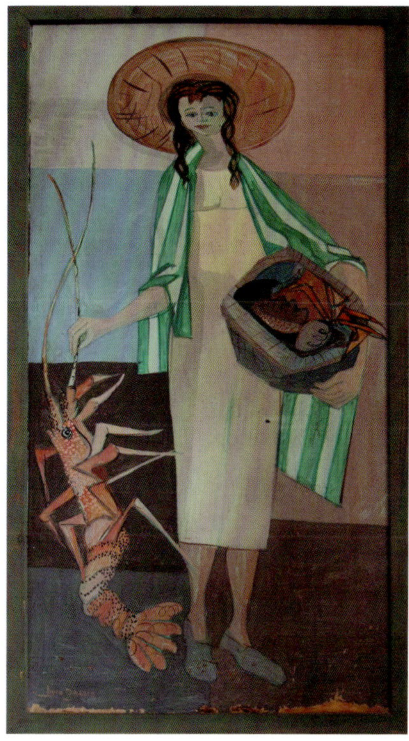

Young Woman with Lobster, Hotel Parrini, Follonica. Acrylic on wood, 63 × 125 cm. Photograph by Francesca Manetti.

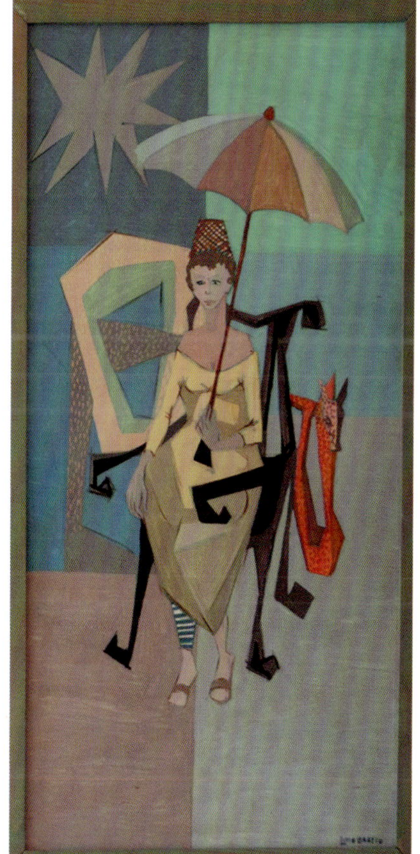

Woman with Umbrella, Hotel Parrini, Follonica. Acrylic on wood, 63 × 125 cm. Photograph by Francesca Manetti.

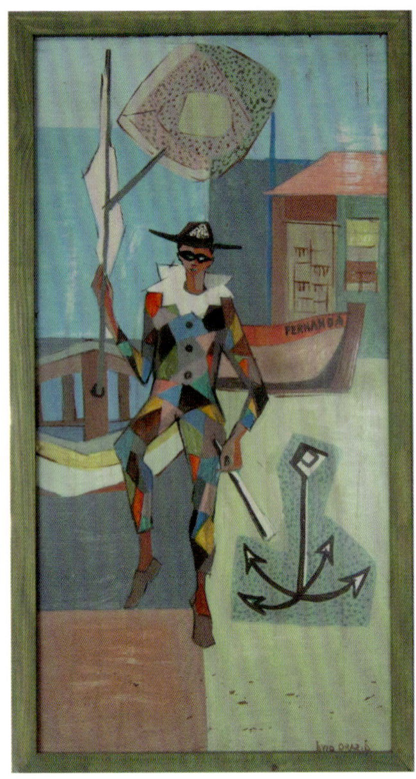

Harlequin, Hotel Parrini, Follonica. Acrylic on wood, 63 × 125 cm. Photograph by Francesca Manetti.

composition, reminiscent of the languid women of Renoir. Four fleshy fisherwomen with shadowed faces gather to clean the catch of the day while one lone fellow cradles a lobster and trident. Over their shoulders we spot more ships near a rocky outcropping. To their right a woman viewed from the back with a ribbon in her hair stands alone carefully stretching the nets between two weirdly patterned trees. Through the ropes we discern the village of Follonica with rising towers of many angled and multicolored rooftops.

The other horizontal composition is painted on tile with its special inner luminous quality. At this same beach we meet a young couple who look right at us! She wears a flat yellow hat and a rose and aqua gown, sitting cross-legged among the oars and nets, beneath a radiant sun. The netting stretches on to the left where we spot clothes drying on a wood pole resting between two scarecrow trees.

The young lady sits with a long-necked boy wearing a three-cornered white hat and a vibrant crimson shirt. He straddles a huge basket of bug-eyed green fish. The boy's half of the composition is completed by a grove of trees with gorgeous Van Gogh-like spiraling leaves. One final pecking bird leans forward to frame the right hand corner.

Livio's next design, and in our opinion his most fantastic, takes us from the beach to the fertile fields of Italy placing his cast of characters in a new environment. Livio crafted a turquoise ceramic framework decorating the base and hood of a large exposed grill for the Hotel Parrini dining room. Across the base of the grill is Livio's ceramic tile rendering of the *cinghiale,* the wild boar so much a part of the native cuisine of Tuscany.

In Livio's interpretation the beast is nearly surreal with wild eyes, blotchy blue hide, and a pink tail and hooves. Most striking is the mane riding the ridge of his back, looking remarkably like a piano keyboard! Above the grill is Livio's most breathtaking

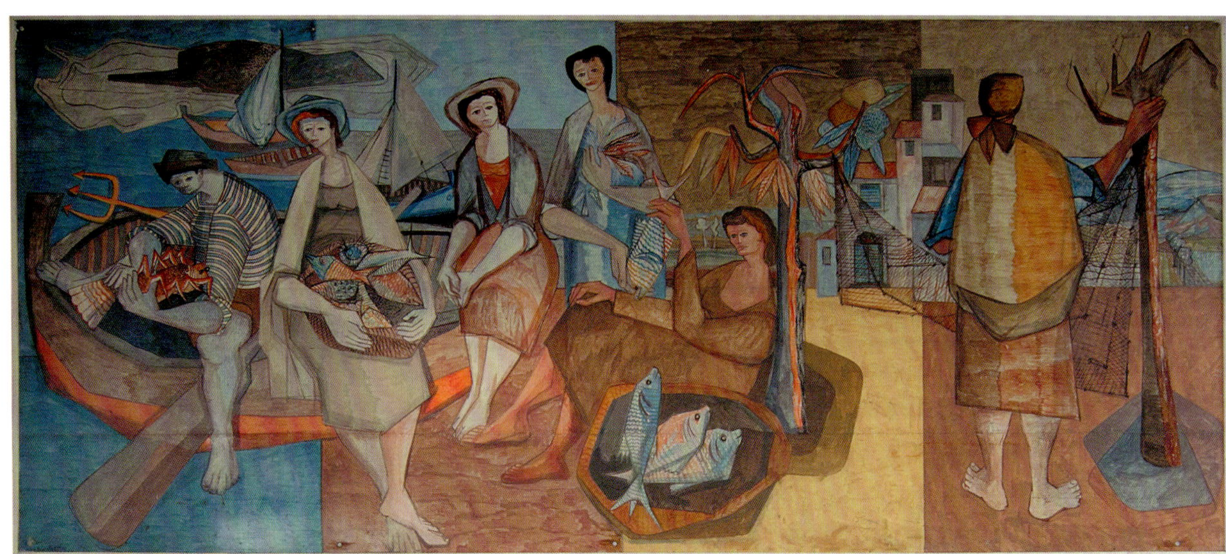

Fisherwomen Frieze, Hotel Parrini, Follonica. Acrylic on wood, 385 × 165 cm. Photograph by Francesca Manetti.

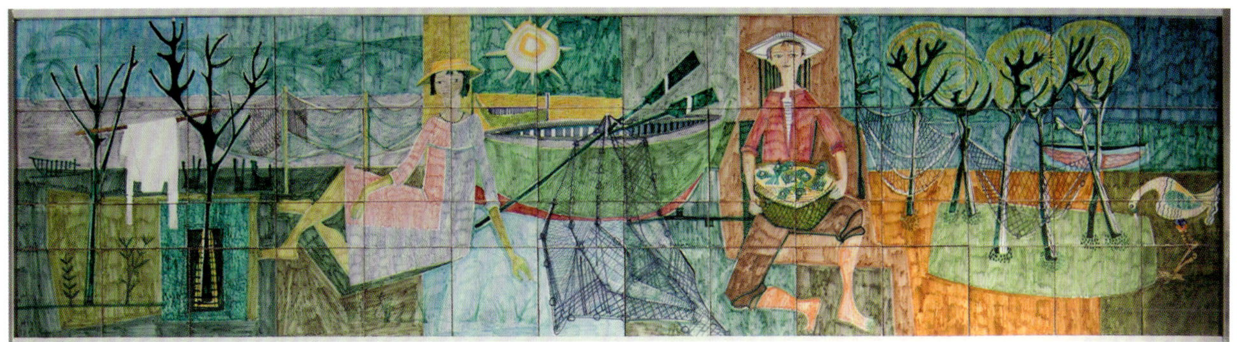

Charming Couple Frieze, Hotel Parrini, Follonica. Painted ceramic tile, 270 × 70 cm. Photograph by Francesca Manetti.

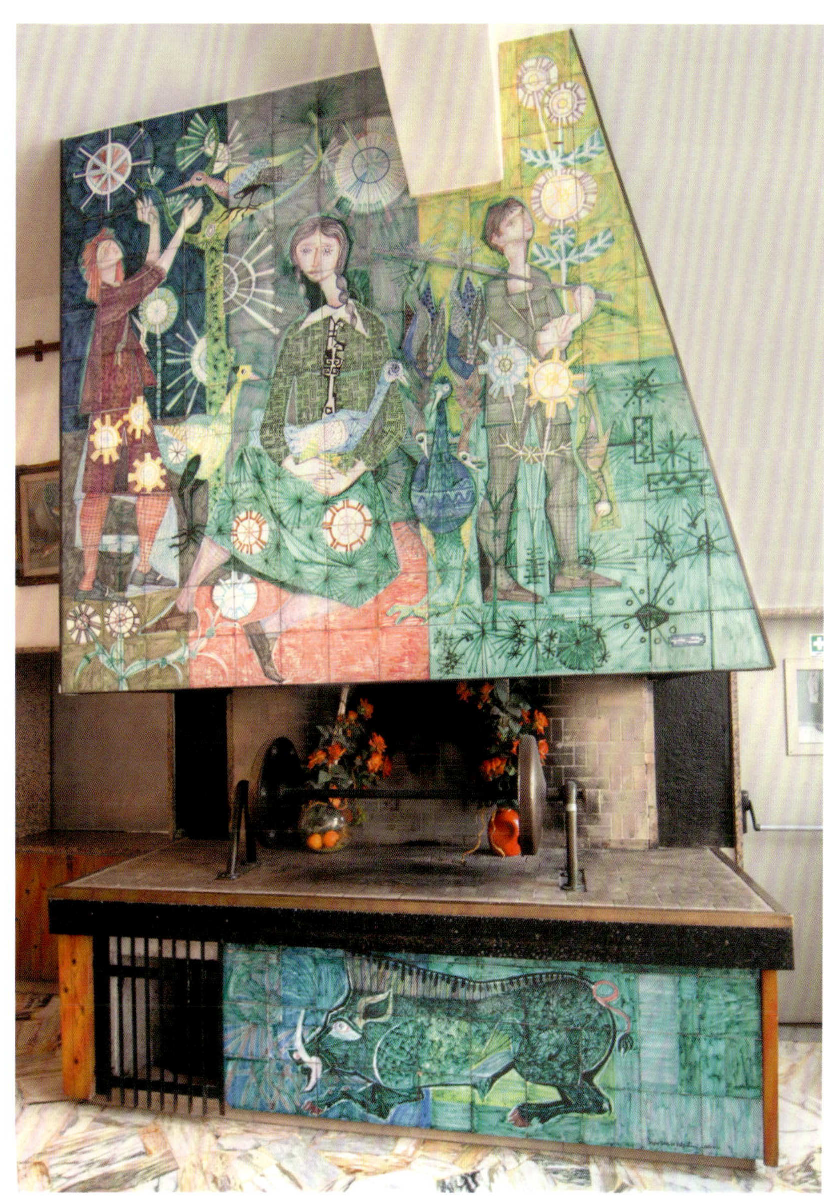

Ceramic hood for grill with wild boar and peasant scene, Hotel Parrini, Follonica. 240 × 260 cm. Photograph by Francesca Manetti.

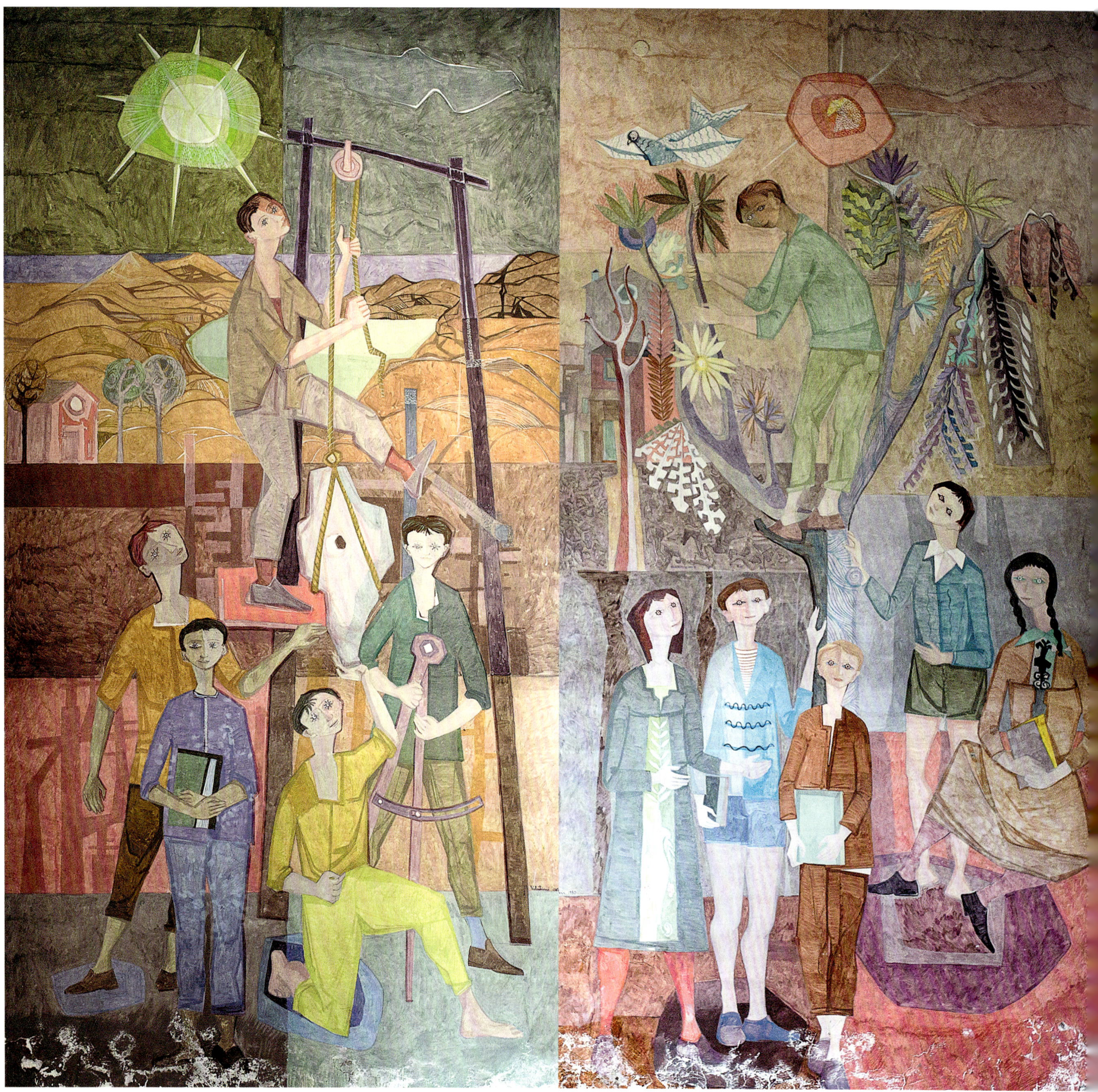

ceramic of all, with a group of peasants perched in a pastoral wonderland. In the center, a lovely girl with braids sits surrounded by a blue crane and a peacock. She is holding a goose on her lap. Around her two young people gather the makings of a meal while sunflowers rise above them. The boy is carrying several limp dead fowl, perfect for grilling. What is wonderful is the return of the wheel-shaped starburst we first spotted in the lobby. Here all three of the figures' clothing is woven with that same pattern. A similar motif floats effortlessly around them, like sparkling sunbursts radiating over a perfect spring morning.

Livio revisited the peasant children again in the frescoes for the Great Hall of the Luca Signorelli Middle School in Orvieto. In the right panel these young people with braids and colorful stockings are enjoying their day climbing trees under that familiar sundrenched sky. In the left panel a group of industrious boys seems to be erecting a monument. These young architects brandish tools for measurement while up on a ladder one lad manipulates a pulley to lift a cruciform stone up from the ground. In both panels the children have small features with long necks and rather sad faces. As always Livio has avoided giving them clothing to identify them with a date or period. Instead, their pigtails, tunics, and shortened trousers might come from any era.

Follonica is home to two of Livio's finest sculptures. On display in the Hotel Parrini is *Struttura di barca* (Skeletal Boat), a wide iron-framed sculpture. In a rare photo of Livio standing on the beach at Follonica, he holds his design vertically. In its original

➛ *The Great Hall of Luca Signorelli Middle School,* 1956, Orvieto. Tempera, approximately 3.6 × 4.5 m. Photograph by Marco Santopietro.

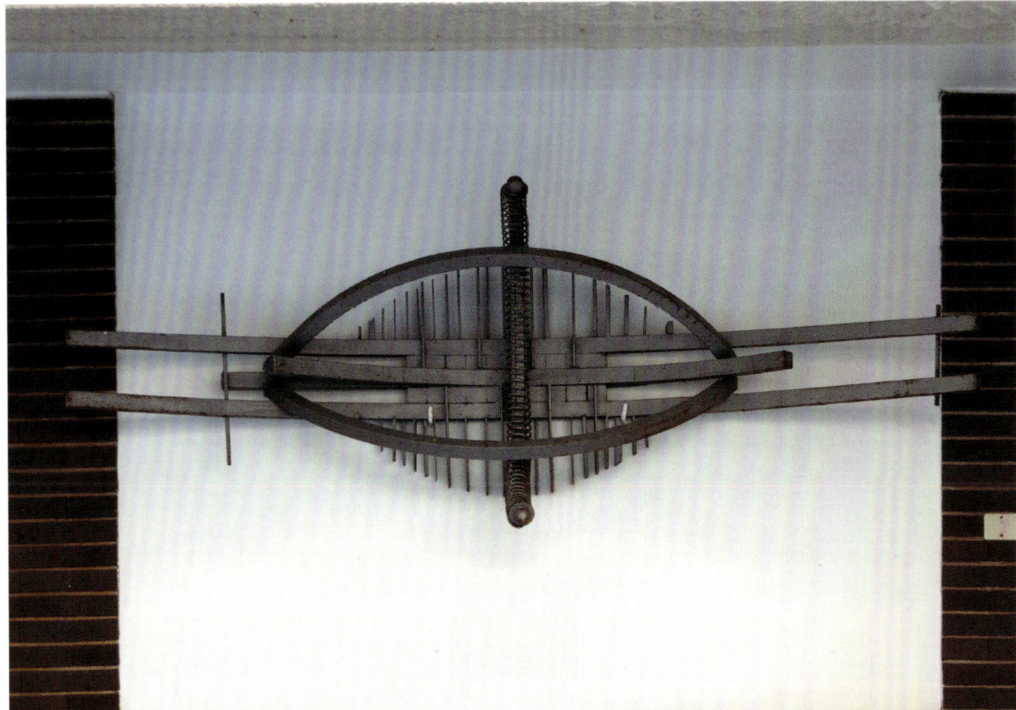

Struttura di barca (Skeletal Boat), Hotel Parrini, Follonica. Forged iron and copper, approximately 3 m. × 76 cm. Photograph by Francesca Manetti.

version the boat had a center copper frieze that is now missing. One does miss the illumination that portion provided.

The overall horizontal design captures the ovoid ship shape of the helm, crisscrossed by metal timbers running end to end and across the body. The boat rests on two very long, thick parallel beams that may represent the horizon line. Bisecting the sculpture is a rounded bar around which coils of metal stretch like a giant straining spring. Is this the mast, buffeted by breezes and whipping sails? As an overall simplified structure of a watercraft, this sculpture perhaps mirrors the style of Piet Mondrian (1872–1944). In his painting *The Sea,* he reduced the wide expanse of water to a series of interlocking shimmers of light and pattern. In the same way, Livio captured the frame, deck, and buoyant quality of a ship gliding across the liquid surface of the Bay of Follonica.

Livio treasured his relationship with the Parrini family. In an e-mail, Maurizio Parrini recalled how Livio remained in touch with his father. At his old friend's passing Livio Orazio returned to Follonica to design Otello's tomb and make a sculpture "in memory of their great friendship."[29] Otello's grave adjoins that of his wife, each marked with their name in raised letters and a ringed doorknocker, as if their souls are waiting to be summoned one more time. Livio's sculpture rises above, with two travertine walls cleaved by a great center open space—the reverse of all those walled in, caged spheres that marked Livio's career.

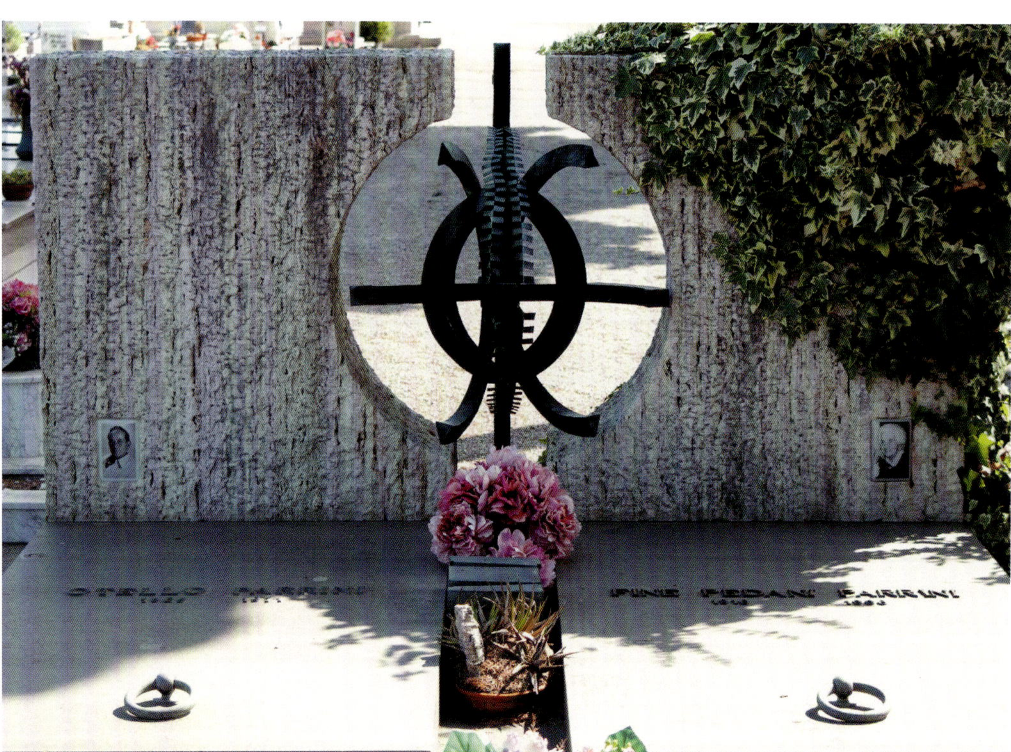

Tomb of Otello Parrini, *Struttura,* Follonica. Travertine, forged iron, and copper, approximately 2.43 × 1.2 m. Photograph by Francesca Manetti.

At the center, seemingly suspended in space, Livio crafted a brilliant blend of iron arms reaching toward and connecting to each tomb—and yet clearly, strongly bound to the inner metal ring as well. Curving out toward the viewer in what resembles a pair of vertebrae is a series of tire track copper attachments, perhaps suggesting the link from birth to the final journey, and their eternal travel side by side.

This was the period in which Livio was back in Orvieto with Flora as his constant companion and his city began to take notice of his artistic contributions. In addition to the commission at the Signorelli Middle School, a number of other significant public works for the city followed. Sadly for the casual visitor to Orvieto, most of these works are behind closed doors and many are being published here for the first time.

Scuola Militare di Educazione Fisica, 1956, Orvieto. Painted ceramic tile 120 × 200 cm. Photograph courtesy of Guardia di Finanza, Centro Addestramento di Specializzazione.

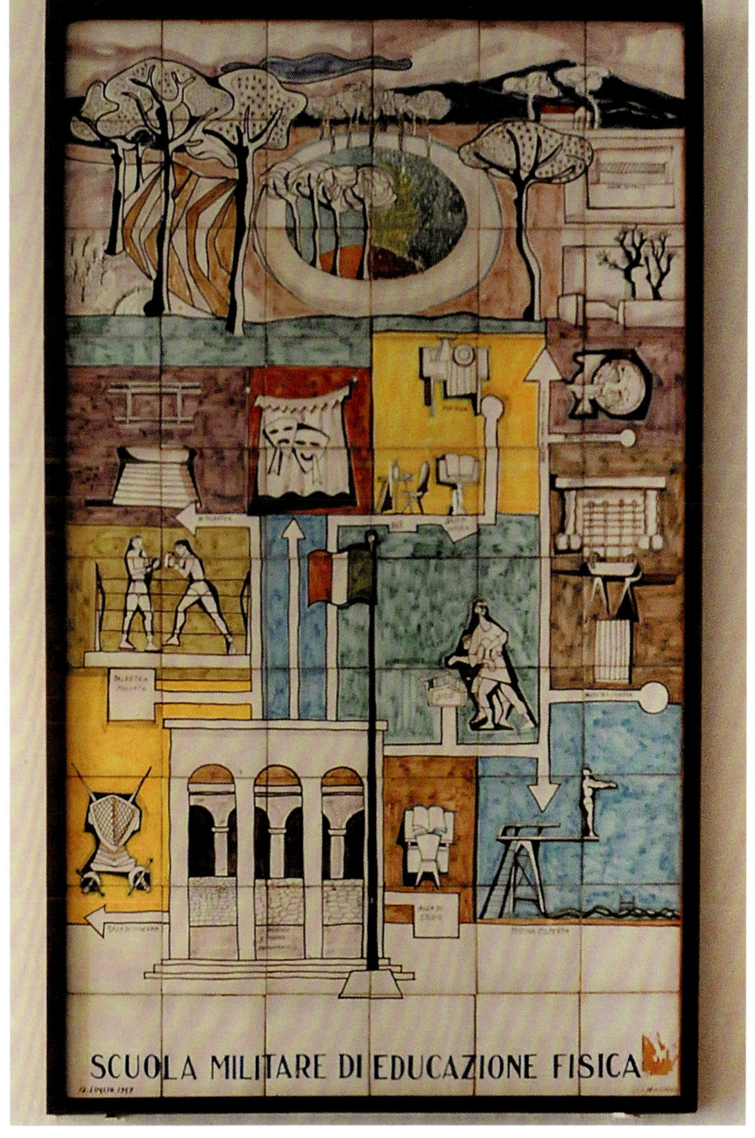

Livio's first commission from the city of Orvieto was for the Scuola Militare di Educazione Fisica that had originally served as Orvieto's revolutionary female physical education academy, the first of its kind. In 1956 Livio completed a large ceramic tile installation, illustrating the various aspects of the educational complex branching out from a loggia in front of which stands the tricolor Italian flag. Arrows draw the eye from one rectangular space to another, each in a unique color and featuring a different activity. In some cases Livio added tiny inscriptions to help identify the room. On the left, beneath a pair of boxers in a ring, he wrote, "*Palaestra,*" clearly linking the school practice to Graeco-Roman history. And the words "*Sala di scherma*" appear beneath the crossed foils and mask used in fencing.

Interestingly not every scene represents a purely athletic activity. Livio also includes a curtain decorated with the traditional tragedy and comedy masks. And to remind us that this is a place for improving both the mind and body, Livio presents a yellow room with a bookstand and what may be a chemistry set, labeled "*Aula di Studi,*" classroom studies.

Across the top third of the frieze, Livio portrays the setting for this exemplary school with an aerial view of the landscape dotted with tall olive trees, a lovely reflecting pool and bright blue peaks in the distance.

To decorate the school's *piscina,* the swimming pool in the same complex, Livio installed a sixty-meter long ceramic wall with stylized

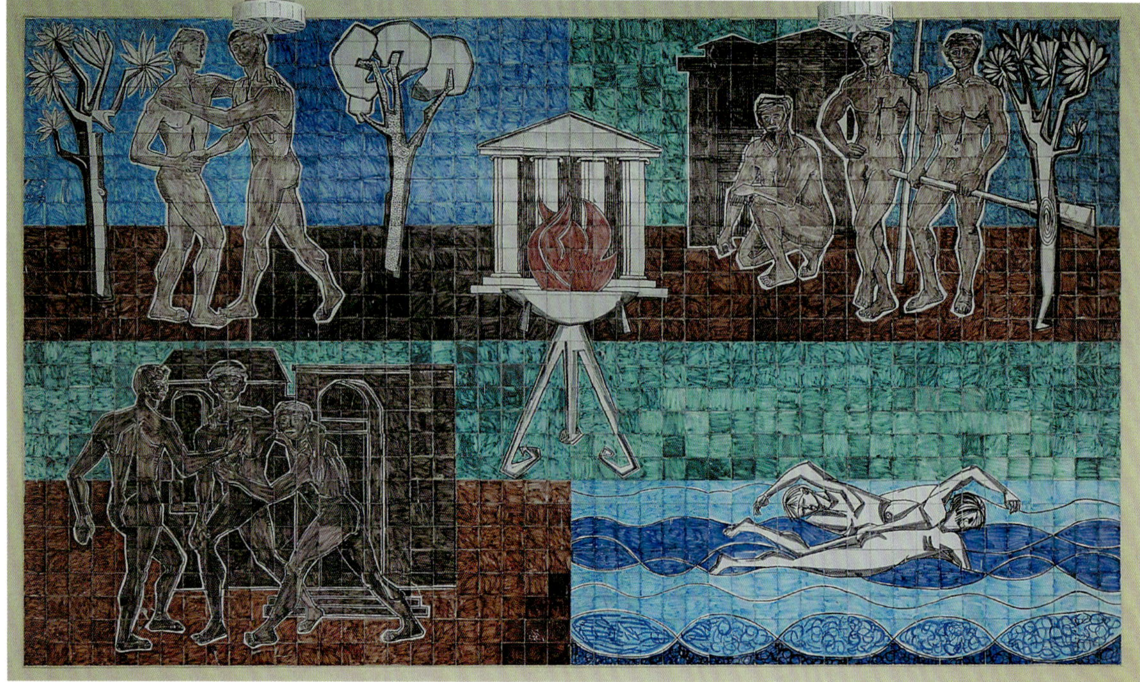

Piscina, swimming pool wall in *Scuola Militare di Educazione Fisica,* 1956, Orvieto. Painted ceramic tile, 5.6 × 9.6 m. Photograph courtesy of Guardia di Finanza, Centro Addestramento di Specializzazione.

athletes in four quadrants. In the manner of an ancient Greek gymnasium, with the columns of a classical temple facade in the background, young nude men engage in a boxing match, wrestle, and pose with the long oars used in rowing. In the final scene swimmers stride past one another in broad waves of color. At the center of the composition stands a flaming brazier on a great tripod, again connecting these Italian scenes of physical competition with the ancient tradition of Olympic excellence.

To illustrate in detail some of the male sports later practiced in this school, Livio decorated one corridor with eight separate scenes done in polychrome ceramic. Each is approximately 95 by 65 centimeters in size. In a very unique manner, Livio designed these figures with fragmented edges as if to simulate the remnants of some ancient wall mosaic.

The first scene shows the *Corsa ad Ostacoli* (Steeplechase) with a muscular runner whose profile face is etched in the shadow of deep concentration. This fellow stretching his limbs across the wooden hurdle is in contemporary athletic gear including spiked shoes. In the right background one spots the edge of the stadium against a fractured blue sky. And most intriguing is what may be a brazen thunderbolt on the left edge. Is Livio making reference to Zeus in whose honor the historic Olympic games were held?

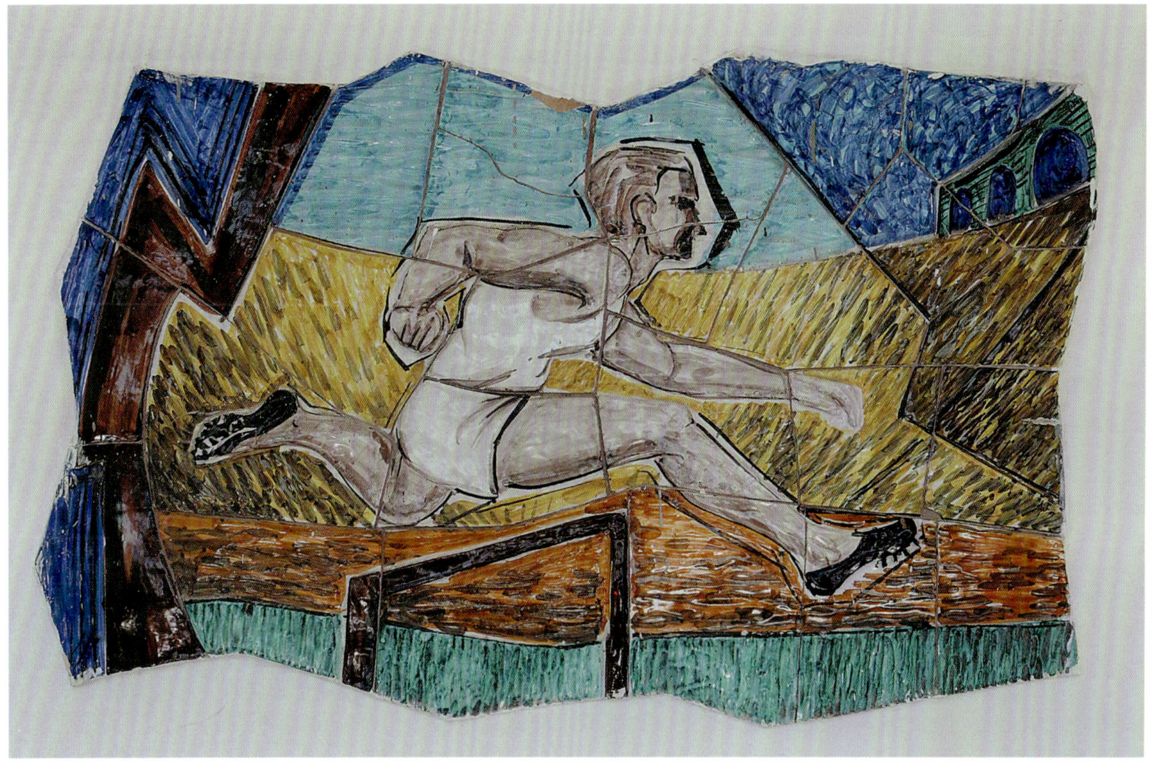

Corsa ad Ostacoli (Steeplechase) in *Scuola Militare di Educazione Fisica,* 1956, Orvieto. Painted ceramic tile, 95 × 65 cm. Photograph courtesy of Guardia di Finanza, Centro Addestramento di Specializzazione.

The next scene is *Volteggio ed Anelli* (Vault and Rings). Noticeably cruder in style than any other piece, Livio's lanky performer hurtles across the horse in a Superman-like pose. A pair of rings dangles overhead. Although the action here is a little lacking, the composition is a strong one with bold horizontal lines etched into the patterned walls and floor.

Next comes *Maratona* (Marathon). The runner closes his eyes in concentration, chin up and pumping his tired limbs. He has arrived in the stadium with illuminated arches on the left while on the right blasts of yellow light burst forth. Did Livio capture a successful photo finish?

In the next event, *Salto in Alto* (High Jump), we view the red-haired athlete from overhead. With arms thrust down to his side, he strains his legs and flattens his torso reaching for maximum height and at the same time casting a shadow beneath him. Livio seemed interested in the environment here with the long bar bisecting the composition and fragmented cubist shapes representing the sky and the cobblestone pavement below.

Pugilato (Boxer) comes next in the corridor. In this signed work the fighter raises his gloved hands before him as he strides forward, one foot higher on a platform. What is striking is that the pugilist is solo; he fights no opponent. Instead the punch of his fist sends out shock waves like the rays of the sun. Or are we to understand this event is staged out of doors? His body is flexed in front of a multicolored wall. One notices in the upper right corner what may be an amphora. We recall that ancient Greek athletes cleansed their skin with olive oil. Is this one more indication of Livio's emphasis on the ancient heritage of such an athletic competition?

Next we find *Salto con l'Asta* (Pole Vaulting). We catch this superb athlete with a surprising calm on his face, almost effortlessly sailing over the high diagonal bar. Here Livio breaks out a full palette of color with the arena arches cast in vibrant orange below a sky modeled in butter yellow with cobalt blue clouds.

Then we encounter *Lotta Greco Romana* (Graeco Roman Wrestling). One chunky brute hoists his competitor above one shoulder and completely over his head. The victim's arms and legs flail about, only connecting one hand with the victor. Here Livio's tones are muted with ivory wrestlers profiled before a coal black background, like something from an ancient Attic vase. Most striking are the decorations framing the scene. At left is an abstract wave punctuated by black dots and cubes. Most importantly on the right Livio again recalled the ancient origin of this sport with large pseudo Greek letters inscribed above his own signature.

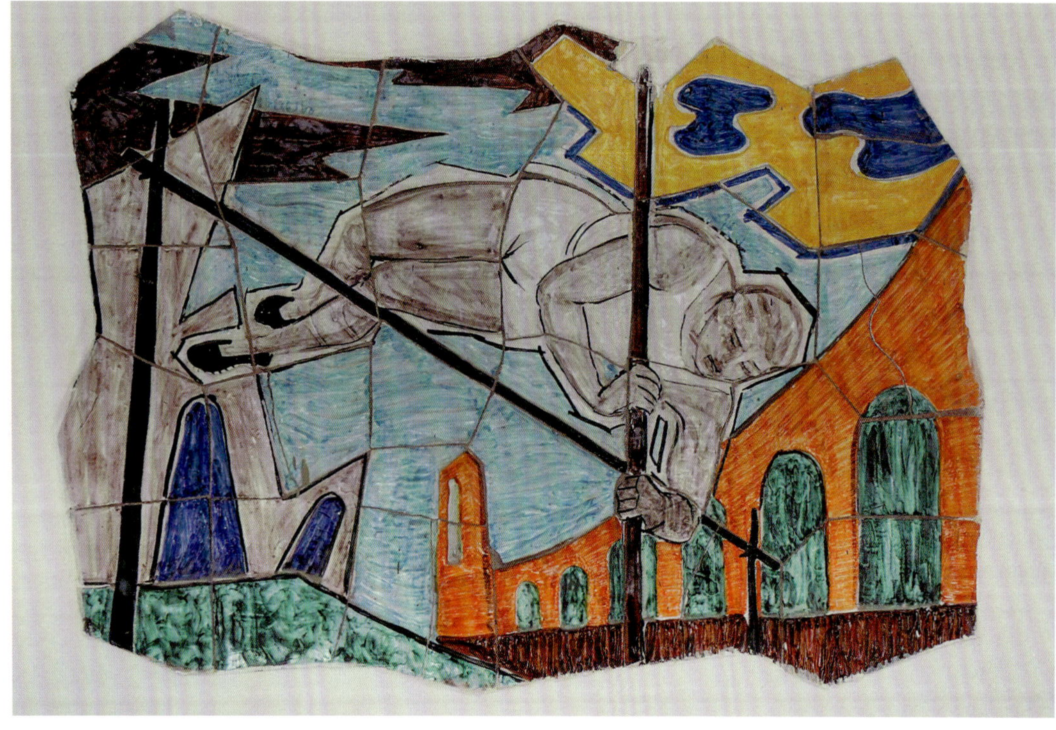

Salto con l'Asta (Pole Vaulting) in *Scuola Militare di Educazione Fisica,* 1956, Orvieto. Painted ceramic tile, 95 × 65 cm. Photograph courtesy of Guardia di Finanza, Centro Addestramento di Specializzazione.

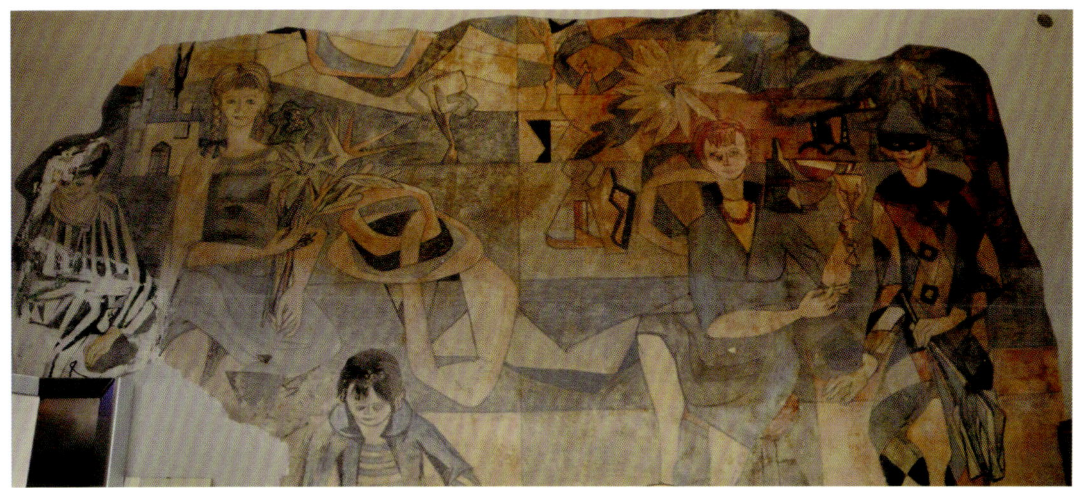

Tempera painting in Caffè del Corso, Orvieto. Approximately 4.5 × 1.82 m. Photograph by Michael St. John.

This remarkable corridor installation concludes with *Corsa 100 M.* (100 Meter Dash). On a track lined with grass and a stone wall, the runner is at the very start of the race, leaning intensely toward his maximum speed. Once again a cast shadow stretches from his left arm down to his feet.

Today this building still features the Roman style loggia so well documented in Fascist-era architecture. But now this structure adorned with Livio's splendid ceramics operates as the Comando Regionale Guardia di Finanza, the training center for the tax police.

Another significant work in Orvieto is Livio's tempera wall painting done for the Caffè del Corso. Today the lower portion is missing but the mural clearly continues the style we saw in the Hotel Parrini and the Signorelli Middle School. On the left a blonde girl with braids holds a cluster of stylized flowers. Next to her sits a brunette woman in a green costume. Below them is a shaggy-haired boy in a striped shirt. His outfit seems more theatrical than a mere sailor's uniform. Unfortunately, the lower portion of this figure does not survive so we cannot tell why he is leaning forward with downcast eyes. Could he be watching us?

Livio tied this disparate group together with a complex twisted ribbon that draws the eye to the right side of the mural. Beneath a huge sunflower, a red-haired woman sits on a three-legged stool and hoists a wine glass, perhaps to toast visitors coming to the bar. Behind her, one notices flasks and bottles of liquor. To complete the scene, Livio returned to the famous Italian character, whom we first met at Follonica. We immediately recognize the Harlequin, best known from the Commedia dell'arte.

Detail of *Harlequin* in tempera painting in Caffè del Corso. Photograph by Michael St. John.

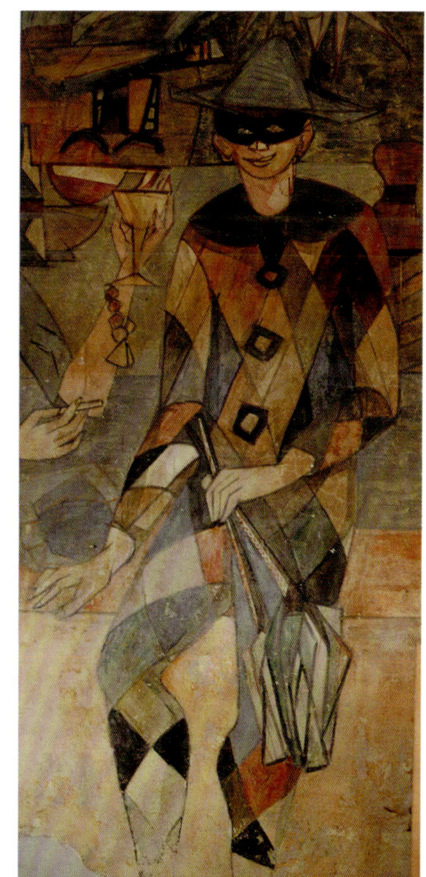

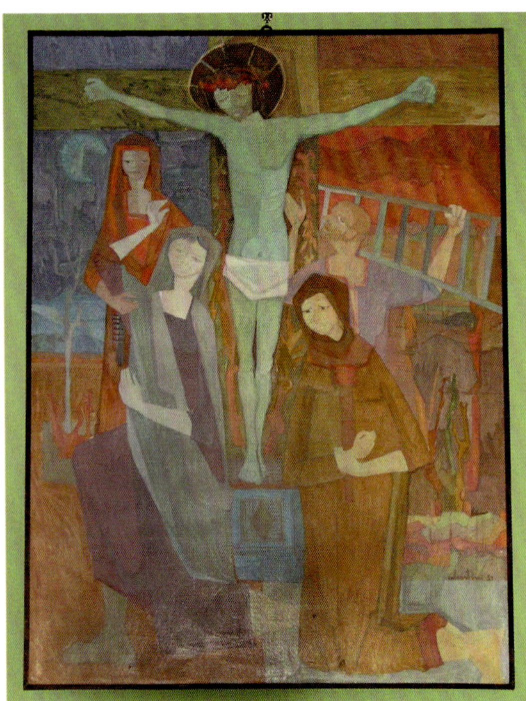

Crucifixion, 1959. Acrylic on panel, 85 × 119 cm. Collection of Rosella Sgarroni, Orvieto. Photograph by Candace Bieneman.

Traditionally he wears a conical hat, black mask, and striking checkerboard suit. What makes this jester so unique is how familiar he is to us, especially in a series of paintings from Pablo Picasso's Rose Period. The character became an alter ego for the artist. However in most of Picasso's works, the Harlequin appears sad-faced; in Livio's interpretation, he wears a broad smile.

With his marriage to Flora in the summer of 1957, Livio's lifestyle was altered, resulting understandably in a fairly dramatic shift in his art. He began to focus on subjects inspired by the family and the spiritual dimension of his life. Lo Presti points out that this marriage illustrates a wise Tuscan proverb; "*chi incontra buona moglie ha gran fortuna,*" (he who finds a good woman is very lucky).[30]

The year 1958 began a period of critical acclaim for Livio's interpretations of well-known Biblical themes. His acrylic painting entitled *Gesu divino lavoratore* (Jesus Divine Laborer), with the traditional theme of Christ working in his father's carpenter shop, is now in the permanent collection of the Galleria d'Arte Contemporaneo della Pro Civitate Cristiana in Assisi. The same year Livio showed his work in the Orvieto Retrospective Exhibition organized by the Istituto Storico Artistico Orvietano.

From this period *Crucifixion* demonstrates Livio's development as an illustrator and storyteller. Behind the massive cross the landscape is bisected into sunset and pure darkness lit by a crescent moon. The Deposition of the Christ is just beginning, with the mourning women gathering below the Savior still suspended overhead. On the right a bearded Joseph of Arimathea has arrived with the ladder hung over his shoulder; notice only he pauses to look at his master. On the left Mary Magdalene and her companion are busy pulling out the lengthy shroud from a blue box marked with the shape of a diamond. In quiet repose, the Virgin Mary kneels on the ground, her face in abject distress and her empty hands held in the same pose that once cradled her son.

Livio represented the body of Christ with great tenderness and empathy. His skin has taken on the pallor of death but his physical form remains muscular rather than racked with torment as countless other artists have shown. One is reminded of Michelangelo's youthful *Pietà* in which Christ seemed almost more at rest than deceased. Around his body and across his brow, Livio sketched leafy featherings of orange and red. Are these the evidence of ghastly torture or might they be Livio's first hint at the tendrils of rebirth and regeneration? Moreover, the Maestro's familiar center circle now becomes a halo of golden light resplendent on this darkest of days.

The Roman School Period: 1960–1970

Reflecting on his time in Rome, Livio recalled being part of a group, the Scuola Romana. One of the co-founders of that school was Giuseppe Capogrossi (1900–1972), who was said to combine primitivism with an intellectual approach to the arts. Another co-founder was Mario Mafai (1902–1965) whose "Demolition" series commented on the Fascist regime under Mussolini. Mussolini had decreed Rome as "the eternal capital of the new Caesars." Il Duce razed whole sections of the contemporary city for the building of triumphal boulevards. In fact, Mafai's studio on the Via Cavour was demolished in order to make way for what is now the Via dei Fori Imperiali.[31] A third member of the Scuola Romana was Antonio Corpora (1909–2004), considered a neo-cubist whose work was thought to be inspired by George Braque.

Livio said, "It's as if I had come alive again from the tragedy of the war so I felt like a little boy. I didn't feel my age; it was like I was born again, as if you started to live a new life."[32] Perhaps one of the most influential Roman School artists was Alberto Burri (1915–1995), who had much in common with Livio. A fellow Umbrian, Burri had also been a prisoner of war during World War II. Like Livio his works are understandably autobiographical, progressing from nostalgic country landscapes to completely experimental constructions in mixed-media. Having served as a medic, Burri was haunted by memories of bloodshed so he crafted his early images out of burlap, stitched together like wounded flesh. In his later work, dubbed *Arte Povera*, Burri used unconventional plastic materials and experimental techniques.[33]

During this time Valentini showed remarkable breadth as an artist producing sculpture in terracotta, wrought iron, and stone, art forms well known in Orvieto. A prolific period of major exhibitions and commissions followed, with Valentini pursuing themes commenting on the human condition with historic references to Mediterranean life and spirituality. One example is a magnificent terra cotta angel, today in the Sgarroni collection. In Orvieto, a town of numerous churches, one encounters angels at every corner. Here, in a nod to Renaissance tradition, Livio surrounded the angel with two types of flowers sacred to Mary: the lily and rose.

Two other important symbols appear in the next ceramic design by Valentini. In 1956 he created *Il filo a piombo* (The Plumb Line) for the Cassa di Risparmio di Orvieto, a banking center located in the Palazzo Ottaviani. This large-scale relief is bisected into two life-sized subjects, divided by gender. On the left a powerful woman with upswept hair and wearing a catenary pleated tunic climbs a massive ladder. Her anatomy seems

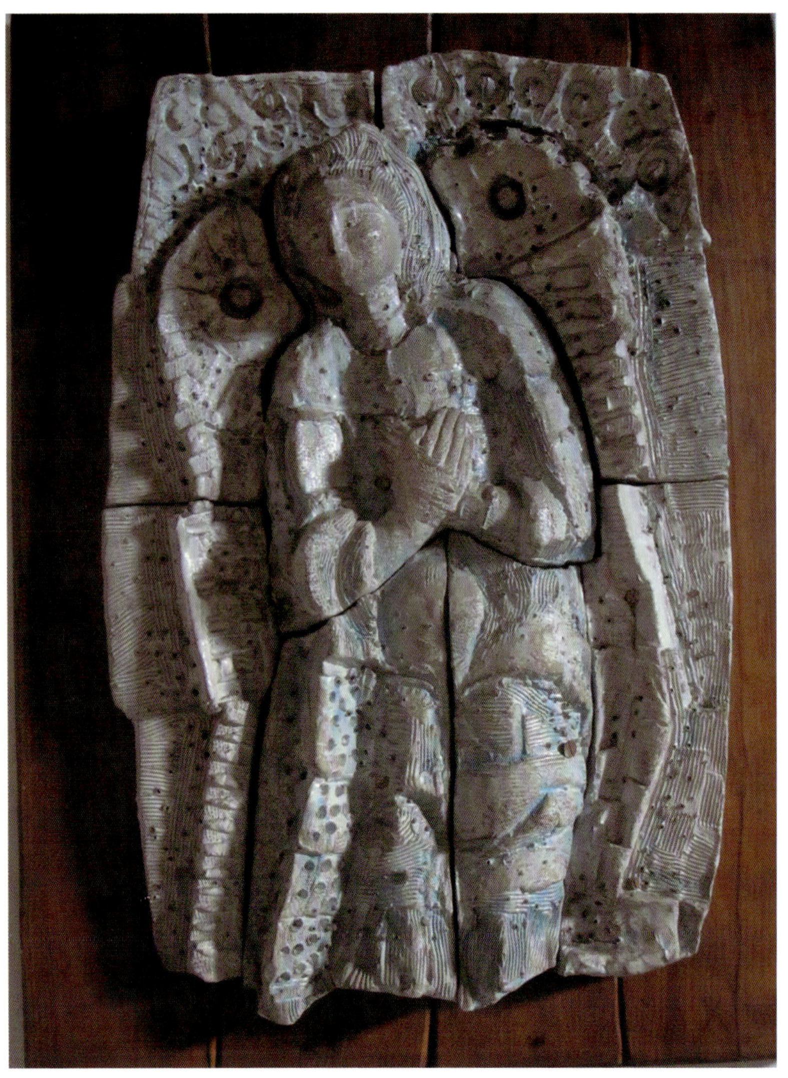

Terracotta Angel. Polychrome ceramic 65 × 45 cm., wood support 78 × 60 cm. Collection of Rosella Sgarroni, Orvieto. Photograph by Candace Bieneman.

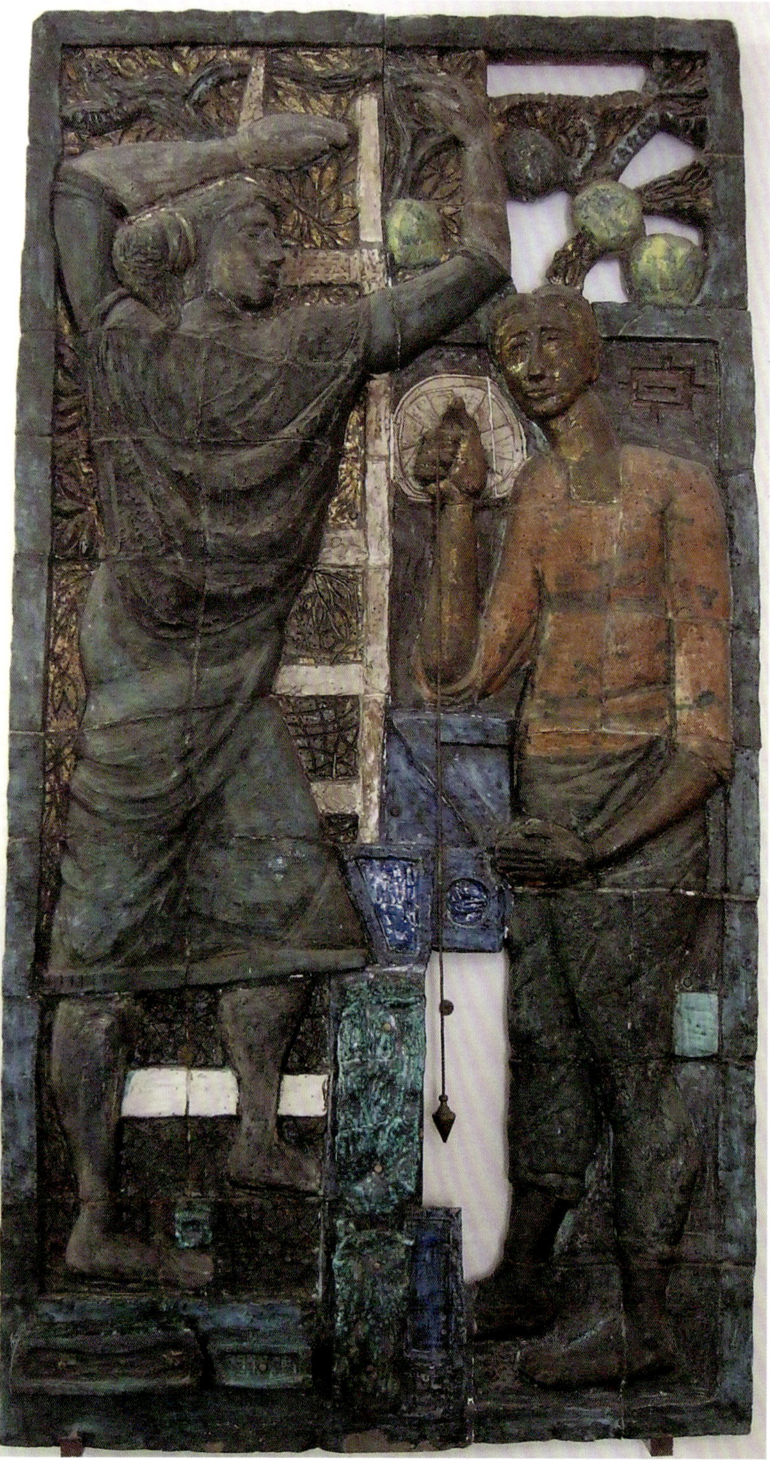

Il filo a piombo (The Plumb Line), 1965. Ceramic, 117 × 234 cm. Courtesy of Cassa di Risparmio, Palazzo Ottaviani, Orvieto. Photograph by Candace Bieneman.

timeless with an Egyptian style profile, thickly muscled limbs and huge flat feet. She reaches dramatically to pluck fruit from a highly stylized branch. Opposite her stands a contemplative man with furrowed brow concentrating on his architectural project. He wields the tools of his trade including an elaborate compass and dangling plumb bob. One is reminded of the pulley and ladder Livio included in his fresco from the Signorelli school. Clearly to Livio, architecture is a male pursuit, perhaps here in contrast to the woman's task as caretaker of the land. On the plaque identifying this work are the words "*simbolo di equilibrio e stabilita*" (symbol of balance and stability). Certainly, the theme of balance is a perfect complement to a bank interior but is Livio perhaps also commenting on the harmony of the intellectual with the applied arts; domestic necessity balanced with scientific pursuits?

We see Livio stretch in an expressionistic manner both in choice of media and technique. Lo Presti pointed out how Livio was influenced by Burri's style at this time. The background behind the man and woman appears almost cubistically shattered with random-looking cracks in the clay. Notice too how cleverly Livio has included a real bronze plumb bob dangling from the hand of the architect. In American art Robert Rauschenberg became famous for combining found objects with painted and sculptural works.[34]

With his work now being recognized outside of the city and perhaps emboldened by the other members of the Scuola Romana, Livio's art afforded him a chance for self-expression and personal catharsis. Most significantly Livio began to explore an autobiographical dimension directly linked to his wartime experiences. It is difficult to separate the suffering Livio endured during his imprisonment from a series of anguished images of the Christ. In 1962 Livio constructed *Crocifisso,* a crucifix from wood, iron, and ceramic for the Church of Santa Maria della Stella e San Pietro Parenzo in the Sferracavallo district of Orvieto. The Crown of Thorns, constructed out of iron nails, tops the Savior's horrific image, resembling a petrified victim with a gaping mouth and twisted rib cage. The iconography proved too controversial and was turned away for display in the new church. It remains in the Valentini family collection.

In 1967 Livio brilliantly continued his metal work in *Cristo* with the entire body of Christ forged out of iron nails. Don Marcello Pettinelli stated:

> Years ago Livio had the idea of using nails to make a cross. This version of the Cross evoked quite a controversy in the Church and the larger community. Some of his critics felt Livio had gone too far and was challenging the existence of God. He did

L'eccidio di Camorena (Massacre of Camorena) 1963. Oil, pigment, pumice on wood, 280 × 300 cm. Courtesy of City of Orvieto.

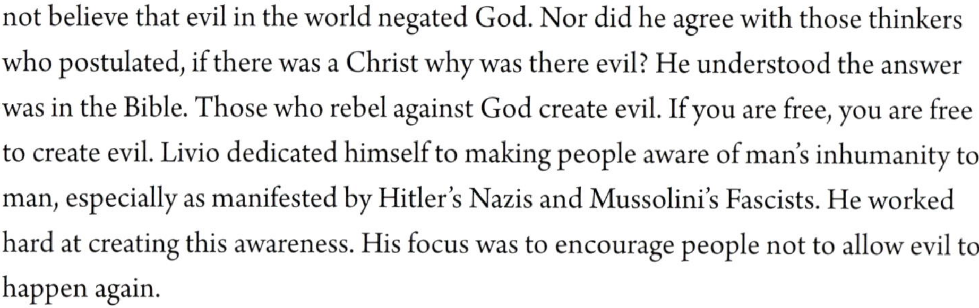

not believe that evil in the world negated God. Nor did he agree with those thinkers who postulated, if there was a Christ why was there evil? He understood the answer was in the Bible. Those who rebel against God create evil. If you are free, you are free to create evil. Livio dedicated himself to making people aware of man's inhumanity to man, especially as manifested by Hitler's Nazis and Mussolini's Fascists. He worked hard at creating this awareness. His focus was to encourage people not to allow evil to happen again.

Livio believed that in reality there is an answer but we may never know what it is. After a moment of reflection, Don Marcello stated, "The nail that nails down does not determine the destruction of what it is nailing."[35] *Cristo* is now in the permanent collection of the Church of San Lorenzo in Milan.

Cristo, 1967. Christ made of forged iron nails, 100 × 70 × 30 cm. Church of San Lorenzo, Milan.

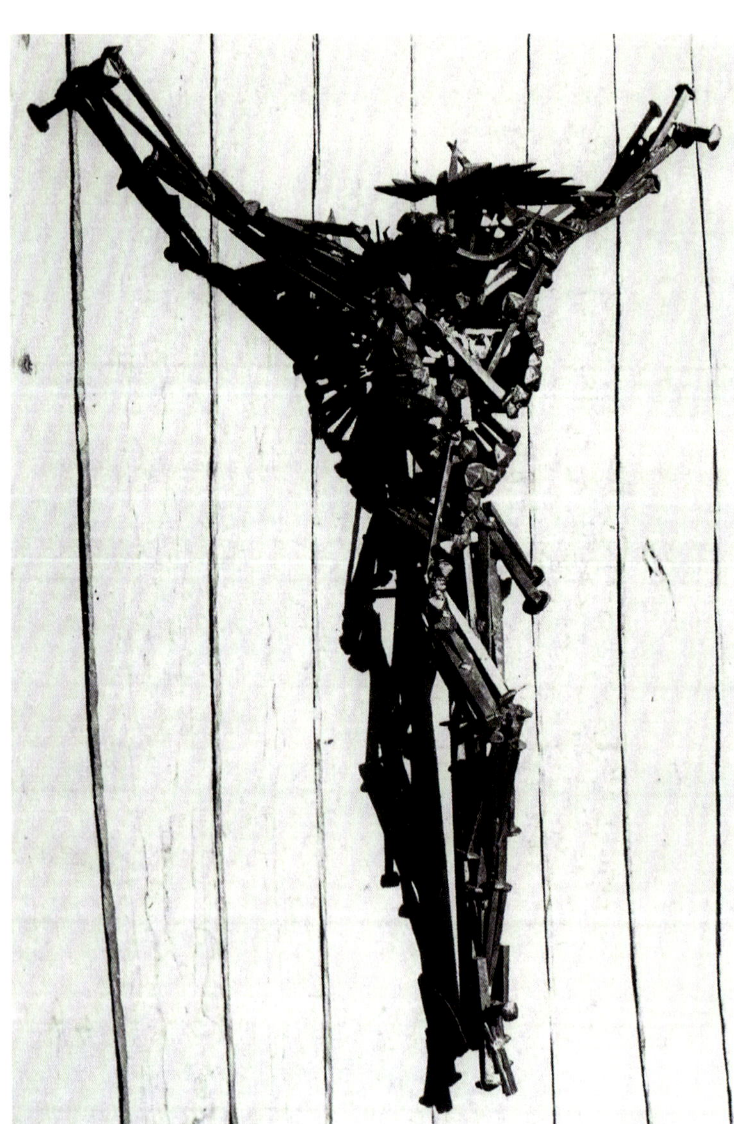

In the same vein, *Crocifissione* (Crucifixion) by Renato Guttuso received a similarly harsh reaction in Rome. The clergy labeled him a "*pictor diabolicus*," a devilish painter, for the shocking quality of this work. The Fascists denounced *Crocifissione* for "depicting the horrors of war under a religious cover." Guttuso wrote in his diary, "it is the symbol of all those who endure insults, jail and torture for their ideas." Guttuso also said, "This is a time of war. I wish to paint the torment of Christ as a contemporary scene . . . as a symbol of all those who, because of their ideas, endure outrage, imprisonment and torment."[36]

In what would become one of the most profoundly personal statements of his career, Livio began to interpret local historic events. Philosopher Pietro Toesca said, "For me, Valentini is Orvieto." In that context Livio Valentini has been described as "an artist who talked about war in order to teach peace."[37]

In 1963 Livio painted *L'eccidio di Camorena* (The Massacre of Camorena), commemorating the anniversary of a tragic day in the city's history. On March 29, 1944, the Fascists arrested seven Orvietani, citizens suspected of having supported the Resistance. These men were tortured and executed at Camorena. When Livio returned from incarceration in Germany, he learned of this tragedy and realized some of those murdered were friends of his, killed in what he termed "a political moment . . . the massacre of seven people because they did not have the same beliefs as someone else." Livio said:

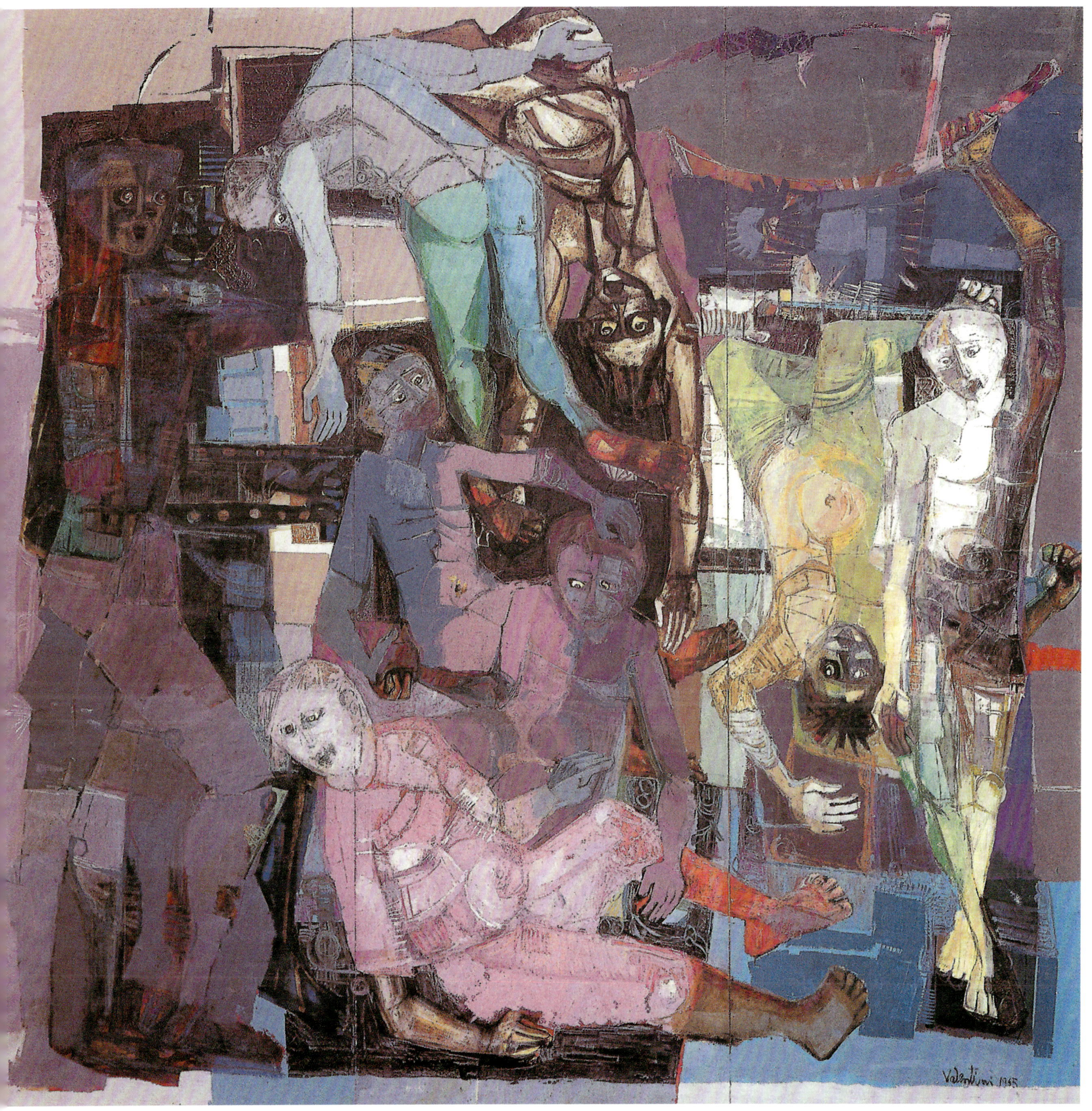
Valentini

> Because they had refused to serve, they didn't want to fight and they didn't want war. Many of them were friends of mine, young people, eighteen to twenty years old. There was also an older person, who had a lot of money. He was helping these people who didn't want war. He was a good person and this moved me. So I took this big canvas and began to paint. It was the only thing I could do to come to terms with this tragedy. They put them on a truck and took them out into the countryside and one by one shot them. It was the Fascists who killed them. The Italians no longer wanted to fight with the Germans. There was something evil about it; they wanted to do something. We'll show you that you can't renounce war. Half of it was a sort of justice; the other half was egoism and violence. There was no reason to kill these seven people.
>
> The only thing I could do was to make a painting. . . . It was a great trauma for Orvieto because there were seven families who saw their sons shot and die. I painted this because I knew what it was like to kill people with a rifle. I knew what it was like to create a firing squad.[38]

In the composition, two soldiers appear on the left, machine-like beings with legs in a lockstep contrapposto, brandishing stylized machine guns. Livio spoke of purposely choosing not to portray the men as German: "these soldiers are really generic, they do not have a uniform identifying them with a particular country or point of origin; they are neutral, they are generic soldiers." His quest was to create "a universal and timeless message."[39] Livio's sources of inspiration for this representation run from Signorelli's frescoes in the Chapel of San Brizio to the paintings done by Pablo Picasso at the time of the Spanish Civil War. He also acknowledged the influence of Francisco Goya and Renato Guttuso.[40]

We encounter seven victims, viewed from every conceivable angle of exposure. For the most part they are stripped of clothing or any other trace of respectability. At first they seem tossed about carelessly, the refuse of man's wrath, in the same way that Signorelli posed the dead in his *End of the World* fresco. But then one notices Livio's unique perspective; these men are interconnected. Reportedly the firing squad took them down one by one, so a hand overlaps the foot next to him; another gracefully connects with the brow of his fellow victim. These men seem to reach out to one another's touch, a final embrace for brothers in martyrdom. Notice the fellow on the far right who extends his long arm up clutching a lonely tree branch. These comrades even in death seem unwilling to give up this place, the city for which they have sacrificed themselves, refusing to fight against what they believed in.

Livio's treatment is definitely connected with Signorelli in his exuberant use of color. In the *Inferno,* Signorelli portrayed demons with bodies adorned in technicolor splendor. These men from Camorena feature a similar multicolored array of skin tones: one has a lower torso of pale blue and the sole of his foot in vibrant red. But Livio's characters are not supernatural. These men are instead hyper-real: they lie there, lips parted, perhaps gasping for a final breath, each with eyes open, vigilantly watching. Do they ask us, "Will you remember?"

According to Livio's friends, Montanucci and Giulietti, there was a significant disagreement in Orvieto over where the painting was to be displayed. Livio said:

> Naturally I got angry because I had given it to them as a present. Part of the issue of where to hang the painting was because public opinion said I was a Communist. Because if you think the way this picture portrays the incident, then you're a Communist. I'm not a Communist but I'm used to being aware of social issues and denouncing those things that are wrong even when they happen in Orvieto. Seven people were killed, without actually providing them justice. It meant they just wanted to kill them. If you say I'm a Communist, okay, I'll be happy to be a Communist.

His painting, controversy aside, became the most widely-known documentation of this massacre. Livio concluded, "There was a meeting with the mayor to talk about the issues. The painting is hanging in the Palazzo dei Sette. They call this the Room of Memory. I thank the mayor for putting it in a safer place, where people wouldn't be arguing about it. I'm happy that it's there and I hope it stays there."[41]

An even more intimate memory is summoned up in Livio's *Stamlager No. 12,* painted in 1964. The correct German spelling is *Stammlager*, but it is sometimes shortened to either *Stalag* or *Lager*, a prisoner of war camp. Here Livio recalled his two friends, Angelo (left) and Umberto (right), being counted every morning. He quoted the guards saying "*Eins, zwei, drei*" and explained that five prisoners were taken away every day for death. Livio awoke one morning to the news that Angelo was dead. "I'm the one in the middle. I made, many many friends there, who are not here any longer. They were not able to overcome that moment." Livio highlighted their anguished faces and emaciated bodies, painted in heavy impasto in sickly greys and brown, the color of flesh as it withers.[42]

Livio concentrated especially on physical torment. One recognizes the exposed rib cage and swollen belly that comes from surviving on only a bit of bread and perhaps

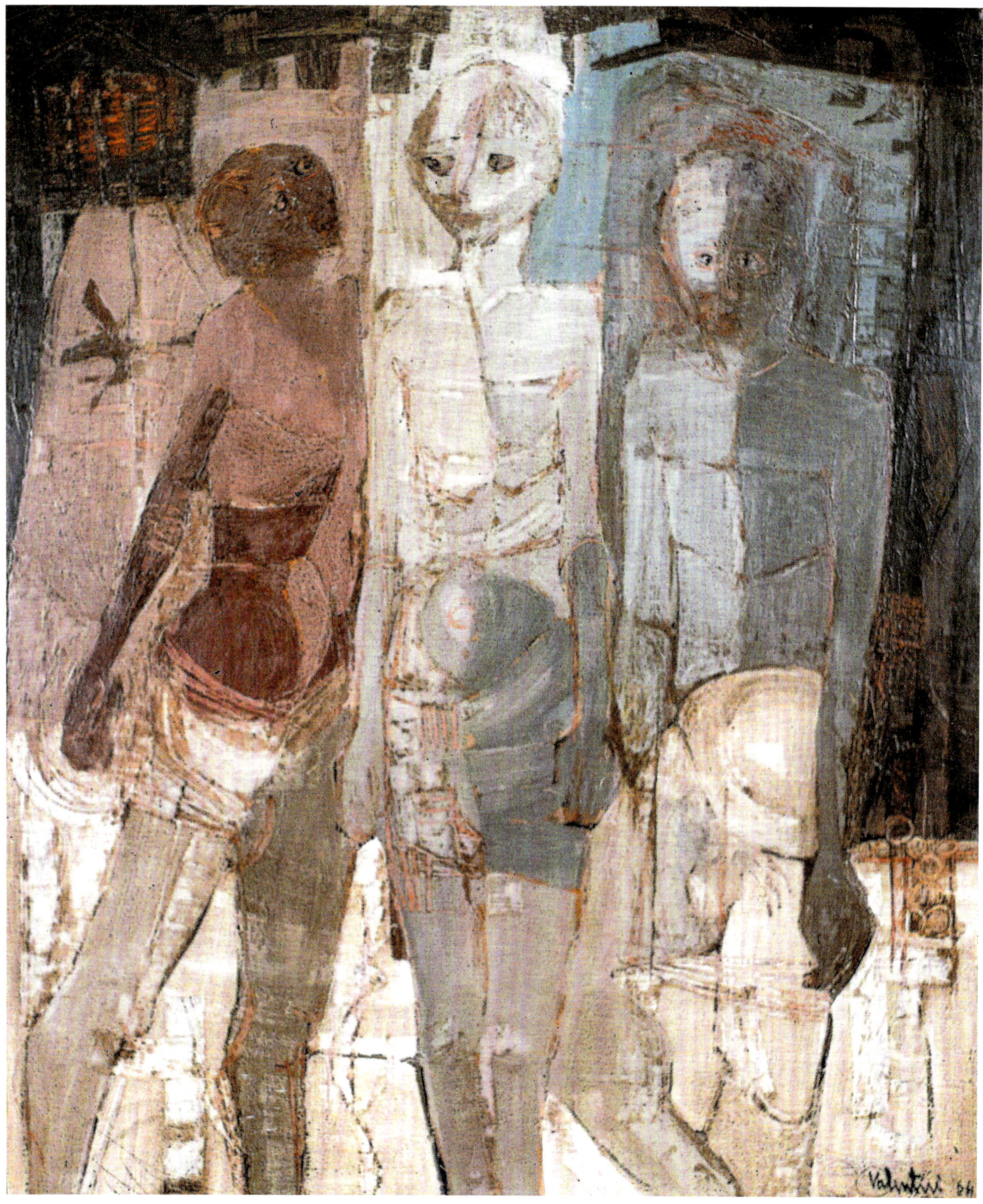
Valentini 64

some soup. In *Ricordi,* the memoir Livio composed for his mother, one of his illustrations shows an exterior view of *Stamlager No.12,* which he labeled "*un vastissimo campo.*" An armed guard stands post before the imposing barbed wire fence while a watchtower looms above. Through the gate, one views a long row of barracks. Also in 1964 Livio took us inside *Baracca No.15*. Using the same impasto shades, he painted two prisoners huddled together, both with shaved heads and haunted eyes. Records indicate Livio's Stamlager 12 may have been the one in Limburg, Germany, used as a transit camp where new prisoners of war were processed, usually detained for a few weeks before being sent to other stalags. Contemporary photographs show the buildings set up with minimal furniture so prisoners slept on cobblestone floors before being transferred elsewhere, like the dreaded Buchenwald. In his memoir, Livio referred to his transferal and remembered they "travelled all around Germany, lastly the area between Munich and Innsbruck."[43]

➛ *Stamlager No. 12,* 1964. Oil, pigment, and pumice on wood, 120 × 100 cm. Collection of the Valentini family.

We believe that these war paintings serve a double purpose: to record the actual events and to serve as a personal catharsis for the artist. He said, "In the concentration camps, there was no way to make photographs. For me to document that experience was something extraordinary. In the morning when I get up, I walk by that painting (*Stamlager No. 12*) while I'm still sleepy and I say to myself, '*Livio, la vita e' bella* (life is wonderful).'"[44]

In 1967, Livio transferred his studio to Rome on Via Monte della Farina near Campo dei Fiore. He was encouraged in this undertaking by Monsignor Giovanni Fallani, president of the Pontifical Commission of Sacred Art. This was probably because earlier Livio had produced some important acrylic paintings showing the young Christ in his father Joseph's workshop.

Livio remained in the capital city for the most part of a year. In 1965 he had sculpted *La strage degli innocenti* (Slaughter of the Innocents), which is part of the Assisi collection. This terra cotta piece represents the massacre of the infants ordered by King Herod with a wild-haired soldier snatching a tiny swaddled *putto* from his mother's arms. Livio's bold design for this glazed polychrome ceramic is utterly unique. He mounted the sculpture on a roughly hewn wooden trough used to collect blood when a pig was slaughtered. Therefore the child sacrifice obviously refers to Livio's experience in Buchenwald. In later years, Livio revisited this subject matter based on the bas-reliefs on the facade of the Duomo. Lo Presti pointed out that in all these works, whether the church processions, the stone layers or *The Massacre of Camorena,* there was a "respect for the sacredness, even in a secular perspective."[45]

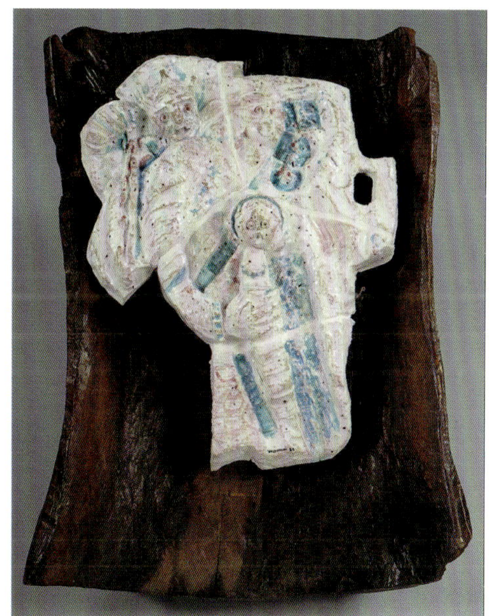

La strage degli innocenti (Slaughter of the Innocents), 1965. Glazed ceramic and wood, 90 × 70 × 35. Courtesy of the Galleria d'Arte Contemporanea della Pro Civitate Christiana, Assisi. Photos by Roberto Vaccai and Mauro Scarpelloni.

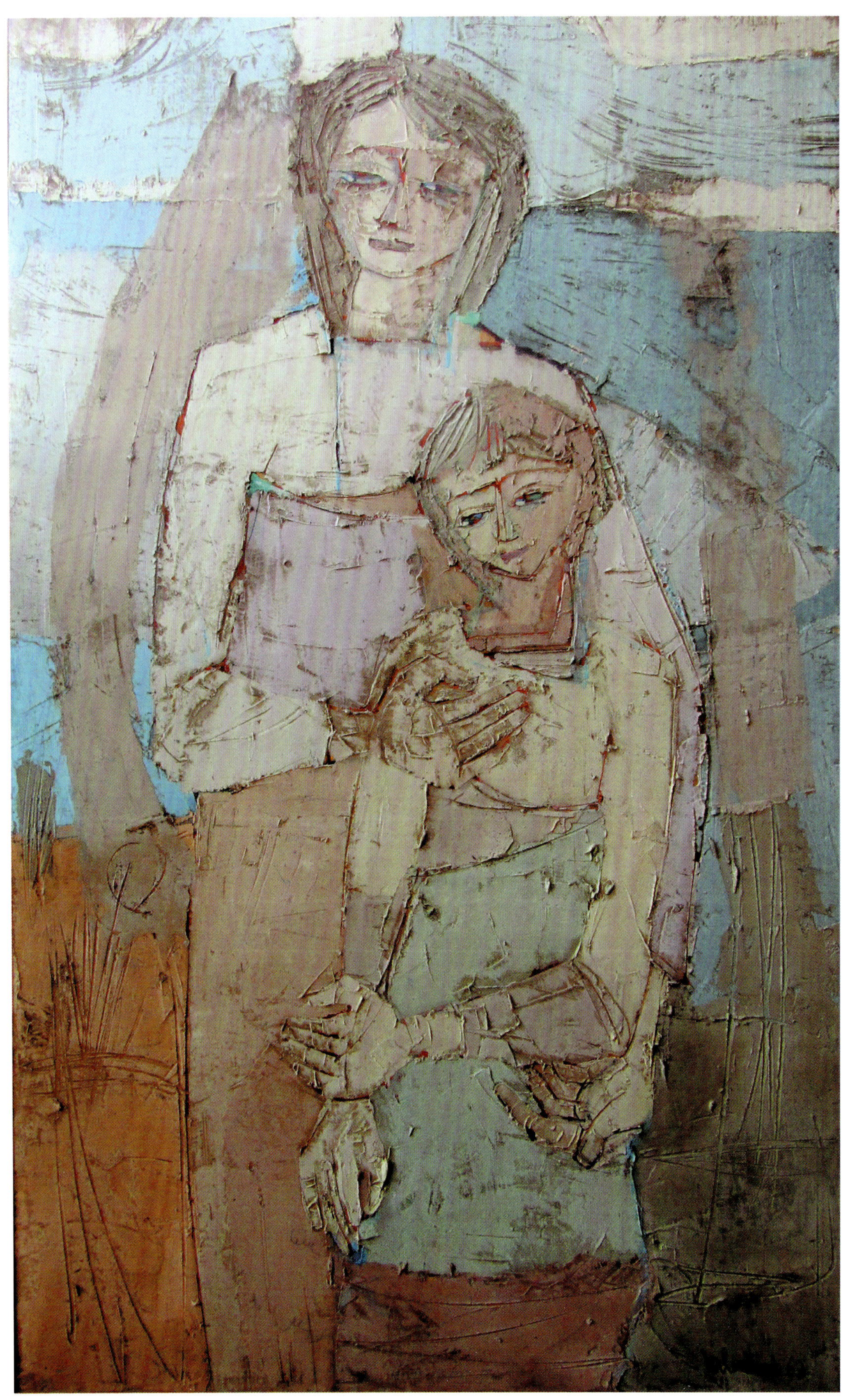

Mother and Child, 1963.
Oil, pigment, and pumice on wood.
Approximately 91 × 76 cm.
Collection of the Valentini family.
Photograph by Silvia Valentini.

Livio found life in Rome too hostile, complaining that his car was often vandalized and, of course, time spent away from Flora and their daughters was painful. He remembered trying to come home for some weekends. In 1963 he painted *Mother and Child,* an impasto work representing Flora and their daughter Silvia. Livio said, "My daughter and my wife are very happy to own this picture; it marks family memories."[46] Regarding that time, Livio said, "I was much younger and I had returned from an odyssey perhaps as complicated as the one I am currently on, in fact, more so, because it was after the Second World War. That's why I was compelled to express something more familiar; something I had missed during the war. These subjects concern themselves with family, a return to normal life after the war."[47]

After a productive but difficult time in Rome, Livio returned to Orvieto with a new studio on Via Lorenzo Maitani, two steps from the gallery of the Montanucci brothers and closer to the Duomo. "After an intense period spent in Rome in contact with the great masters of the twentieth century, De Chirico, Guttuso, and others, I came back to Orvieto because it is a formative city, because its monuments, its works of art are just a step away from the townspeople, because when you take that step the monument becomes personalized to each person. To the young I say, Orvieto forms you because in this city there is universal art, not in the small things but in the characterization of art."[48]

As Livio settled back into Orvieto with his family, his artistic focus was one of new beginnings. In this context Livio revisited the theme of carding the hemp, which he first explored as a very young man. The cover of the bulletin of the Rotary Club of Orvieto honoring the years 1950–1972 reproduces Livio's etching *San Giovenale.*[49] Livio shows a mature man cranking the traditional wooden rope-making wheel, an obvious, and literal, metaphor representing the logo of Rotary. The historic tower of the Romanesque church looms above his shoulder while young women and two children observe. This symbolizes the young people who are helped by Rotary's civic generosity.

The theme of rope making continued to fascinate the Maestro. In 1985 for the book *Orvieto: progetto per una città utopica,* Livio created a new illustration showing the now-famous industry. Here we recognize the young man, barefooted and in shorts, raising his hands overhead, each wrapped in the freshly twisted hemp rope. In this case Livio set the scene at the foot of the cliff with the San Giovenale church high far above. The view from this precipice over the valley beyond is known as one of the most striking for tourists. Perhaps this composition is a reference to the soaking and softening of hemp stems in the Paglia River. It is a brilliant composition encircled by Livio's tondo pattern, marking a bright, wheeling halo of light from the sun rising beyond the tower.

For another *Utopica* illustration, Livio chose to honor the celebrated vineyards of Orvieto. In the foreground a young man shoos away a flock of birds while his companions begin the harvest. Over their shoulders hang vines heavy with enormous clusters of grapes. In traditional Umbrian cultivation, grape vines were trained to grow up the supportive branches of maple trees. Of course our memory turns back to those boyhood days in Livio's artistic education. We recall Professor Benini encouraging young Livio because he drew grapes that were realistically thick and plump. All those years later, Livio remembered and gratefully so do we.

The Pictorial Cycle, "Germination": 1968–1970

In his new studio Livio created the theme of what he called "environmental considerations," natural germination.[50] During this brief period Livio delved into naturalistic works: paintings, terra cotta sculptures, and graphic series. Each piece features some sign of life and the theme of generating and regenerating. Livio explored the images of rebirth in nature, what Massimo Duranti called "the eternal mystery of continuity." In his essay, "Joie de Vivre Regained," Giorgio Di Genova wrote, "to be born in Umbria means to enjoy a special relationship with the land; this is possible because the Umbria region is one of the few on the Italian peninsula not to touch the sea."[51]

In *Germinazione,* painted in 1968, Livio used mixed-media to show an organic, embryonic form, the live seed splitting, sprouting, and rising upward. The brown earth nestles the precious seed of new life. Coming from an artist whose life experiences had included such hardships, it is not difficult to interpret this as self-revealing. His country had been war-torn, his city had weathered countless regimes, and systems of belief had come and gone. And yet the earth nurtured life, regardless of these setbacks. And so, in much the same way, Valentini had triumphed over adversity.

Take note of the shadowed, dimensional ring of color because it became a repeated shape. Livio acknowledged that he did not recognize this shape right away. In the Cycle of the Birds, this pattern haunted Livio's imagery through his remaining career, including his time in Aiken.

In the ceramic sculpture, *Formella,* completed in 1970, Livio used two such curves bound together, perhaps even chained together. Of this style of terracotta, Livio said there was "a need to research, to explore ceramics. It had been necessary to rediscover ceramics after the Renaissance, after the medieval period and after the Etruscans. At a certain point many people needed to try a new message, which could be formulated with ceramics. I was part of the group of artists who proposed this new type of ceramics."[52]

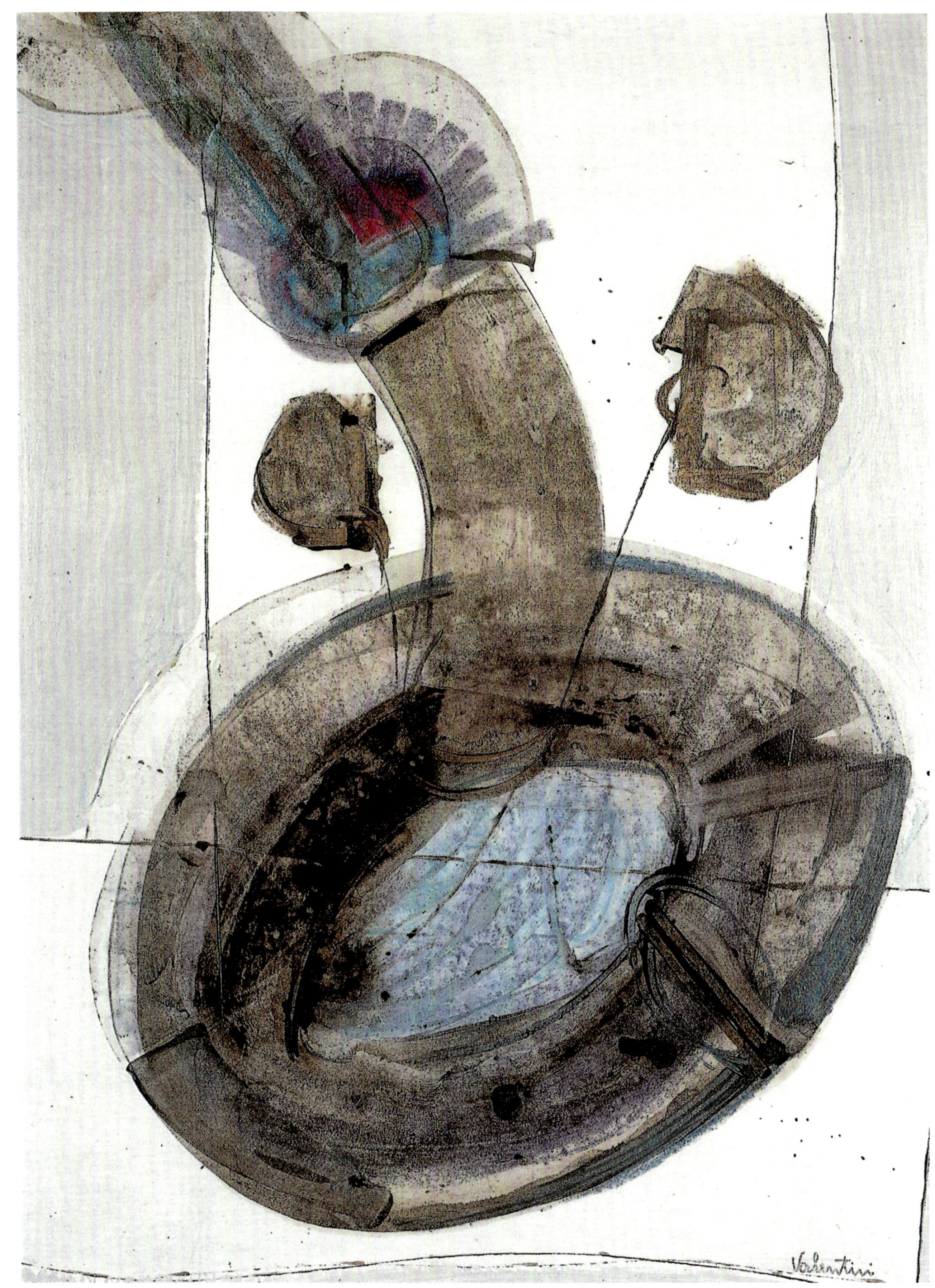

Germinazione, 1968.
Mixed media, 100 × 70 cm.

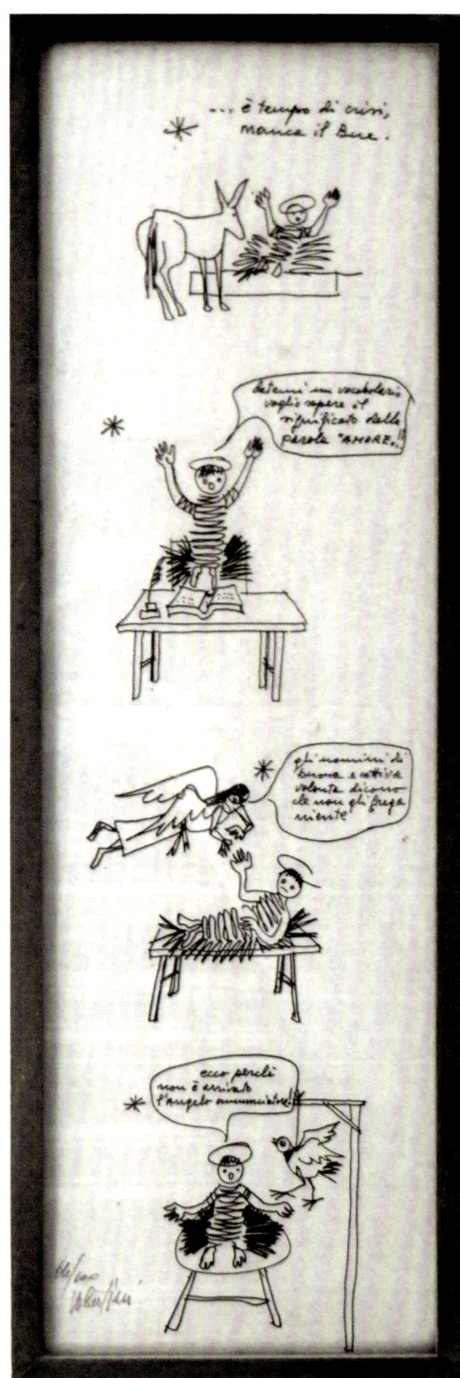

Story with the Christ Child. Print on paper, 57.5 × 20 cm. Collection of Luca Crescini. Photograph by Thomas Gerish.

In a 1982 BBC documentary about Livio's art, it was pointed out that he, perhaps unconsciously, repeatedly created the rounded shape. Livio reflected, "This was very personal to me. This curved element had been present in my mind almost constantly because it looks like the posts around the extermination camp. They held the electric wires used to keep people from escaping from the death camp."[53]

In the last work from this period, we turn to a set of novelty drawings, more in the tradition of Livio's postcard interpretation of the Duomo suffering from too much wine. In four scenes, created circa 1970, Livio shows the Christ child speaking in vignettes from what seems to be a Christmas crèche come to life. This framed design is in the collection of Luca Crescini, son of Antonio Crescini, the *marmista* (the marble man) from whose business in Baschi Valentini purchased marble for his sculpture.

In the first scene the Christ child in the manger, speaking to the donkey, exclaims, "There's a crisis, the Ox is missing." Scene two shows the *Bambino*, whose swaddling clothes and halo look more like a t-shirt and beret, saying, "Give me a dictionary, I want to know the meaning of the word love." Notice he is seated at a child's writing desk with quill and paper.

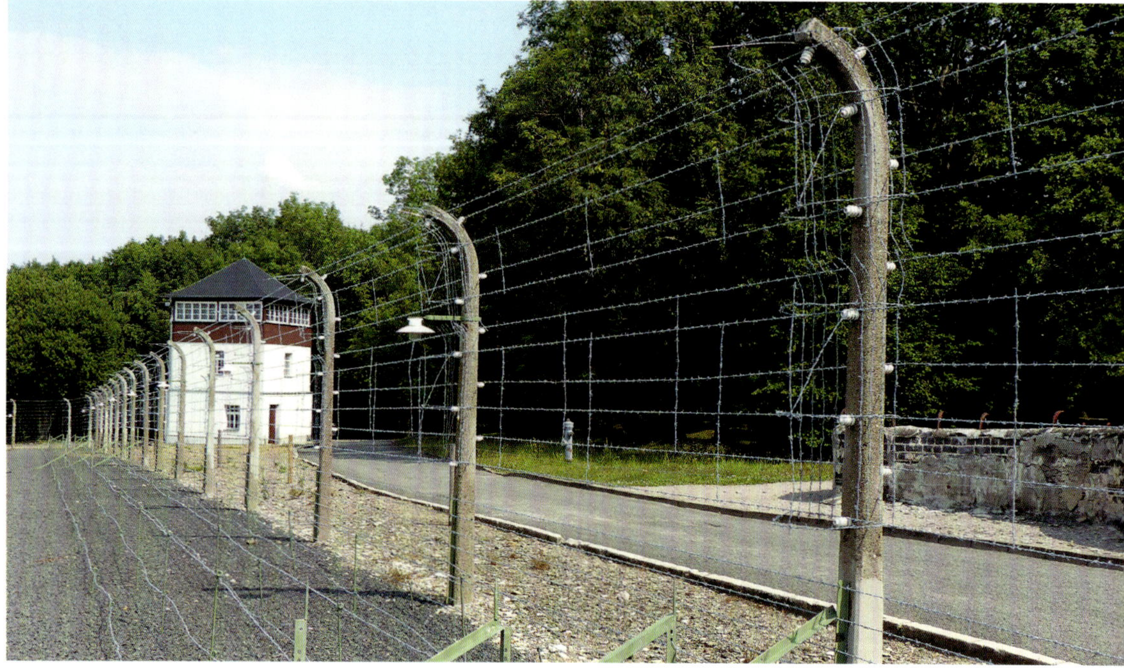

Fences with electrical wires at Buchenwald. Photograph courtesy of Dr. Bernd Gross, Wikimedia Commons CC-BY-SA 3.0.

Those of us who remember Livio's whimsical sense of humor can imagine the smile on his face as this series unfolded. In scene three the Child, back in his manger, looks toward an angel, who proclaims "men of good and bad will say they don't give a damn."

Scene four has Christ speaking from beneath what resembles a stage prop. As the infant says, "That's why the angel of the annunciation hasn't arrived," over the cradle dangles a bird on a wire. This poor bird's plight seems a very natural way to segue to his next art period, the one for which Livio became famous.

The Cycle of the Birds: 1970–1980

We turn now to the subject matter for which Livio became best known and most honored. While Livio was on the faculty of the Istituto d'Arte, he created a cycle of prints and paintings with the wounded bird as the central theme. In each case the birds are caged or tortured. As we have noted, in the image of the cage, he was repeating the form of the curved fence posts of Buchenwald that he had unconsciously appropriated. Clearly these imprisoned birds mirror the hardships Valentini endured in World War II. But why did he choose the birds?

For explanation consider his 1954 *Venditori di uccelli* (Bird Sellers), where merchants display their birds in ornamental cages. As we have theorized, viewing this otherwise innocent moment in the public square may have been the spark for his obsession with the trapped birds as, "a metaphor, alluding first to violence and to being in prison."[54] It is helpful to consider the environment in which Livio was creating these images. As always one must focus on Livio's heritage as a child of Umbria, and especially as a descendant of the Etruscans.

Paintings on the wall of the *Tomb of the Triclinium* in Tarquinia show an outdoor occasion where birds flit among the revelers. Livio said, "In the tombs we have the representation of a bird; there's delicate poetry in it. There's a big message of an advanced civilization. The Etruscans were a civilized people." Furthermore in the frescoes of the *Golini Tomb*, since moved to the National Archaeological Museum in Orvieto, game birds are strung up in preparation for a funeral banquet.[55]

The other concept of Etruscan origin is the practice of augury, the belief that the flights and songs of birds could reveal the future. Today even the language of Italy recalls this important custom; one often hears the phrase *auguri* meaning good wishes.

In order to understand how significant a role birds played in the Umbrian diet, a visit to the underground caverns of Orvieto reveals great numbers of *columbaria,* pigeon

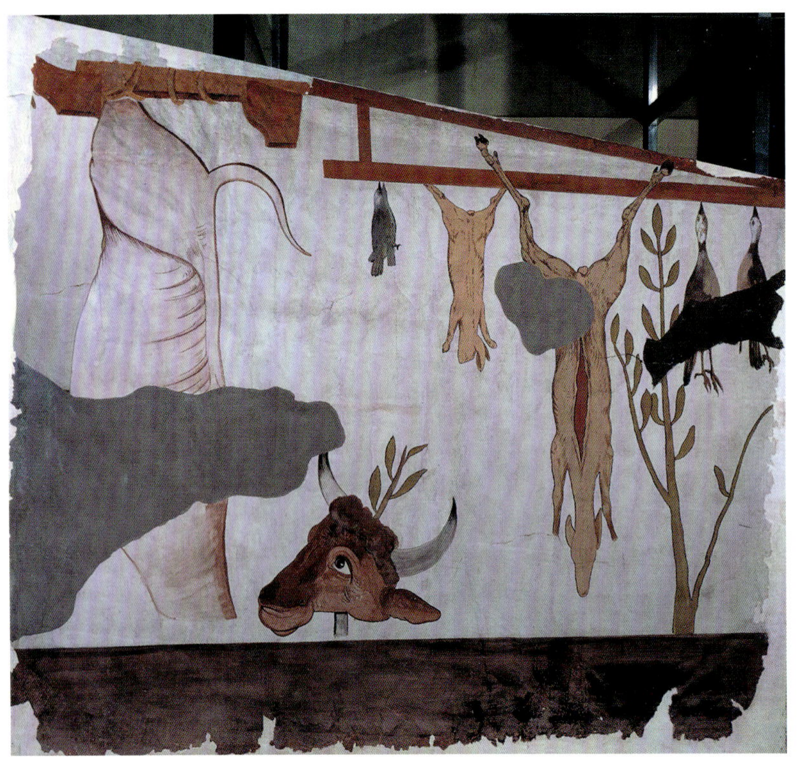

Tomba Golini. Drawing by A. Cozza. National Archaeological Museum, Orvieto. Photograph courtesy of Soprintendenza Archeologia dell'Umbria.

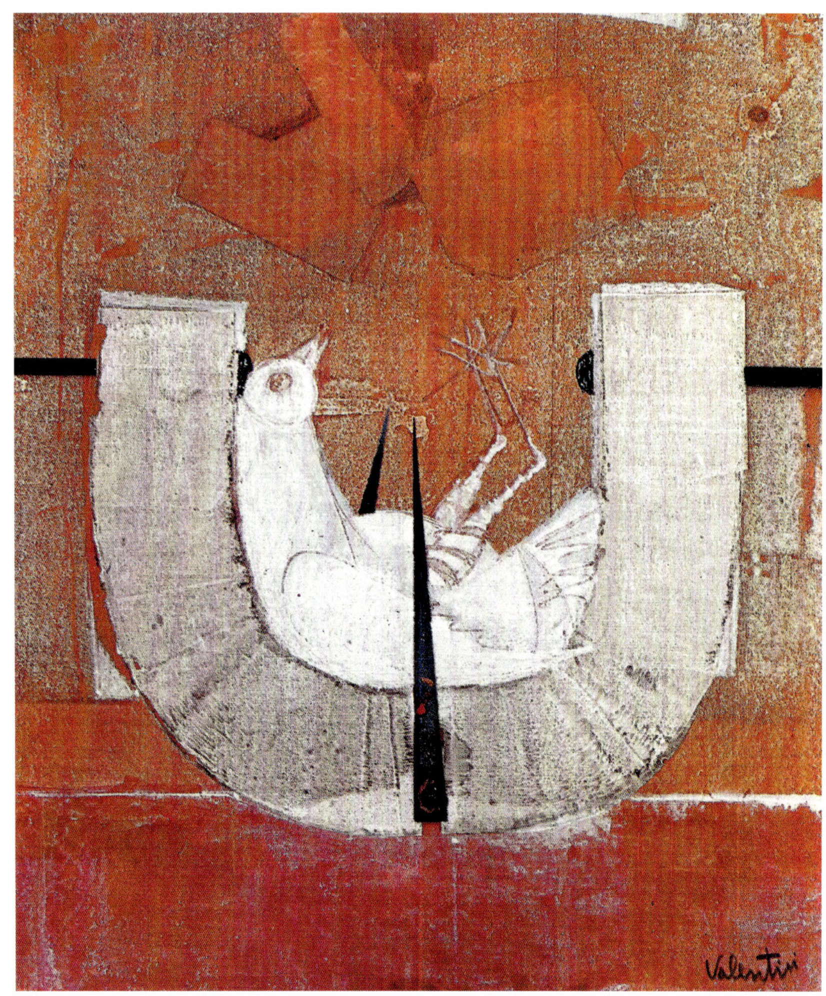

Costrizione (Compulsion), 1972. Oil, 50 × 60 cm. Collection of the Valentini family.

cotes carved out of the tufa stone. Clearly the use of game birds endured from antiquity to recent times in Italy. According to Livio's friends, Valeriano Venturi and translator Erika Bizzarri, most of Italy remained *contadina* (peasant) while Livio was growing up. These birds were terribly important to the locals as their major source of protein.

But for Livio the artist the birds became his metaphor. The prints and paintings are so vivid in their combination of vulnerability and violence. In some cases they are merely captive, trapped in their portability; whether it is two birds in the familiar curve of a basket, or with multiple cages, stacked one upon another. Then came the birds specifically behind bars or expired, cradled in the undeniable "U" shape of the Buchenwald curve.

Livio commented, "These are the birds I did for eight years, always the same motif. I used them because it was necessary for me to express the negative in life, which bothered me, because I always thought about these things. So I had to express these thoughts in painting. At night I would wake up suddenly, worried about the same problem, of being a prisoner. So this was like medicine, this was my invention. I imagined a bird, the most fragile and free element in the world. But instead of imagining it free, I imagined it as a prisoner, imagined it tied up, nailed, constricted . . . I became famous for these birds."[56]

Some of Livio's most brutal representations hauntingly beckon back to previous artworks. *Una morta e una viva* (One Alive, One Dead) reveals a pair of birds, imprisoned before the magnet-shaped arch of the concentration camp fencing. Livio movingly spoke about this:

> It's a motif which is apparent. It reminded me of two friends of mine, men who were prisoners like me, two people I knew. One morning they told me Armando had died. They gave me the news. Raffaele was my other friend. And I said, "What about him?" They said, "He's alive." So this contrast—one dead, one alive impressed me. As if there was a reward, one is dead but one is alive. It's like a stupid consolation but psychologically it was important because they could have both died. . . . It might sound stupid because one person had died but under those circumstances, it was a joy my other friend was alive. So there's a paradox but at that moment it was very important.[57]

Finally reaching a near saturation point with dozens and dozens of such illustrations, there came a single, brilliant reminder of the depth of Livio's metaphor of loss. In his painting *Uccello crocifisso* the poor bird is not merely bound by its legs, but is sacrificed,

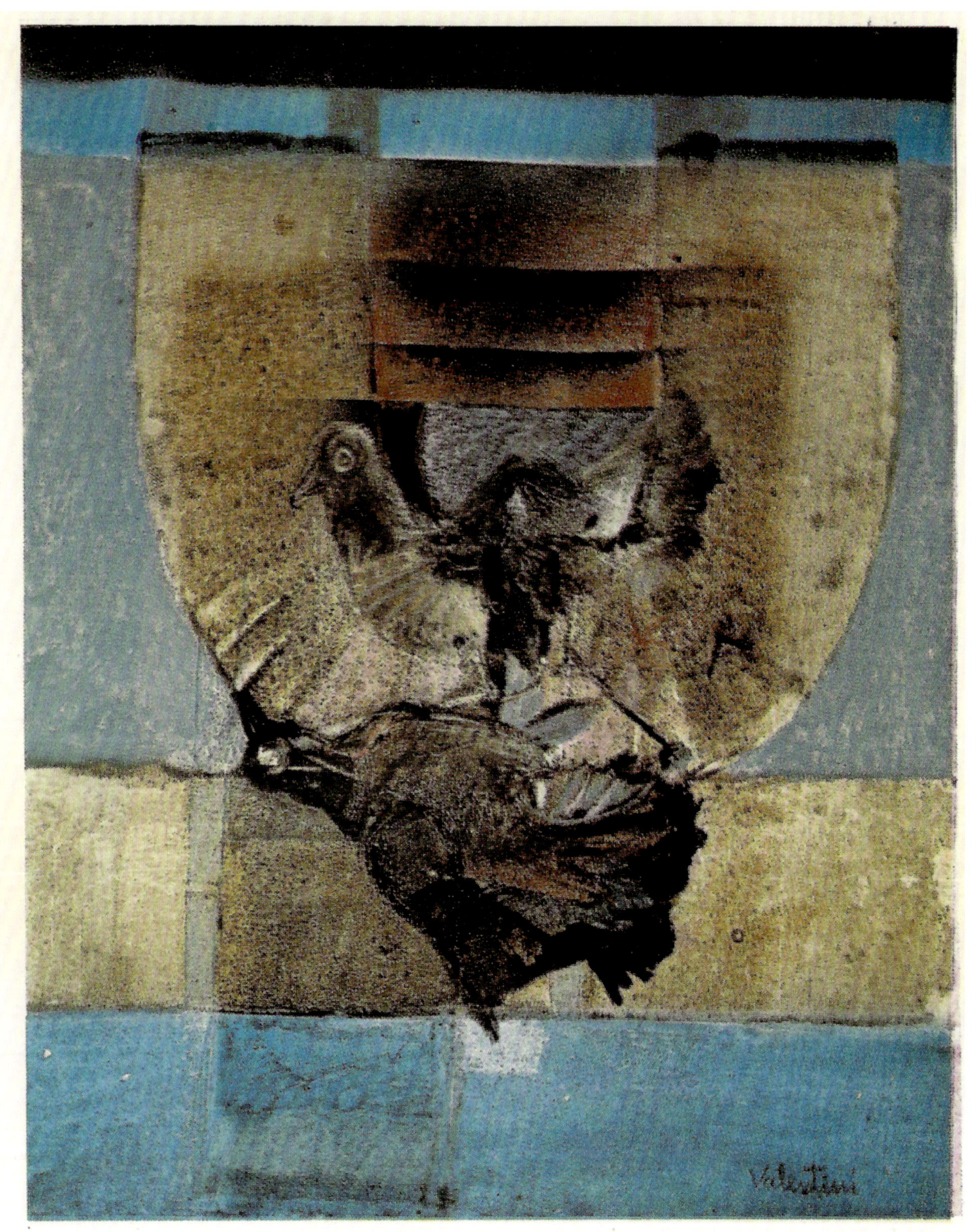

Una morta e una viva (One Dead and One Alive), 1970. Oil on canvas. 40 × 50 cm. Collection of G. Rapaccini, Terni.

quite literally crucified, reminiscent of Livio's exploration of the Christ motif during his Roman School period.

This one image with the bird like a slain savior leads us to an examination of the spirituality in these now iconic studies. Tracing the origin of Livio's Bird Cycle is like trying to deduce why Michelangelo returned again and again to the *Pietà* or Picasso to the bull. Some art historians have compared Livio's birds to those portrayed by the surrealist Max Ernst (1891–1976) or the cubist George Braque (1882–1963). We contend Livio's birds are more specifically about his upbringing, physically and spiritually, in the environment of Orvieto.

As evidence, let's consider some of Livio's renderings regarding the cathedral and events in the Piazza del Duomo. One print shows birds gathered about the *Madonna and Child Enthroned (La Maestà) and Six Angels,* a brilliant bronze and marble group directly above the center portal of the Duomo. As birds will naturally do, they settle at

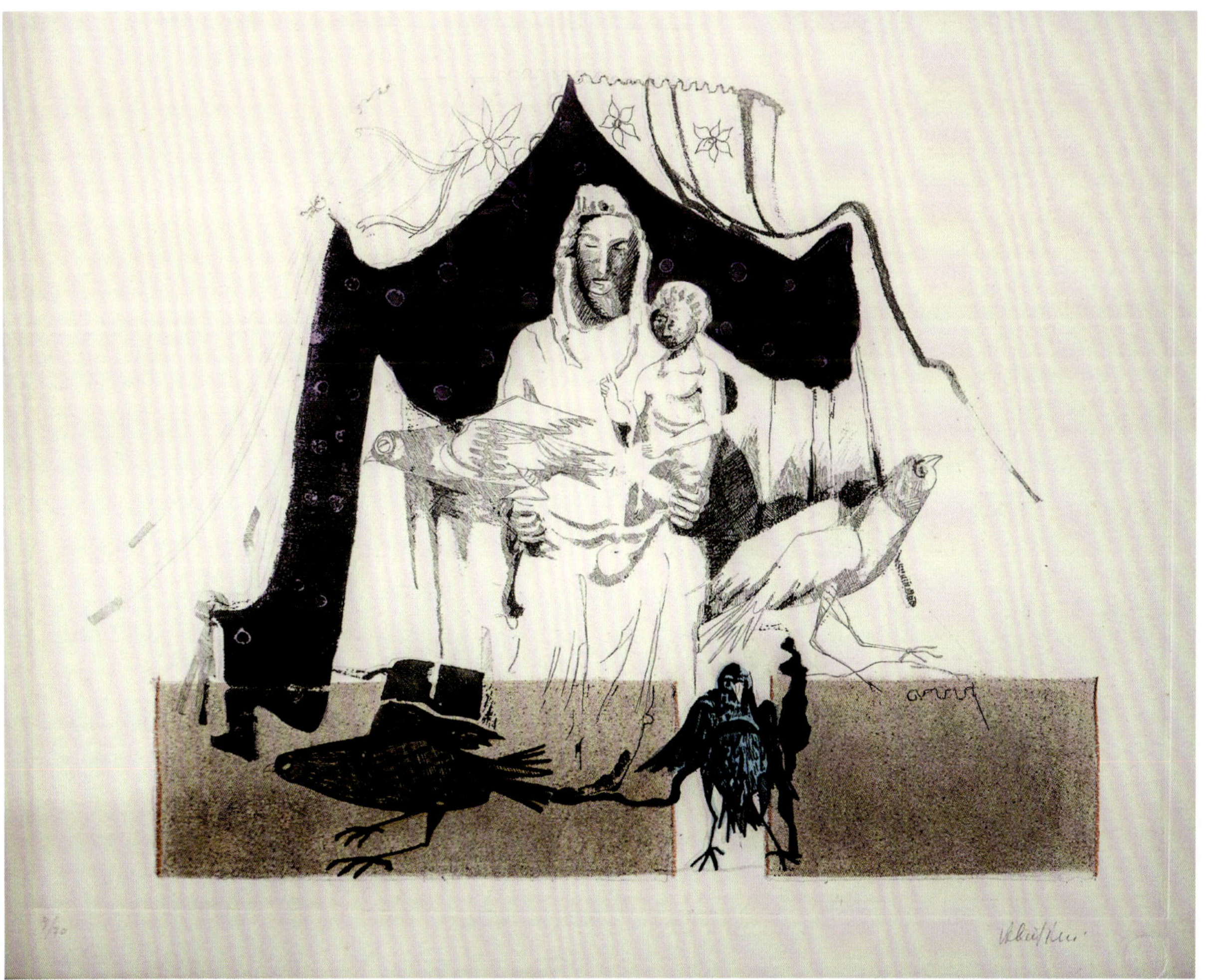

Madonna and Child Enthroned (La Maestà) with Birds, 1997. Hand-colored etching, 69 × 56 cm. Collection of Patsy and Ron Lewellyn. Photograph by Michael St. John.

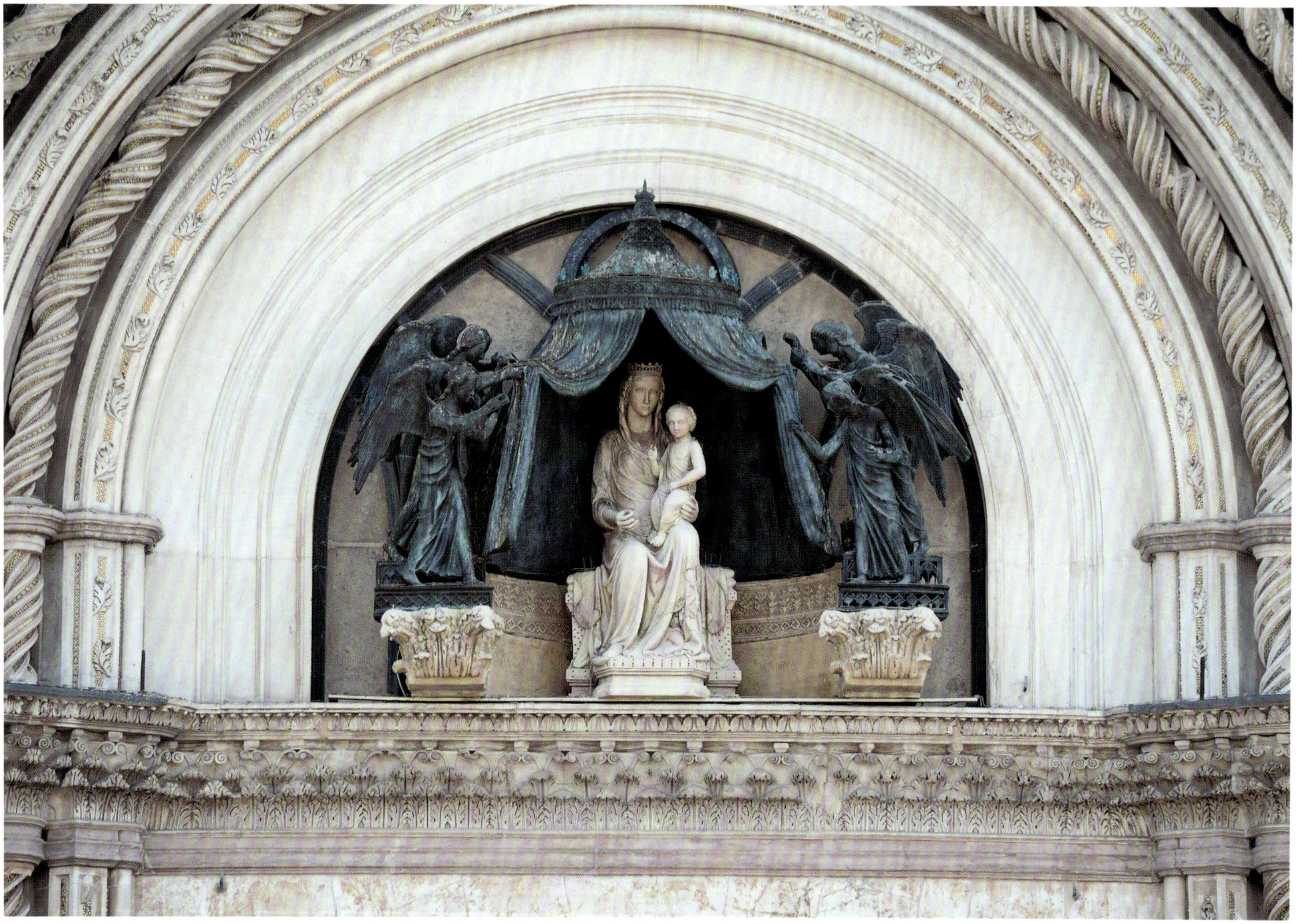

Madonna and Child Enthroned (La Maestà) and Six Angels. Statue over main entrance to the Cathedral, copy of the original now in the collection of Museo dell'Opera del Duomo, Orvieto. Photograph by Michael St. John.

the feet of the outdoor sculpture. One even dares to rest on the arm of the Madonna opposite the Christ child. Similarly in an illustration from the book *Orvieto: progetto per una città utopica,* Livio shows the view of the facade he enjoyed upon leaving his studio on Via Maitani. On both sides large birds cling to the high walls on light posts. A photograph captures how realistically Livio has represented this moment.

The spiritual aspect of Livio's attachment to the subject of the birds can be explained by describing a recurring festival in Orvieto. Every spring, Orvieto celebrates the *Festa della Palombella,* which originated in the fifteenth century and commemorates Pentecost. Stretched over two days, this festival takes place fifty days after Easter and

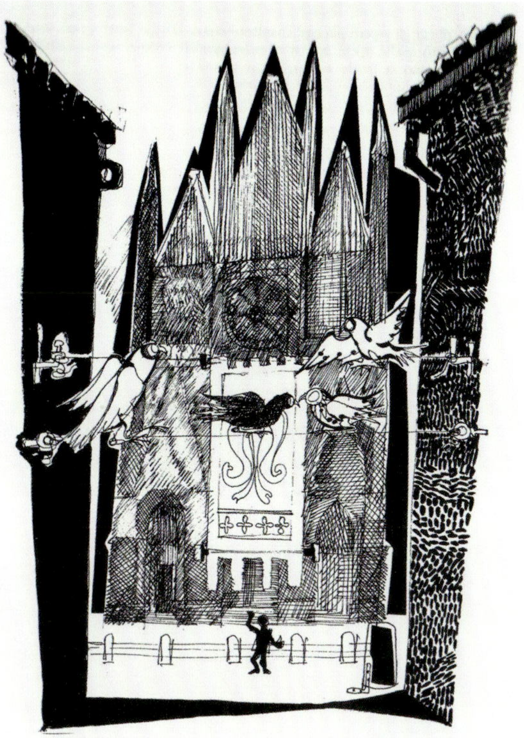

Birds on the Via Maitani from *Utopica.*

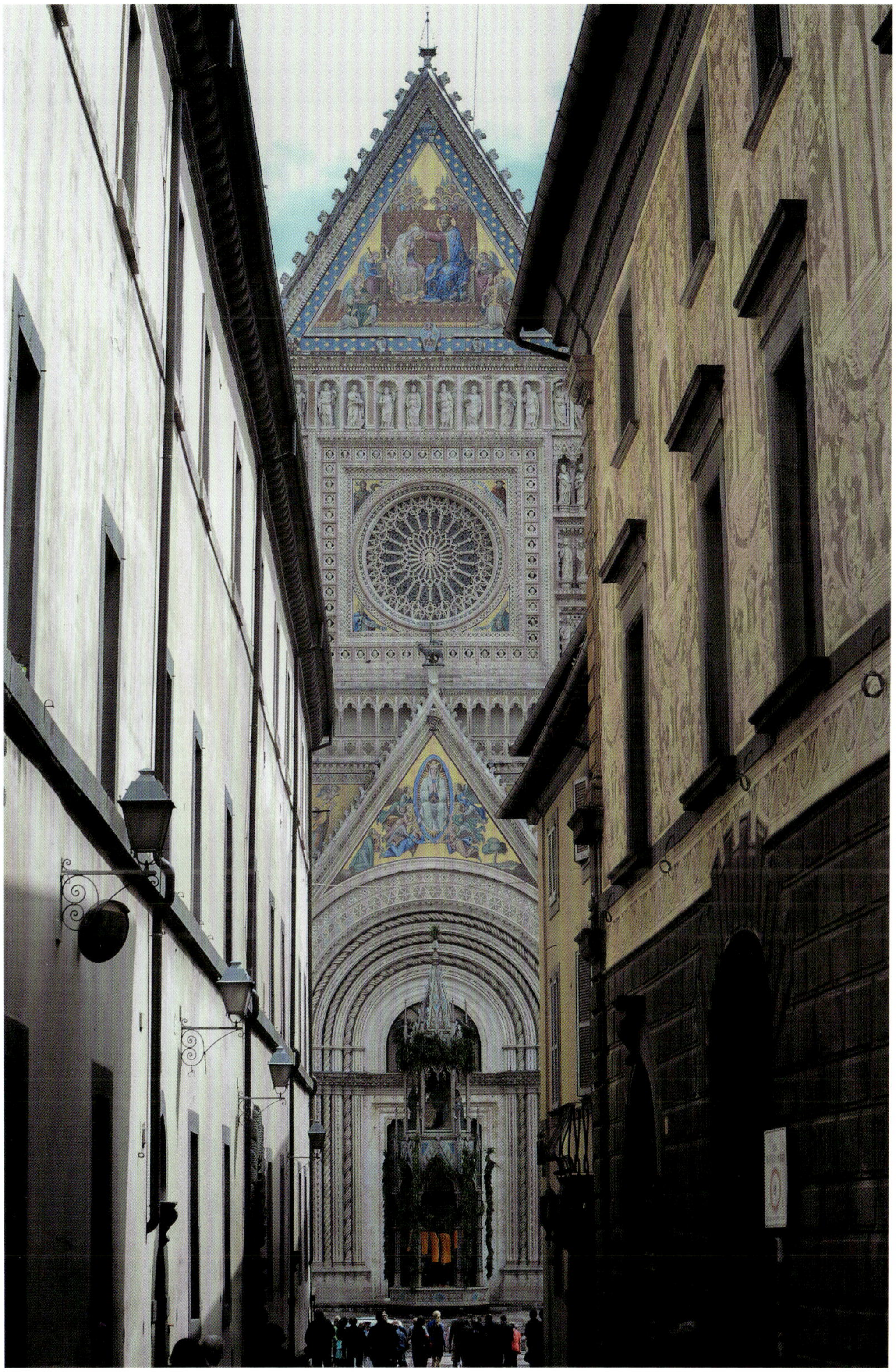

View of the Duomo down Via Maitani. Photograph by Michael St. John.

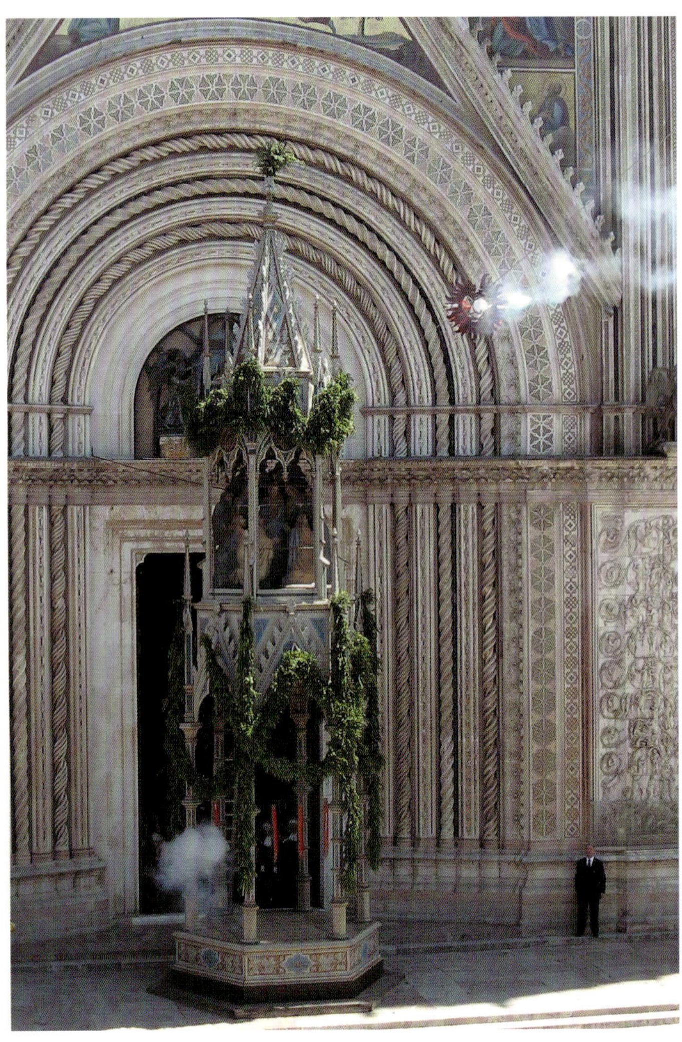

Wooden tabernacle in front of Duomo for Palombella (Pentecost) as caged dove approaches. Photograph by Erika Bizzarri.

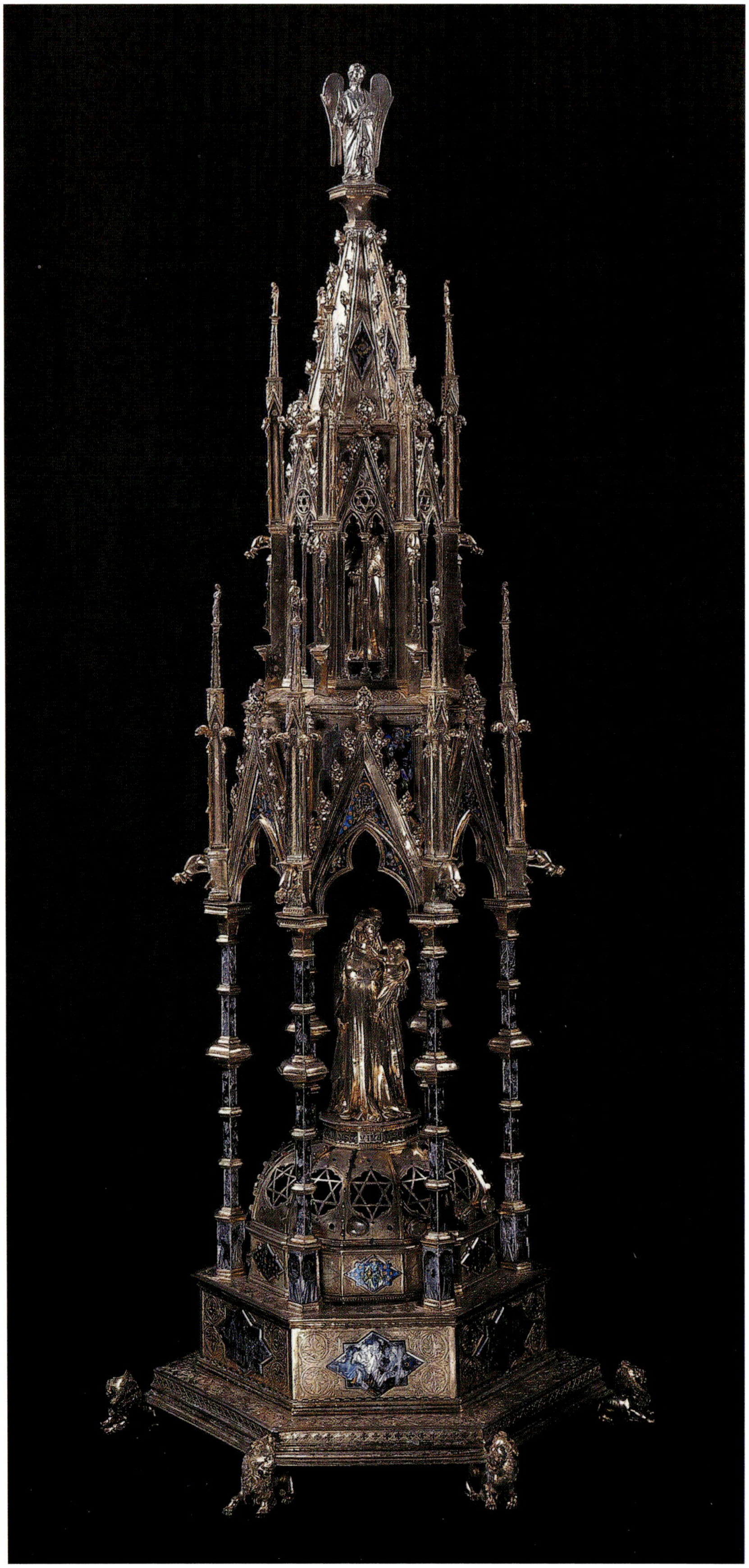

Reliquary of San Savino from the fourteenth century. Collection of Museo dell'Opera del Duomo, Orvieto.

almost matches the grandeur of the Corpus Domini. On the Saturday before Pentecost, the *Palio dell'Oca,* a competition on horseback, is held. A small parade of the Corteo Storico features an extraordinary performance by men exchanging colorful banners accompanied by drum and trumpet. Costumed medieval peasants are particularly important to our story, because one fellow carries a white dove in a blood-red cage.

Sunday morning brings the Palombella proper, a festival introduced in 1404, probably with ancient ties to a pagan fertility celebration. In 1524 the noble Giovanna Monaldeschi della Cervara willed her family estate to Orvieto with her wish for this event to be celebrated annually.

On Saturday, before the palio, a wooden tabernacle is set up before the Duomo with traditional statues of the Madonna and twelve apostles. This Gothic-style structure is based upon the fourteenth-century *Reliquary of San Savino,* designed by the goldsmiths Ugolino di Vieri and Viva di Lando. The wooden shrine, now festooned with fresh garlands, represents the *cenacle,* the upper room where the Last Supper occurred and where Christ established the rite of the Eucharist, which was followed by the Crucifixion and Resurrection. According to Christian tradition, seven weeks later, in this same cenacle, the Madonna and apostles gathered. This is the Pentecost, when the Holy Spirit descended on the apostles in the form of tongues of fire, giving them "tongues" or languages to spread the word.[58]

At noon on this Pentecost Sunday, an extraordinary ceremony is performed using the cenacle and the caged white dove from the day before. Preceded by medieval trumpeters and the valets, white-wigged gentlemen in baroque dress, the bishop of Orvieto begins the sacred event precisely at noon by waving a white linen cloth from a balcony opposite the Duomo. At this signal, a painted shrine representing the Empyrean sky opens up above the Church of San Francesco. Small fireworks go off around a Plexiglas tube which contains the white dove with trammeled wings, all surrounded by a metal frame matching the sunburst around the monstrance. It sails down a 1000-foot wire across the piazza. When this device hits the cenacle, a larger burst of fireworks explodes and tiny flames appear over the heads of the apostles. The startled bird is taken down and born about the square for public devotion. According to custom, upon the dove's safe arrival, the bishop presents it to a recently betrothed couple, auguring them for a happy and fertile marriage. Ancient tradition holds that a successful flight foretells a fruitful harvest for the region as well.

This ceremony is performed directly before the facade Livio shows in his *Utopica* imagery and only a few steps down from his studio. It seems this dove became Valentini's

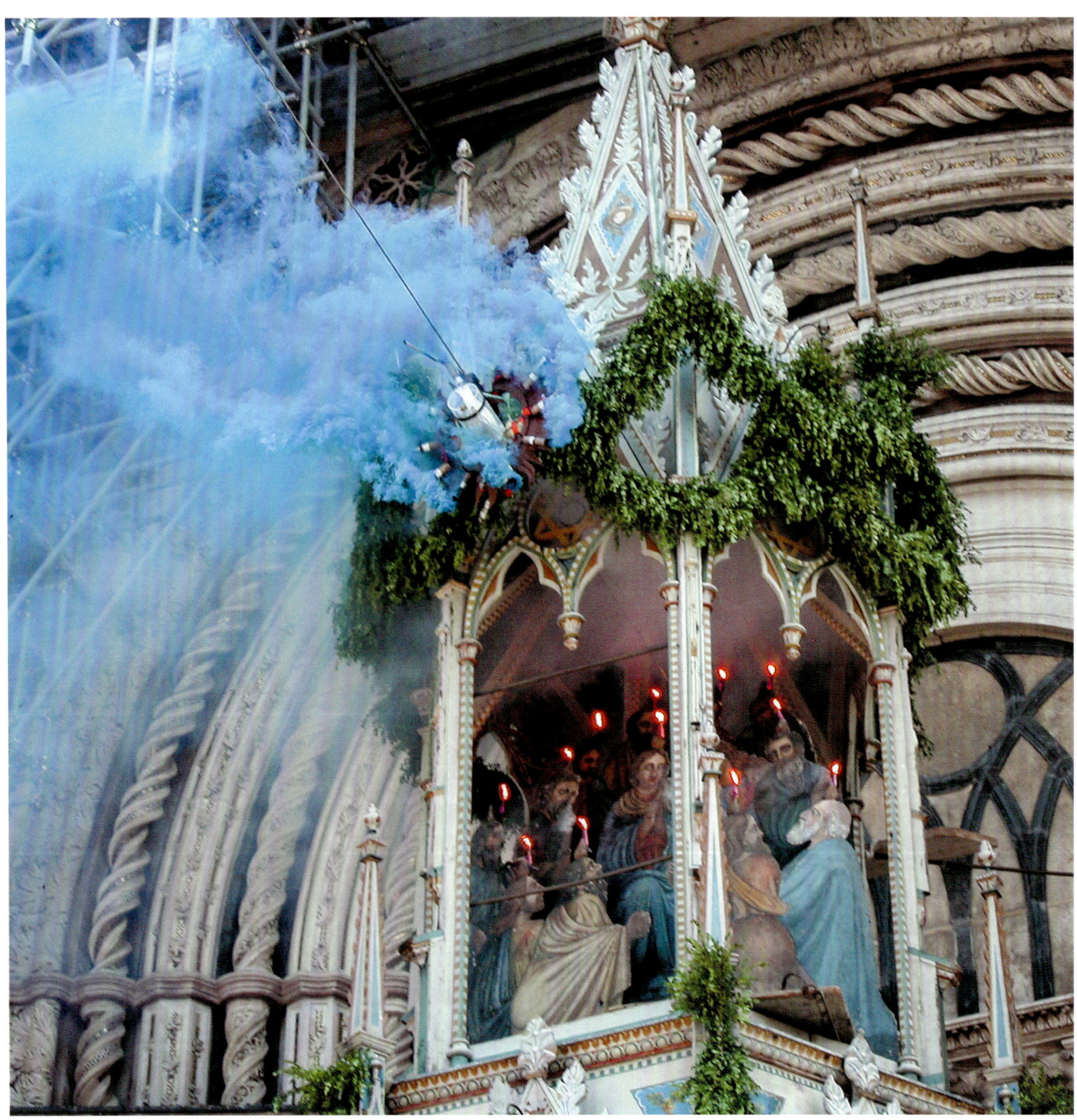

Flames light above the heads of the Apostles. Photograph by Ron Williams.

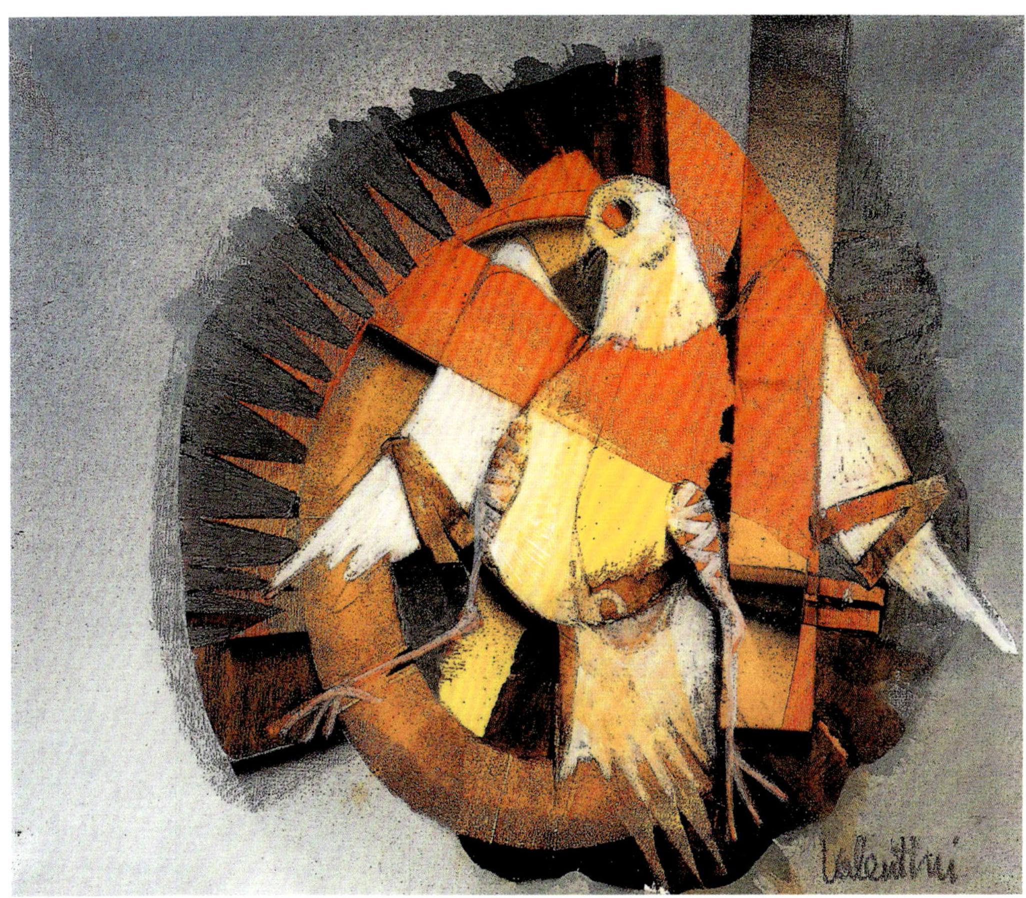

La Palombella 1980. Mixed media on canvas, 50 × 60 cm. Collection of Valentini family.

bird of the spirit, the bird of peace, which he usually showed as wounded or in danger, his comment on the violence of the twentieth century.

As if to complete a full circle exploration of his fascination with this annual festival, in 1980 Livio painted *La Palombella.* Comparison with the real dove contraption shows how remarkably this all helps illuminate Livio's imagery. The live dove is imprisoned in the tube (the cage), surrounded by a sunburst aureola mirroring those infamous rounded walls. The dove hopefully survives inside that plastic tube although, ironically, if one thinks of the terror the live dove must feel as it hurtles over the heads of the crowd, accompanied by sparklers and eerie blue smoke, it even resembles the bombast of war. Is there really any great difference between Livio's tortured birds and this controversial ceremony? Livio himself marched in such city spectacles going all the way back to his teenage years.

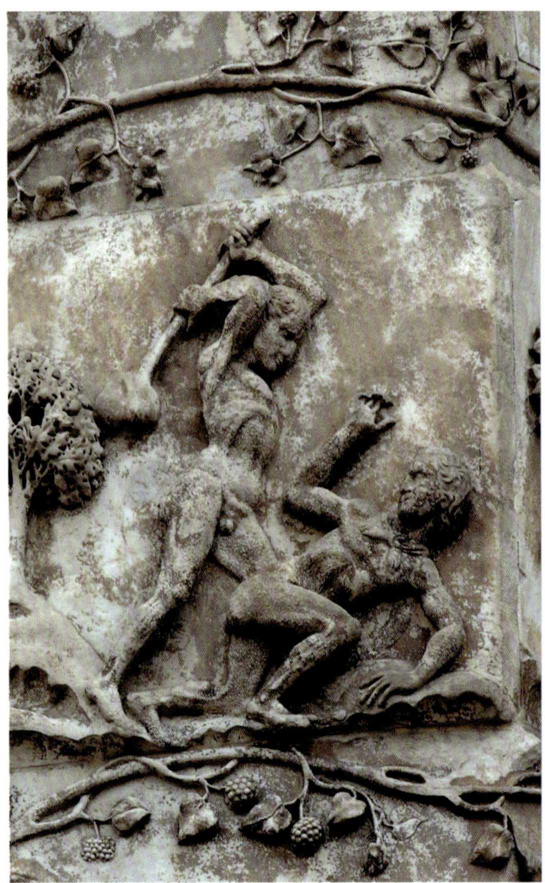

Maitani, *Cain and Abel.* Marble bas-relief on facade of the Duomo. Photograph courtesy of the collection of Museo dell'Opera del Duomo, Orvieto.

The Etchings:

Iconologies of the Cathedral of Orvieto—1977

If anyone should doubt that the remarkable birds of Maestro Valentini bear a direct connection with the cathedral and her public arts, let's move on to Livio's Iconology series. In 1977 Livio designed an exhibit entitled *Iconologie del Duomo di Orvieto* (Iconologies of the Cathedral of Orvieto), which included ten etchings exploring the Biblical themes in the bas-reliefs on the facade of the Duomo, which were sculpted by Lorenzo Maitani. Valentini reinterpreted the *Slaughter of the Innocents,* supplementing the horror with a child on a cross and adding a soldier wearing a contemporary costume. Notice his gas mask and machine gun.

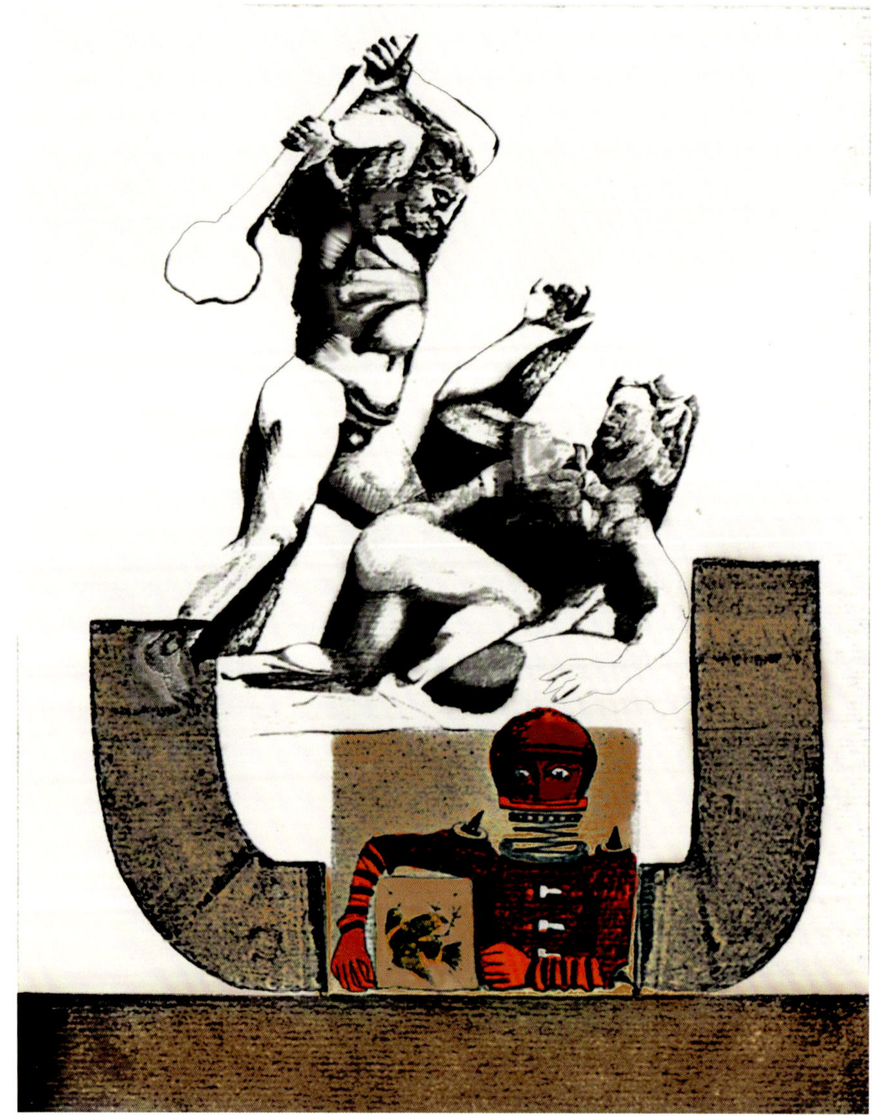

Cain and Abel, 1977. Hand-colored etching, 50 × 60 cm. Color reproduced by Michael St. John.

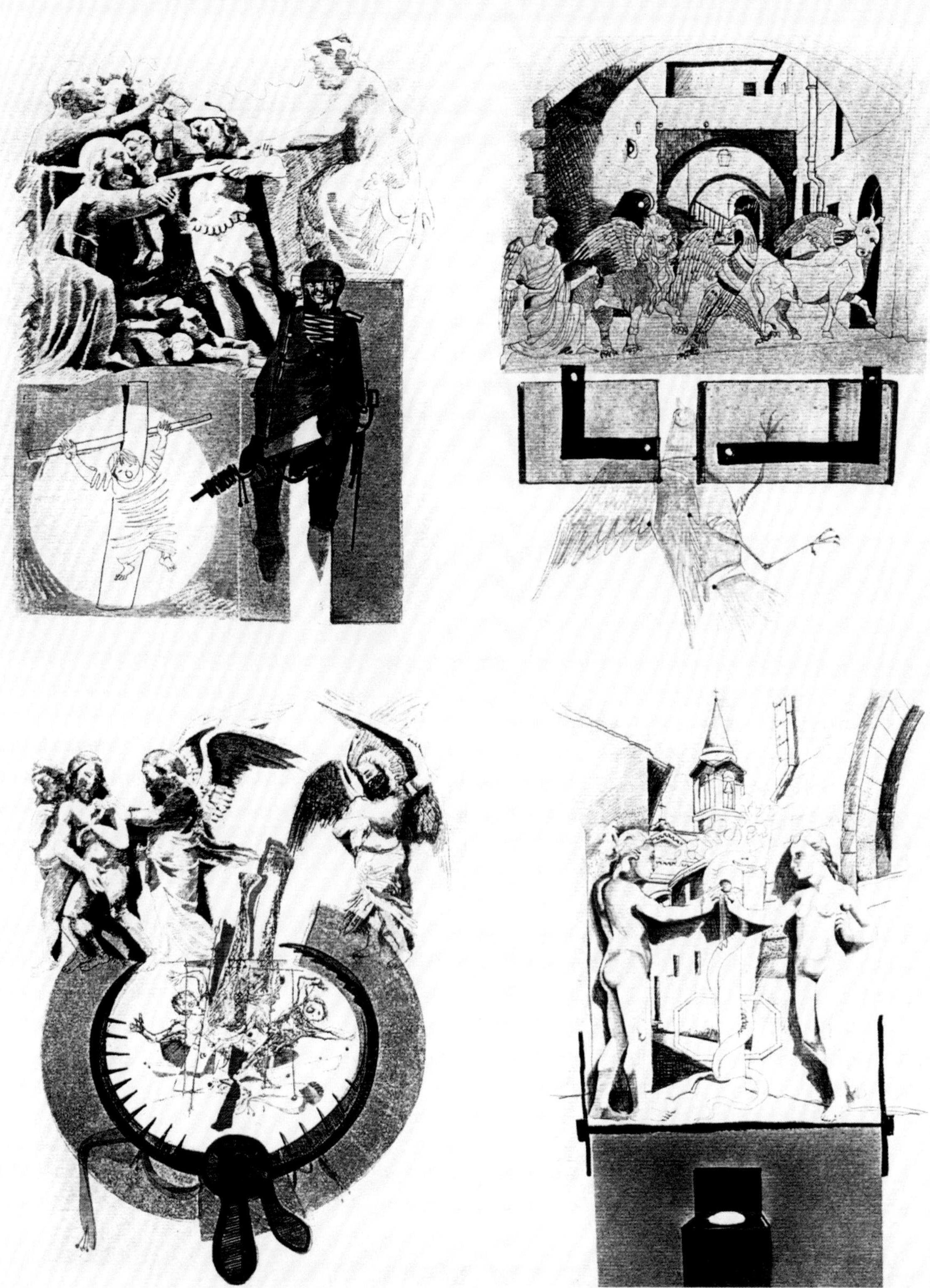

Four hand-colored etchings from the Iconologies of the Duomo: *Slaughter of the Innocents, Expulsion from Eden, The Four Evangelists,* and *Adam and Eve,* 1997. Each is 50 × 60 cm.

Similarly in Valentini's *Cain and Abel* another modern soldier appears; his helmet resembles that of an astronaut. This soldier holds the caged bird, Valentini's icon, now ringed by the walls of war. That bird, victimized, symbolized, became Valentini's spiritual totem.

Birds often appear in Christian iconography. For example St. John the Evangelist's icon is an eagle. In his next print Livio co-opted the symbols of all four Evangelists from the facade . The winged man, the attribute of Matthew, the winged lion, usually seen as Mark, the winged ox representing Luke, and the eagle of John parade through the street. In the distance appear the great arches of the medieval city and down below the poor bird is crushed by a metal frame.

In both pagan and Christian iconography, the bird is often identified with the soul. Livio said, "You can take the bird as a symbol of the human soul, not free to fly, to move as it wished to. There were too many things which were restraining it, which were tying it to the earth and not leaving it free." For the Maestro, as we have quoted him earlier, these birds stand in for man in this violent world.[59]

Indeed this bird has become Livio's familiar. Tortured, as was he, fired upon, as was he, and just as transcendent as he, the artist of Orvieto, became! Livio took us from the humble bird sellers to the processions where for centuries Orvietani have moved rhythmically through the streets, bearing images of the saints, of Christ, of the dove of the Holy Spirit itself. The environment and pageantry of the cathedral offered Livio enlightenment and redemption. In a sort of dialogue of the divine, the Maestro offers the same to his audience.

When we first met Livio in 1997 he was introduced to us as Maestro Valentini and we always tried to honor that title. Only years later did we inquire about how one came to be known as an Italian maestro. Was it an honorific title granted as one rose up through the ranks of achievement in a certain field? Did it require the seal of approval from some mysterious governmental agency? Erika Bizzarri explained that the title of maestro signified a teacher at the grade school level. As one of the founding fathers of the Istituto d'Arte in Orvieto, Livio taught drawing from 1970 to 1979. He became known as Maestro Valentini and the name endured even after he departed the institute.

One wonders if his close association with the young people of Orvieto led Livio to choose some of the new themes to explore in his art. It is our contention that his extended interaction with the students, who were constantly challenging the values and mores of the day, influenced his treatment of these subjects.

Continuing his interpretations of sculpture from the Duomo facade, Livio visited some of the most pressing moral issues of his time, weaving them into the proto-Renaissance originals. While Maitani's *Adam and Eve* still share the tempting fruit in front of the tree of the knowledge of good and evil, in Livio's version they are transported to the square in front of the Church of San Giovanni. Below their feet appears an open display case in which lies "the pill."

Livio remarked, "I took the liberty to represent a different setting, Orvieto rather than the Garden of Eden, as if to say they are us, not someone else; these people represent us. That's the constant problem of original sin. Of course in these last few years it has undergone a tremendous existential shock. . . . Because of the advent of the birth control pill, because man has now taken on the task of controlling birth and population, original sin has significantly changed in its meaning, the concept of birth and life."[60]

According to Massimo Duranti, Livio "interprets messages from the art of the past." In our discussion of the Cycle of the Birds, we listed several of Livio's appropriations from Maitani's bas-reliefs. Duranti explained, "Here Livio literally 'tears off' pieces of sculpture from the facade of the Cathedral and redesigns them. They are episodes from the Bible which are full of death and violence."

Livio modernized these works with his own contemporary images of the birth control pill, astronauts, heavily-armed soldiers, and of course, the birds perched on sculptures or trapped in cages. Through these ten etchings Livio found a way to address what Duranti refers to as "the widespread human condition of pain and vulnerability which the artist anxiously and helplessly observes."[61]

To Maitani's *Expulsion from Eden,* Livio added an explosive centerpiece. A light blast resembling a thunderbolt strikes a group of terrified people with arms flailing about. Livio encircles this episode with the brown encampment wall pierced every few inches with sharp jags of metal. Clearly Livio modernized the moment when mankind was thrust from the Garden of Eden and the piece shows them walled inside the darkest of places while bombs descend from the sky.

Livio revisited the suffering of Christ two more times. Taking us again to witness *The Crucifixion,* nails drip down from the pierced hand of Christ on the cross and pile up menacingly on the floor below. On closer observation one can detect the faint skull-like faces of other victims of modern violence, overwhelming in its scope. In *The Resurrection,* as is tradition, the focus is on the wounds of the risen Savior. In this case Livio introduced an additional character lying on the steps below. A shadow-faced wraith is wrapped from head to toe in an unraveling shroud. At first this seems to represent Christ in the tomb before he rose from the dead. But in the context of these pieces, perhaps Livio is reminding us of others who have felt pain, like Lazarus, the Biblical lepers, or perhaps some contemporary brother whose agony seems beyond our intervention.

Next we recognize the winged archangel *St. Michael,* wearing armor and raising a sword overhead, as he stands astride a dragon. This is Livio's interpretation of the bronze statue of Michael by Matteo di Ugolino da Bologna that stands on the facade of the Duomo. In this print the dragon materializes inside an egg shape and next to him is one of Livio's iconic birds, as lifeless as the slain dragon.

In Livio's etching *One of the Damned* we find a modern example of anguish. A male hangs tortured across a cruciform frame, head dangling and limbs twisted. The jaws of a Maitani demon gnaw on his raised left arm but Livio added the green-tinted carcass of a serpent, a universal symbol of evil, spiraling about him. Anyone of a classical bent is reminded of Homer's tale of Laocoön, the Trojan priest killed by sea serpents with his two sons. But in Livio's contemporary reimagining, the serpent is draped like a preserved specimen, head encased in a plastic bag and tagged for preservation. When this piece was on display in the Etherredge Center, Livio explained that he was thinking there are "other serpents which are much more dangerous nowadays."[62]

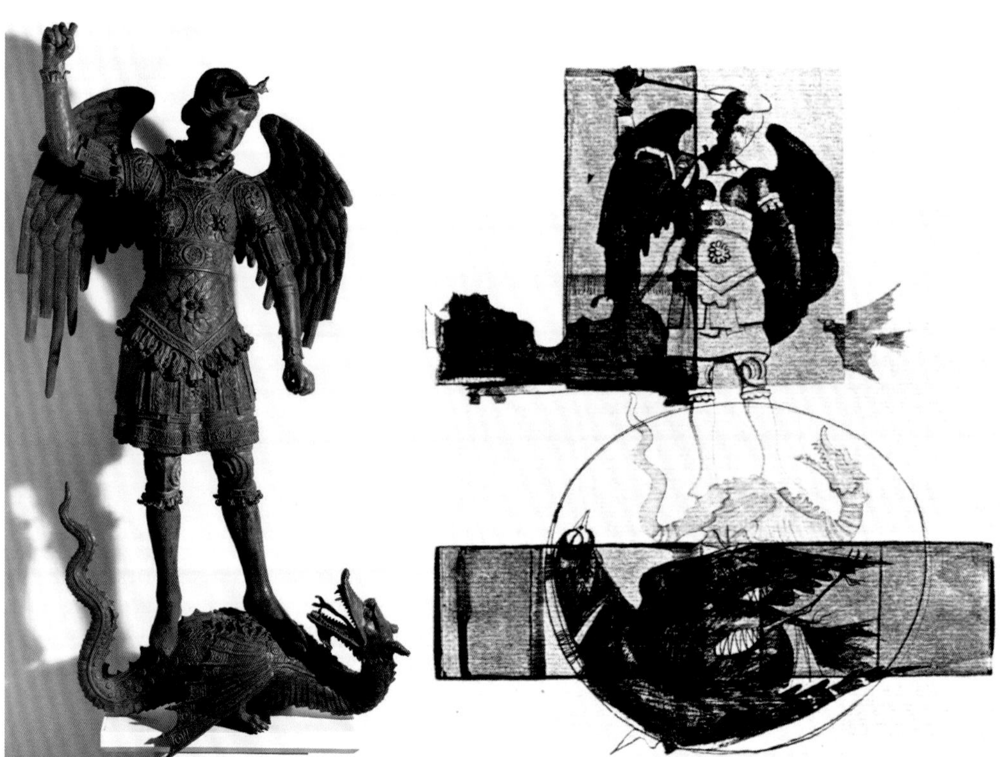

St. Michael and the Dragon. Hand-colored etching, 50 × 60 cm. Matteo di Ugolino, *St. Michael Archangel and the Dragon.* Collection of Museo dell'Opera del Duomo, Orvieto.

Combining the Biblical sins of man with the horrors of warfare and envisioning the proto-Renaissance overlaid with contemporary morality, these ten hand-colored etchings are an example of Livio's intention to denounce violence. Livio embarked upon an important period in which he was concerned with contemporary issues and used his art to express his views. 1978 brought his participation in the "Festival of Two Worlds," under the aegis of the Artists for the Rights of Man working with Amnesty International. One year later came a trip to Berlin to visit the wall. In 1979 he retired from the Istituto d'Arte but retained his title of maestro. A 1980 monograph, *Un muro, l'eccidio degli Uccelli* (The Wall. The Massacre of the Birds) resulted from this period of brave new self-expression.[63]

The Signorelli Period: The New Representation—1980–1991

One could consider the Iconology series and Livio's moral pronouncements a prelude to the groundbreaking Signorelli project. It was as though, having harvested the best images from the Cathedral's facade , the doors were now swung open, and Livio entered and began gleaning from the Renaissance frescoes within. This next project required him to come to terms, artist to artist, with one of Orvieto's superstars. In order to celebrate the seventh centenary of the Cathedral of Orvieto, Valentini undertook a reinterpretation of the famous frescoes by Luca Signorelli (c.1445–1523). In the early Renaissance Signorelli heralded a new age of sophisticated and scientific knowledge. Consensus among art historians places him as a pioneer in the understanding of human anatomy and proportion. He flourished just before the predominance of Leonardo (1452–1519) and Michelangelo (1475–1564).

According to Livio, "This cycle of paintings is in the cathedral of Orvieto in the Chapel of San Brizio. Work was done between 1499 and 1504. It was a Tuscan painter, Luca Signorelli, who was entrusted with the work . . . a real masterpiece that can be compared with Michelangelo's *Last Judgment.* The Last Judgment, the stories of the Antichrist, paradise, hell and the Resurrection are depicted on the four walls. There are three types of beings in this context, men, both good and bad, angels who are all good, and demons who are all bad. These are the three elements which compose this great work."[64]

Livio stated, "When the new spirit of the Renaissance emerged, this new concept was to represent historical as well as political things. . . . One sees scenes of conflict and contrasts, of struggles between aristocratic families vying for supremacy and control. Partially inspired by Dante, the combative archangels and demons were intended to help educate the masses."

These frescoes tell the story of the end of the world, the apocalypse, which Signorelli stages in Renaissance costume. The end of the world is preceded by the preaching of the antichrist who is shown here with the devil whispering in his ear. The antichrist promised false miracles and in the end was destroyed along with the whole world.[65]

According to Livio, "Signorelli depicted contemporary politicians. That's probably Pope Alexander VI, a Borgia, to whom the devil is whispering. The pope reportedly had a connection with the Mafia. So that represents the saying, the right hand doesn't know what the left hand is doing."[66]

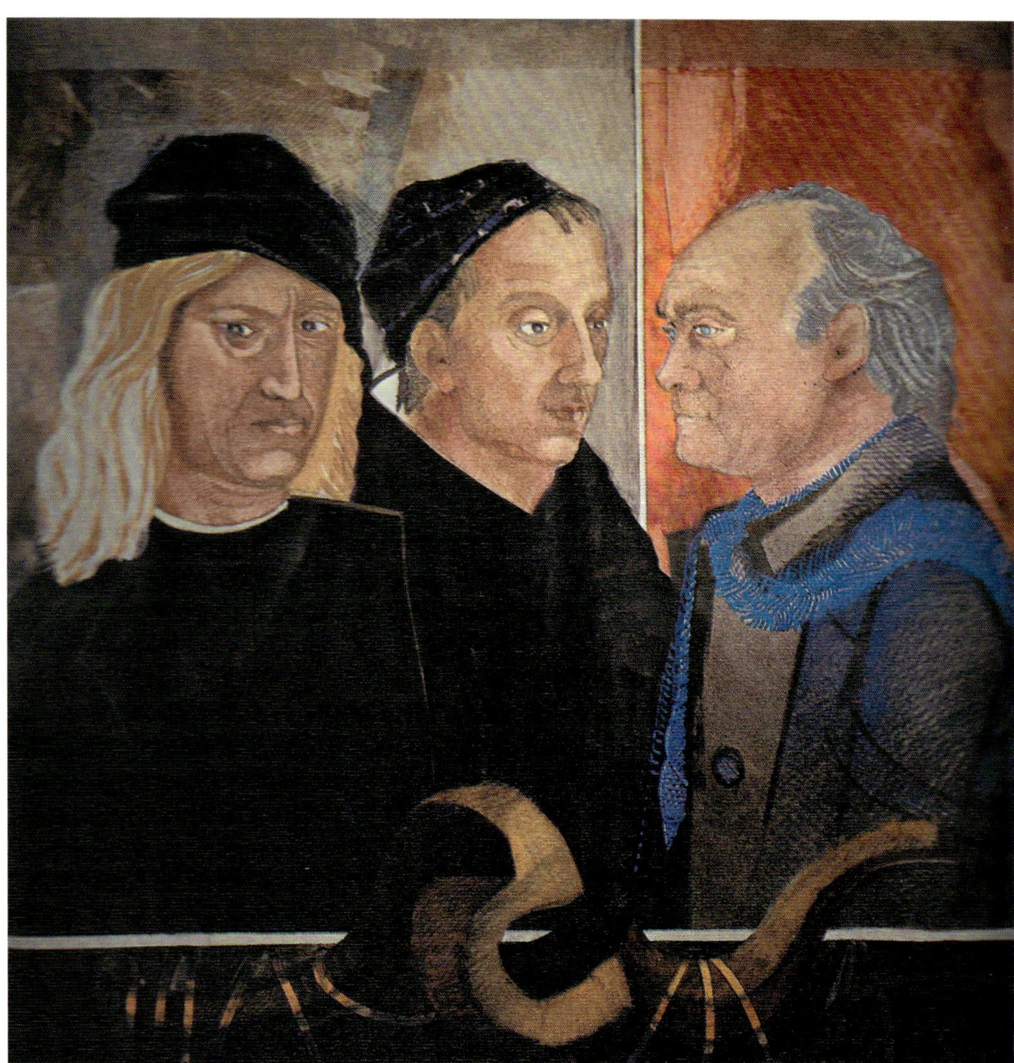

Self-portrait together with Luca Signorelli and Fra Angelico, 1985. Oil and acrylic on canvas, 150 × 142 cm.

Livio stated:

> At a certain point in my life I made a really heroic decision. I sort of ignored my humility and became presumptuous. I decided to try and follow this artistic auteur, this artistic Signorelli. In other words I took Signorelli's subjects, bringing them into my own historical period. I reinterpreted the various aspects, which made this work so important. I went to Signorelli and I said, "I am Valentini" and together arm in arm we went along this journey. It was a really splendid trip, as I discovered how our forebears thought and I discovered much to my surprise that art is always art. Thoughts will change, culture will change, but the concept of giving life to a plane surface, a flat surface, to make it come alive is always the same and you almost have to have that inborn.[67]

In a moment of wonderful enthusiasm for his heritage, and perhaps recognizing the inherent hubris of reimagining Signorelli's masterworks, Livio created a self-portrait as a part of the project. The Maestro shows himself in profile, draped in a blue scarf and coming face to face with Luca Signorelli and his predecessor Fra Angelico (c. 1395–1455).

According to Graham-Collier, "Livio and Signorelli, were they able to sit down together and close the gap of the centuries, would find themselves brothers-in-arms when it comes to feeling for, and making visually manifest, the two sides of our nature. The figure of man is the motif of power, designed to express the destructive passions which drive us, and at the same time symbolize the potential, transcendent goodness of the human spirit."[68]

In a campus lecture Livio once referred to the astonishing accomplishments of this handful of artists who hailed from Umbria and Tuscany. Livio listed, "Signorelli of Orvieto, Michelangelo of Tuscany, Giotto of Assisi, Piero della Francesca of Arezzo, Leonardo from Vinci, a perimeter not of the biggest distance in kilometers but it contains an atomic bomb of these geniuses who have written the history of our life." In one brave step Livio acknowledged his own entrance into the pantheon of Italian regional talents.

Livio selected just a few central Signorelli characters to analyze. In his painting, *L'ascoltatore curioso* (The Curious Listener), we meet a man in multicolored tights with ribbons at the knee, standing near the antichrist. Livio said, "This was a living model whom the painter used in different situations, sometimes as a man, sometimes as an angel, sometimes as a devil. This model doesn't look like someone from another period but paintings should not become dated. This could very well be the figure of a man today but it's from 1499. He looks like a football player!"[69]

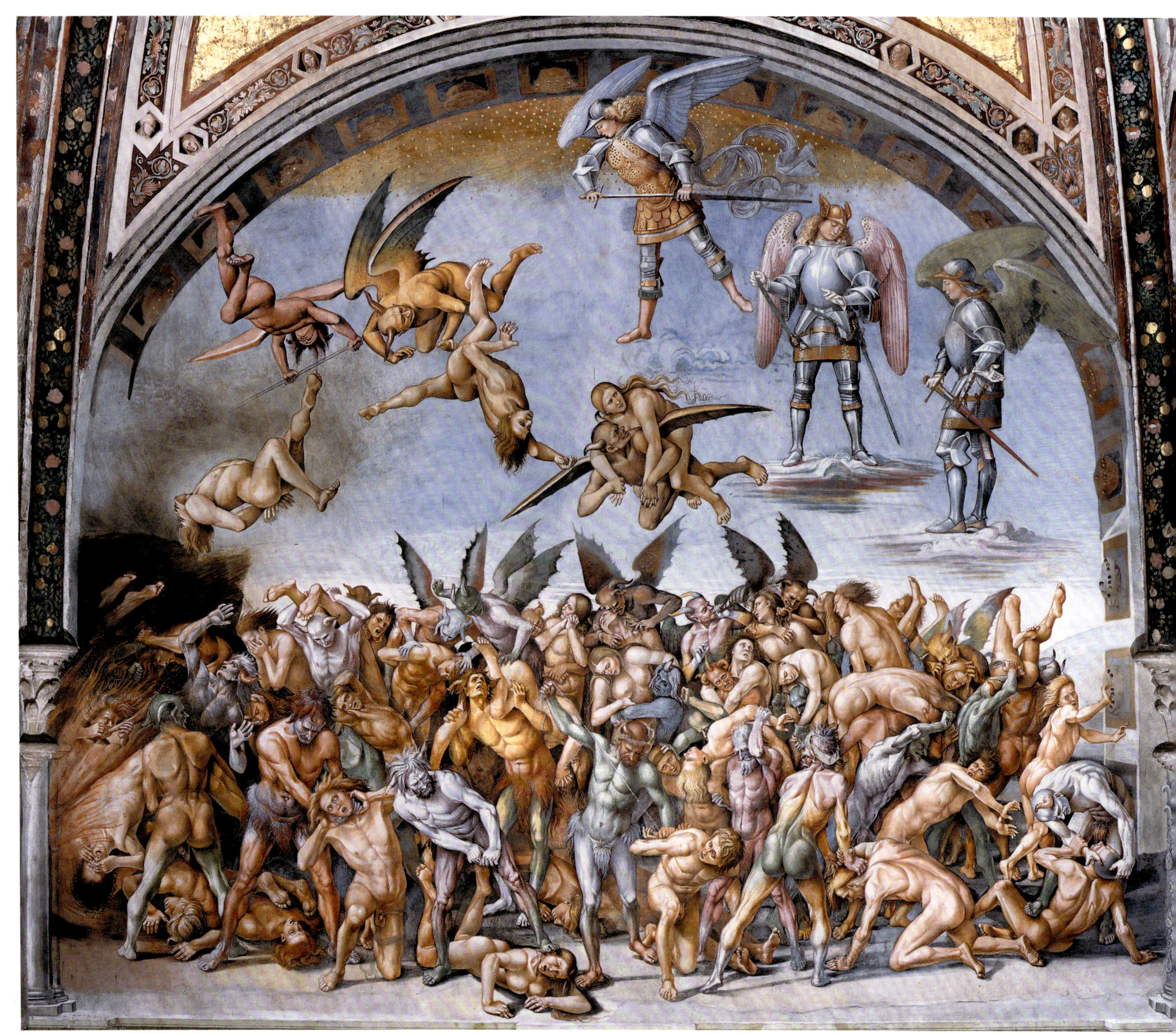

Signorelli, *Inferno* (The Damned Cast into Hell). Photograph courtesy of Museo dell'Opera del Duomo, Orvieto.

The other Signorelli fresco that seems to have especially intrigued Livio is *Inferno* (The Damned Cast into Hell). Giorgio Di Genova observed, "It might be said that Valentini triumphed over the hell of his memories by studying the Hell Signorelli painted on the walls of the San Brizio Chapel."[70] Here Livio zeroed in on the face of a demon dragging a young woman to perdition. Legend records that the woman had been Signorelli's girlfriend before spurning him. As revenge, he immortalized her as the so-called Whore of Babylon, being taken to eternal damnation. In the Etherredge Center Livio and his wife Flora seemed eager to explain these timeless issues both Signorelli and Valentini highlighted.

Next comes *Figura di angelo "guardiano"* (Guardian Angel) from 1984. Hovering at the top of the *Damned Cast into Hell* are the three archangels Michael, Raphael, and Uriel, floating on clouds standing guard over the underworld lest any wayward soul escape. In the *Book of Revelation* (20:1), Michael is the leader of an army of angels. Traditionally Uriel controls the keys to the gates of hell. Here each angel sports full military dress and weapons befitting their role as guardian warriors.

Valentini appropriated the center figure of the silver-armored angel with miniature golden wings adorning his helmet. Livio charmingly captured the angel's rather reticent face and yet ironic position of holding two weapons at the ready. Notice the subtle change of color in the angel's wings from a pink into a pale blue bordering on purple. Closer observation reveals tiny silver dots among the feathers. This became significant when Livio revisited the angel in *Galassia.* One wonders if his points of light are meant to mirror the three-dimensional golden spheres peppering the firmament above the angels' heads. Throughout the frescoes in San Brizio, Signorelli referred to the horrifying cosmic disruption of the apocalypse. In *Il Finimondo,* Signorelli filled both corners with explosions of the heavens. On the right, quoting the *Book of Revelation,* is a crimson crescent; the moon has become as blood. On the left the stars of heaven are spiraling to earth, like a flood of streaming comets. When Livio moved to Aiken to paint *Galassia,* his heavens became equally dynamic in coloring and chaos.

Valentini presented another such celestial being, this time borrowed from the *Resurrection of the Flesh.* Livio captured an angel playing the long clarion trumpet to awaken the dead. He found certain details, like the triumphal banner with its red cross and multiple ribbons swirling in the air, particularly fascinating. But above all notice how Livio obsessed over the astonishing musculature of the angel. He almost completely stripped the angel's body and wings of color, using bold transparent outlines. Observe the golden spheres that polka dot the heavens overhead and the way Livio framed his angel in the semicircular pattern he revisited in *Galassia.*

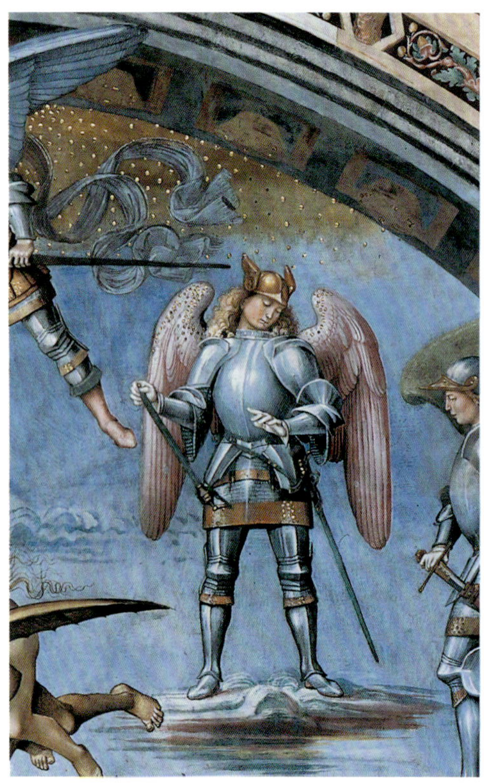

Signorelli, *Figura di angelo "guardiano"* (The Guardian Angel), from *Inferno*. Photograph courtesy of Museo dell'Opera del Duomo, Orvieto.

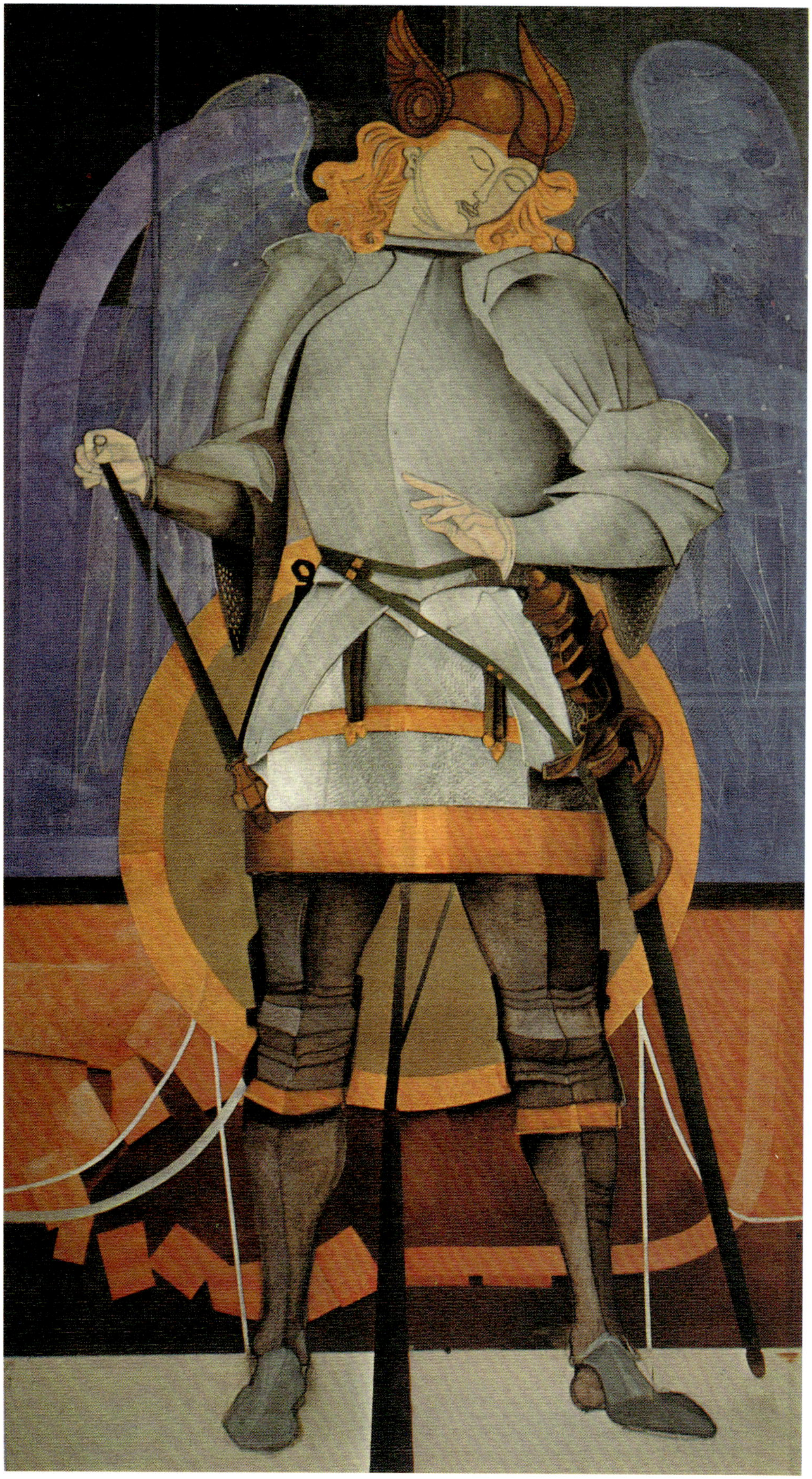

Figura di angelo "guardiano" (The Guardian Angel), after Signorelli, 1984. Oil and acrylic on canvas, 150 × 280 cm. Private collection.

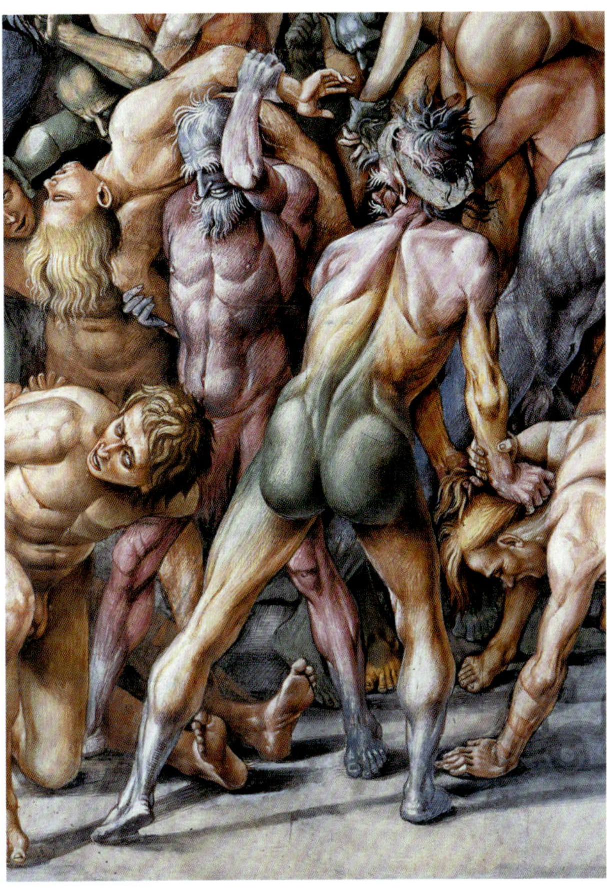

Signorelli, *Figura di demone* (Figure of Demon), from *Inferno*. Photograph courtesy of collection of Museo dell'Opera del Duomo, Orvieto.

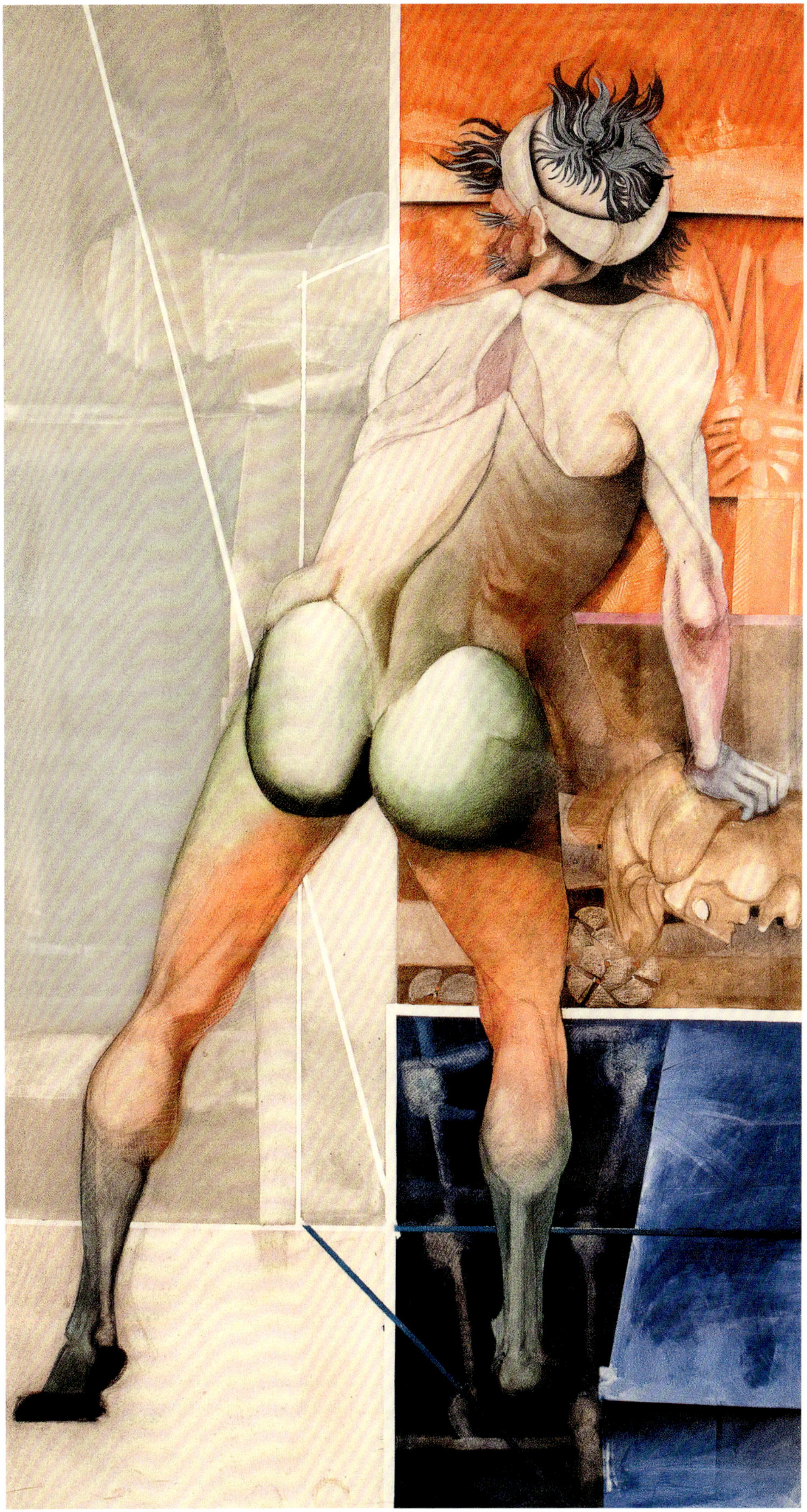

Figura di demone (Figure of Demon), after Signorelli, 1985. Oil and acrylic on canvas, 150 × 280 cm. Collection of Hotel Duomo, Orvieto. Photograph by Marco Santopietro.

Livio famously introduced *Figura di demone* (Figure of Demon) in 1984. Here Livio shifted his focus to the ground where a startling confrontation erupts with demons inflicting excruciating torments upon the damned souls. Livio selected the demon who dominates the right half of the group with his muscular backside turned towards us while he yanks the blonde hair of his victim. Signorelli's figure has become iconic not only for the remarkable realism of his musculature but for the multicolored hues of his skin, said to resemble the colors of rotting flesh. Livio could not resist accenting the strange metamorphosis of one colored body part blending into the next in a contrasting shade. His attention above all focused on the gleaming green buttocks.

Clearly Livio was particularly fond of divine demons because when he was asked to illustrate the *Utopica* book, he chose to include them again. What is so novel is the palpable lightness he brought to the formerly grave imagery. Now the devil whispers into the ear of the antichrist as both stand in the middle of an Umbrian square, observed by barefooted figures.

The guardian angel has become remarkably feminized, cradling one of Livio's iconic birds in the manner of a Madonna and Child. Strangely, the bird is wrapped in a tube-like affair with rivets and pointed projections mirroring those on the space suit of the soldier in *Cain and Abel.* And finally, the bat-winged demon who seized the so-called Whore of Babylon now seems happy to transport her on his shoulders in a sort of joy-ride over the city. Signorelli's originals have become uniquely Livio's. The five hundred year metamorphosis is complete.

About the same time as he was quoting directly from Signorelli's work in the chapel, Livio painted a simple tondo reminiscent of his earlier religious works from Assisi. In *St. Thomas and the Birds* we see the great lover of nature's creatures bend his body forward to cradle a dove in a gentle embrace. Years later when he turned to the magnum opus *Galassia,* Livio gathered these same beloved images: the angels, the demons, and the explosive heavens, for an astonishing reunion of theme and purpose.

The Barilla Installation

Parma: 1988

When Livio discussed the Barilla pasta project it usually resulted in broad smiles and even broader puns. During George Custodi's introduction of Livio at a lecture dealing with his artwork for the Barilla Company, George mentioned "pasta." However, Livio thought he heard "Basta." "Basta?" he asked. "No, pasta!" Laughter came naturally with this subject. The project was called *Strategie d'immagine,* literally "Strategies of Image."

According to Livio, Parma, Barilla's home base, "makes more pasta than anywhere else in the world." Livio shared, "Mr. Barilla called one day because he wanted to retain me, he wanted me to modernize the symbol of his business. He had about forty thousand square feet to use for the project. He asked how I was going to represent the high quality of this pasta. I designed an exposition and I presented it to him and he looked very doubtful. Mr. Barilla told me, 'I'd have to spend a hundred million lire (or eighty thousand dollars).' Livio responded, 'Yes, I know, Mr. Barilla, that you would need to spend that much money.' Mr. Barilla retorted, 'But you wouldn't have any idea how much money I would lose if this thing doesn't do its job.'"

Livio continued:

> So I became very worried because of the great responsibility. But I believe in my work so I went ahead with it. Since pasta is extruded as a paste through a block of copper I used copper structures distributed around the exhibit like a landscape and structures made out of glass to contain the pasta. But instead of the spaghetti hanging straight up and down we put it in sideways so you could see the end of the spaghetti rather than the entire length of it. The little pasta was contained in geometric forms and in this entire transparent structure. Barilla came down to see how I was doing and he said to me, "This doesn't look very promising. I don't see my name Barilla written anywhere." I told him an exposition such as this did not need to have his name on it. Due to its quality people would know only Barilla could come up with an excellent display like this.

And in telling this tale, Livio laughed. "So in the end Barilla became very pleased with the way this turned out and he shook my hand and told me congratulations, very good job. Barilla made a lot of money out of this project. It was a great success!"[71]

The Flight into the Quaternary (*Fuga nel Quaternario*): 1990

In 1990 the director of the Forte Spagnolo in L'Aquila asked Livio to create a special exhibition of his works. Coming to examine the facility, the Sala Elephas, the Maestro was struck by the skeleton of a mammoth in the museum. Livio said, "When I saw this enormous animal I asked the director, 'what are you going to do with it?' It was twelve feet high, this Mediterranean elephant. Bellissimo. He lived six hundred thousand years ago."

Livio described his feelings:

> So I said to the animal, "I have to do an exhibition with you." And the elephant said, "no, it's not a good idea." Because he dominated the scene and he was so imposing, it was absolutely impossible to compete. So I went out and I said "there's just one way to make it possible. The only way is for me to do an exhibition with paintings and sculptures that resemble you." So I began working, thinking about and trying to understand my own historical past, setting aside, ignoring the future of history. The historical past is something we all know but the difficult thing was to give it an aesthetic meaning. The wrong way would have been to copy the archaeological finds. I began to imagine a surreal world, color, substance, structure and that's how this wonderful adventure began. Our two elements, the elephant skeleton and my art works, belong to this great cycle, here and there. This animal of six hundred thousand years ago said, "Okay, I feel better now" and I felt a lot better too. And it was a really successful show.[72]

The new theme brought out an expressive, textured quality in Livio's ceramics, with organic shapes which could have been unearthed after centuries. *Struttura flessibile* (Flexible Structure) resembles the skeleton of man when he has just developed the ability to stand upright. Livio gave the title *Fuga nel Quaternario* to a wall installation of four round ceramic plaques. Later at a demonstration for USCA students, he revealed the techniques involved in such sculptural works. Using a wire cutter to slice smooth clay slabs, a process he traced back to the Etruscans, Livio created cavern-like shapes that writhe across the flat disks. Horizontal bands of dark glaze add a sense of stability while clay organs sprout from overlapping slabs, buttoned into place by tiny clay balls, which Livio pierced by inserting a wooden dowel. Another example of these ceramic disks is in the permanent collection of the Museo Magi 900 in Bologna.

In the same way, a four-panel grouping entitled *Da Fuga nel Quaternario: Storie di creazioni* (Flight into the Quaternary: Stories of Creation) features a surprising burst of lemon, lime, and orange colors. Each square uses dimensional mixed-media work, held in place by fish-eye buttons, like the clay spheres mentioned above. Clearly these dots of color, like those first used by Signorelli, were becoming a Valentini characteristic.

↞ *Da Fuga nel Quaternario: Storie di creazioni,* 1989. Mixed media on panel, 200 × 200 cm.

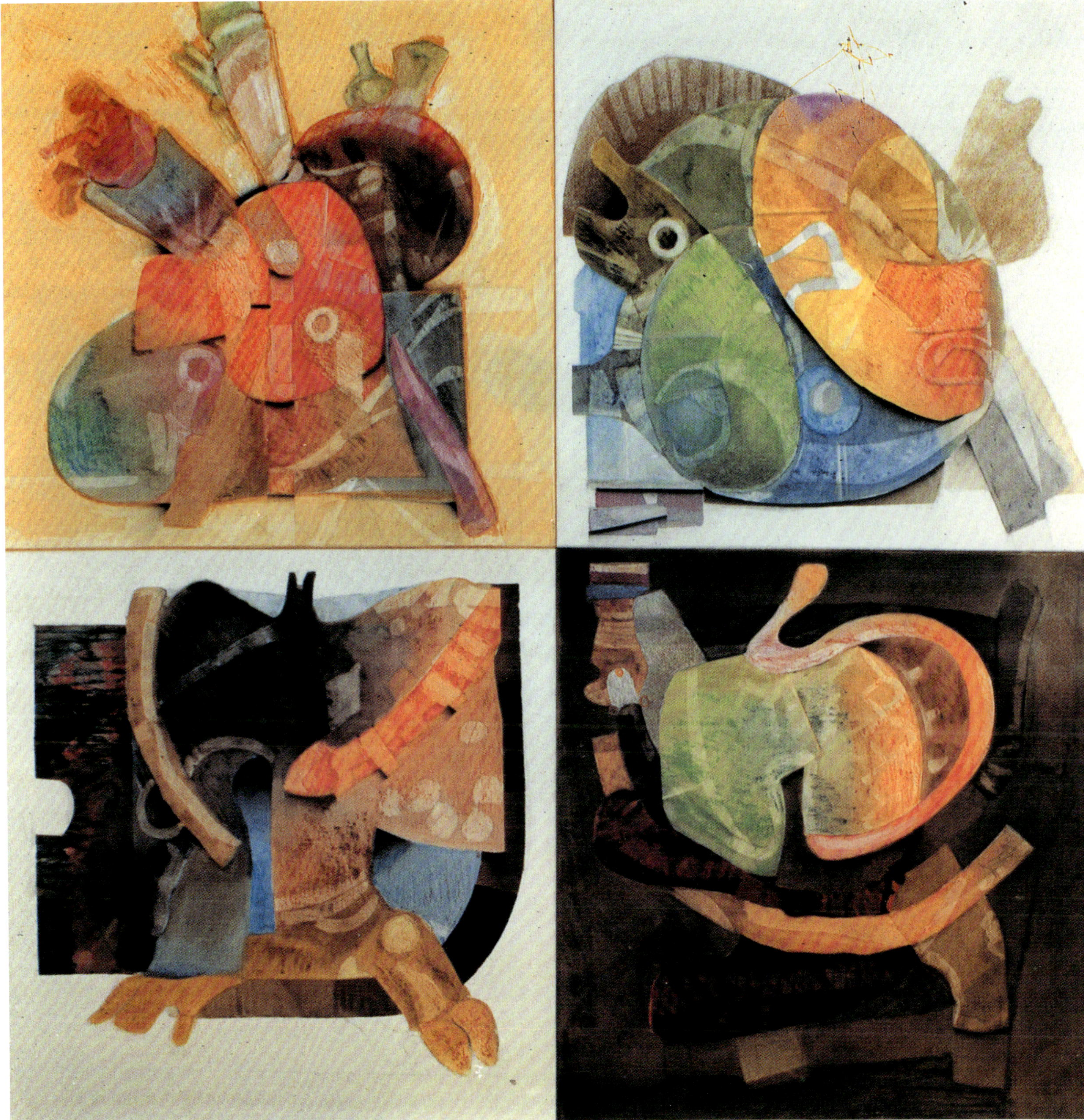

As an example of the Maestro's later works, let us examine the multi-media *Paesaggio cosmico e microcosmo* (Cosmic Landscape and Microcosm). This painting reveals an assortment of influences from the past as well as hints of the new style Livio later debuted in Aiken. In the upper left corner we recognize an angel cloaked in transparent washes of layered color. The cosmic angel's head looks much like the astronaut helmet we saw in his Iconology series. And close inspection may even reveal a Picasso-like face, with eyes staring forward while at the same time turning in profile.

In addition Livio introduced the motif of a running colored band, probably inspired by decorative ribbons in Signorelli's *Resurrection of the Flesh* fresco. Through a floating cloud we detect his microcosm of nature. A bracketed branch crisscrosses a stalk of flowers with red stamens and tiny curling leaves. At the same time beneath the branches is a metallic hinge secured with a pair of screws; this is clearly a bit of the "technology" Livio loved to discuss. When the chance came for Livio to visit Aiken, many of these very same references were used in his various commissions.

CHAPTER FIVE

Livio and Aiken

When Valentini came to the University of South Carolina Aiken campus in 1997, he chose the theme of *Odissea,* his odyssey to the United States for the American debut of his art. The grand opening and reception for Livio's show on November 13, 1997, was the culmination of the Orvieto delegation's visit to Aiken. It gave center stage to the Italian artist whom they had insisted be the focus of the exchange. It also introduced Livio to the people who became so important to the next period of his life and art. However the exhibit and reception did not happen without its moments of great anxiety.

Livio's show was huge, curated by Professor Al Beyer and filling both floors of the Etherredge Center. It consisted of nineteen paintings, twenty ceramic sculptures, and twenty-three lithographs. Professor Beyer and his student assistants unpacked eleven crates of art and finished their initial placement for the display, but when Livio and Flora arrived they disapproved. So the paintings had to be taken down and the ceramics moved into new positions. Livio preferred to hang the show in the Italian manner, with all the works of art hung with a consistent bottom line. Livio and Flora shifted everything around in the gallery and only then were the paintings hung and ceramics displayed in the specially-designed cases.

A frightening situation arose just before our grand opening. Due to its rarity we worried about insurance and security for this important Italian collection. The day of the opening we discovered a ceramic platter missing from the entrance wall; it was a very significant work because Livio had painted the title *Odissea* across its face. We alerted the campus police and prepared an official report for insurance coverage. Only later did we discover George Custodi, with Livio's permission, had taken the piece to his home to see how it looked before he purchased it. Of course no one had bothered to inform anyone at the university about this plan!

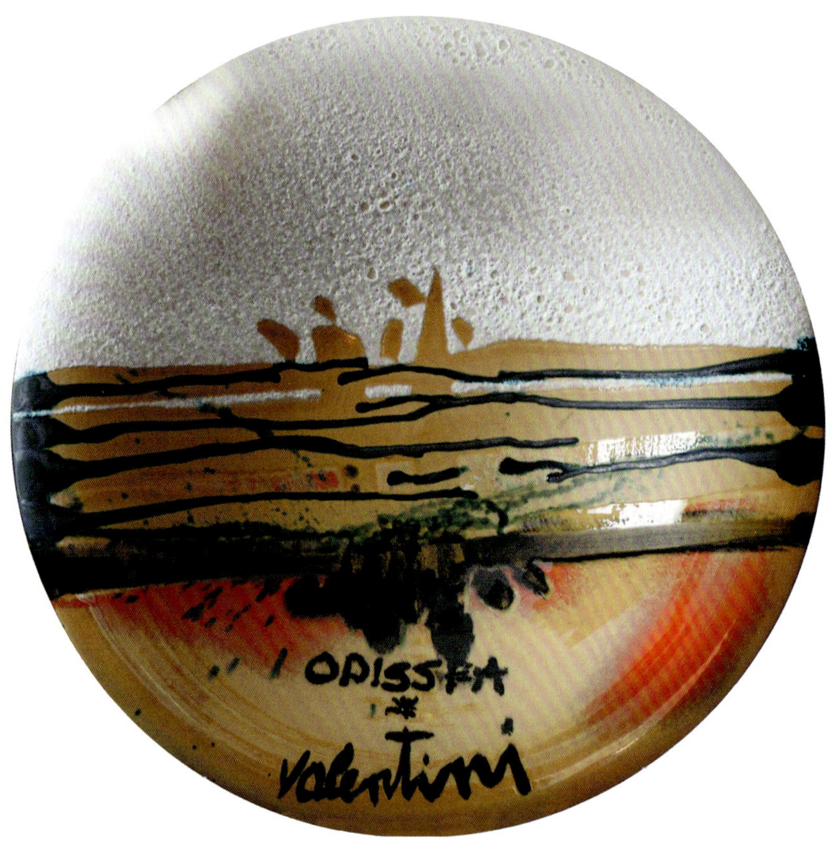

Odissea signature platter, 1997. Ceramic with oxide glazes, 53 cm. in diameter. Collection of George and Sandi Custodi. Photograph by Michael St. John.

The grand gala that evening honored Livio and Flora and the official Italian delegation with Mayor Cimicchi as well as members of the Orvieto city council and officers of their Rotary Club. The university and Partners in Friendship had approached the Odissea project as a unique opportunity to promote education on all levels. Before Livio's arrival, John, George Custodi, and Art Lader from Aiken High School had given lectures for the USCA Continuing Education program. They spoke on the history of Orvieto and Livio's artistic importance. In addition Massimilla Townsend taught conversational Italian lessons for the community. As part of our educational outreach, Livio had agreed to hold several ceramic demonstrations for elementary, high school, and adult classes.

When Valentini arrived we involved as many academic departments as possible, and arranged opportunities for him to visit local schools. All of this was to advance the long-range goal to internationalize USC Aiken, to allow our students to experience influences from around the world and to encourage them to consider studying abroad.

The campus newspaper, *Pacer Times,* welcomed Livio with the headline, "Benvenuto Signore Valentini." The article described a number of on-campus lectures and art demonstrations accompanying the *Odissea* exhibit. The poster for one of Livio's first "cultural conversations" trumpeted, "USCA goes Etruscan!" The *Pacer Times* article explained, "Students can welcome this remarkable man and his wife to our community by taking advantage of the many opportunities he is offering our campus."[1]

Furthermore the planning committee decided the *Odissea* gala would serve to raise funds to support our international educational goals. Many committee members contributed sections to the commemorative catalogue edited by Erika Pauli Bizzarri and printed in Florence, Italy. Livio produced a beautiful poster for the exhibit. The USCA music department arranged for a fine quartet to perform mostly Italian works.

Even the menu for the gala was an opportunity to educate our guests. The offerings were half Italian, half American, with bilingual name cards for each dish done in beautiful calligraphy. A special chef assisted campus food services with the preparation of Italian dishes: prosciutto, tortellini, and crostini. Naturally Orvieto Classico wine was served. An army of campus and community volunteers made all of this possible but there was a last minute hiccup. We had ordered freshly-prepared gelato from Five Points in Columbia but the caterer forgot it; one of our volunteers made a last minute save.

When Livio and Flora arrived that morning to find banquet tables bisecting the lower gallery, they strongly objected to serving food at an art show. Such a thing would simply not be done in Italy! We later joked that we averted an international incident by offering Livio a comparison from the Italian Renaissance. The noble patron Lorenzo de Medici traditionally hosted events of magnificent splendor honoring the finest artists in Florence. Luckily the complimentary comparison appeased Livio's alarm and the event proceeded. Despite these snafus the evening was one of the most elegant and unforgettable in the history of the University of South Carolina Aiken.

Livio reflected, "It almost became a diplomatic incident. I couldn't understand why in an art show there would be a banquet with food and wine. But Alexander, with a lot of patience and as a gentleman, explained to me this is the way it is in the United States, this is a normal thing to have. So he gave me the possibility to reconnect myself to some facts of the Renaissance, so luminous and important. . . . With a lot of humility on my part, I proposed we start the new Renaissance of Aiken. This became a spiritual and cultural renaissance."[2]

As part of the *Odissea* exhibit, Valentini introduced eleven prints in Aiken with a portion of the proceeds going to Partners in Friendship to support the high school

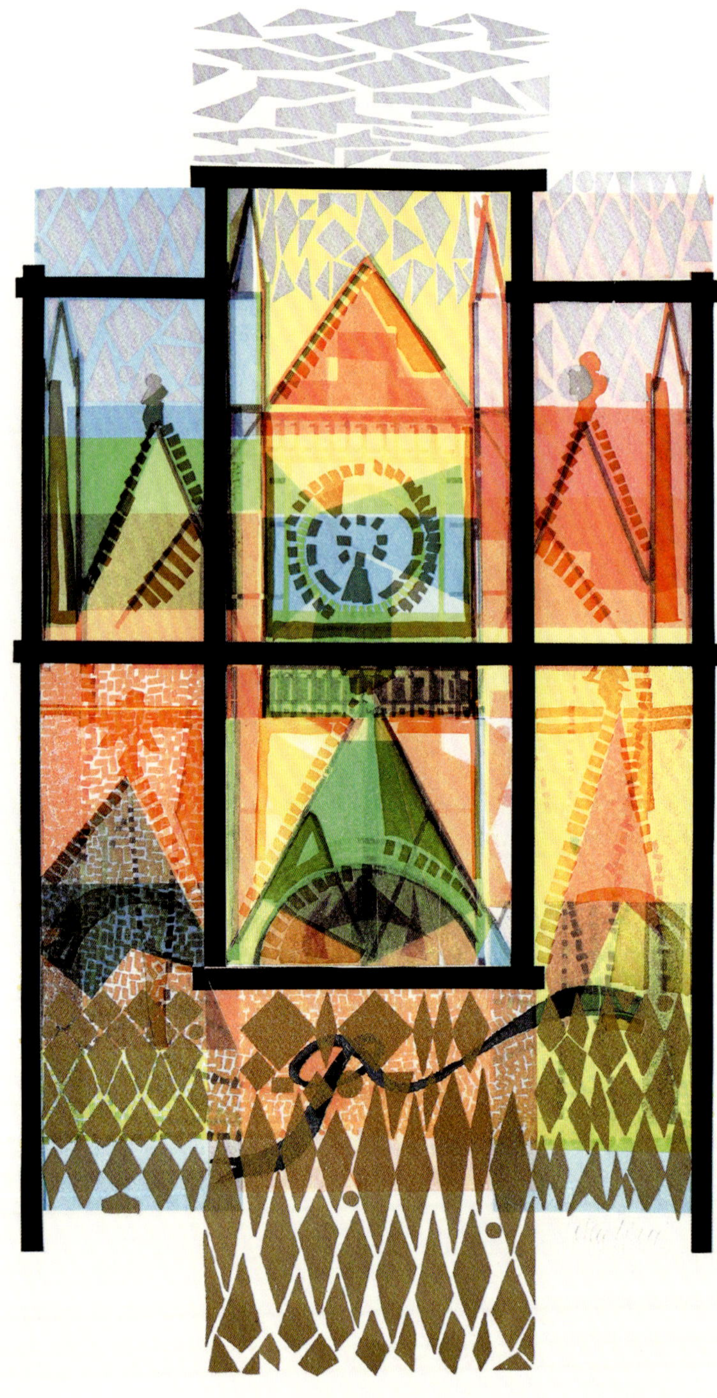

Luce delle pietre (Light of the Stones), circa 1990s. Seriolithograph, 70 × 50 cm. Collection of USC Aiken. Photograph by Michael St. John.

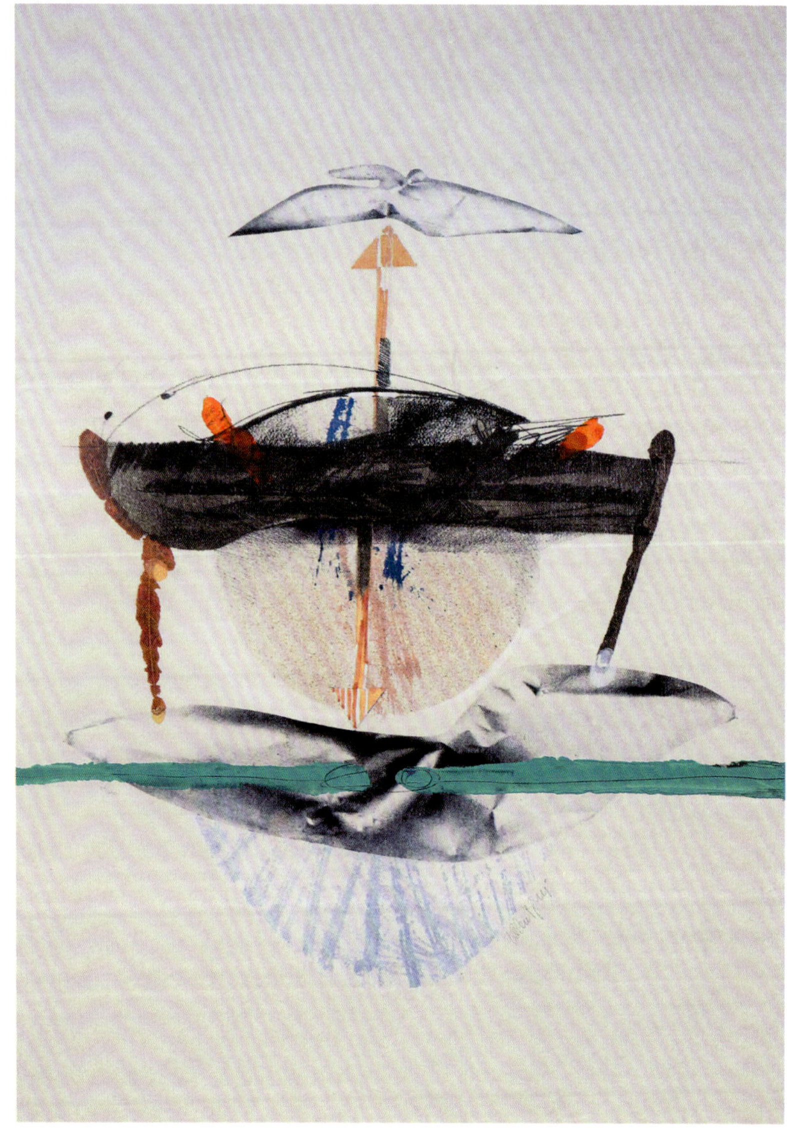

I luoghi dello spirito (The Places of the Spirit), 1995. Mixed media on lithograph, 96 × 70 cm. (Collection of USC Aiken). Photograph by Michael St. John.

exchange programs between the two cities. Livio gifted a complete set of these prints to the university's permanent collection.

Luce delle pietre (Light of the Stones) captures the essence of the magnificent Duomo. Valentini reproduces the facade of this beloved landmark in the translucent colors of stained glass. Traditionally every Gothic church features a triple gable design to represent the Holy Trinity and a rose window at the center honoring the Virgin Mary. The cathedral in Orvieto is inlaid with luminous marble, a light-reflecting stone, and encrusted with original gold mosaics. In the same way Valentini overlaid this print with a brilliant patina of gold and silver.

In another print, entitled *I luoghi dello spirito* (The Places of the Spirit), Livio explained some of the forms were "symbols of things we have in our memories that come to have meaning for us." We asked, "Isn't that a bird, his bird, floating across the top of the scene?" Livio responded, "It depends on what your background is, what context you have. Up here is the dove, which has always been a symbol of spirituality. . . . Here we have a round shape; it could represent the wafer of the Host in Roman Catholic mass." He added, "When you are using symbols, they may be personal but also should refer to the general world around you so that other people will be able to understand and interpret them. This composition doesn't necessarily give you a symbol with only one specific meaning and which is tied only to the Church or a certain political theme. This is the freedom of the spirit, the places of the spirit."

When asked about the technique Livio had used to produce these lithographs, he described drawing on a transparent film, which was used to transfer the images to a zinc plate. Each individual color required its own plate. In the USCA collection we have *Uccello,* a rare, original example of such a plate and its black ink imprint. How remarkable to see the strong yet subtle line work without the layers of color that would follow.

In *The Places of the Spirit* Livio hand applied wound-like shapes of bright color onto the surface of each individual print. The band of teal that bisects the work is also hand painted with a stylus piercing the color's surface. Consequently each buyer owns a unique print that has been individually personalized.[3]

Livio's symbolic dove dominates many of the lithographs he brought to campus. For example *Finestra da aprire* (Window to Open) is one of Livio's most complex prints. There is an almost oceanic woodcut style to the background pattern, reminiscent of the work of Paul Gauguin. A pastel rendering of the dove appears at the center of the work. Surrounding the bird is a metal-framed, jail-like structure. Notice the rusty red wounds at each sharp point of iron. The illusion of three-dimensional bands and bolts reminds

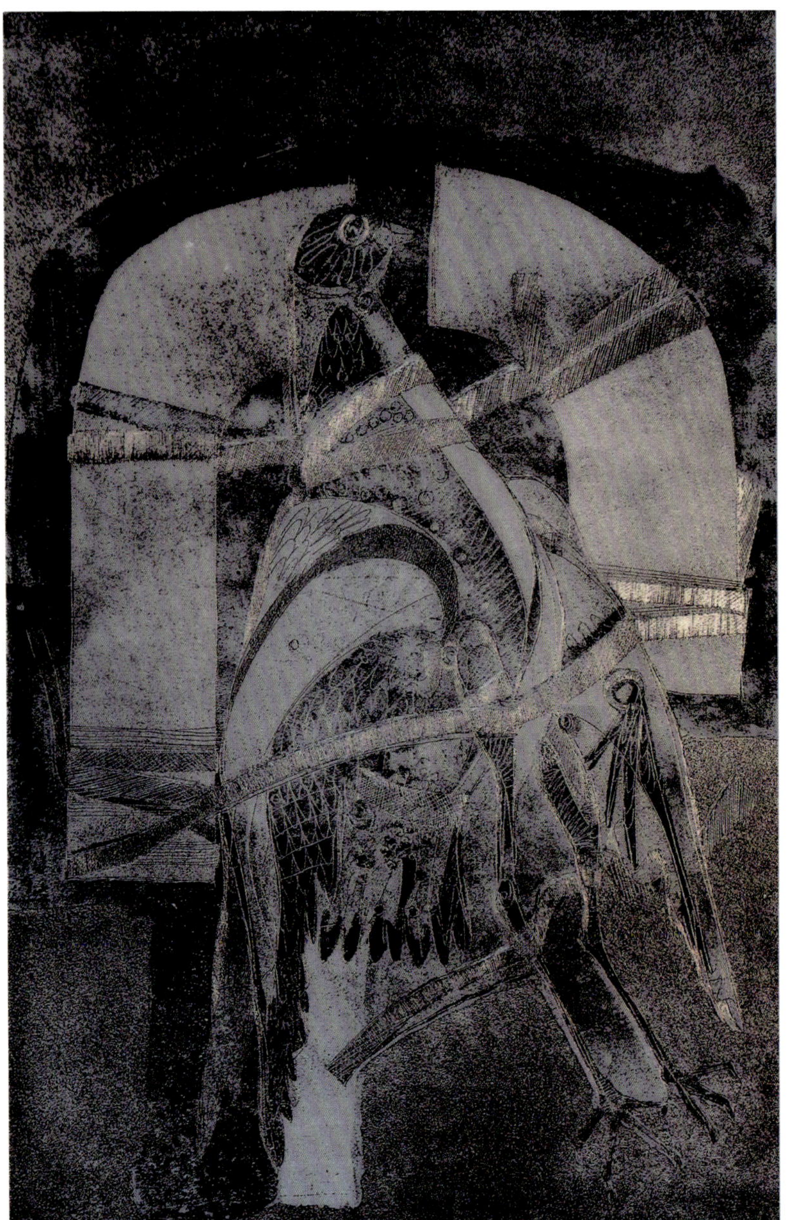

Uccello (Bird). Zinc plate, 31.75 × 49.5 cm. Collection of USC Aiken. Photograph by Michael St. John.

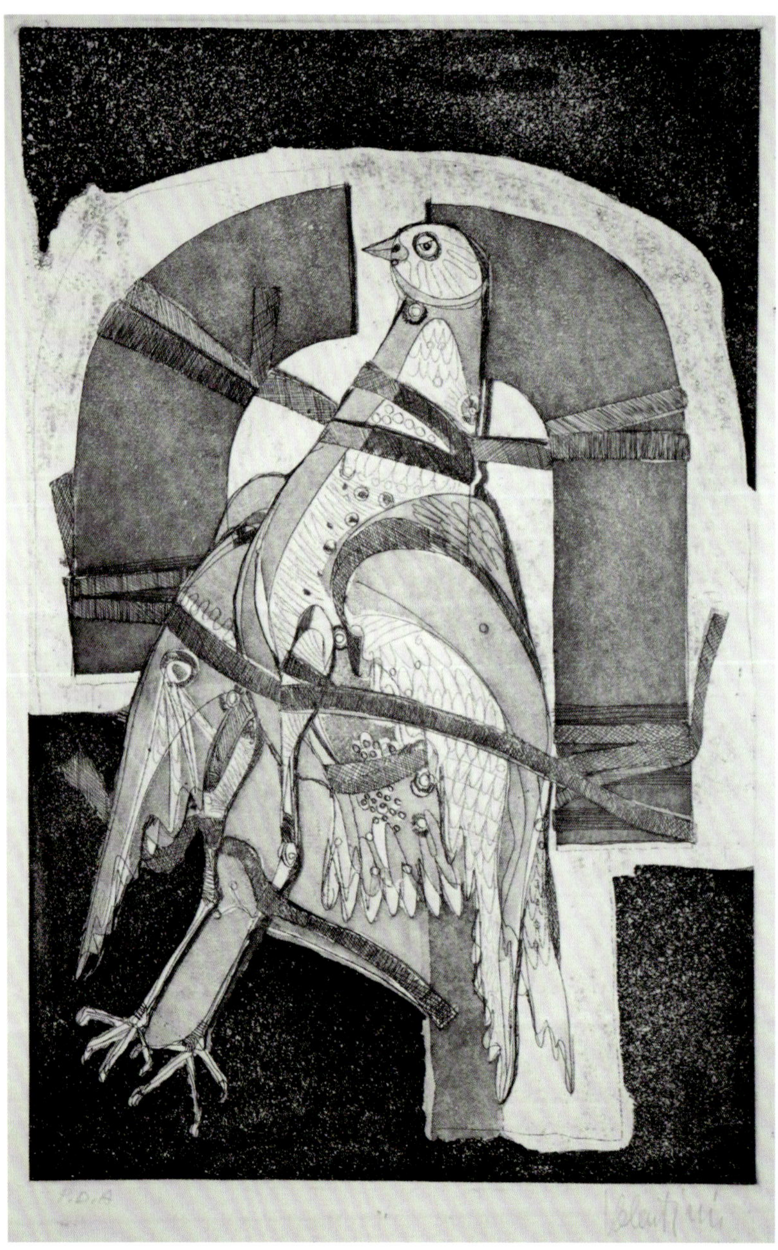

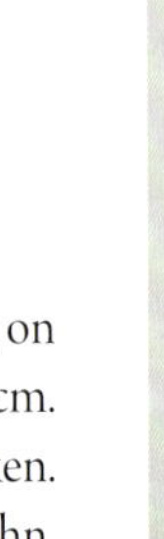

Uccello (Bird). Etching on paper 31.75 × 49.5 cm. Collection of USC Aiken. Photograph by Michael St. John.

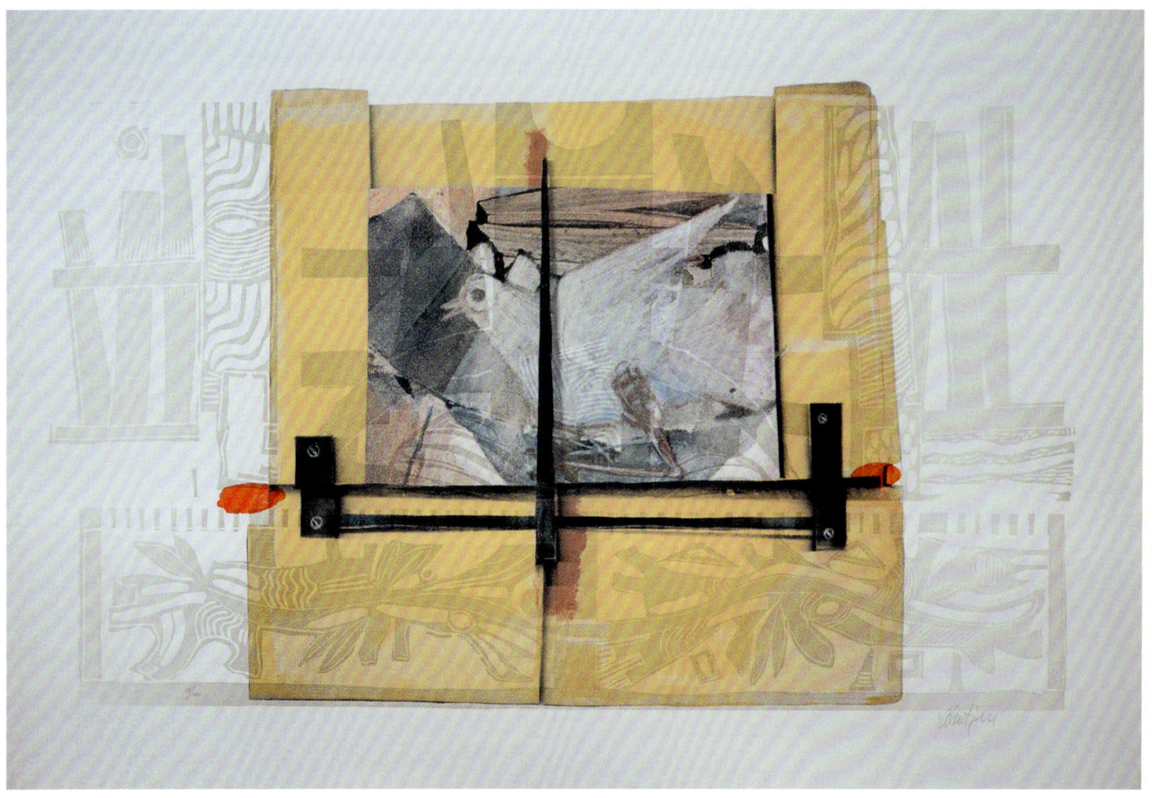

Finestra da aprire (Window to Open), 1992. Woodcut lithograph, 63 × 90 cm. Collection of USC Aiken. Photograph by Michael St. John.

us that Livio produced numerous sculptures in forged iron. Here the viewer is left to contemplate if and at what point escape is possible.

The *Nido* (Nest) yields a sort of printer's secret. Certainly, the golden tones of grasses and leaves remind us of a well-built nest. But hidden along the left side is the lower body and legs of the same dove. Clearly Valentini is challenging the viewer to a hunt for the ethereal dove.

Uccello nel nido (Bird in the Nest) is much more than a peaceful nature study. One notices the womb-like oval nest and within it the shape of the egg. In contrast to that life force, Livio stressed the theme of imprisonment with the poor bird's legs bound up with bands. Notice the orange toned Buchenwald curve in this highly stylized example.

In another nod to the Church, *Spiritualita* (Spirituality) resembles shattered shards of stained glass. There are numerous layers of color and interpretation here like some Rorschach test of the celestial realm.

From the spiritual to the natural world, Valentini explored all varieties of experience. *L'alfiere del vento* (Standard Bearer of the Wind) captures the feeling of the

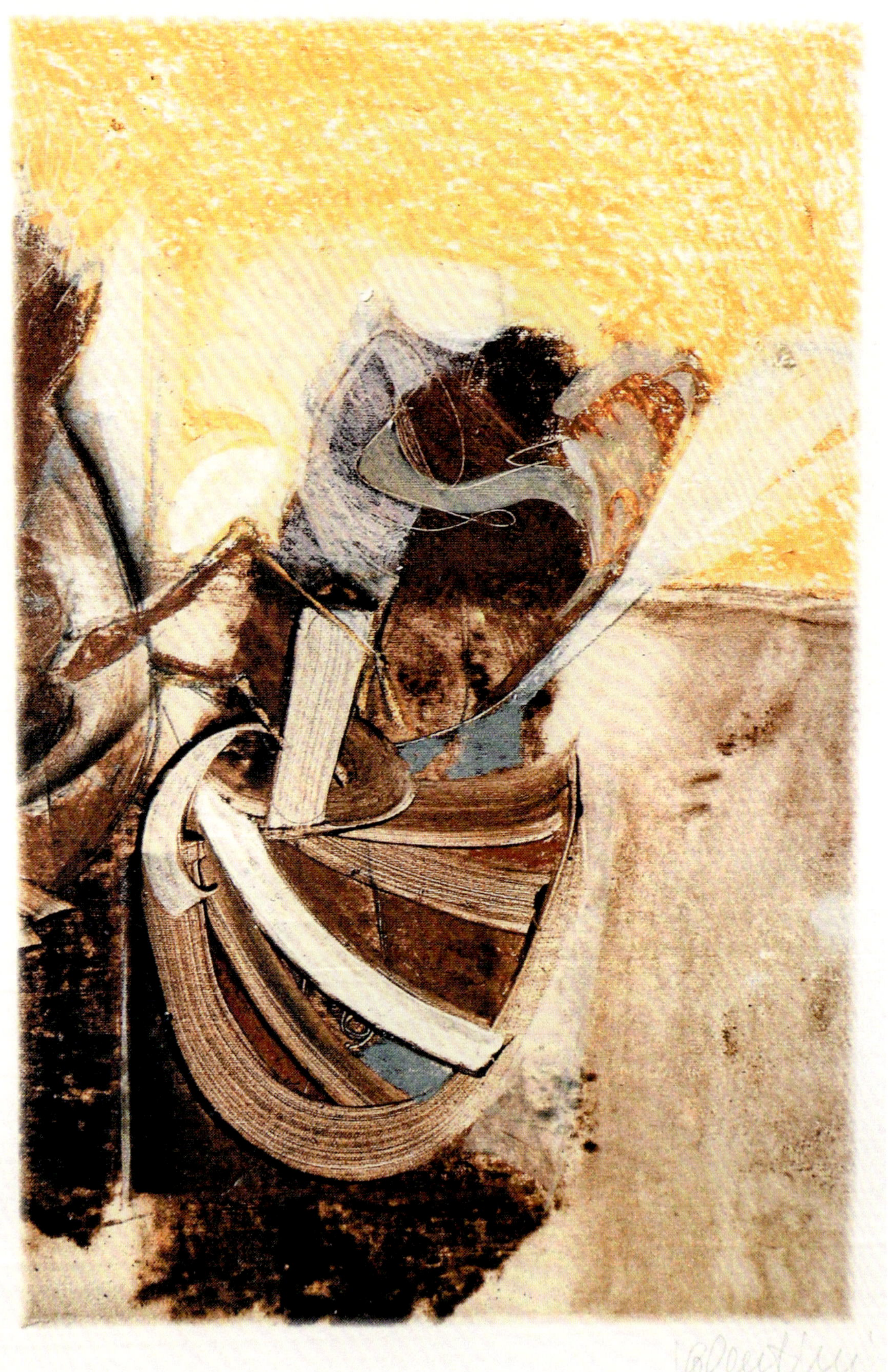

Nido (Nest), circa 1990s.
Lithograph, 70 × 50 cm.
Collection of USC Aiken.
Photograph by Michael St. John.

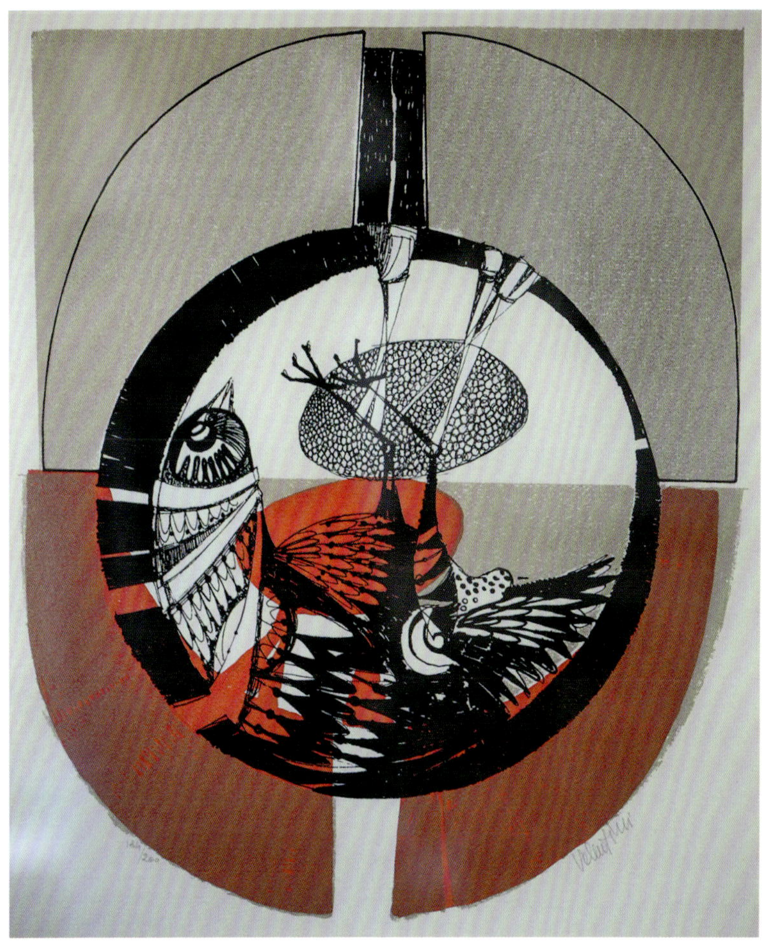

Uccello nel nido (Bird in Nest). Serigraph, 75 × 56 cm. Collection of USC Aiken. Photograph by Michael St. John.

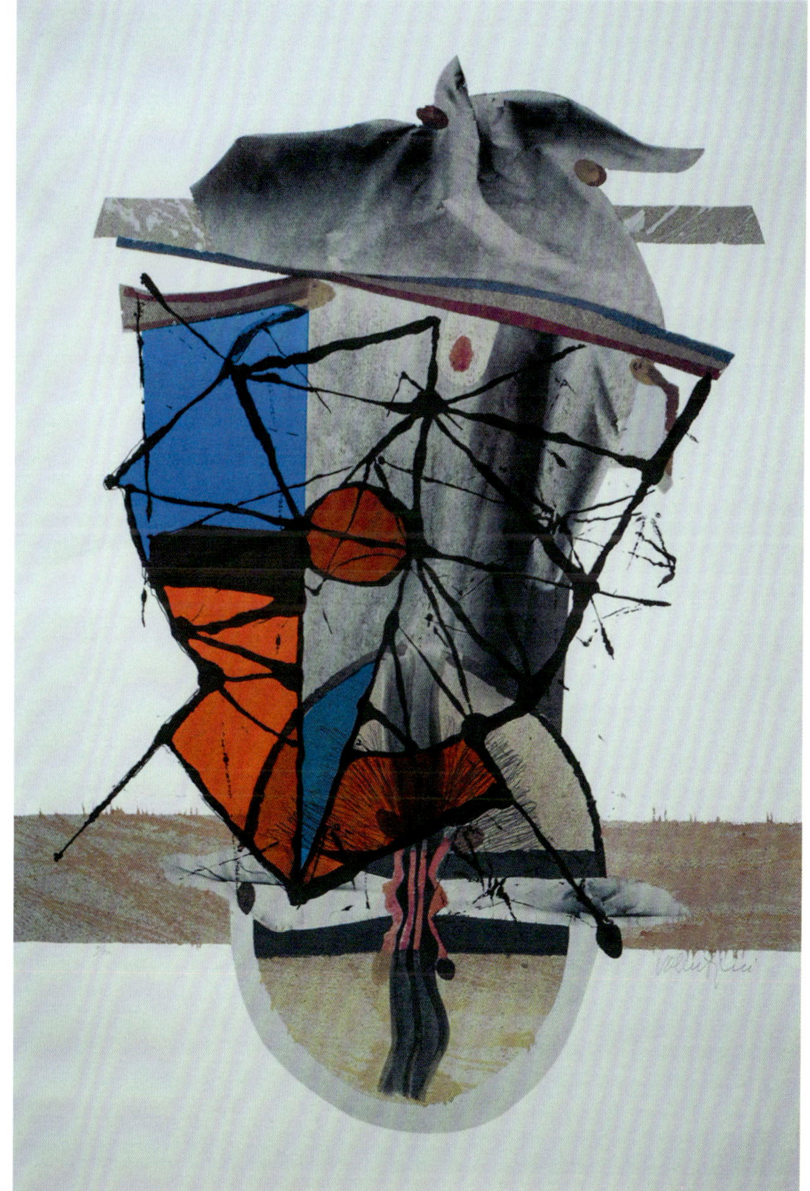

*Spiritualit*à (Spirituality), 1990s. Lithograph, 62 × 44 cm. Collection of USC Aiken. Photograph by Michael St. John.

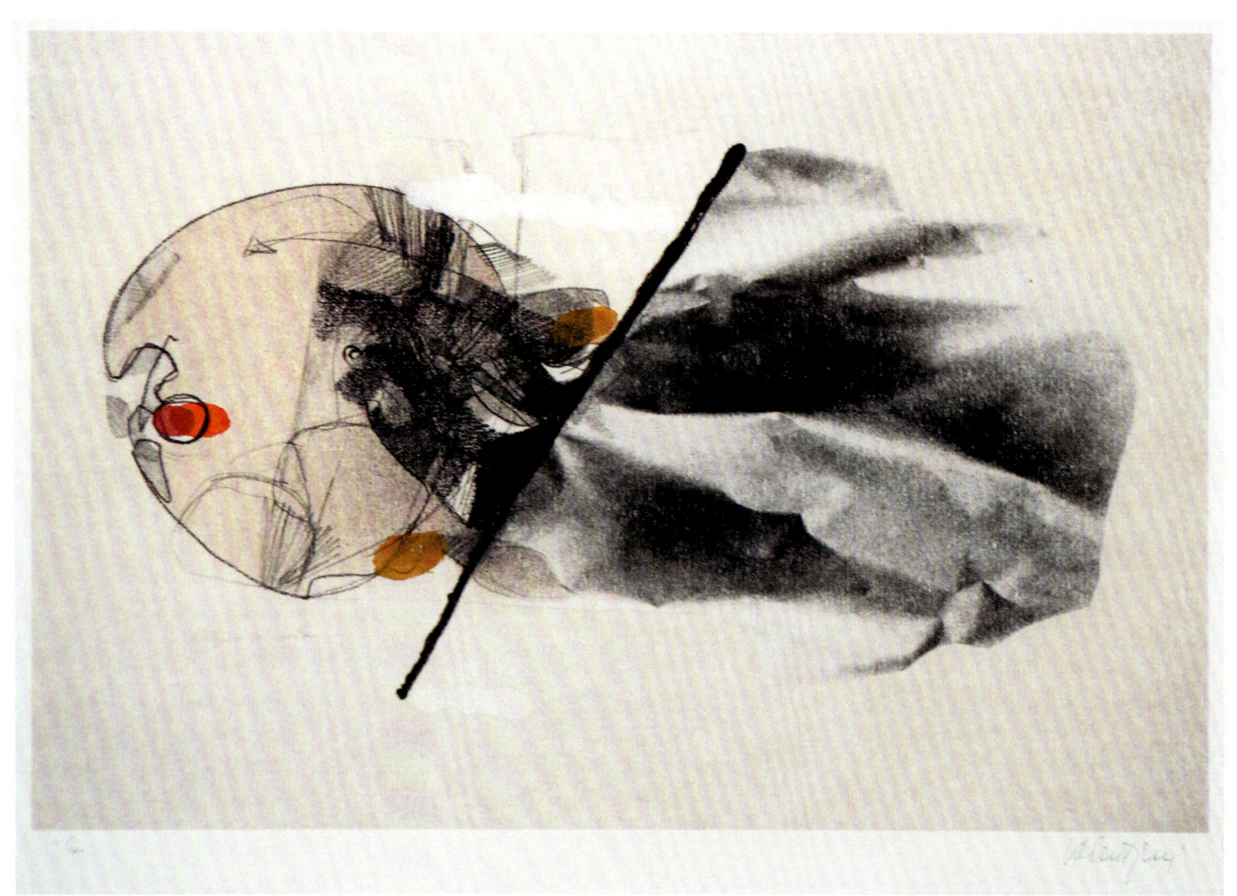

L'alfiere del vento (Standard Bearer of the Wind), 1995. Lithograph, 70 × 50 cm. Collection of USC Aiken. Photograph by Michael St. John.

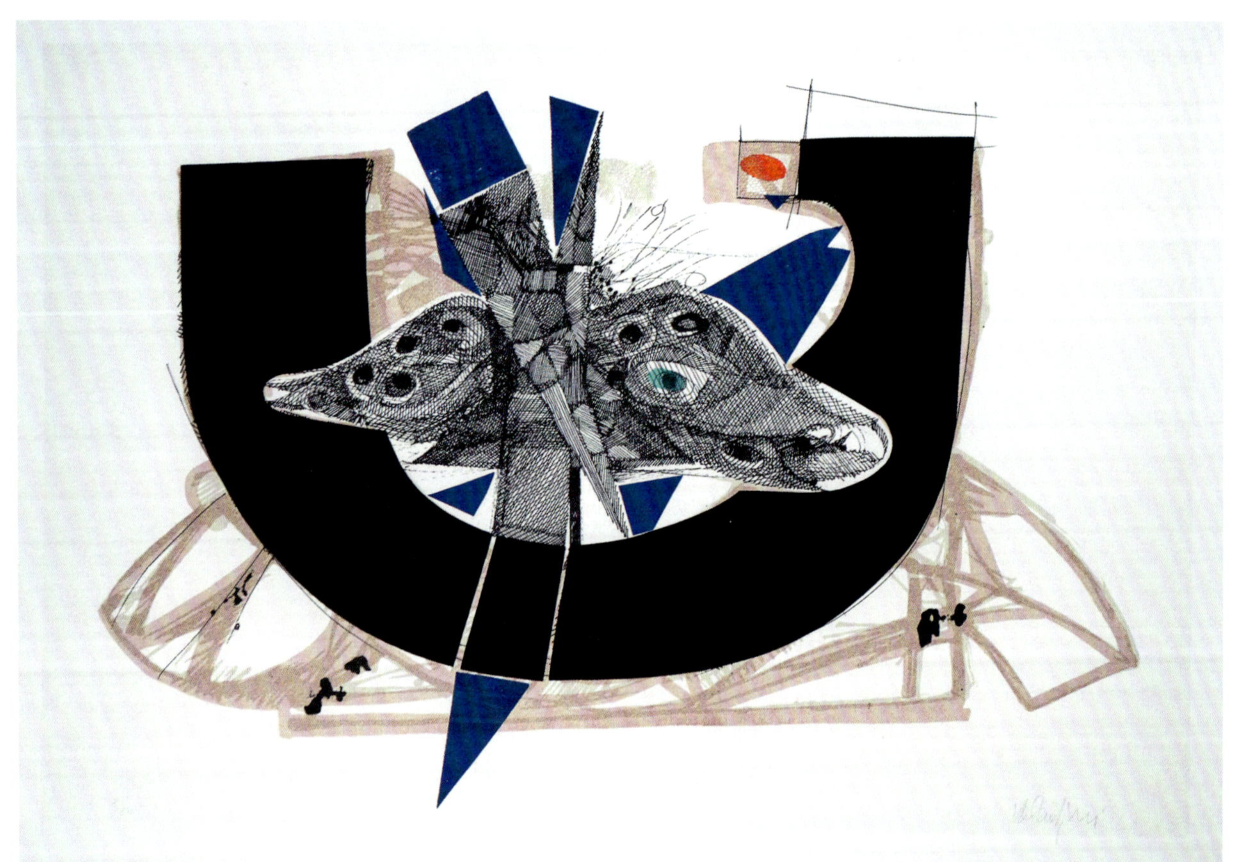

Farfalla notturna (Moth), 1994. Seriolithograph, 56 × 75 cm. Collection of USC Aiken. Photograph by Michael St. John.

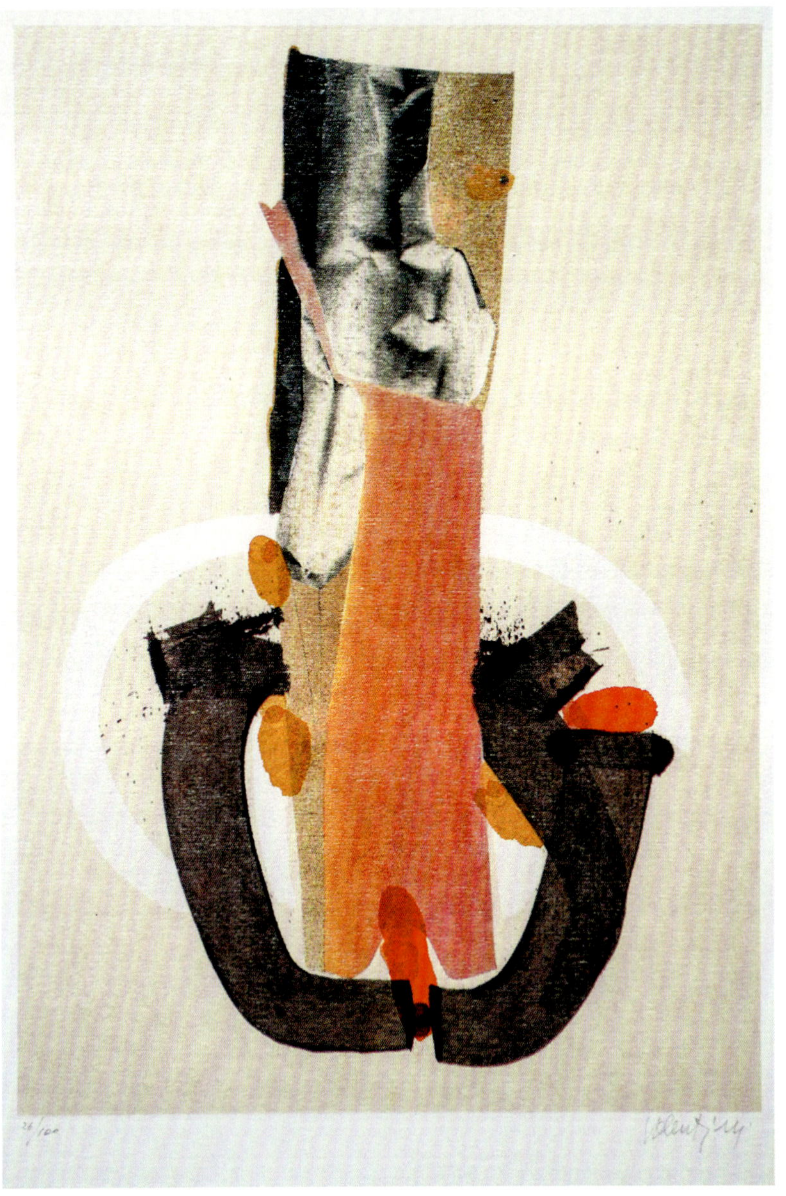

Germinazione No. 2 (Germination No. 2), 1996. Lithograph, 50 × 70 cm. Collection of USC Aiken. Photograph by Michael St. John.

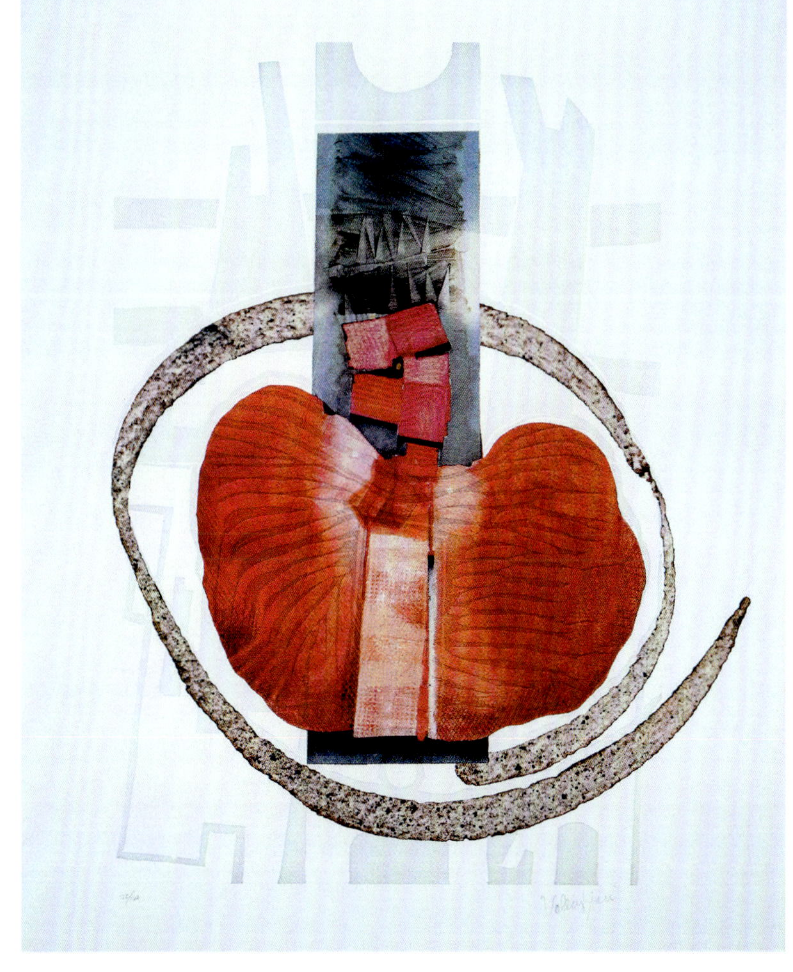

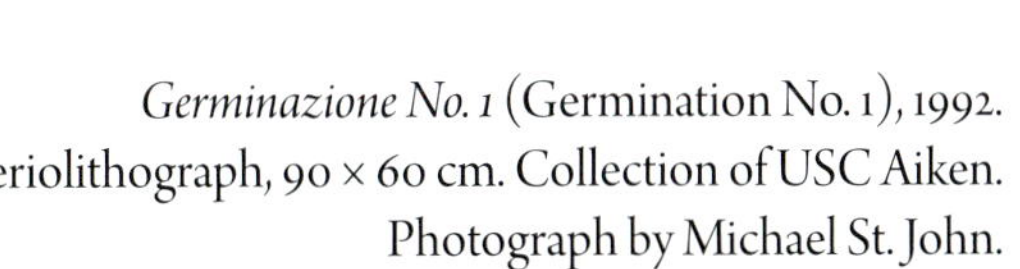

Germinazione No. 1 (Germination No. 1), 1992. Seriolithograph, 90 × 60 cm. Collection of USC Aiken. Photograph by Michael St. John.

flag-snapping breezes of Orvieto. When one lives on a precipice one thousand feet high, his art should take on the sensation of flight.

Similarly, *Farfalla notturna* (Moth) embraces the quiet in nature. With wings of filigree delicacy, this almost mythical sprite sparkles with peacock shades against the dark sphere.

From that same thematic ovoid shape, so many of Valentini's characters emerge triumphant. Three examples are the bird from the nest, the angel from the clouds, and finally the seed from the earth itself. In *Germinazione No. 2* (Germination No. 2), an orange stalk with the texture of crumpled paper rises skyward, again from the dark, rich, erupting earth. The same action occurs in *Germinazione No. 1* (Germination No. 1) against a background of subtly shaded architecture. In this case the seed, walled around by a stone colored, nest-like band, seems to throb with nascent life itself. This shape continuously evolves as we observe, at one point resembling a human heart, or is it a pair of lungs? And as if to remind us to remember the spirit, what might be the Crown of Thorns materializes at face level of the trunk. For Valentini both the breath of life and the conquest of death rise from the same sacred source.

In *L'angelo* (The Angel) the main figure flies along on brilliant white wings before a background of Byzantine gold with ribbons twisting in the wind behind her. Livio individualized this print with two tiny drops of red, one directly overhead, and the other at the center of a large blooming flower in her hand. In addition oval bands of yellow and blue encircle the angel.

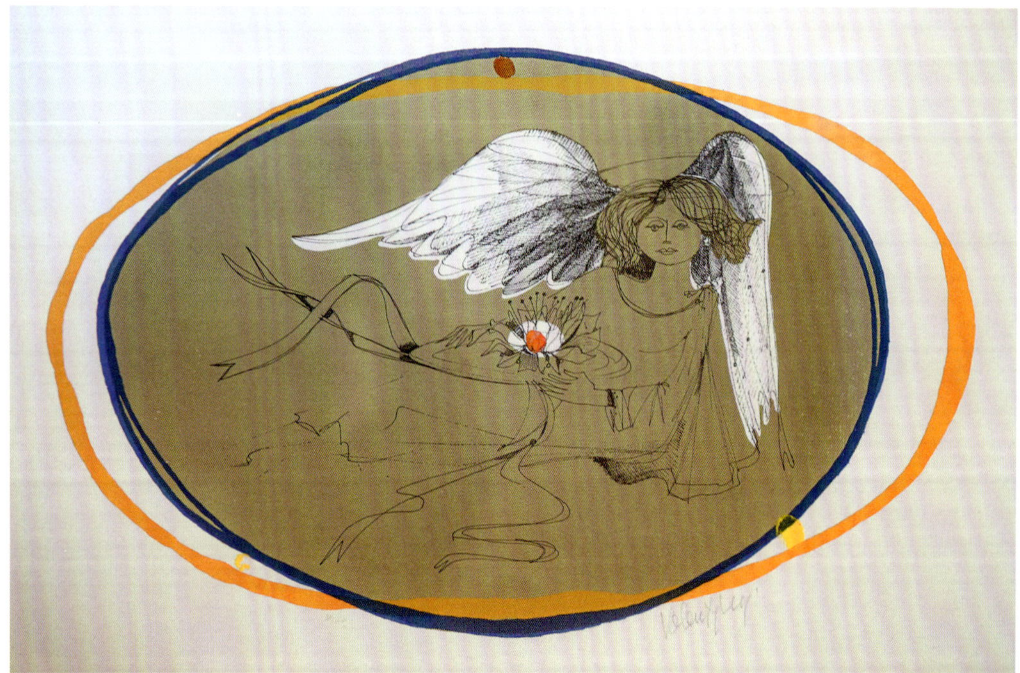

L'angelo (Angel), circa 1990s. Seriolithograph, 50 × 70 cm. Collection of USC Aiken. Photograph by Michael St. John.

Several of Livio's paintings including *The Places of the Spirit* were reproduced on wine labels as a part of an annual fundraiser for Partners in Friendship. For a number of years Partners contracted with distributors for bulk orders of specific white and red Italian wines and labeled them with local designs featuring the Aiken-Orvieto relationships. These efforts raised impressive sums of money to provide scholarships for the high school exchanges between Orvieto and Aiken.

Always generous of spirit, it was satisfying to see Livio interact with his admirers although it required planning on our part to ensure a translator was at his side. At a lecture on campus Livio explained, "I already know three words in your language: *grazie* (thank you very much), *buon giorno* (hello) and *bella* (beautiful) and that's it!" Livio offered a metaphor for himself and his art, "I am like a bird, a migrating bird, lit by an idea, a human and cultural idea. And so therefore it's not necessary to know your [English] language but to be just simply human. And to be able to communicate beauty and aesthetics and culture."[4]

Livio's tiny knowledge of English and ours of Italian was a constant concern. To help remedy the lack of Italian on our part the university introduced a series of classes to our foreign language curriculum taught by Silvia Powledge. There were times when Livio's lack of English resulted in humorous situations. At one of his first public lectures to a group of grade school students, George Custodi had prepared Livio with a few English phrases. Erika Bizzarri introduced him to the children and his first word to them was "goodbye"—nice and loud. Erika and George jumped in to explain to him and the confused children the difference between hello and goodbye. After all, in Italian *ciao* can mean either hello or goodbye. So he began again, "Hello!" His tales of being an artist from so far, far away enchanted the children.[5]

As part of his outreach during his first time in Aiken, Livio taught his ceramic techniques to middle and high school classes and demonstrated his painting style for university and continuing education classes. Speaking at his first lecture on our campus in November of 1997, a guest inquired as to what those now well-known dots represented. Erika Bizzarri translated for Livio that night, "He discovered that if you draw simply one line on a piece of paper, that line is not fixed, it sort of wanders around. Until you put a spot of color on it, which in a sense nails it down, gives it a key pivotal point on which to center your attention. And once he discovered that, he put the dots everywhere!" Livio laughed as he told this story.

He then went on to discuss how he borrowed images from the cathedral. Erika translated, "Those are my dots and Signorelli was doing dots about five hundred

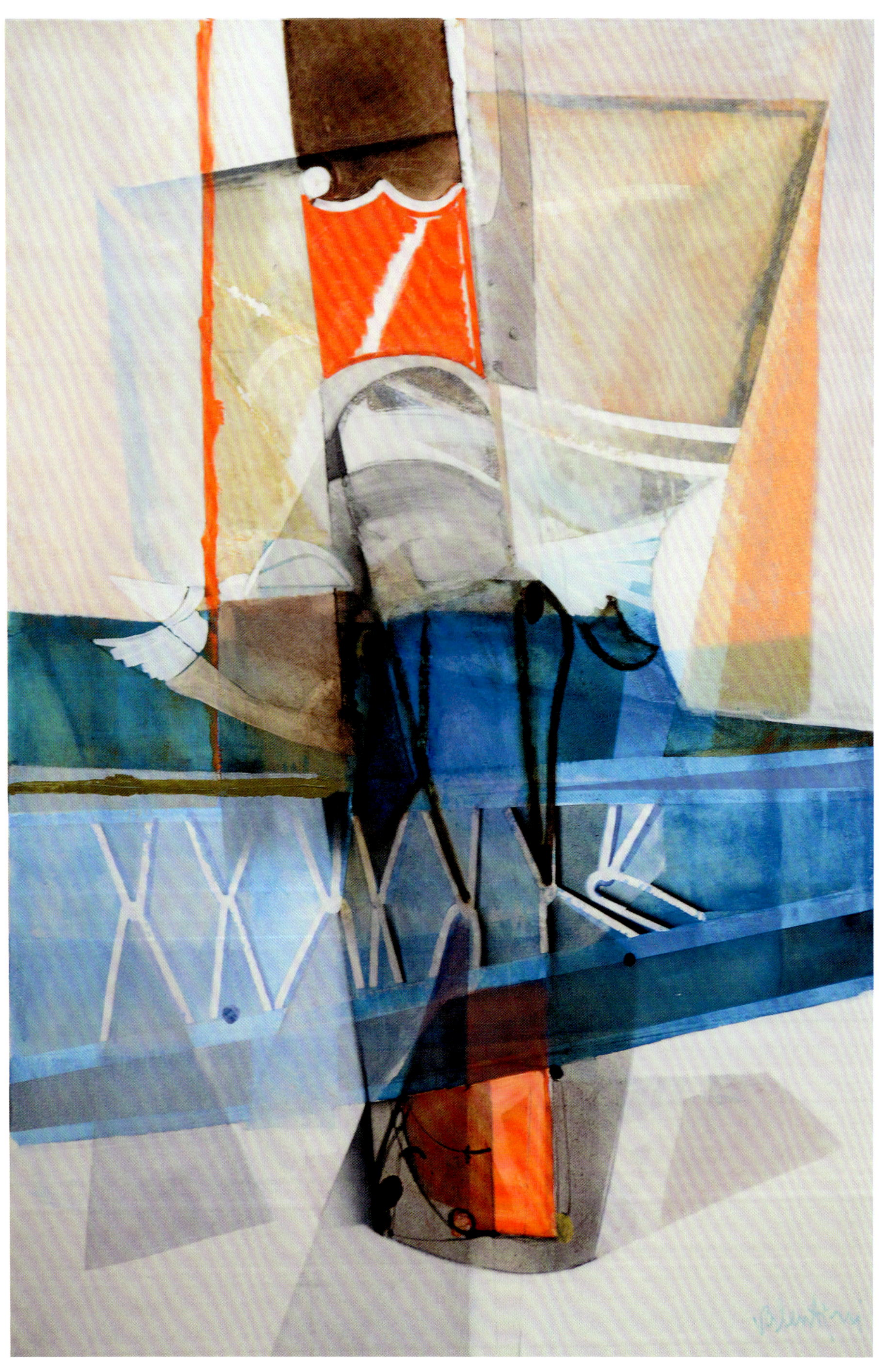

Odissea, 1997. Acrylic on canvas, 152 × 102 cm. Collection of USC Aiken. Photograph by Michael St. John.

years ago." She added, "Signorelli and Livio both have that same mastery of design or draftsmanship which ties them together. They both commented on the world around them. I think you'll see that in the exhibition."[6]

One of the last acts Livio performed before returning to Italy was to present the title piece *Odissea* to the university's permanent collection. This painting is in his recent, almost surrealistic style with a copper-colored tube projecting vertically through the plane; one notices a light effect highlighting its shape. Just behind it is a metallic cutout studded with tiny screws. The vertical copper tube conflicts with a swath of vibrant blue sweeping from side to side. Everywhere Livio scattered his painted dots in black, white, yellow, and blue, some solid, some transparent.

Among such vivid colors and shapes one still must rely on *dietrologia,* searching for the deeper meaning of his *Odissea.* Only on closer examination can one detect the ethereal wings of his spiritual bird fluttering about the abstract shapes. It helps to remember that Livio came from a city with ancient roots reaching back to the Etruscans, who practiced augury, the belief that the actions of birds could reveal the future. In a unique bit of contemporary augury, a yellow and gray bird crashed into our own rose window in the gallery just before the Valentinis first arrived. For long after, the dusty shape of the bird's wings remained illuminated on the glass. One wonders how the Etruscans would have interpreted such an omen. Certainly Livio and Flora were astonished when Jane Schumacher walked them upstairs to view the clear shadow of outspread feathery wings still shining through the glass. Flora asked if the bird had fallen. "Is it dead?" Jane said, "Yes . . . it happened about a month ago," to which Livio responded, "*misterioso*" (mysterious).[7]

Finally, as reminder of his imprisonment, bound into that blue banner is a band of barbed wire. This gentle man could not help but reveal the haunting shapes from those years of oppression. Every painting by Valentini serves as a form of self-portraiture and we are fortunate to have *Odissea* in our permanent collection. It now hangs in the Etherredge Center downstairs gallery.

In one of his many lectures on campus, Livio explained that the original title of this work was the *Odyssey of Technologies,* concerning contemporary technologies brought about by science and used by man, rapidly consumed with such greed until they are no longer needed, but obsolete. Livio said, "This is a philosophy not simply visual but intellectual. The painter interprets, and therefore creates a document of history, a narration of what's going on in the world about you. So art always has to belong to the period of history when it's being produced. His colleagues, fellow artists who had not yet understood this importance, said you'd better go be a barber because you've got a brush and when you use it, you'll even earn some money." Livio laughed and said "*scherzo*." Erika, translating, said, "He's joking, of course, but you know that."[8]

At the grand gala, Livio said, "Contemporary man has his odysseys. In my personal situation, coming to America has been my own. It's a tiring journey with sacrifices involved. It has been a real trip with Elliott and friend, Georgio Custodi, and also my wife. But it's been a joyous voyage and this gala bears witness to my odyssey."[9]

A significant number of Livio's works were purchased during the time of the exhibit at the university. Later faculty members from the art department were able to establish an arrangement for the remaining paintings and sculptures to be placed in a local art gallery.

It just so happened that the *Odissea* exhibit overlapped with another long-planned event in the Etherredge Center. The university had agreed to display several panels from *The NAMES Project AIDS Memorial Quilt.* Richard Maltz had written an original composition to be performed in the theater accompanied by a special slide show choreographed by Elliott. We didn't intend to involve the Maestro at the time, but when Livio learned about the event, he volunteered to participate. That evening as the crowd exited the theater, USCA students began reading aloud from the list of names. The audience found that *Trofeo,* one of Livio's large paintings, had been draped in a dark cloth, put into "mourning." A printed sign indicated his support for the cause. Erika told us if he had known about the event in advance he might have produced an original composition for the occasion. This generous reaction illustrated the Maestro's great sensitivity to the student body and confirmed our initial idea that we needed to bring him back to the university as an artist in residence.

In the summer of 1999, following the Italian delegation's visit and the *Odissea* show, Liz Benton, the chairperson for the tourism committee for Partners in Friendship, arranged for a small group from Aiken to visit Orvieto and the surrounding areas. The primary purpose of the trip was to demonstrate a commitment to an ongoing exchange with Aiken's partner city. Additionally this trip provided the opportunity for the chancellor to negotiate with Livio to serve as artist in residence. For several of us it was our first trip to Italy. Liz and her husband Rick did an outstanding job of ensuring the entire trip exceeded our expectations.

Our home base was the Locanda Rosati, an agriturismo inn on a hill several kilometers outside of Orvieto. Driving down to the city, Orvieto suddenly appeared out of the clouds like an eerie space ship. At an agriturismo the vegetables and most other foods served to the guests are produced on the property or on farms in the vicinity. This restored farm villa, owned by Giampiero Rosati and his sister Alba, demonstrated the best practices of Italian hospitality. The communal evening meals were always a feast including antipastos, pastas, numerous vegetables, and a variety of meats such as rabbit, lamb, guinea, and beef. For the vegetarians, there were pizzas, omelets, and quiche. Generous amounts of local red and white wines were always served. We spent many enjoyable evenings around these tables after long days visiting the surrounding areas of Umbria and Tuscany.

The first several days were spent touring Orvieto and meeting with many of the members of the delegation who had visited Aiken. Of course the first stop was Livio's gallery, located on Via Maitani across from his painting studio, where we spent time with Livio and his wife, Flora. It was here we also met his daughter Silvia who, when not working at school, frequently helped manage the gallery. A highlight of the trip was the exploration of the Etruscan underground caves and the necropolis located at the bottom of the cliffs. Claudio Bizzarri, an archaeologist and anthropologist, led these excursions. He has done much work in making the underground areas accessible to tourists. He is the son of our friend and translator Erika Pauli Bizzarri. His father and great-great-grandfather did significant work on the Etruscan culture. Claudio and his wife, Alba Frascarelli, later taught at the University of South Carolina Aiken as visiting professors in the spring of 2000.

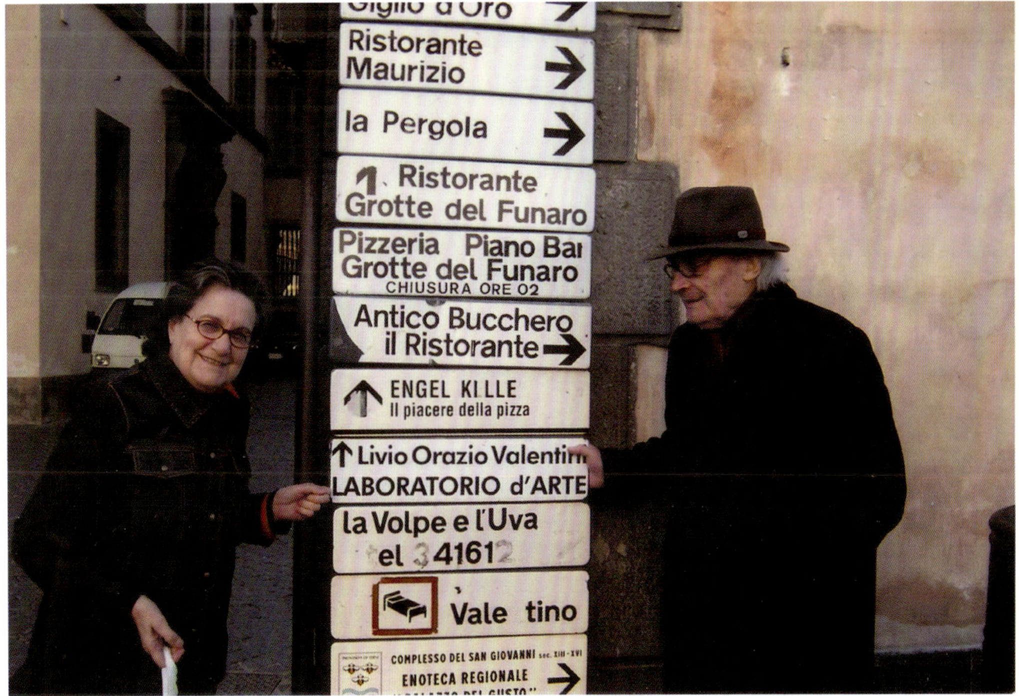

Flora and Livio Valentini in Orvieto at the time he was invited to become artist in residence for USCA. Photograph by Bob Alexander.

Excursions included trips to the hill towns of Umbria and Tuscany. We visited Assisi, known as the holiest hill town in recognition of St. Francis, Italy's patron saint. In Florence we saw many of the art treasures of the Renaissance masters. We drove to Civita di Bagnoregio, the ancient city on a hill, isolated by earthquakes in the seventeenth and eighteenth centuries. Nearby we visited Bolsena to see the church where the Miracle of Bolsena occurred as well as the volcanic lake. On the drive to Siena we toured the famous Piazza del Campo where the Palio horserace is held twice a year and continued on to Monteriggioni, whose medieval walls still stand. We travelled by train to Rome where we toured many historic landmarks and museums. Of course we visited other Tuscan hill towns famous for Italy's best-known wines. Many members in our group thought these days were the best part of the entire trip.

Our mode of transportation was a fifteen-passenger van with an Italian driver coordinated by Rick Benton who spoke some Italian with a southern accent. Rick gave the driver a typed schedule for each day. According to Rick this was a unique concept for the driver who was used to "winging his way." There were moments when none of us, including Rick, had a clue whether his best efforts had really communicated the intended message. We usually arrived at our destinations after a certain amount of excitement including missed turns and circuitous routes.[10]

When one explores the projects Livio undertook during his early years, it is clear he developed relationships with the businesses located near his studio. He created paintings for the Caffè del Corso, the Ristorante Maurizio, and the Trattoria Etrusca, and in more recent years, a large number of his sculptures and paintings were installed in the Hotel Duomo. Naturally in such a neighborhood, the Maestro established a system of patronage with his fellow businessmen. As an example of Livio's commercial cunning, he designed a special menu cover for the Ristorante Maurizio. He portrayed an angel amusingly presenting a platter of spaghetti and meatballs. This is only one of many such clever designs.

Adjacent to Livio's gallery was the Trattoria Etrusca, owned by his friend Giovanni Massaccesi, who collected the Maestro's art by bartering meals with him. Livio had a seemingly unending account. In this restaurant we successfully negotiated the arrangement for him to serve as artist in residence at the university. Bob and Leslie were Livio's guests, accompanied by Flora, the Bentons, and Erika Bizzarri who translated the discussions and the formal documents. Of course nothing of a serious nature was discussed until we dined. Livio ordered for everyone. The meal included porcini white sauce over *umbricelli,* a local type of pasta, followed by roasted vegetables and grilled lamb chops drizzled with extra virgin olive oil. What a way to negotiate! We reached an agreement for him to come in the fall to teach classes across the curriculum and to do demonstrations in the public schools as well as lectures throughout the community. In addition the university provided a private studio for his personal work and assisted him in obtaining commissions.

Livio's arrival on October 1, 1999, was auspicious to say the least. The university found exactly the right place for him to stay during his extended time as artist in residence. Barbara Sue and Brad Brodie generously offered their guesthouse which featured a Charleston-style porch opening onto a nice garden with huge oak trees. A welcoming committee had prepared the house for his arrival. The beds were made, the kitchen was stocked with some of his favorite foods, and a new espresso coffee pot with a tin of Italian coffee awaited his enjoyment. A variety of Italian wines and cheeses were laid in for his daily use. Livio's flight from Rome to Atlanta was scheduled for deplaning around 4 PM. Accounting for the time for getting through customs, he should have been in Aiken by 7:30. The committee had decided to gather at the cottage around 7 PM to welcome him with a light dinner.

John Elliott and George Custodi were commissioned to meet Livio in Atlanta and drive him to Aiken. They called to say the plane had arrived on schedule and as soon as Livio cleared customs they would be leaving. The second call explained there was a slight problem because of the language barrier. George was finally allowed to meet

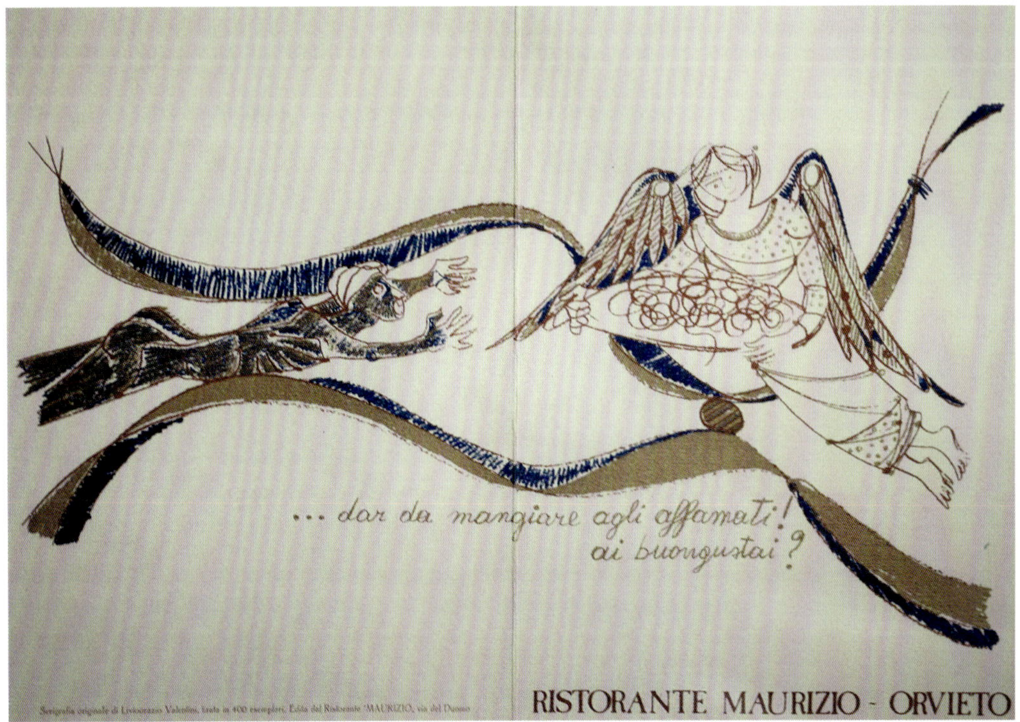

Angel with Platter of Spaghetti and Meatballs, on the menu of Ristorante Maurizio, Orvieto, 1982. Silk screen, 25 × 35 cm. Collection of Jack and Janet Morris. Photograph by Michael St. John.

Livio and help with translating. The third call indicated a problem with the luggage. After a long hiatus and after the welcoming committee had gathered at the cottage, the fourth call had a more panicked tone. It seemed some of his luggage either had been lost or stolen between customs and the luggage carousel. Eventually after filing a claim for lost luggage, Livio and company left for Aiken. They reached the guesthouse around 10:30 PM.

Exhausted and frustrated, Livio was finally in Aiken. Unfortunately his one missing bag contained all of his art slides and lecture notes. Livio was most upset because the bag also contained his cheeses, sausages, and wine. He had carried it with him for the entire trip until the point when he rechecked his luggage for the claims terminal. Livio remembered a "very pretty young woman who had x-rayed the bags and insisted he put it on the conveyor belt." It never arrived at the other end.

The committee members helped him get settled in the cottage. We shared some of the prepared food and said our good nights. Livio was left to wonder what was next for him in the great adventure he had undertaken in Aiken. Bob arranged to take him to

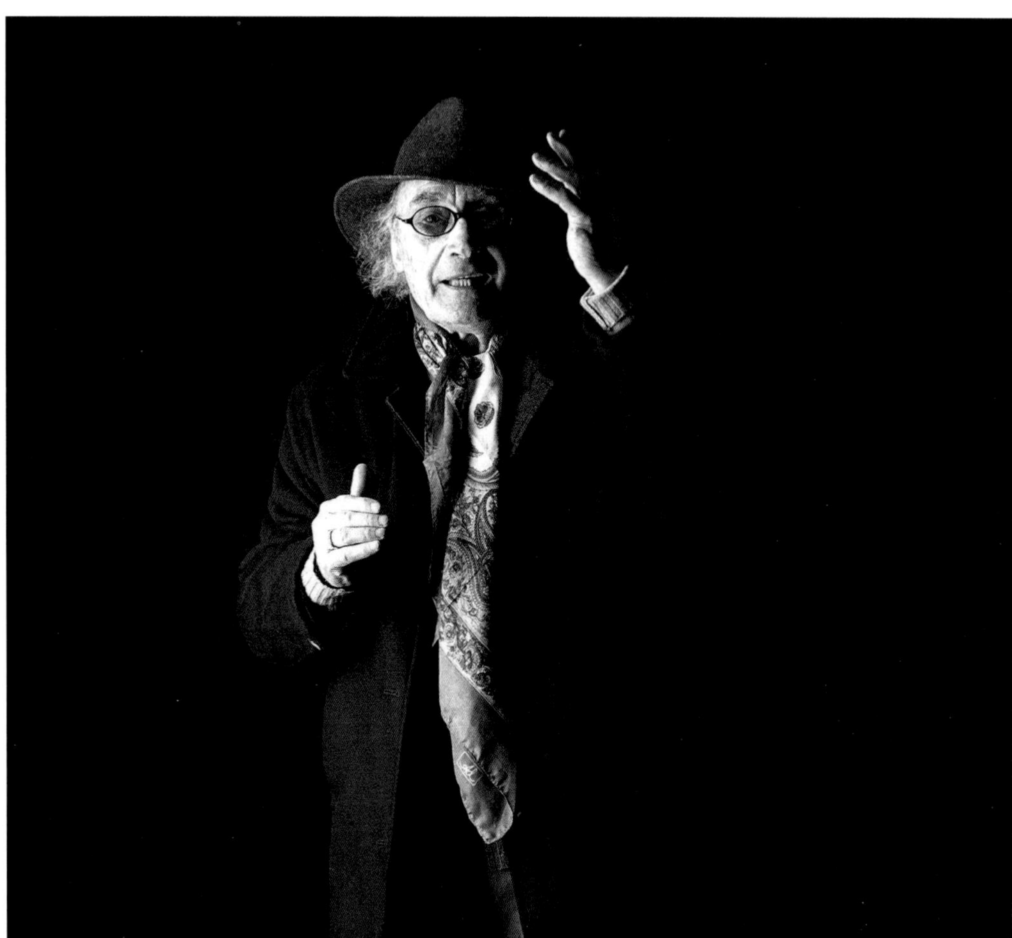

Livio with glasses, hat, and scarf. Photograph by Giancarlo Pancaldi. Photograph courtesy of the Valentini family.

the university the next morning. The first failure in communication dealt with the exact time of departure. Arriving at 8:00 AM, Bob started a pot of coffee and waited at least thirty minutes before knocking on Livio's bedroom door. Livio was shocked to see Bob but he got up and had some coffee and pastries. Eventually they left for the university and Livio told Bob he was not accustomed to getting up at such an ungodly hour. Ten o'clock was more to his liking. Even though his cottage was two blocks from Bob's home, we made other arrangements for him to get to campus.

John assumed the major duty of transporting Livio to the university. Livio was always late and frequently misplaced items such as his satchel, watch, glasses, his sketchpad, or his hat. Every day with Livio involved transportation to and from his university art studio, scheduling his meals, and preparing him for any upcoming social events. It quickly became clear we were going to need to expand our Italian vocabulary, especially with terms specifically oriented to the arts. This evolved into what John called the "*come si dice*?" ("How do you say?") game. Livio had invested in the tiniest English/Italian dictionary as a gift for him. One day John attempted a conversation in his broken Italian and Livio gave him a curious look. Haltingly John said that when he encountered a phrase he didn't know in Italian, he substituted something from his undergraduate studies of ancient Latin. "That explains it," Livio exclaimed. "Now I know why you talk like Julius Caesar!"

Many others in the community pitched in from time to time to shuttle Livio back and forth. Sandi Custodi, Silvia Powledge, Tamara Cannon, Jane Schumacher, and Mary Alice Lockhart were prominent among the community members who generously served as his chauffeur. Livio epitomized a stereotypical absent-minded professor and demonstrated the typical Italian disinterest in time.

Several years later, Silvia Powledge, an Italian and Spanish faculty member and his primary local translator, had a similar problem with a unique twist when she went to pick up Livio at the Carriage House Inn. "There was a fountain in the courtyard right in front of his room. As normal he had forgotten something and he had to keep going back in. He came out . . . 'finally, I'm ready to go' . . . put his hat on, then his scarf. And when he heard the fountain, he said, 'Oh, no. I have to pee. That noise makes me have to go . . . now I have to go back.'"[11]

One morning John picked up Livio from his downtown apartment. It was autumn and the gardener had just planted a bed of pansies beside the entrance. A comment was made to the Maestro about the beautiful flowers. Livio's face grew dark and he paused and said, "They planted those in the concentration camp. I always wondered why they would feed the flowers but not feed us." Being in the presence of such a man every day brought a new opportunity for learning about remembrance and compassion.

Livio inevitably received a warm reception as our students and Aiken residents gradually came to know him. "I'm here at the university and I do not speak your language but I speak with everyone, because there is a kind of gesticulating for Italians, there is the ability to draw and paint and there is humanity and spirit and sentiment. We have in our language many things that help us to communicate."

On October 7, 1999, Livio spoke to the Town and Country Club at the Etherredge Center. In a moment of candor Livio shared personal memories of his incarceration:

> In the extermination camps, when the body suffered from hunger and did not want to respond, there was no joy; all the sentiments were basically a flat line. So I understood you don't die from starvation, from lack of food. You die before that, you die before hunger kills you. You die because you have lost all of your emotions, all of your feelings.
>
> A person becomes like a desolate desert. There is nothing left that is pretty to look at. It's worse than hunger. Therefore, having experienced that, I understand very well a person doesn't need anything. I don't need money; I don't need food. But I need feeling and emotion; that is the food of life, of the soul. Many times emotions are confused, and are substituted by vices, by food, by drink, by all these things that are not necessary. I was fortunate enough to have survived this trial.

Once again came the familiar metaphor, "I was like a bird going across the ocean, who finds his place and begins his life, without knowing if someone will give him money or work. All the things we need, we have within ourselves. We have it within our feelings and that is happiness." Livio's personal artistic odyssey was expanding to involve all of us who knew him. Everyone at the university and those who met him about town learned to embrace this dear seeker of freedom with his remarkable collection of illuminating artworks.[12]

Livio went on to say, "This group is composed entirely of women, which for me is a very unique experience. It demonstrates that a group of women is more beautiful than a group of men." This brought laughter and applause. "Certainly more desirable, more charming. You have real substance, particularly as women who are active and want to understand life. You speak together about your problems and therefore are a vital form of humanity. I am honored to be among you."[13]

Livio explained to them why he was using actual prints rather than projected images for his presentation. "In my adventure of coming to Aiken I lost a piece of luggage which had my CDs with all of the images of my works, so you cannot see them today. If a miracle happens, you might be able to see them later. I'm very upset about this but we have to be patient." A miracle did happen and Flora was able to send duplicates of his CDs and copies of his lectures by Federal Express.[14]

One of our daily responsibilities was to coordinate his meals. Feeding Livio was always an adventure as we struggled with the language and came to understand his food preferences. On his first visit, a group of professors, foolishly, decided to take him to one of our local Italian restaurants. He ordered a selection featuring three different dishes and was quite surprised to have them all served on the same plate. He tasted all of them with curiosity but little comment. When we were finished he asked to speak to the chef. Somehow, again foolishly, we thought he intended to offer his compliments on the authentic cuisine. Instead it was necessary to delicately translate when he asked the poor man, "did you intend to make it taste that way?" This was our first and last visit to any Aiken Italian eatery with our distinguished gourmand.[15]

One of his favorite spots was a Chinese buffet on the south side of town. He loved their fresh vegetables, and he could see things before putting them on his plate. The worst part was when the bill arrived with fortune cookies. It was a nightmare trying to translate those "sayings of Confucius" with any Italian wit.

On one occasion a meal downtown inspired a Valentini original painting. A group of us from USCA took Livio to the Stoplight Deli and everyone ordered sandwiches. Each arrived with a wooden toothpick adorned with a plastic flower top. Livio was fascinated by this "only in America" decoration and asked to keep them. The result was *Lunch with Five Friends,* an abstract arrangement of table-top-like cubes. The longer Livio stayed in Aiken, the more inclined he was to experiment with mixed-media. Here the multi-colored pics are glued to the surface, a reminder of a special day at the deli.

Lunchtime was tricky and involved getting a quick meal for Livio and scurrying back for our afternoon classes. One Aiken restaurant he enjoyed was the Swan, a combination luncheonette and

Lunch with Five Friends, 1999. Oil and acrylic on paper, 100 × 70 cm. Collection of USC Aiken. Photograph by Michael St. John.

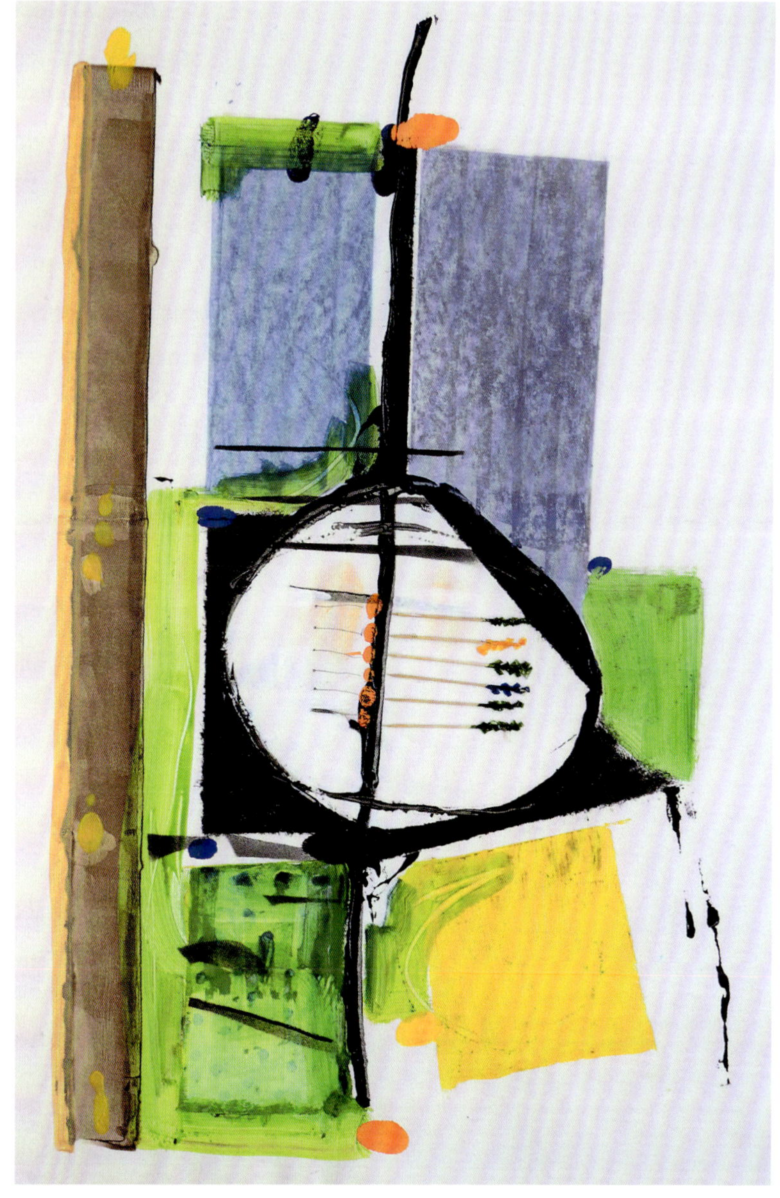

antique shop. They served an English menu, so he would start with *tè caldo* (hot tea). Then he usually was content with half a turkey sandwich and the soup of the day. One day he tried to converse with our young waitress. We explained to her he was an artist visiting from Orvieto. She piped in that some of her people were from Italy. "From where?" he inquired. She explained her great grandfather had come from Sicily. "Ah," he said, with an odd look on his face as she went to place our order. We asked him, "why the curious expression?" He simply said in English "cowboy," acting out the universal symbol for raised pistols. We realized he was referring to the common belief that the Mafia ruled Sicily, but he only mentioned it well beyond her earshot. Yet another English word we didn't realize Livio knew![16]

We were on the way to Augusta one evening for dinner when suddenly a huge rainstorm swept over the car. Out of nowhere and to the rhythm of the windshield wipers came a clear baritone voice singing: "Stormy weather"—in English! Livio, sitting in the rear seat, was smiling so proudly. One of us responded, "Livio, how do you know this song?" "From the radio," he explained. The automatic reaction was, "So Livio, all this time you've been able to speak perfect English?" "Yes," he laughed.

One day the chancellor and some art faculty took him to Bobby's, a famous barbecue restaurant. We promised Livio that the food was quintessential South Carolina cuisine. We did stop short of telling him it would be a gourmet dining experience. As you enter the restaurant one has to pay for the meal in advance. All of the food is on the buffet line. There was a substantial array of vegetables and starches as well as hash and at least two kinds of pork meat, pulled and chopped with Bobby's special sauce. The drill was to grab a paper plate and help yourself. We sat down at a long table in the huge dining room and encouraged Livio to sample all of his choices, which he gladly did. We feasted on some of the best barbecue and side dishes you will ever enjoy. Livio very carefully tasted each dish. He found the rice, the hash, and the pulled pork suited his tastes best and went back for more.

As we finished and were leaving, the owner, Bobby Griffin joined us and shared his secrets for cooking quality barbecue. In the course of the conversation he walked Livio over to a huge boar's head, which adorns the wall of the dining room. He asked Livio to reach up and touch the boar's chin. Livio did, only to have the tongue of this gruesome-looking animal drop out of its mouth into his hand. His first reaction was to jump back in alarm. Then he insisted on repeating the experience half a dozen times until most of the customers nearby were in tears from laughter at his clowning. Livio seldom went anywhere without showing his wonderful sense of humor.

On the trip back to campus Livio told us he really enjoyed the food but disliked being served on paper plates with plastic utensils and cups. He insisted we never take him anywhere to eat unless they used ceramic plates, metal utensils, and real glasses. He was adamant that food served any other way was not worth eating, a lesson none of us ever forgot.[17]

On the first night Bob invited Livio to his home for dinner. He had the audacity to fix a pasta dish. In addition to baked salmon and asparagus, followed with a salad in the Italian tradition, our first course was umbricelli pasta with a white porcini sauce. Livio sat in the kitchen sipping an Orvieto Classico wine while we prepared dinner. He was fascinated by our work on the salmon and salad. He took particular interest in the sauce for the pasta. In several instances he made what turned out to be excellent suggestions. Livio instructed that one should add red pepper flakes and dried rosemary to the olive oil and cook it on medium heat so their flavors infuse the oil before adding in the mushrooms and the white sauce. We have adopted and added to his suggestion over the years. The dramatic moment in the evening came when we removed the pasta from the stove and drained it in the sink. Bob's usual next step, according to how he had been taught by his mother, was to rinse the pasta to remove the excess starch. Livio leaped across the room shouting, "*Basta!! Basta!!*" He communicated through sign language that rinsing was not permitted because it destroyed the true taste. Taking his adamant advice we learned he was correct. Pasta should never be rinsed and the sauce adheres better if you add a cup of pasta water. One of the key lessons learned from our friendship with Livio and other Italians is to listen to their suggestions about cooking. Even an absent-minded Italian professor of art knows more about cooking pasta than the average American.[18]

Food played a central role in all of our lives during Livio's time in Aiken. The several years he spent at USCA were extremely busy with lots of dinner invitations and community social activities. Nearly everyone who met him sooner or later wanted to give a dinner party in his honor. One of the most memorable was at the home of David and Dorothy Ridley. It was a celebration of his art. As soon as the Ridleys became aware of his commitment to return to Aiken, they commissioned Livio to do a sizable painting for their living room. It was a grand evening with several guests invited to see the unveiling.

Dorothy Ridley made the following observations when asked about her relationship to Livio and his work. She commented on how they met:

> First of all we were members of Partners in Friendship and when they had the Odissea exhibit and reception, I was impressed with his art before I ever met him. I loved his

art, the way he took ancient themes and combined them with contemporary thought and expression, the way he handled the paintings from the Duomo and made them entirely different. So I was really impressed with his art. I met him again walking down Laurens Street. He was saying "*Bella, bella, bella*!" He was so cheerful and loved Aiken from the start. He was a very warm person and easy to get to know.

I'm always intimidated by someone who has such obvious talent. He was a man who lived well, loved life and was very proud of his accomplishments, proud of his contributions to the world of fine art. Of course there was the language problem because I speak no Italian and he spoke no English.

He was here twice for dinner. Because I felt comfortable and loved his art, I commissioned him to do a painting for us. I thought it was going to be just what I wanted, a lot of dead space. He had seen our house; he knew what we liked. He knew who we were so I was sure he was going to give me exactly what I wanted. When I received the painting in the mail, I was disappointed because it filled every inch of space with

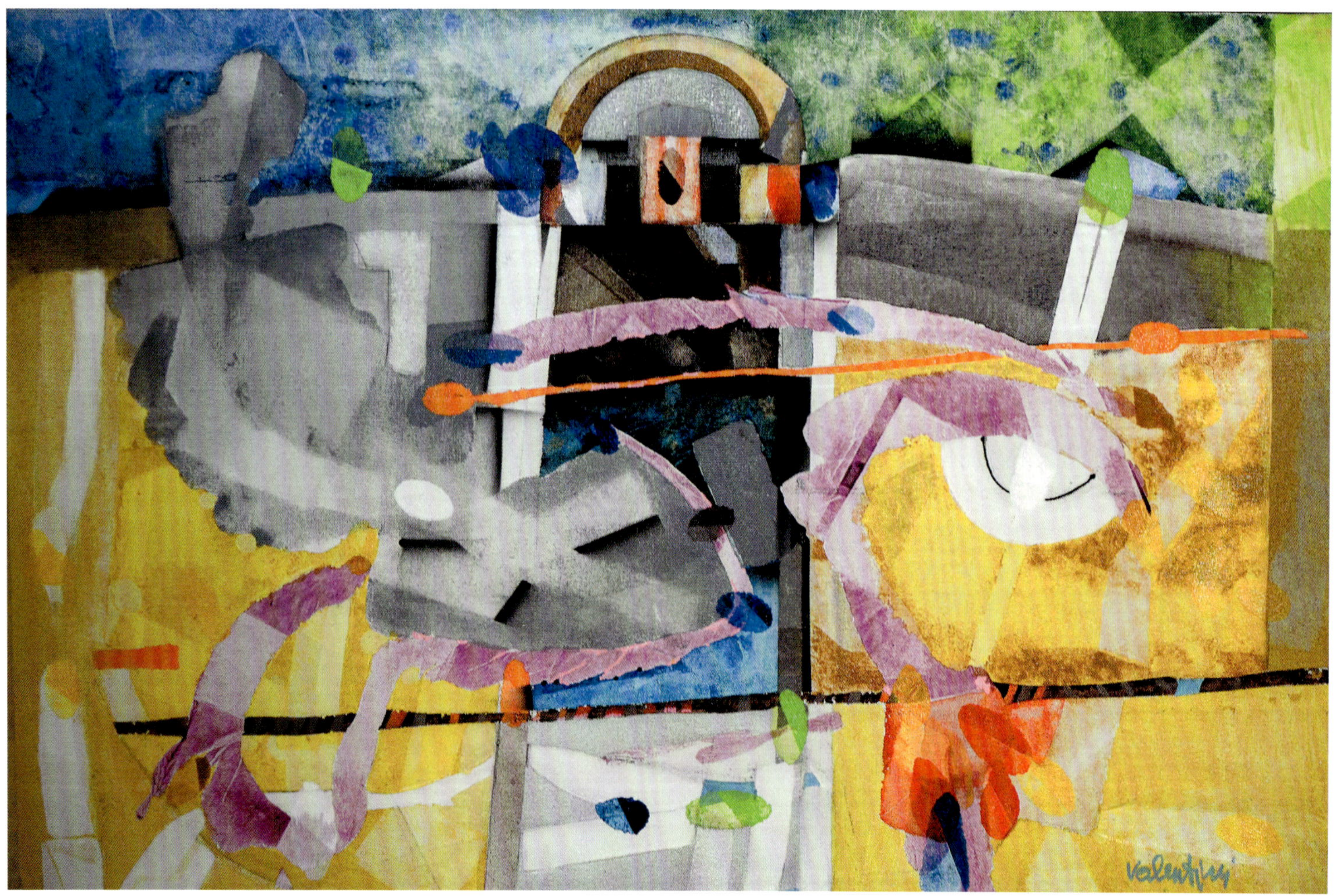

La valigia della felicità (Suitcase of Happiness), 2000. Mixed media on canvas, 61 × 91 cm. Collection of Dorothy Ridley. Photograph by Michael St. John.

> bright colors. It was a very contemporary piece and I had a real problem with it. He sent along a letter explaining the title, *La valigia della felicità* (Suitcase of Happiness). He said, "Aiken is just so happy. . . . I have to show a happy picture." So that's exactly what it is. It's sort of like a Matisse . . . filled with wonderful joyous color and actually, I have grown to like it a lot. But it took me some time . . . it wasn't so much that I didn't like the piece . . . he did not give me what I hoped for. That I'm sure was a result of poor communication.

This is a perfect example of what we can characterize as Livio's Aiken style. The canvas explodes with bold color: squares of sunny yellow and verdant green adorned with orbs of blue, orange and red. Livio's Aiken works are often self-referential with the artist visually quoting himself. This painting serves as a triptych in which on the lower right we spot the arrow and wafer from *The Places of the Spirit* and on the left the dove's wing from *Odissea*. But rising above all, atop the dark chasm at the center of the work, is a golden arch. Some interpreted this as a bridge, perhaps intended to honor Partners in Friendship.

Dorothy recalled, "He made some interesting comments about our house. He liked our contemporary décor, that it wasn't chintz and flowers. He said most people have a more traditional look. We don't, because I don't know how to create it. We're pretty black and white in our house and find it easy to live with."

That particular evening Livio gave a discourse on the purpose of art in private homes and the difference between good contemporary art and the "horse art" he had seen in so many homes in Aiken. Livio was never shy about expressing his feelings on this subject. One can only imagine the type of reactions he received to these statements. The various defenses and explanations of the value of realistic art focused on horses did not faze him. He indicated that part of his mission in Aiken was to educate the community toward a better appreciation of art and its value for the enrichment of our souls. On this particular evening he was surrounded by many disciples of his perspective. The painting was unveiled to an enthusiastic group with a very positive response.

As we moved to the dinner table the conversation continued along the same line of thought with some serious exchanges about why we valued art. There were alternating points of view: the first was the basic concept that liking a piece of art was sufficient reason to buy it; the second, grander, concept was that art transcends self-centeredness and causes one to reach out for a better understanding of one's place and purpose in the world. It was a conversation often repeated and expanded upon over the course of many

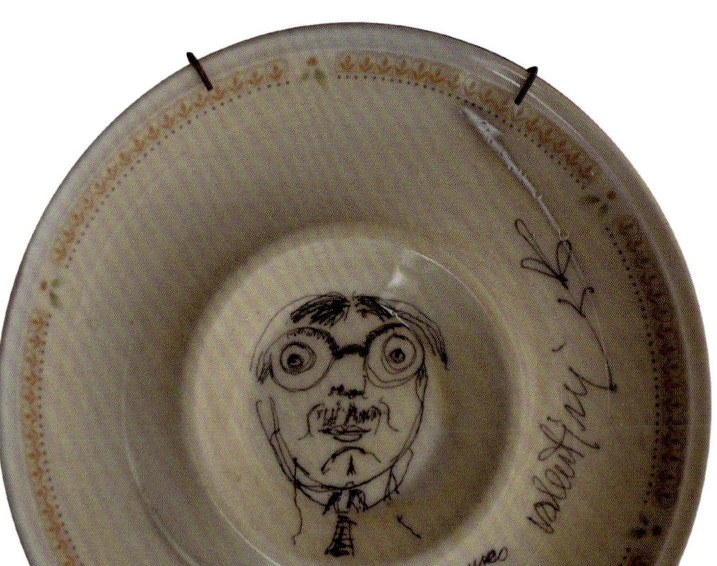

Livio's birthday sketch of Bob Alexander on Dorothy Ridley's tea saucer, 2000. Collection of Bob and Leslie Alexander. Photograph by Michael St. John.

evenings throughout the years. As we began coffee and dessert we noticed Livio had become quiet and was engrossed in drawing something on the bottom of his coffee cup saucer. We stopped and watched with amazement. He never looked up or said a word until he had finished his drawing. With a few deft strokes Livio had captured a very amusing caricature of Bob's professorial features: his glasses, trim moustache, shirt collar, and patterned tie. It's unclear why he made the then-chancellor look so wide eyed! Perhaps it was to record how surprised Bob was over the fuss that was being made over his sixtieth birthday? On the rim of the saucer, Livio wrote: "Per il tuo compleanno. Albero del tipo sempre verde" ("For your birthday. An evergreen tree"). Clearly Livio seemed impressed by Bob's youthful vitality!

Dorothy described the scene, "He was doodling on my saucer from my good china. I was trying to peek over to see what he was doing and thought 'Oh! That's alright it will wash off.' But I realized even if it would wash off there's no way I could do that. It would insult the Maestro as well as my wonderful guests. I was just sorry he didn't draw my portrait. I mean really, after all, I thought I was the pretty one in the group. But clearly he didn't see in me what he saw in Bob."[19]

He presented the birthday portrait to Bob with a "bit of fanfare" and said goodnight for the evening. We made our apologies to Dorothy and David with a polite laugh. Later, we offered to buy them a new saucer for their fine china but they generously declined. We kept the "portrait" for our Valentini collection.

On another occasion at Bob's home, when Livio saw a preliminary study for the official chancellor's portrait by noted artist Michael Shane Neal, he decided that the study did not resemble his good friend and resolved to do his own! The result is Livio's stylized and utterly abstract version of his friend Bob.

We are reminded of the story of Michelangelo Buonarroti when he was at work on the portraits of Lorenzo de Medici and his brother Giuliano. At the time these sculptures were considered ill-conceived because people who had known the brothers said they looked nothing like their portraits. Reportedly Michelangelo responded, "No one will know how they looked in a thousand years."

So what had Michelangelo—and now Livio—done in their approach to a portrait? It seems that in each case the artist was more interested in the sitter's personality than outward details. Livio's style in contrast to Neal's realism illustrated his desire to push the limits of traditional representation and open viewers' eyes to a deeper reality and more expansive form of art.

To these points Livio's abstract and stylized portrait shows his use of mixed-media techniques to accomplish his goals. A thumb-shaped tree of evergreen at the top center of the work might well be a clever reference back to his own birthday sketch of Bob scribbled on the Ridley's tea saucer! Three carefully-cut miniature squares from a previous printed work are arranged side by side at what might be hair and eye level. The face continues as a fleshy orange spot stretching down the center leading us to where Livio pasted three more rectangles cut from another of his prints. Might his repeated use of three shapes refer to Livio's awareness of Bob's spirituality? Having a theological education, Bob clearly identified himself as a man of faith. To Livio a reference to Bob's vitality and spiritual beliefs surely would have been more authentic than a carbon copy of his friend's glasses and hair. Livio's portrait of Bob is an example of his goals in Aiken: to introduce residents to new styles of art and to expand the range of art appreciation and their various collections.

Another memorable evening was dinner with the Brodies, whose guesthouse Livio lived in that year. As we gathered around the table for dinner just before the Thanksgiving season began, Livio asked to be allowed to say something. He was very emotional. He started by saying he had noticed most American families said a prayer of thanksgiving before they sat down to eat. This had touched him deeply and as he wiped away his tears he said, "In Europe we do not take time to show our gratitude." He then proceeded to say a lovely prayer in Italian, which needed no translation because we all felt its power and understood the true meaning of his words.[20]

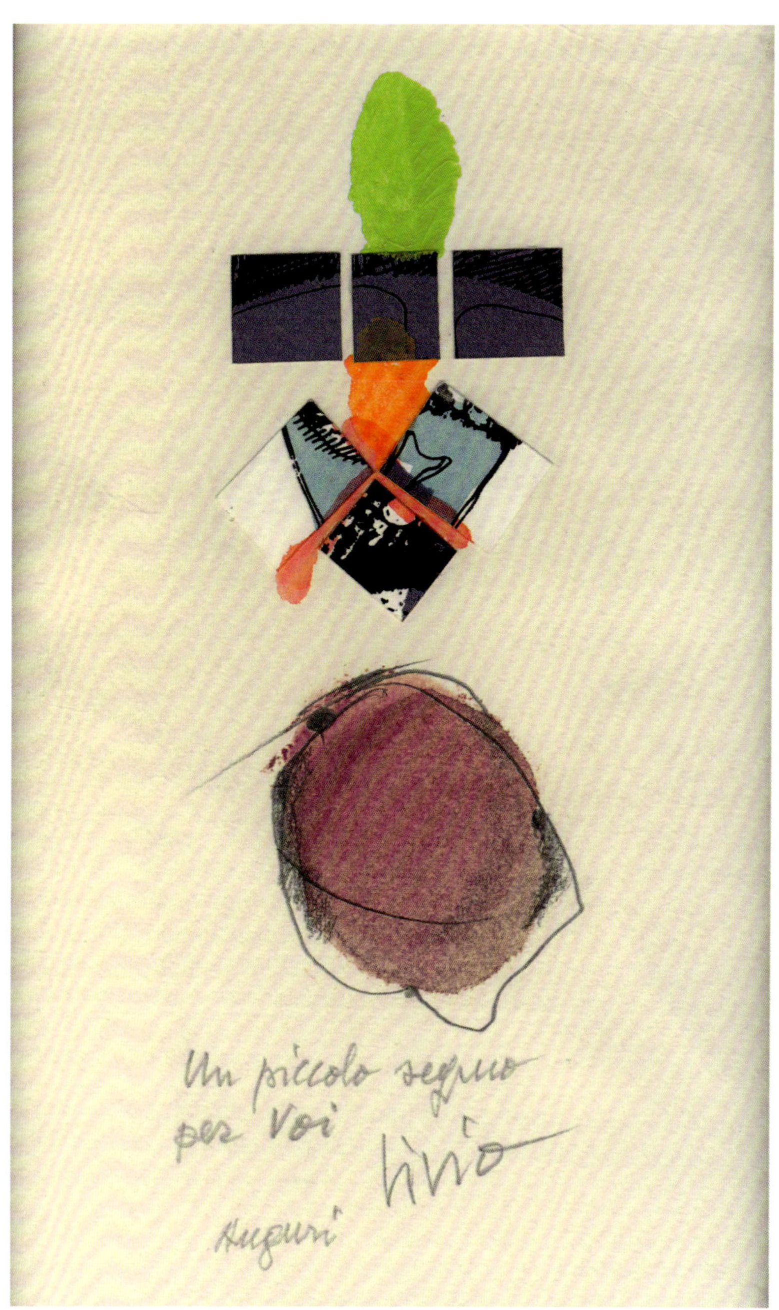

Birthday Portrait of Bob Alexander, 2000. Acrylic and mixed media on paper, 26 × 17.75 cm. Collection of Bob and Leslie Alexander. Photograph by Michael St. John.

Most southerners, if honest with themselves, would acknowledge college football as their second religion. Livio's time in Aiken would not have been complete without the experience of the pageantry and liturgy of this game. On October 2, 1999, soon after Livio's arrival for his stint as visiting artist in residence, we arranged for him to accompany us to a University of South Carolina football game along with a new faculty member, Sandra Fields, and the Custodis. We played "Ole Miss" that October night. Our seats were in the board of trustees' suite, which provides an unequalled experience of the game. As was our custom in those days we had rented a fifteen-passenger van. Along the way to Columbia our discussion centered on the upcoming game and our team's chances of winning. Livio listened and said very little. We neared Columbia and the traffic began to crawl, and the congestion was similar to what he had experienced in Atlanta. Livio perked up and wanted an explanation for all of the cars and people. He had some difficulty with the idea of so many people coming to a college football game. He was really overwhelmed when we arrived at the stadium and walked through the crush of fans. We took the elevator up to the box seat level and just as we started down to our seats the team ran onto the field with the band playing the theme from *2001: A Space Odyssey*, or as it was known to Livio, *Thus Spake Zarathustra*. He walked to the railing and opened his arms wide in a papal-like stance, then taking his hat off waved enthusiastically to the more than 81,000 fans. Livio was so overwhelmed by the festivities and the cheering that he wept! Later we assured him this was not arranged especially for his grand entrance; indeed this was the way each home football game was introduced. Whether he bought our explanation is still a question because he certainly embraced the moment with great enthusiasm.

For the first half most of our time was spent explaining the rules of the game to him while George translated. George gave Livio a good sense of the essence of American-style football. Livio particularly liked the television screens and instant replays. At halftime we joined the board members and their guests for barbecue. Of course here the barbecue was served on ceramic plates and was much more to his liking. He seemed to thoroughly enjoy hobnobbing with all of the "important" people of the university system.

During halftime the university marching band gave one of its classic performances. As the band concluded it was clear the Carolina Gamecocks had a very enthusiastic new fan from Italy. Unfortunately the final score of the game was "Ole Miss" 36—South Carolina 10. The most exciting part of the experience was the trip back to Aiken. Livio regaled all of us with his interpretation of the meaning of American football. He explained that the game was a metaphor for the history of the United States. The game was about territory, winning or losing it. Each team had the same goal: to take the most real estate, and thus to score the most points in order to win. In doing so one team fought to gain yardage while the other team was determined to stop them. For him it was the story of cowboys and Indians and America's struggle through the decades of early history to establish our boundaries and determine our place in the larger world. With this perspective in mind he said it was easy to understand why Americans took their football so seriously. Livio saw it as something imprinted on our souls.[21]

In the second and third years of Livio's residency, he lived in an apartment at the Carriage House Inn in the center of downtown Aiken. This location made his daily life more convenient as he was close to numerous restaurants, shops, and friends of the university. This was also easier for those providing transportation. To insure his comfort we introduced Livio to several key merchants and shop owners. As one would expect he charmed them immediately with his personality and wit.

Anne Thomason, who owns and operates the Carriage House Inn, one of the top-ranked inns in the nation according to *National Geographic Traveler,* generously offered one of their nicer apartments for Livio's accommodations. At the time Anne's daughter Elizabeth ran the inn and basically adopted Livio, as did most of the staff. Livio found it easy to be adopted by her because she was a beautiful young woman who enjoyed the attention he showed her and he likewise. She would check on him and ensure he was comfortable and had the things he needed. One of the staff members, Willy, took a special interest in Livio because he was a good tipper. Willy kept a close eye on him and reported regularly to the university. With Willy's cooperation there was little of Livio's activity we did not know about. When it was time for Livio to return to Italy, the staff always lined up to bid him farewell. There were not many dry eyes in the house.

Livio began each day at the New Moon Café, which is owned and operated by Chris Alewette. For those who have never been there, the coffee shop seems caught in a time warp. When you enter, you get a sense for what Haight Ashbury must have felt like in the sixties and seventies. This was Livio's favorite place to have breakfast, which usually consisted of coffee with cream and Italian biscotti cookies. Chris added the cookies to the menu just for Livio. When we asked her to feed Livio any time he came by and to keep a running tab of his expenses, she readily agreed. Such an arrangement seemed a convenient way to make certain Livio received the basic sustenance he required. As a regular he knew most of the early morning customers, and they him. He would always greet them enthusiastically even on those days when he strongly resisted getting out of bed. There is no way to know for sure what the final tab was because when we tried to settle with Chris she just laughed and said she never started a ticket. It was her gift to the university! In thanks for her generosity, Livio presented her with a piece of art that now hangs in her living room.

Rick Osbon, a young alumnus of USCA and strong supporter of his alma mater, solved the issue of clean clothes for Livio. Rick's family owns Osbon's Cleaners, only a few blocks from the Carriage House Inn. He insisted Livio bring all of his dirty clothes to them. As often as twice a week they did both his laundry and his dry cleaning. He was the cleanest Italian artist in Aiken and at no cost to him or the university. Recently Rick has been elected mayor of Aiken and continues to support the Orvieto-Aiken partnership.

Lionel Smith Ltd. was the clothier of choice for Livio during his time in Aiken. The shop is known as one of the finest clothing stores up and down the eastern U.S. seaboard. Smitty, the founder and owner, has clients from all over the east coast who call him at least once or twice a year to pick out and ship them the latest fashion additions to their wardrobes. Smitty is the consummate salesman. Livio and Smitty met and liked one another. On his first visit to the store Livio purchased a hat and scarf made in Italy. On special occasions such as the birthdays of faculty colleagues or when he was returning to Italy, Livio would buy ties and other sartorial gifts. On his walks about downtown Livio would frequently stop in and visit with Smitty and his staff.

Then there was Sandy Harris' Guest Cottage, which specializes in fine linens. Sandy and Tony, a physician, became close friends with Livio during his first visit to Aiken. They commissioned him to do several paintings over the years. Sandy remembers:

> It was exciting to have Livio Valentini in Aiken and see the exhibit at the Etherredge Center. I determined I had to have one of his paintings and couldn't afford an original at the time but I did buy one of his early prints, *Germination,* which we have hanging in our home. The friendship between George Custodi and Livio is really what drew us to him. Both their stories were similar, Livio being in a concentration camp and George's father being in another. It's a wonderful story and a "God thing" . . . a term I came up with to describe Livio's connection with Aiken and some of the people here. It was sort of a spiritual cross-culture. A lot of his personal emotions are reflected in the paintings he brought to our community, feelings similar to those that developed between him and the people of Aiken. Certainly he introduced a new kind of art to a lot of people who didn't necessarily associate it with Italy until visiting Orvieto. When they went to the Duomo and saw the Signorelli Chapel, they began to understand what was happening within Italian art.
>
> Sandi, George, Livio, and I went to our condo at Kiawah. The beaches are wide with white sand and he enjoyed walking and picking up shells and driftwood. We had

> George to translate but sometimes Livio would tell us something and George would say, "Oh, they know what you mean." We were all hoping we knew what he meant. It was true we all had a spiritual connection. . . . In addition to the Aikenites being affected by Livio's work, his art changed once he came to town. Before, he painted birds trapped in cages and there was less color.

Sandy reflected on the different images people have of our country as they contrast the large cities with the rural open spaces. "Many Europeans think they have an idea of what the United States is like and they really don't unless they are fortunate enough to come to a wonderful small town in the South. They get to meet people and experience their warmth and genuine hospitality. People welcomed Livio not because he was a great artist from Italy but because they liked him as a person. I think that made his art evolve to another level. He genuinely loved so many people in Aiken and they loved him."[22]

One day John and Al Beyer took Livio shopping at Chris' Camera Shop on Laurens Street. Livio picked out one of the better and more expensive cameras available. To their shock when it was time to pay, Livio pulled out a stack of one hundred dollar bills from the side pocket in his cargo pants. Livio handed the money to the clerk, expecting him to take the appropriate amount for the purchase, which he did under their watchful eyes. It was obvious something needed to be done to protect Livio and his money. The next day George helped him open a bank account. From that day on George managed his non-university financial affairs, especially the money Livio received for his various commissions.

Another friend on Laurens Street who played a significant role in Livio's Aiken period was Toni Jerome, owner of the Artists' Parlor. As one of his earliest supporters she displayed some of his paintings and pottery and did much to promote his work during his first year here. The gallery was located two doors from the New Moon Café.

Arnold's Gallery, owned by Trish Arnold, became the semi-official location for people who wanted to purchase any remaining works from the *Odissea* show. She displayed his work for several years until Partners in Friendship took a more active role in promoting his art. They hosted a number of shows featuring Livio's paintings as well as fine Italian wines. The proceeds supported our international student exchanges. Joan Bondor coordinated this project for Partners in Friendship. Joan recalled, "There was a slight misunderstanding concerning [the] marketing [of] the prints. George asked me if I would take charge of them. I explained how these works of art should be stored and what I thought should be done with them. Livio said, 'she's the right person to keep these prints.'" Joan went on to say, "I've had them ever since and it's been quite a responsibility." Over the years Joan coordinated various exhibits and sales of Livio's art.[23]

Livio became the unofficial Italian ambassador to downtown Aiken. He was very much at home and extremely well received by the local merchants. Everyone who shared their hospitality played an essential role in helping Livio's art transition from the anguish of war to a new realm of bright colors and hopeful expressions, which typified his Aiken period.

This new positive outlook inevitably began to change his subject matter. How could Livio abandon the birds, his chosen metaphor for freedom and a theme that dominated so much of his career? In an interview with Alessandro Bosi, Livio said, "The birds? I hate them. I have hated them for some time. Every so often at night I dream of strangling the whole lot. Then in the morning I find I am thinking intensely of a cage. It is the same ambiguous relationship established between Conan Doyle and his favorite creation, Sherlock Holmes." From Livio's perspective, because Doyle was so intricately tied to his character Holmes, the only way he could free himself was to kill off his creation. Having done so Doyle ultimately had to resuscitate him. Clearly Livio's birds had a similarly ambiguous hold on him. "I have painted too many birds; too many to continue; too many to stop. I am nailed to my birds like one of my birds." But then came his immersion in Aiken and its people. From the painting *La Principessa* on, he never included the tormented birds again in any of his works.[24]

During his first visit as artist in residence, Livio developed plans for a new painting, an interpretation of the city. Livio began a large acrylic work ultimately named *La principessa nel sole di Aiken* (The Princess in the Sun of Aiken). Principessa was his nickname for a large live oak tree he admired in Hopelands Gardens.

While giving a special lecture to a group of USCA students, Livio traced the development of this project:

> The problem was trying to interpret a monumental tree in Aiken. . . . The task was to give meaning to this tree, communicating information about the quality of life in the city of Aiken.
>
> So I needed to create a sense of dignity which emanates from the sun and refers to moral and spiritual richness. The tree has lived for many centuries and has seen many generations. This tree cannot talk but knows a lot about the city. Therefore this condition must be represented in some way. So the tree resembles a monarch

La principessa nel sole di Aiken (The Princess in the Sun of Aiken), 1999. Acrylic on canvas, 193 × 152 cm. Collection of USC Aiken. Photograph by Michael St. John.

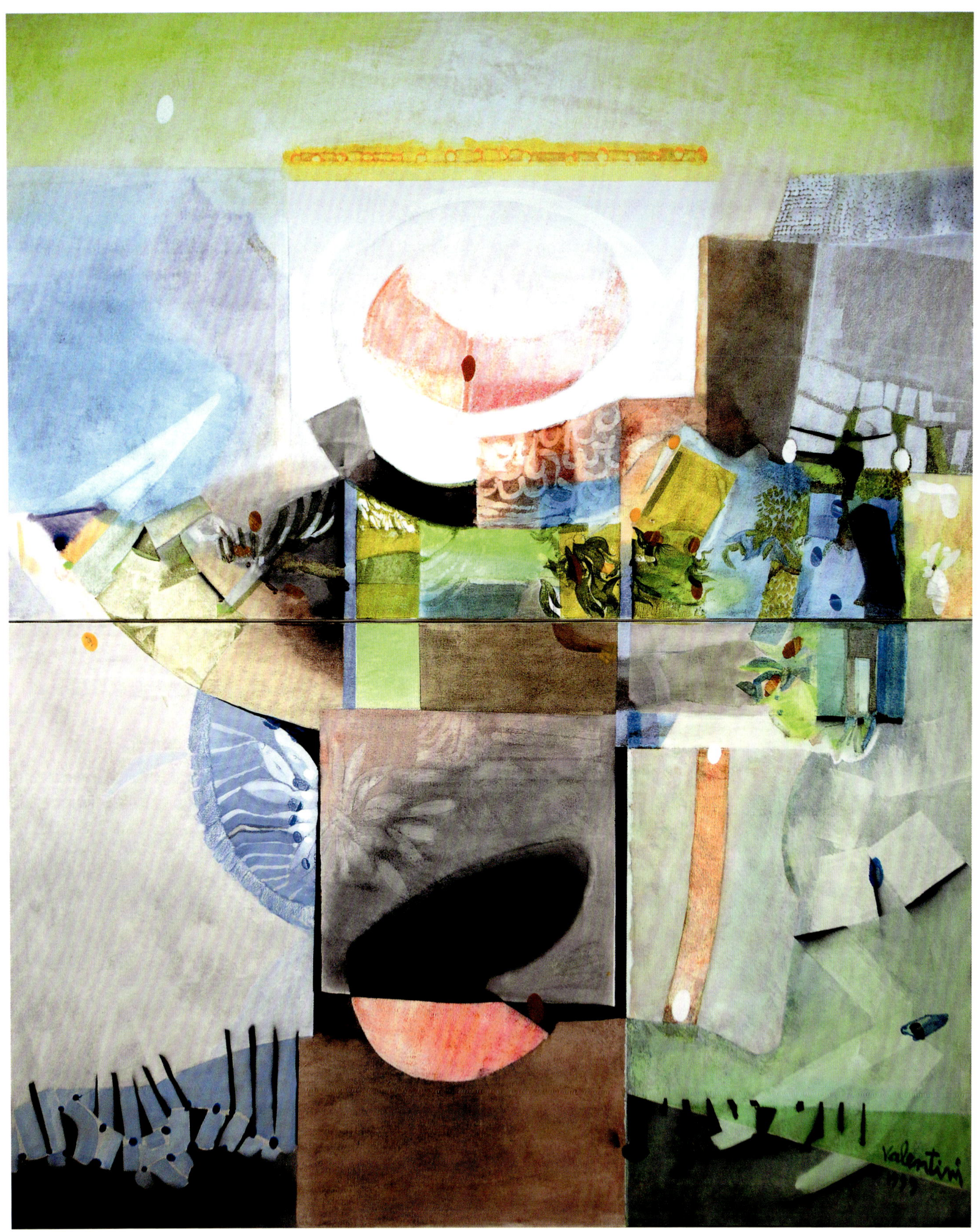
Valentini

> commanding her subjects with royal power. Or one might compare it to a big general with medals, wreaths, and flowers.
>
> Commissioned by Alexander, the original title of the work was *La regina nel sole di Aiken*, later to become *La Principessa*. . . . The unique heritage of Aiken is its special combination of nature and people. However, the city has not yet contemplated creating public monuments. . . . Even though they're experiencing problems because of new developments, it is clear they love nature very much. The city has a certain appearance with its golf courses, horse races and all that goes with nature.

Lest it sound like Livio was criticizing Aiken, he went on to say, "The structural aspects of the city are less important than its natural setting. There is no distinctive architecture here but there is no need to go to the avant garde, to compete with the natural setting of the city."

Livio said, "*Principessa* is a work I have labored over with a lot of love." The tree features a great cavity in its trunk, delicate wisps of foliage and below, the shapes of all the people who have passed beneath it for so many years. He said, "It's a synthesis, a representation, . . . not something to be forgotten but a work to be discovered."

When Livio heard that some Aikenites found his art hard to understand, he said:

> Americans have told me my paintings seem to be a little too complicated. I am not offended because painting is complicated. But you can make it less so if those who find it complex are informed and allowed to study it. If you study artistic movements in Europe and America, comparison will allow one to better understand the techniques involved. You might understand what a number of artists are doing right now. This group of artists, they're not all nuts, but responsible people. By looking at these artists you understand the world is changing. Because in Europe *La Principessa* would not be strange or too avant garde but basically a normal work from an artist who constantly questions the current culture.

While working on *La Principessa* Livio also conducted numerous seminars on campus, gathering both young people and non-traditional local artists, with whom he was glad to share his philosophy of life and art. Livio wished that those participating in these seminars might experience what it means to do "Great work with great enthusiasm. I hope also for meaningful communication of ideas. I hope human beings will get to know each other better, to love one another."[25]

At another evening lecture Livio continued to explain his use of a tree as a symbol for Aiken, a tree in which the beauty of nature and spirituality resided. Livio compared the tree to a medieval shield decorated with emblems of both Aiken and the university, which he appreciated for its cultural role. He wanted to leave *La Principessa* as his memento, as a town shield of the city of Aiken.

His idea was to show the essence of the tree as a noble entity. Therefore he decided not to depict it as it actually looked, which would have been easy for him to do. Instead he wanted to pursue the tree's meaning and the life quality it represented. Livio adorned the tree with medal-like shapes, like those typically worn by humans to signify their status and importance.

Livio mentioned the abstract forms famous Dutch artist Mondrian (1872–1944) used in his early tree studies and how they influenced him to eliminate various details from the work. For example there is the element of the knothole, the only realistic part of the painting. Livio explained that other portions of the composition are more ephemeral: "This is the moon as imagined, and that's the sun as imagined. The sun has been humanized." Livio stated, "Between imagination and substance, this work was born. Aiken does not have traditional monuments, its trees are its monuments."[26]

After Livio finished his tribute to the trees of Aiken, he turned his attention to Spoleto, the annual celebration of the arts in Charleston. Joan Bondor, Sandy Harris, and her friend Carolyn Dietrich, a member of the Spoleto committee, arranged for Livio to exhibit some original work in the 2001 Piccolo Spoleto. This was not Livio's first time with Spoleto; his first was in Italy. In 1967 he accepted an invitation from Gian Carlo Menotti, founder of Spoleto Festival USA, to exhibit his paintings at Menotti's Festival of Two Worlds. Livio and Gian Carlo were contemporaries although Menotti was nine years older. During an interview in Charleston Livio quipped, "Gian Carlo might say, 'I am not older than Valentini, but rather grander than he.'"[27]

The show was in the Dock Street Theater Gallery. Livio spent the better part of two weeks in Charleston. Because of the language limitations and Livio's lack of familiarity with Charleston, the committee made special accommodations for his housing. Gary and Carolyn Dietrich offered their home, within walking distance of the Dock Street Theater, for Livio and his escorts to use. Several couples volunteered to spend three days assisting with his schedule and meals. There was always one person who spoke some Italian. Joan Bondor recalled that she and her husband Ted escorted Livio. "We had a translator from the College of Charleston who was with us every day and evening. This young professor attended the show, explained who Livio was and answered

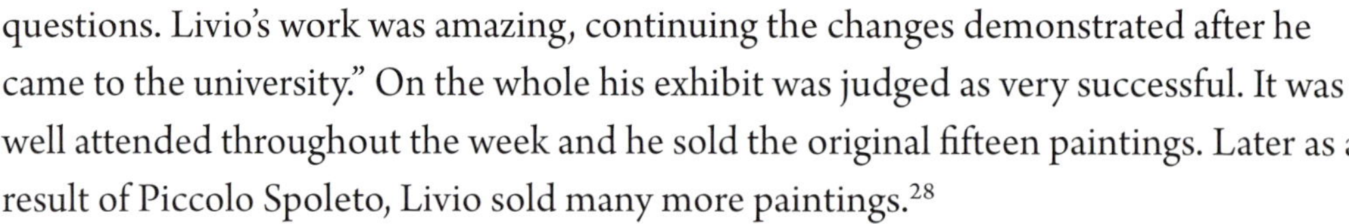
questions. Livio's work was amazing, continuing the changes demonstrated after he came to the university." On the whole his exhibit was judged as very successful. It was well attended throughout the week and he sold the original fifteen paintings. Later as a result of Piccolo Spoleto, Livio sold many more paintings.[28]

According to Silvia Powledge, "One of the happiest experiences for Livio was his time at Piccolo Spoleto. The three days I spent with him walking every morning to the art show, I watched him interact with people from all over the world. Some people were foreigners, others from throughout the United States as far away as California; it was a joy to watch the paintings being sold one after another. It was amazing how people would not even hesitate; they just loved those paintings. Some people actually asked him if there were any more available and did he have a website. It was such a success. I remember seeing his eyes watering because he never expected to be treated with such respect."[29]

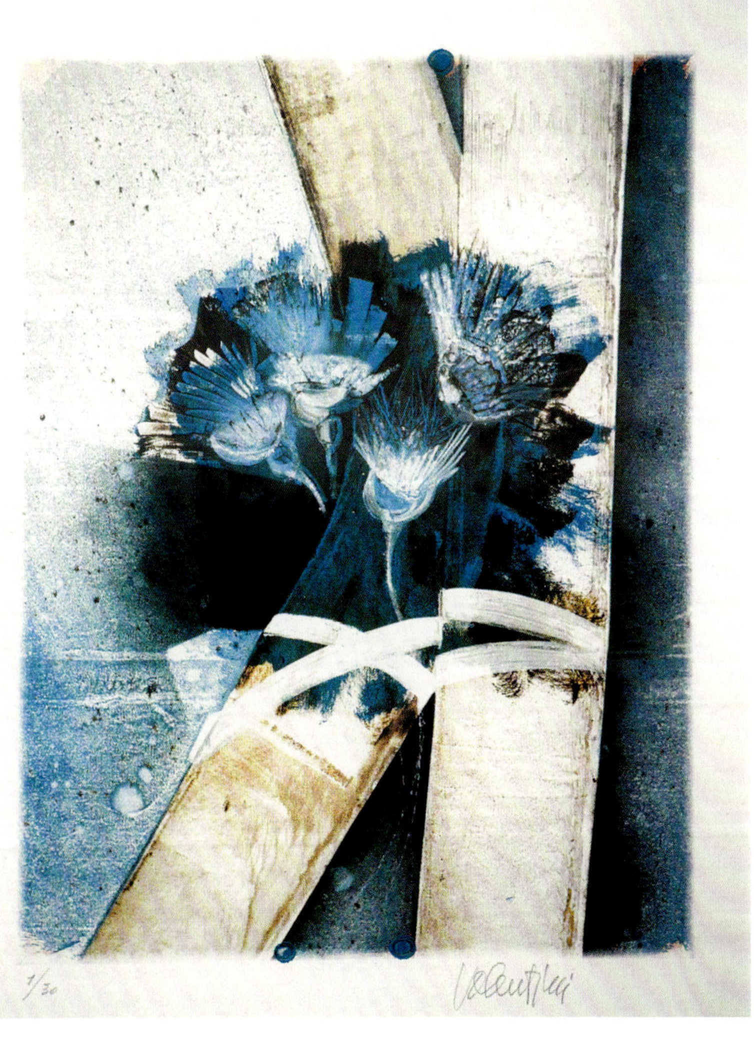

Cardi blu (Blue Thistles). Lithograph, 32 × 41 cm. Collection of Bob and Leslie Alexander. Photograph by Michael St. John.

Benjamin and Jerry Dell Gimarc, friends from Columbia who are sophisticated collectors, attended his show and spent time with Livio. They later invited us to their Charleston home a few blocks from the exhibit where Livio gave a magnificent discourse on contemporary art and the many ways it enriches our lives. Had it not been for the translator the essence of the discussion would have been lost. Several years later while the Gimarcs were traveling in Italy, they stopped by Livio's studio and purchased a limited edition print. The print shows four unusual *cardi,* blue thistle flowers bound to two pieces of birch wood. The Gimarcs continue to speak fondly of the time they spent with him in Charleston.[30]

Often the language limitations made for some interesting experiences. One evening in Charleston several of us from Aiken spent time with Gary and Carolyn Dietrich and their friends, the Royals. The focus of the conversation was on big game hunting in Africa. Livio was perplexed by most of the conversation and had a hard time understanding the interest in hunting and killing these animals. Sandy Harris remembers a similar reaction from Livio when they visited Carolyn in Cameron, South Carolina, to work out some of the plans for the Spoleto exhibit. "On our way to the beach we went by Carolyn's plantation home where Gary was hosting a big dove shoot and all these people were out in the fields shooting. It sounded like a war. And Valentini said 'Oh, oh, what is this slaughter, what is this slaughter?'" The discussions that evening were animated but civil with neither side conceding much to the other.[31]

Later the same evening at dinner Livio, who had been sitting beside Barbara Morgan, the second district solicitor, realized he had completely misunderstood what a solicitor did and what the term meant. Somehow, whether serious or not, he had assumed it meant someone who was a member of the "world's oldest profession." He jokingly proposed that on their return to Aiken the two of them should go for a walk in Hitchcock Woods naked. When we clarified that her profession involved arresting and prosecuting people who made such solicitations, he showed an unusual amount of humility and made numerous apologies. We all had a great laugh.[32]

One of the more interesting evenings during Piccolo Spoleto was a late dinner after the opening of Livio's show. We had a young Italian professor acting as our translator. She and her husband, a graduate student from Australia, suggested we dine at the new restaurant called Fish. Everyone agreed and off we went for a good meal at the end of a very long and tiring day. When we arrived we were told it was closing. While we were discussing our next move Livio was busy drawing on one of the menus. He had drawn a fish with the characteristic Valentini flair. At that moment, the owner came by and was intrigued by what he saw on his finely crafted menu. Bob quickly introduced Livio as an internationally-renowned artist and an exhibitor in Spoleto. The owner insisted we come upstairs and let the staff "create a delightful dinner" for us. We were seated in a small private dining room. A few minutes later the chef said the first course would be a light fish soup and some special breads. He gave us several wines he thought should accompany the meal. We chose an Australian chardonnay in honor of our translator's husband. When the soup and breads were served we tucked into the food as though we had not eaten for days. Everyone agreed it was some of the best we had ever tasted. Certainly we had a sufficiency with that single dish. Moments later the chef appeared with a platter filled with three different kinds of fish, all local to Charleston, along with another platter of roasted vegetables. Despite our earlier protestations, we ate everything that was put before us. Just when we were sure there could be no more, the owner brought out the pastry chef, his wife, and she presented us with several plates of her specialty desserts. Again we feasted. Interestingly there had been no discussion of price at any point. As the meal came to a close, the one who was to pay the tab, Bob became keenly aware of the potential financial disaster he faced. At that moment the owner and the chefs came out and told us what an honor it had been to serve the wonderful Italian artist Valentini and his friends. He asked Livio to autograph several menus for the chefs and indicated he would be framing the Fish menu and hanging it in a prominent place in the restaurant. When Bob asked for a bill the owner said a nice tip for the chefs was all that was required. They received a very generous amount. What an evening! Good food and art transcended all language barriers.[33]

Silvia Powledge remembered a reception they had for Livio in a house close to the water attended by some important officials from Charleston. "Livio was looking at the furniture, looking outside through the window, enjoying every little moment. He was so excited. I'll never forget, he'd say, 'there was so much potential in the South.'"[34]

At the end of the second week we returned with Livio to Aiken. The return trip required driving through the countryside between Orangeburg and Aiken. Livio asked about the poverty he was observing in some of the shacks and old dilapidated tenant houses. He wanted to know the role race played in what seemed to be crushing poverty for so many rural South Carolinians. With our bambini Italian and a well-worn dictionary of Italian and English, we tried to share with him some of the "Old South's" early history. We talked about the plantations, slaves, and the continuing vestiges and resulting problems we face today that had their genesis in that period of our history. Such a discussion would be difficult under any circumstances. One can only imagine the struggle we had with the language barrier.

This was a subject Livio returned to on numerous occasions, especially in political science class lectures. There the focus was on Italy's role in Africa and its colonial empire. For Girma Negash's political science class, entitled Art and Politics, Livio showed examples of his work, illustrating the power of art to educate and inspire young people. Movingly Livio began his lecture by apologizing to Negash, who was born in Ethiopia. Livio spoke of his regret at the position Italy had taken against Ethiopian freedom.

The students were fascinated by Livio's themes of "the lack of liberty" and the universal theme of violence possible in "any time, any country, any civilization, and how these situations repeat themselves." Livio said, "It seems impossible that people can't remember events like these." He explained, "Every painting has a political, social and qualitative function . . . we have to pay attention to the cultural value and spiritual meaning of things."[35] In the Maestro's lectures, our USCA students learned of his visions not of doom but of rebirth, not of bitterness but of hope and humanity. A few weeks later

Negash came to the studio to present Livio with a bronze plaque of appreciation on behalf of all the students in his class.

One day Livio and John were having lunch with Negash. He has an obvious accent which led us to realize everyone at the table had a different accent. Negash said travel back and forth to the United States had become increasingly complicated. He joked that people kept asking him where he was from and he had started saying he was from Kansas. Livio loved this story and learned to say, "I am from Kansas." Later we shared this story with Jane Schumacher, the executive director of the Etherredge Center. Jane was exceptionally kind to Livio, checking in on his progress as he painted in his studio next to her office. She associated Livio's Kansas story with her favorite film, *The Wizard of Oz*. Later she found the perfect gift for him, an apron printed with "I don't think we're in Kansas anymore, Toto." Livio laughed and laughed.[36]

Friendships were the coin of Livio's realm in Aiken. Over the years Bob's son, Rob, and Livio developed a close relationship. Rob is nearly six feet tall and has very broad shoulders and weighs 240 pounds. Livio used to tease Rob and call him his three-door armoire. In return sometimes Rob would lift Livio up and twirl him around like a rag doll. They seemed to enjoy messing around in a playful manner. There was always a lot of laughter when they were together. If he had not seen Rob in some time, Livio, always the romantic, would ask for an update on what he was doing. Livio was especially interested in who Rob was dating and how they were getting along. The reports he received never seemed to disappoint him.

In the late spring of 2001 Livio came to the Alexanders' for dinner, joined by George Custodi, Rob, and two of his close friends, Jimmy Hartley and Thomas Coleman, who were active in the youth wing of the Episcopal church. The three young men were on their way to serve as counselors for the summer at the Bishop Gravatt Conference Center and Camp. The evening was planned with a twofold purpose in mind: first, as a time to celebrate the work they would be doing with young people and second, to introduce them to Livio. The evening was a major success on both points.

With George translating, Livio regaled us with stories as we enjoyed a typical summer dinner of grilled salmon, corn on the cob, salad, and good Italian wine. He had us all doubled over with his humorous observations about his exploits as a young man before the war. Soon he moved to more serious topics and began querying each of the young men about their plans for the future. He urged them to take seriously the influence they would have on the lives of the children in their care for the summer. He reminded them they had "an incredible responsibility."

He began to tell stories about his wartime experiences, something he did not normally do. That night he had a message, a lesson for the three young men. He began by sharing how he and his comrades were captured when they refused to continue fighting for the Germans after Italy declared they were quitting the fight. He held us all spellbound as he told how the German soldiers gathered the Italians together in the school yard and threatened them with huge cannons. Then he related how they were force marched and crowded into cattle cars as they were moved to the death camps.

He mixed humor in the story as he told how he and his Italian comrades were assigned to cook for the German officers. The officers ate very well. For the times and circumstances they had excellent food and wine. Not so for the cooks who did not get to share in what they prepared, at least officially.

Livio delighted in telling how he and his friends smuggled food to their fellow prisoners by slicing potatoes, onions, and occasionally meats into very thin pieces and concealing the food in their leg wraps. Once they returned to the barracks they would unwind the wraps, remove the food and cook it by "slapping it to the side and top of the pot bellied stove," the prisoners' only source of warmth. The guards became suspicious when these Italians did not suffer the same illnesses as many of the others. They searched Livio and company, watched them more closely, and generally harassed them but did not discover their secret. Finally one of the guards, a huge sergeant who had never missed a meal, pleaded with them to tell him how they were cheating the system. According to Livio in this version of the story, which differs slightly from the memoir, they left the camp with their secret.

While we all shared a laugh at their cleverness, he moved on to stories of torture and daily executions in the death camps. He talked about how many of his friends were taken out and shot after having been beaten nearly to death. He reflected on the evil and inhumanity that surrounded him. More importantly he spoke "about the evil of the Holocaust and the millions who died because of Hitler and his minions who had become the embodiment of evil. It surrounded all of society and for unspeakable reasons we collectively failed to confront it in its very beginnings." Livio concluded by looking each young man directly in the eyes and saying to them with powerful emotion, "You must promise me you will do all you can to keep this evil from ever gaining any kind of control in the world again! We all must do what we can to stop it before it begins!"

Recently in a conversation at a wedding with these same young men, they stated that the evening with Livio had a major impact on them. One is now studying to become an Episcopal priest and the other two are working full-time with non-profit youth organizations. They fondly remembered his stories and his challenge. The artist painted and sculpted with words as well as with his brush and his clay.[37]

Another important friendship for Livio resulted from a political reception and fund-raiser held for senator Thomas Moore at Rye Patch in October 2000. Livio attended as a member of our delegation from the university. The goal was to expose him to another of the customs in South Carolina, barbecue and political stump speeches. Livio was taking it all in and as usual was asking many questions about the event. He was quite charming as he met the different politicians. He was becoming one of the university's secret weapons in our ongoing task of winning political support for our several causes. Once politicians met him and experienced his enthusiasm and innocence, they generally wanted to spend more time with him. Politicians found it easier to respond more favorably to our requests when his name was mentioned.

In the course of the afternoon Bob was telling someone about Livio's time in Buchenwald. Long-time state senator John Drummond was standing behind Livio and overheard the exchange. He tapped Bob on the shoulder and asked him to tell Livio that he also had been a prisoner at Buchenwald during the same time. He was shot down over Germany after recording numerous kills as a U.S. Army Air Corps ace fighter

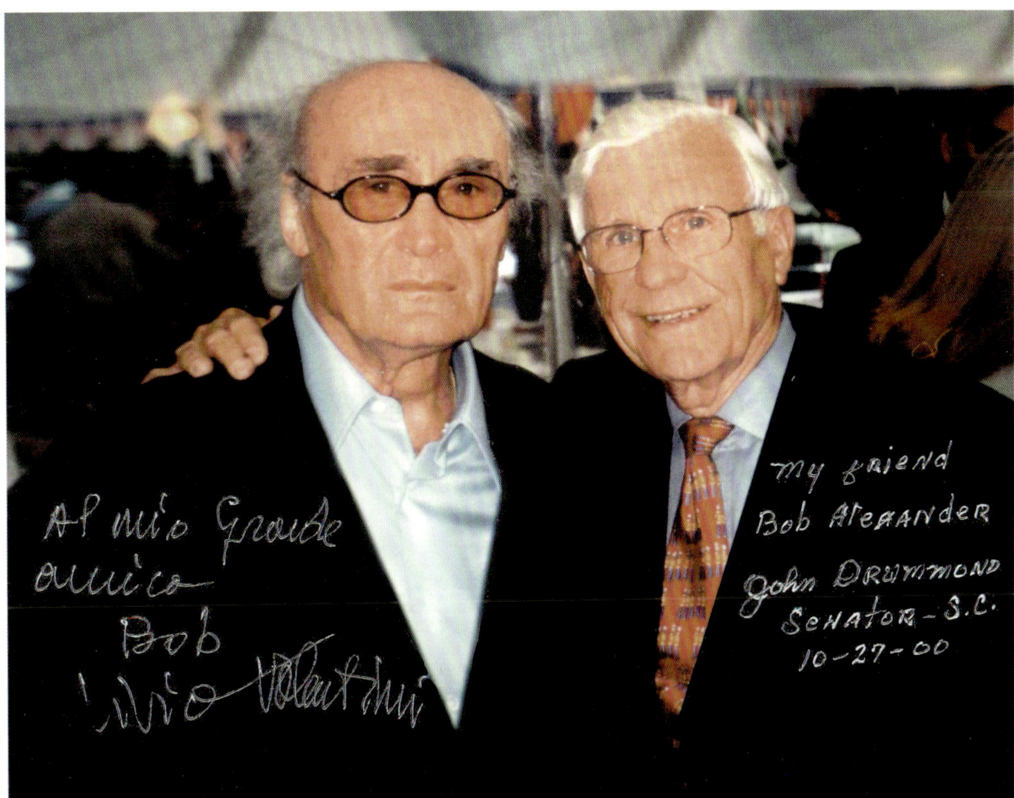

Livio Valentini with Senator John Drummond. Collection of Bob Alexander.

pilot. As Senator Drummond and Livio were introduced and Livio heard of their shared experience, they embraced each other and wept. The rest of the afternoon was spent with the two of them talking about this awful time in their lives. They discussed how Americans were segregated from Europeans in the death camp. They talked about the number of comrades who were either shot or died from the extreme conditions. This exchange was one of the most touching moments we shared with Livio and continues to be a vivid memory. From this meeting they developed a close and lasting friendship.

Partners in Friendship not only played a key role in introducing Livio to Aiken but many of its board members became his close personal friends. For example Joan Bondor chaired the art committee with the specific goal of setting up a series of exhibits for Livio. These shows were in community galleries. Consequently Joan got to know Livio and his art better than most:

> People began to appreciate his art and a number of patrons in Aiken commissioned original works. Sometimes they were surprised. I think he tried to figure them out and he visited many of their homes in an effort to personalize their work. He made their homes much more interesting because our art collections tended toward horses, golf, older prints, and antique maps. It was hard for some people to adopt this contemporary idea. They did so because they began to understand him and love him for who he was and what he did. It reflected their affection for him. He added so much to all of our lives.
>
> I have been asked how I thought his art changed. I saw it change a lot as many people did.

Having dealt with the prints he brought from Italy and then observing his work in Aiken, Joan became keenly aware of Livio's transformation.

> The colors had changed. They became much more vibrant. He started using more mixed-media and different types of paper. He opened up to a brighter world, a freer world. It made me wonder about this sudden change. I think it was Aiken and her people. In Orvieto, we experienced an enclosed atmosphere. The narrow streets, the tall buildings, no trees, a fascinating place with so much history but so different from what we have in Aiken. The USCA campus quadrangle is relatively small with beautiful plantings, trees, and walkways. You can stroll from one place to another.

> The first time Livio came to Aiken he went to Hopelands Gardens and was blown away by the old trees, one of which became his subject, *La Principessa.*
>
> Two things happened when he came to Aiken. He was in a different type of geographical environment. Our downtown has wide parkways. He enjoyed larger and more open space with the parks and the campus. The people provided an uplifting experience for him. Everyone made him feel welcome and they invited him into their homes for dinners and parties. His art became freer.
>
> He had a personal freedom in Aiken he never experienced in Orvieto. He had no restrictions. He actually became his own person, not a person directed by anyone else or influenced by anyone else. He brought the baggage of having been a prisoner still searching for freedom. He blossomed in Aiken into a different personality. If Flora had seen him here she probably would not have recognized him. It was all nurtured by his coming to Aiken and his experiences with the university.[38]

While artist in residence, Livio received several special commissions from the community. One of the most unique was a composition entitled *Mother Theresa.* Janet Augeri Morris remembered finding her husband, Jack, huddled with Livio in their kitchen engaged in a deep conversation, even though neither spoke the other's language. Soon after Livio delivered his one-of-a-kind drawing of the beloved religious icon, pointing out that it wasn't intended to look like her. But it did capturing the image simply in deft strokes of charcoal and a minimum shade of blue pigment. The woman affectionately cradles a child, perhaps every child, in her arms. But why did Livio leave the image so incomplete, with just a hint of the infant? Livio explained this drawing was unfinished because Mother Theresa's work was unfinished. The Morrises are delighted to possess a portrait of the recently elevated Saint Theresa!

Sandy and Tony Harris own a significant collection of paintings from Livio's Aiken period. Because they had been so helpful to him during the Spoleto exhibition, he presented them with *Il grande oceano* (The Great Ocean), in which he captured a brilliant South Carolina sunset. The great orange disk of the sun partly recedes behind a gauzy mist. The sea horizon is represented in fleeting slashes of brown and blue. In the foreground the cool, pale, sandy beach makes a perfect

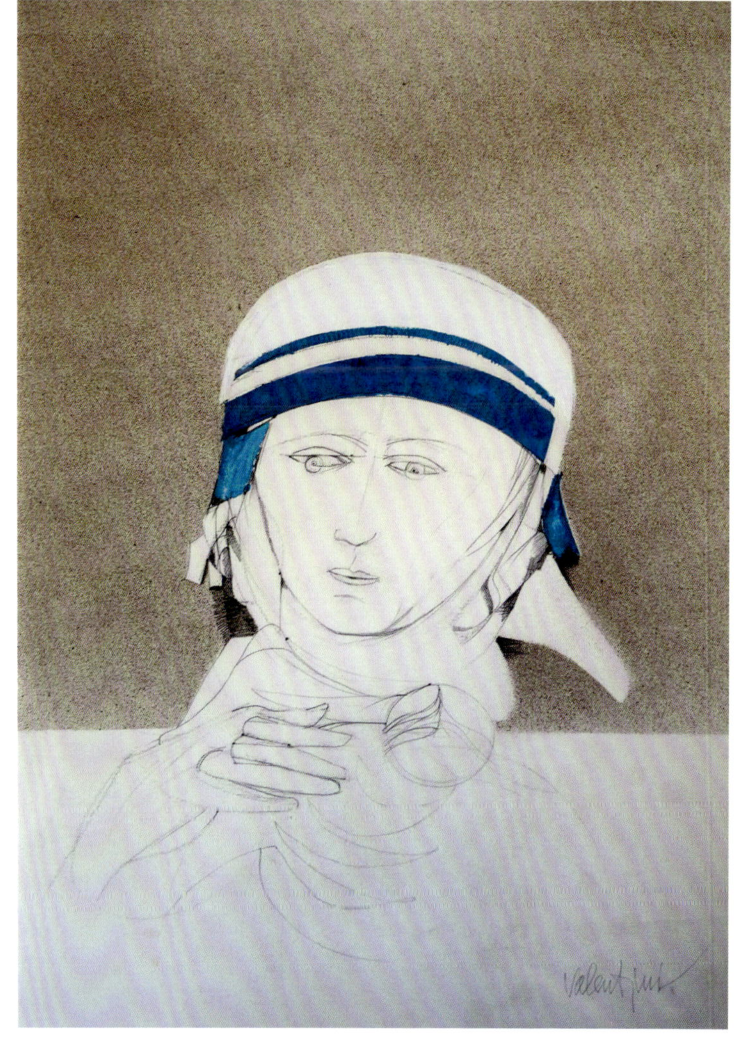

Mother Theresa, 2003. Acrylic on paper, approximately 50 × 76 cm. Collection of Jack and Janet Morris. Photograph by Michael St. John.

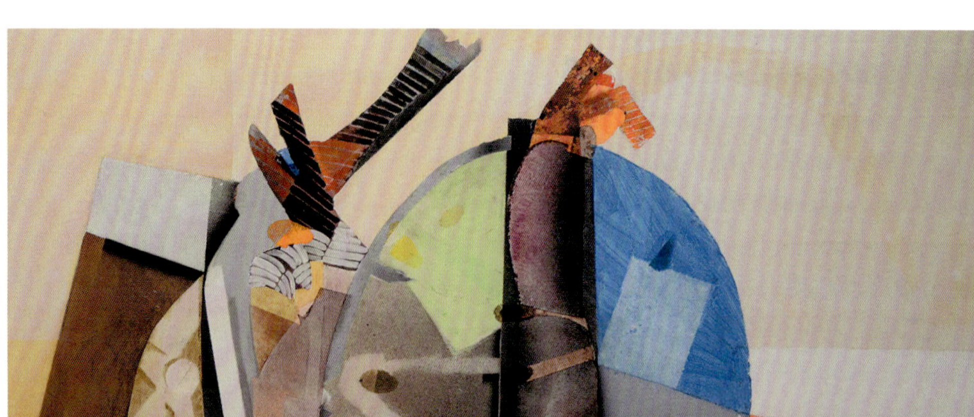

La poetica dell' equilibrio (The Poetic Balance), 2000. Acrylic on canvas, 120 × 91 cm. Collection of Tony and Sandy Harris. Photograph by Michael St. John.

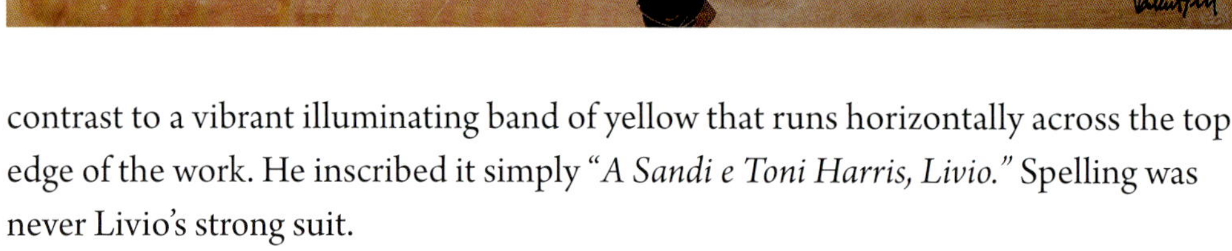

contrast to a vibrant illuminating band of yellow that runs horizontally across the top edge of the work. He inscribed it simply "*A Sandi e Toni Harris, Livio.*" Spelling was never Livio's strong suit.

The Harris family also decided to commission an original work by Livio entitled *La poetica dell' equilibrio* (The Poetic Balance). In the new intense colors that characterize this period, Livio unveiled a beautiful oval of cobalt blue and mint green floating in the middle of a plane surface over which chunks of red, ochre, and purple play. A remarkable three-dimensional-looking tube rises up at the center, bisecting the composition into two regions. Livio explained that this represented their marriage, the tying together of their partnership. Livio had begun revisiting some of his earlier ideas, so one is reminded of the sculpted ceramic tondi from his *Da Fuga nel Quaternario* series. Watching Livio visually examine the balance and dynamic duality of marriage takes us back to the way he and Flora described their fifty-year-long relationship.

↞ *Composizione floreale* (Floral Composition), 2007. Mixed media on panel, 53 × 71 cm. Collection of Tony and Sandy Harris. Photograph by Michael St. John.

As a second gift to the family Livio created *La poetica dell' equilibrio di un giorno* (The Poetic Balance of a Day). For the second time he captured the orb of the sun

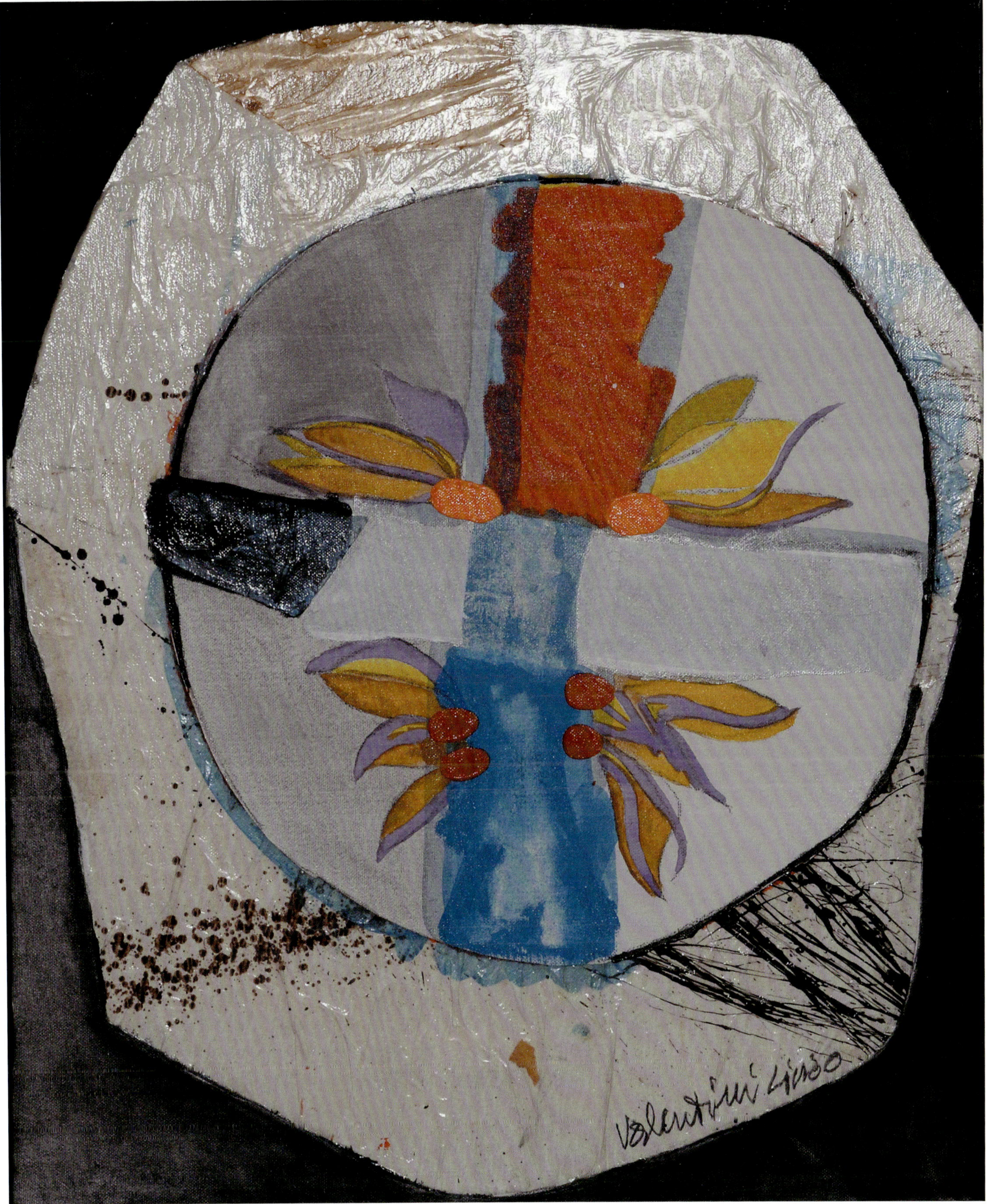

balanced above the horizon with an intense blood-red slash directing our eye to the mixed-media sands below. Here Livio experimented with varying textures of pasted paper, cellophane, and thick, melting brush strokes that are, for the Maestro, unprecedented.

Finally we include *Composizione floreale* (Floral Composition), in which Livio quoted several of his own previous themes. Above all one is struck by the familiar center circle, ever present since the bird cycle. We have traced its use from the concentration camp walls to the seed of *Germination* and to the tondo, which now marks Livio's gravesite. In this case Livio seems to have encapsulated the surface beneath a sheath of transparent cellophane, adding texture and depth to the work. Also notable is the dazzling variety of ways with which he applied color. Hand-painted yellow petals trimmed in contrasting purple sprout from behind a jewel-toned cross. In a technique he also used in *Galassia,* he spattered trails of paint drops across the surface. In a most unique touch he has inscribed "Livio" in the orange paint on the upper portion of the cross. To finish Livio accented the cross with red-orange fingerprints; they might mirror the seeds of a Van Gogh sunflower or become the wounds of the Crucifixion. Is this piece about the sun and vegetation or eternal life itself?

Other members of Partners in Friendship, Bob and Kay Moody, collected several of Livio's works over the years. They hosted him at their mountain home in North Carolina. One evening the Moodys took Livio to a restaurant where music majors from Brevard College served as the wait staff. After dinner, the young women serenaded the group with excerpts from Italian opera. In gratitude, Livio presented the Moodys with an especially lovely print of one of his angels, *L'angelo* (The Angel).

Autumn in the Mountains, another small painting in their collection, refers to the time of the year of his visit. In autumnal colors Livio painted his miniature impression of the mountains. A tiny tree rises up in a blaze of orange while below he has arranged yellows, tans, reds, and lavender. Livio was revisiting familiar themes but note that they are not merely repeated. In this case the transparent washes of pigment meld together to form the unmistakable curve of the Buchenwald walls. Should we be surprised to find such a grave symbol in an otherwise lighthearted design? Even in a gift to acknowledge the

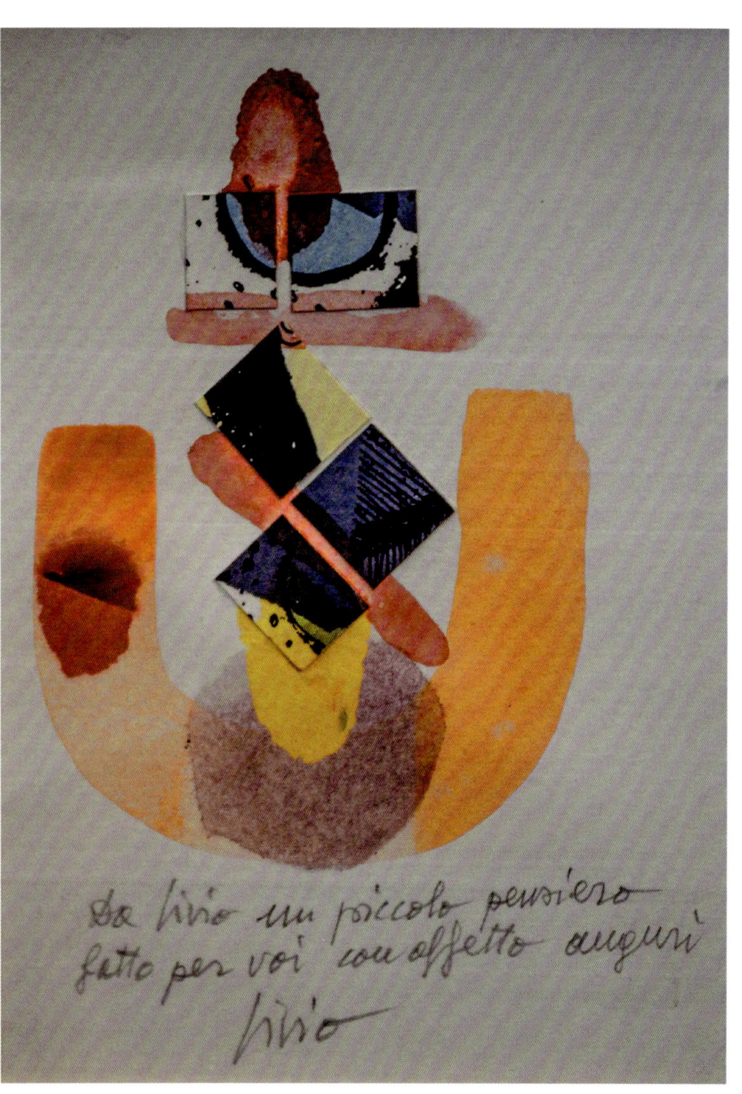

Autumn in the Mountains, 2000. Acrylic and mixed media on paper, 15 × 20 cm. Collection of Bob and Kay Moody. Photograph by Michael St. John.

kindness of friends, Livio could not seem to avoid the imprint of his years of suffering long ago. Livio inscribed the painting: "*da Livio, un piccolo pensiero fatto per voi con affetto auguri*" ("from Livio, a little thought made for you with affectionate wishes").

The most impressive piece of the Moody's collection hangs above the fireplace and has been dubbed the *Celebration of Life*. The color scheme is rich like other examples of the Aiken period; Kay referred to them as "happy colors." The most extraordinary feature is the frieze of wine and champagne foil caps that anchor the base of the painting thus insuring its classification as a mixed-media work. Most prominent of these is a Charles Krug foil. These were souvenirs Livio appropriated when dining with his Aiken friends. There are the traditional thumb print spots of color but in this case he has enriched them with two tiny green tesserae, mosaic tiles originally from Italy.

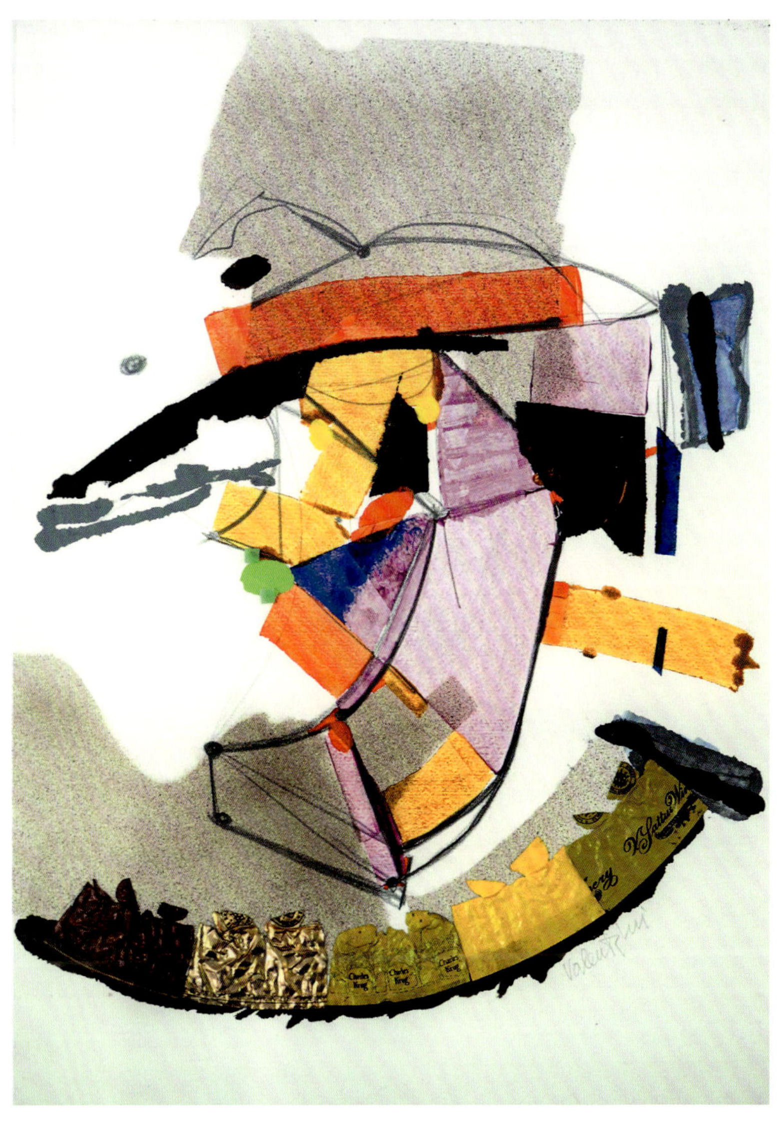

Celebration of Life, 2001. Acrylic and mixed media on canvas, 61 × 81 cm. Collection of Bob and Kay Moody. Photograph by Michael St. John.

In addition to the original paintings commissioned by Aiken collectors, several people purchased Livio's limited edition prints. Among the most popular was a print also shown in the book, *Orvieto: progetto per una città utopica* (Orvieto: Project for a Utopian City). In this print the Duomo rises high on the hilltop. In the valley below a group of citizens wave their hands and hoist banners blowing in the wind. Overhead two distinctive Valentini symbols float: his iconic dove and a hovering angel. The facade of the cathedral is hand painted with bright yellow thumbprint shapes while at the feet of the men he placed a smaller vivid blue dot. Each addition is *uno alla volta,* one at a time. In this way Livio has given each print his unique blessing. In comparing several copies of this print we observed that the color shapes differ slightly in size and placement making each a one of a kind creation. Taylor and Leslie Garnett who hosted the first Orvieto delegation are one of several Aiken families who have this hanging in their home.

Joan and Ted Bondor purchased the original painting *Paesaggio astrale #15* (Astrale Landscape #15) from the exhibit of Livio's work at the Aiken Center for the Arts. This piece continued to demonstrate his fascination with the universe. At the center of the composition Livio unveiled the shape of a planet adorned with metallic gold with green and purple stripes. At the right edge one detects a fantasy eclipse with a Carolina

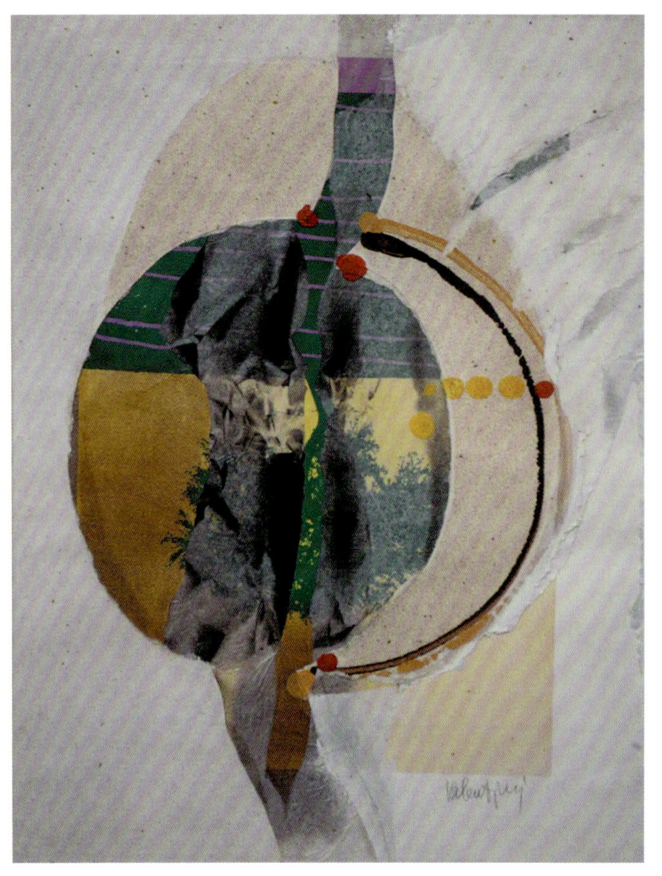

Paesaggio astrale #15 (Astral Landscape #15), circa 2000. Mixed media on paper. 53 × 71 cm. Collection of Joan and Ted Bondor. Photograph by Michael St. John.

crescent moon passing over the resplendent green planet. Again Livio uses the punctuation of yellow and crimson dots to highlight the importance of the moon. At the top and bottom, ribbons of lavender and gold suggest the connectivity to the other planets in this particular solar system. This seems to be the precursor to his journey through *Galassia* and Mars. *Marte, pianeta immaginato* (Mars, Imagined Planet) was Livio's centerpiece theme in the Mostra in 2004.

Liz and Rick Benton purchased *Rebirth* when Livio displayed his later works at the Aiken Center for the Arts. Again the Maestro chose mixed-media to revisit a theme he first pursued at the Istituto d'Arte. His portfolio of studies of the egg, with a variety of shades and contrasting colors, helped him obtain his credentials for full-time teaching. Here a trio of eggs appears side by side but also overlapping one another. The left egg seems to be cut out from an already existing print in which abstract shadows of brown speckle the surface. The egg on the right is cut from transparent cellophane like a diaphanous yolk. Livio outlined this egg with thick white pigment and accented its surface with vertical dribbles. Each egg is clearly a flat cutout yet by juxtaposing them he creates a dimensional illusion. The center egg especially seems to occupy space. At its core rests a perfect stone black circle. Erupting around it a variety of abstract shapes of teal, red, and orange float about, with a translucent, cellophane sphere hovering both behind the left egg but over the black core.

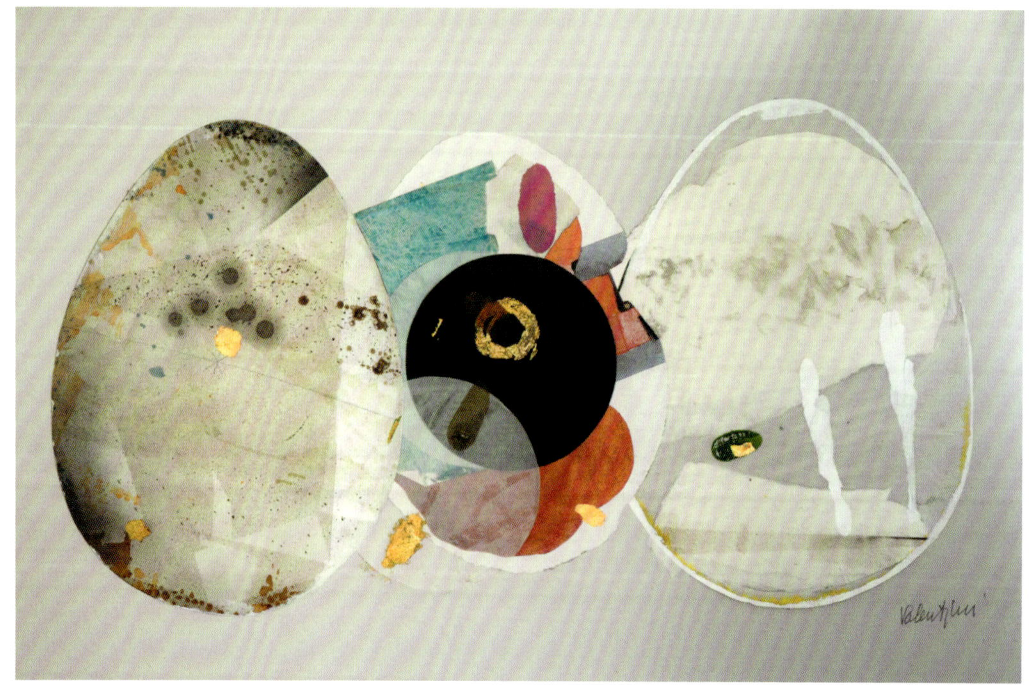

Rebirth, 2000. Mixed media on paper, 99 × 63 cm. Collection of Rick and Elizabeth Benton. Photograph by Michael St. John.

Most intriguing are the recognizable Valentini accents, those gentle tweaks of thumb-sized purple and green spots. Finally, and most importantly, Livio has added tiny circles of gold leaf. Each egg shows some unique touch of this precious material, which gleams in the light like no other media can. Gold leaf is the traditional adornment of Renaissance triptychs, imparting a quality of divine light to its subject matter. Is this remarkable collage Livio's trilogy of germination and transformation, his testament to the sacredness of life? We have come a long way from the boy who intuitively understood the Italian grape, from the outer skin to the flesh beneath. In the same way here, these eggs evolve and glow with the breath of life itself.

Rich and Johnette Viviano own two original compositions. *Tensione spirituale* (Spiritual Tension), features some of the same characteristics as Livio's *Spirituality* print. The familiar illuminated grey cloud is bound up by orange, red, and blue bands and studded with thumbprints of silver, cobalt, and burnt sienna. As in so many of his Aiken works, Livio has added mixed-media elements of pasted paper, perhaps for the purpose of healing over spiritual wounds. Then, using a technique from *Galassia,* Livio has spattered the surface with strokes of thin black pigment, accenting the dramatic tension the title implies.

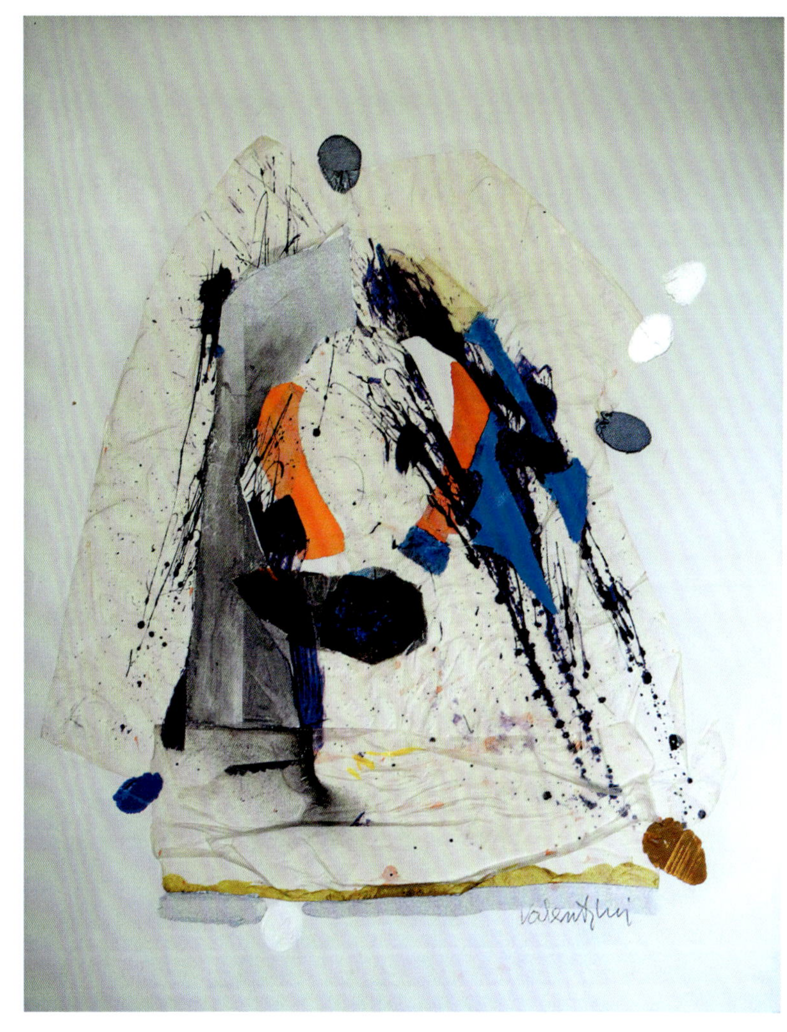

Tensione spirituale (Spiritual Tension), 2004. Acrylic and mixed media on paper, 53 × 69.5 cm. Collection of Rich and Johnette Viviano. Photograph by Michael St John.

In *Realtà allo specchio* (Reflected Realty) we recognize bits of Livio's vocabulary as shown elsewhere: The Mediterranean sun is mirrored from the *Il grande oceano;* the teal bands from *The Places of the Spirit.* We appreciate how expressively Livio has applied the acrylic colors to the paper, alternating between heavy and airy brush strokes. At the center a writhing pink and red pod seems to throb with life, harkening back to the *Germinazione* series. Flame-like fingers enfold the center orb, crafted from paper collage. These vivacious, spontaneous bursts of shape and color stand in strong contrast to Livio's earlier compositions about control and restraint.

One of Livio's most important collections belongs to George and Sandi Custodi, who treated Livio and Flora like members of their own family. Considering how close the Custodis and Valentini families were, it seems appropriate that George purchased Livio's intimate *Laceration,* created at the time of Flora's surgery. George inherited from

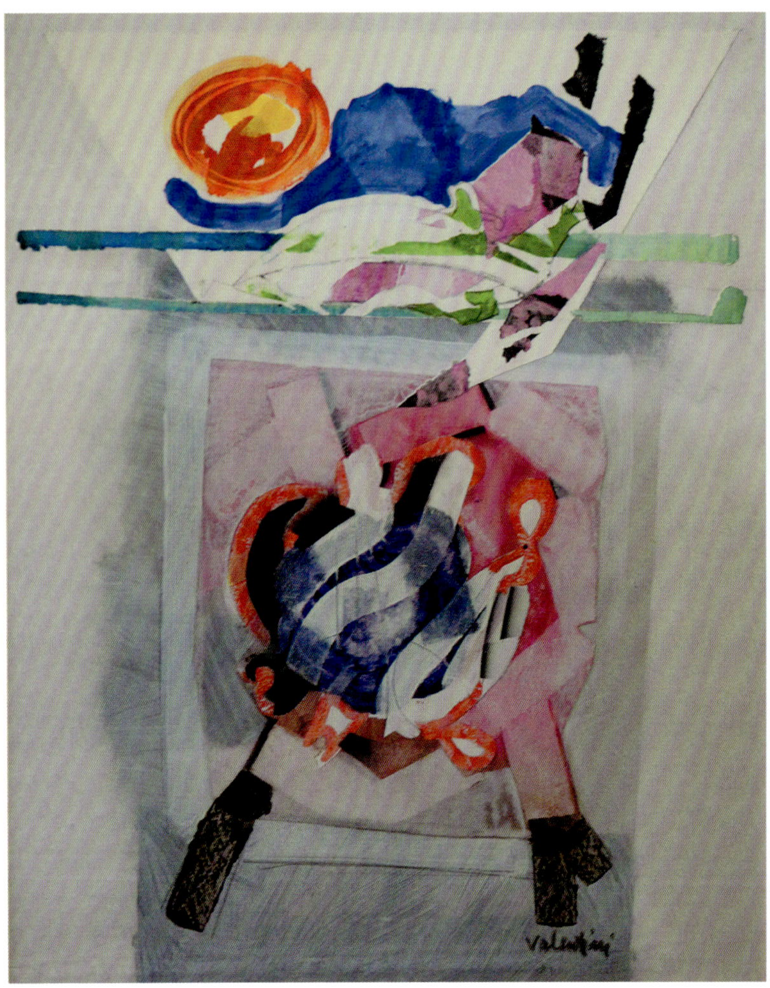

Realtà allo specchio (Reflected Reality), 2001. Acrylic and mixed media on paper, 69 × 97 cm. Collection of Rich and Johnette Viviano. Photograph by Michael St John.

Pia Custodi *Incontro sulla riva* (Meeting on the Shore), the very first work Livio sold professionally.

The Custodis also own the *Odissea* plate, which served as the focal point for his initial exhibit in the Etherredge Center. At the heart of the brightly glazed tondo rises the glittering facade of the Duomo, seen as if filtered through brilliant sunlight along the tufa horizon. Livio even includes the cast shadow of the cathedral spires leading down to the calligraphic title with his bold signature.

Another piece in the Custodi collection reminds us of Livio's interest in such sciences as astronomy and geology. An astonishing painting resulted when he learned that Mt. Etna, located on the east coast of Sicily, had become active once more. In his first year of military service as reflected in *Ricordi,* his memoir, he was fascinated with the role the volcano played in the life of the Sicilians. Livio's version here shows the famous volcano erupting with bubbles of radiant orange against which spikes of stone resemble the broken towers of some toppled cathedral. Within the crackling volcanic crust one detects strata of varying vivid shades of grey, red, and blue. Anyone who has ever visited a volcanic site will recognize the authenticity of Livio's choices of color.

Two smaller and much calmer works attest to Livio's fondness for the members of George's family. Livio dedicated a lovely study of a pair of *Uccelli* (birds) to Sandi Custodi, with the inscription: "*A Sandy, Donna a rischio linguistico con amicizia e stima profonda*" ("To Sandi, woman at linguistic risk, with friendship and deep esteem").

This was Livio's comment on Sandi's early attempts to master the Italian language. In an airborne ballet two birds drift together on the breeze intertwined within an overall egg-like shape. Each bird, with intricately patterned feathers, holds the leafy twig of an olive branch, the universal symbol of peace.

One of the smaller works resulted from George and Sandi's son, Stefan's visit to Livio's workshop. When the young man commented that he had never seen Livio paint, the Maestro proceeded to demonstrate his technique. Livio spent only thirty minutes completing this wonderful treasure. On the spot he created an airy abstraction of both opaque and transparent aqua and violet waves. Bobbing to the surface of these currents of color, a lavender pyramid perhaps represents the sail of a ship on the far horizon. Valentini inscribed it: *per Stefano. "Un simbolo libero, Livio"* ("To Stefano, a symbol of freedom").

A pair of prints with a man stretched out on a rack-like device is the most alarming of the works in the Custodi collection. We recall Livio saying he had chosen not to show human beings tortured, so instead he substituted his famous birds. And yet we have the artist's proof and *Print #26* from a limited edition of fifty, clearly showing this poor soul suffering in physical torment. In the Renaissance drawings of Leonardo da Vinci, it was common to find a human specimen with exposed bones and organs. The best example is *Vitruvian Man* with a male stretching his limbs to mirror the shape of a perfect circle inside a square. In this case Livio's design resembles something rather more like a scene from a modern version of *Frankenstein*! Elaborate pulleys lead down to shackles on the victim's hands. His widespread knees are twisted within a pair of crossed beams nailed between huge flattened metal planks held in place by hinges and screws.

So what is the purpose of this print, effectively unprecedented in Livio's body of work? The anatomical details are extraordinary, with the effect of an X-ray revealing the poor fellow's organs in his abdomen, the bones in his legs, and his face, reduced to a ghastly skull. Clearly physical torture is the theme since Livio includes leather thongs and a Roman-style *flagrum* (sometimes called the cat-of-nine-tails) near the man's waist. Such a weapon has traditionally been linked to the whipping Christ endured before his Crucifixion. Is this a remarkable and highly unique return to Livio's earlier Crucifixion scenes?

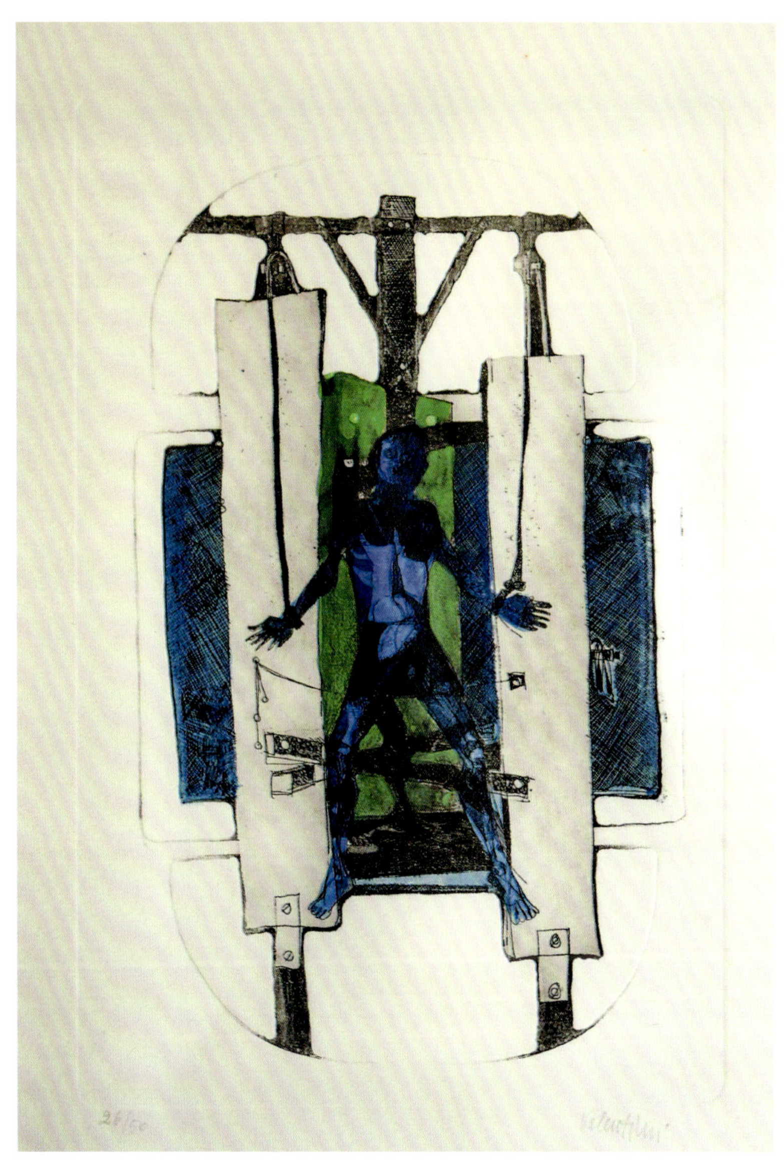

Tortured man, circa 1960s. Print with added color, 53 × 74 cm. Collection of George and Sandi Custodi. Photograph by Michael St. John.

One should note that in the second print Livio has added muted colors. A sickly green appears on the plank directly behind the victim while his skin is tinted a ghoulish blue. Finally to help the viewer understand the circumstances of this situation, Livio adds an additional detail. Over the man's shoulder, right next to his haunted face, appears a dark spiky-haired phantom with glowing eyes. From the shadows one sees his great claw clutch at the man's left shoulder. Is this the devil or could it more generally represent the inherent evil in mankind? While not all of these are of the

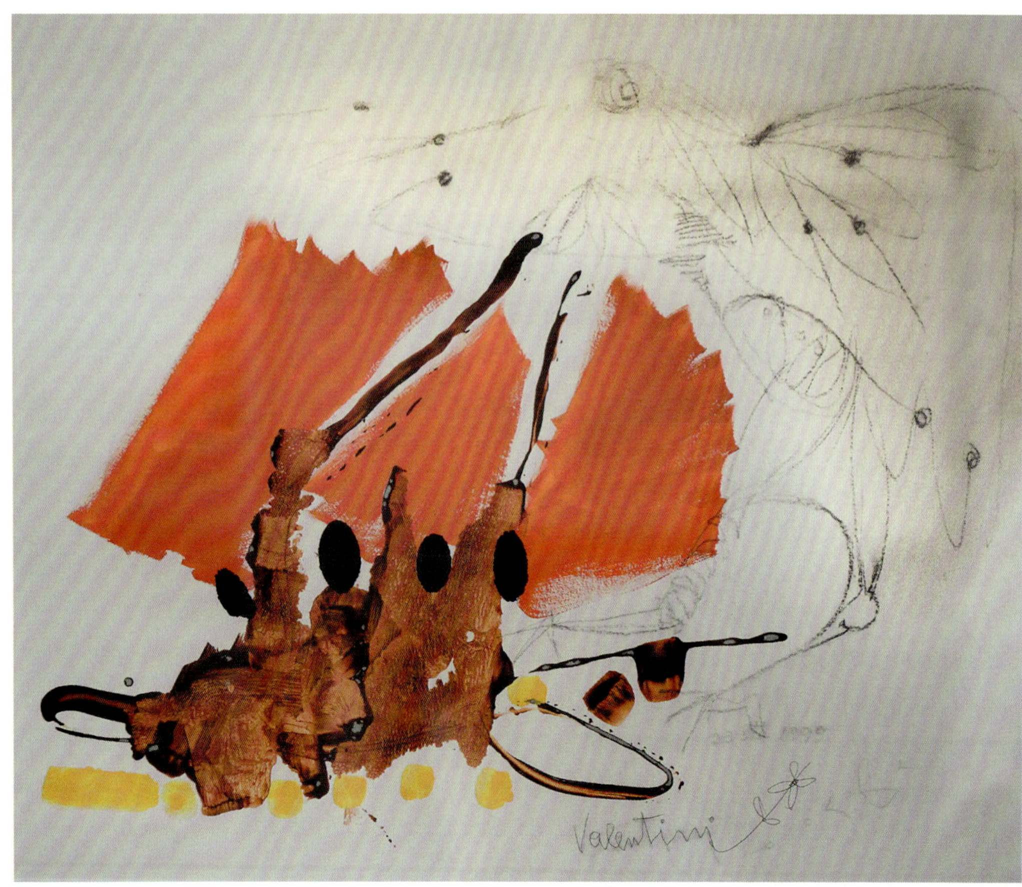

The Red October, Oct. 23, 1999. Acrylic and pencil on paper, 99 × 86 cm. Collection of Bob and Leslie Alexander. Photograph by Michael St. John.

Aiken period, the Custodi collection exemplifies Livio's creative range. They all speak to his spiritual journey.

As part of his responsibilities Livio conducted a painting seminar on campus for community artists, most of whom were already accomplished and hoping to learn more about his technique. Early the first morning he joined Leslie Alexander in exploring the natural materials she had gathered, including a bundle of pine straw. She had begun her painting with a fluid acrylic he referred to as Bordeaux red. One will recall Picasso saying Livio painted with the colors of wine. Very quickly Livio took over the work, making abstract spirals in burnt sienna. While he painted he also performed, so he joked, "No, not Siena, Orvieto!" He began using torn paper towels and a brayer—a roller typically used in print making—to absorb part of the color and create a transparent effect.

Next Livio added bits of the pine straw, needle by needle, using them to create a delicate tint on the textured surface. He then applied thick droplets of black acrylic.

More paper and rolling turned them into four fat egg-shaped dots. He finished with tiny points of paint that he brushed into golden squares. Finally over the entire composition Livio added a dream-like charcoal rendering of the bird, with broad fluttering wings punctuated by his signature hand-drawn dots. The project had begun as an Alexander but became *The Red October,* an original Valentini when he signed and dated it "23 Ott. 1999." This painting hangs among several in the Alexanders' collection.

Determination and Friendship, the first work the Alexanders commissioned from Livio, seems to quote from elements he admired in Aiken. Working on a large scale, Livio used masking tape to weave a lattice of orange and brown bands. Behind the walls

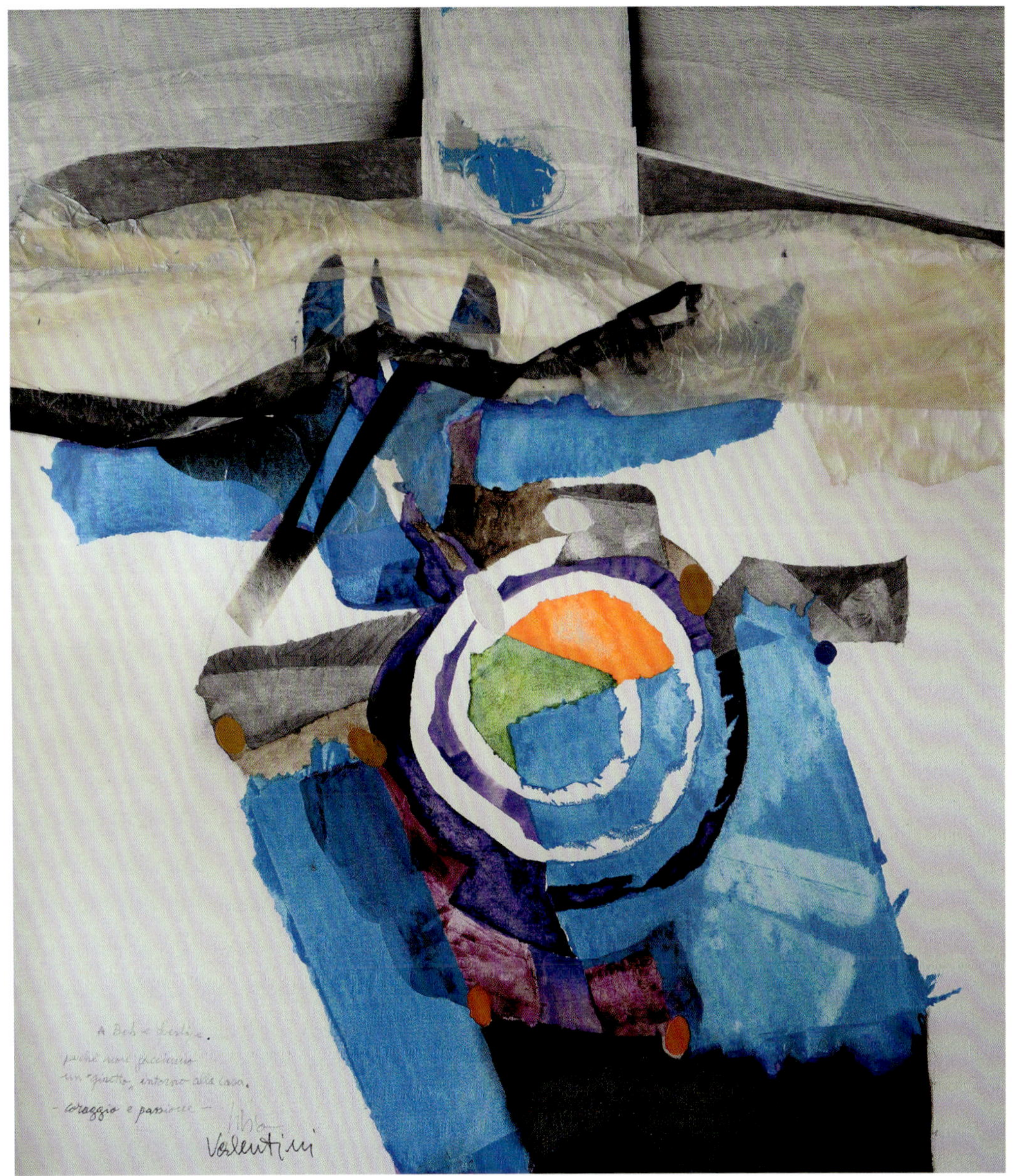

Passeggiata, circa 2000. Acrylic and mixed media on canvas, 89 × 79 cm. Collection of Bob and Leslie Alexander. Photograph by Michael St. John.

of this garden one detects a tiny growing branch from which a fresh bud is sprouting. The technique here and the pale green shade seem a direct reference back to Livio's *Principessa.* He inscribed this lovely work with the words: "*Volonta e amicizia*" ("Determination and Friendship").

In another mixed-media original, *Passeggiata,* Livio combined broad rectangles of blue, grey, and black behind a vivid white spiral, reminiscent of the ellipses with which we illustrated Livio's life story. In rotating the spiral appears to have gathered areas of orange, green, purple, and crimson. Livio glued a swath of transparent cellophane, which sweeps across the upper portion of the painting like a great storm cloud threatening the landscape below. This painting seems to reflect a stroll around the Alexanders' Aiken neighborhood. Livio explained the central spiral with his inscription: "*A Bob e Leslie, perché noi facciamo un giretto intorno alla casa. Coraggio e passione, Livio Valentini*" ("To Bob and Leslie, because we're taking a walk around the house. Courage and passion, Livio Valentini").

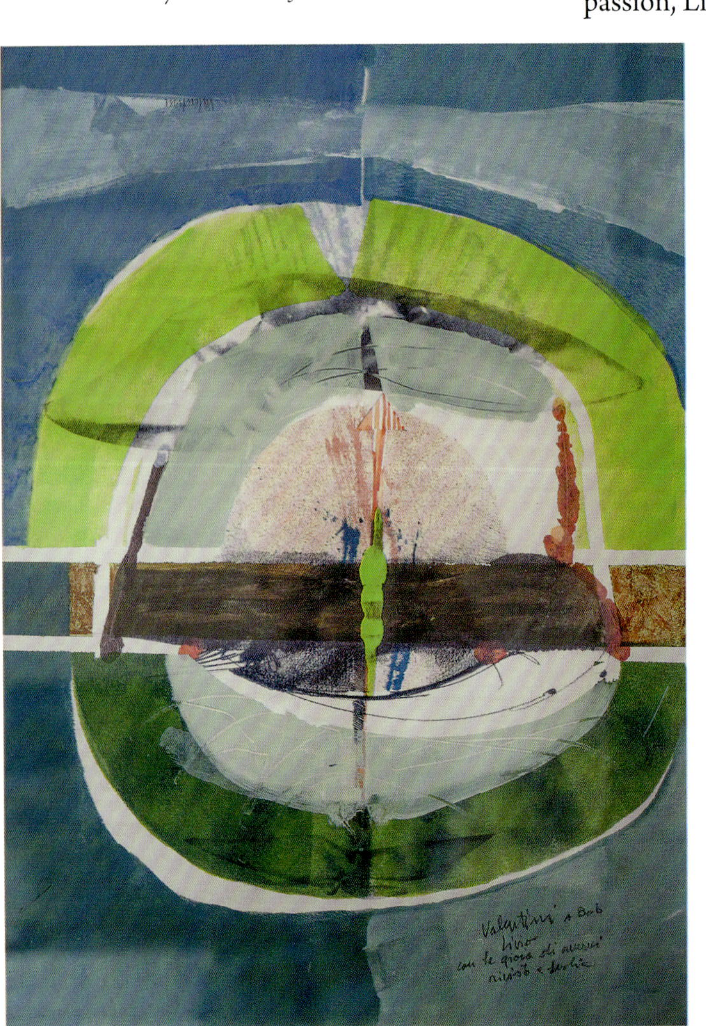

Inverted Spirits, circa 2004. Mixed media on lithograph, 96 × 70 cm. Collection of Bob and Leslie Alexander. Photograph by Michael St. John.

Another example in the Alexander collection, *Inverted Spirits,* was a gift Livio presented to Bob on his final visit with Livio in Orvieto. Originally one of *The Places of the Spirit* prints, Livio turned it upside down and painted it over in teal and shades of green. The painting is inscribed: "*A Bob e Leslie con la gioia di esserci rivisti*" ("To Bob and Leslie with the joy of seeing you again").

Since we know Livio was influenced by many of his European contemporaries, it is reasonable to ask if he may have been aware of the Russian Marc Chagall (1887–1985) and his upside-down world. Towards the end of his life Livio was prone to revisit earlier works, overlaying original prints with new media or completely repainting others. As a matter of practicality his family became concerned the results might be more destructive than creative for his legacy.

Illustrative of his family's concern, several people in Aiken added different versions of *The Places of the Spirit* to their personal collections. George and Sandi Custodi's copy features vibrant added colors as well as a significant symbol. A wide swath of orange links the fluttering dove above down to the earth below. Surrounding that earthly domain, Livio uses a repetitive shape that appears in many of his most significant works: a dominant green curve that mirrors the electrical fences of Buchenwald.

Jack and Janet Morris also own a personalized *The Places of the Spirit.* Here the earth seems to have broken open with rays of light leading the eye up to the dove and the red wounds. In addition Livio has added the bright blue point of a ship's sail. In early Christian Rome the iconography of the boat signified the Church carrying one's soul to God. How meaningful to have woven such an important symbol into a work concerning the spirit.

While in many instances Livio quoted earlier works or revisited themes that permeate his corpus, the dominant factor of his Aiken period was the way he changed his approach to color. If Picasso's observation of Livio mixing his colors with the wine had validity years ago, it was even truer after his time in Aiken.

As Livio's Aiken translator Silvia Powledge spent more time with him than many of us. She remembered the first time Livio was introduced to her:

> I did not know what to think about him because he was unpredictable. He had a wonderful sense of humor. I remember when I started speaking Italian to him he said, "Oh! You are an American but you speak in Italian. Where did you come from?" I told him I was here teaching but I had been born in Italy and my parents immigrated to Argentina. So he said that I was a citizen of the world. He taught me all about art because I didn't have much of a background. I learned a lot from him and I value his work.
>
> Every time he started a project at the university, he repeated the phrase; "You need to have courage in art." When he talked about courage, he meant you had to be true to yourself and hope people would understand your feelings. He also said art could be interpreted in many ways; different people got different vibrations from a painting. . . . At first I did not understand him because I was not familiar with his style of art . . . I watched him work on different pieces and started to understand what he was doing

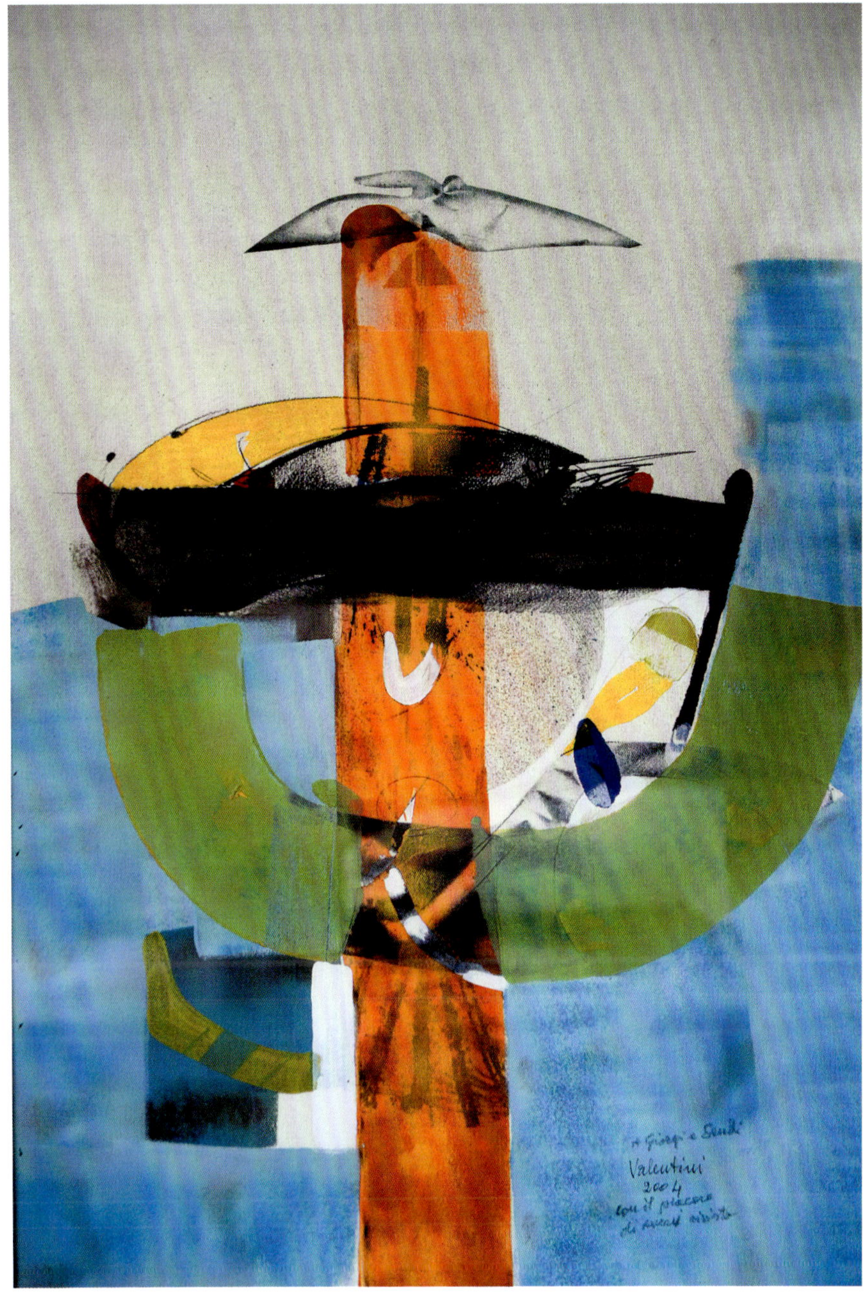

I luoghi dello spirito (The Places of the Spirit), 2004. Mixed media on lithograph, 96 × 70 cm. Collection of George and Sandi Custodi. Photograph by Michael St. John.

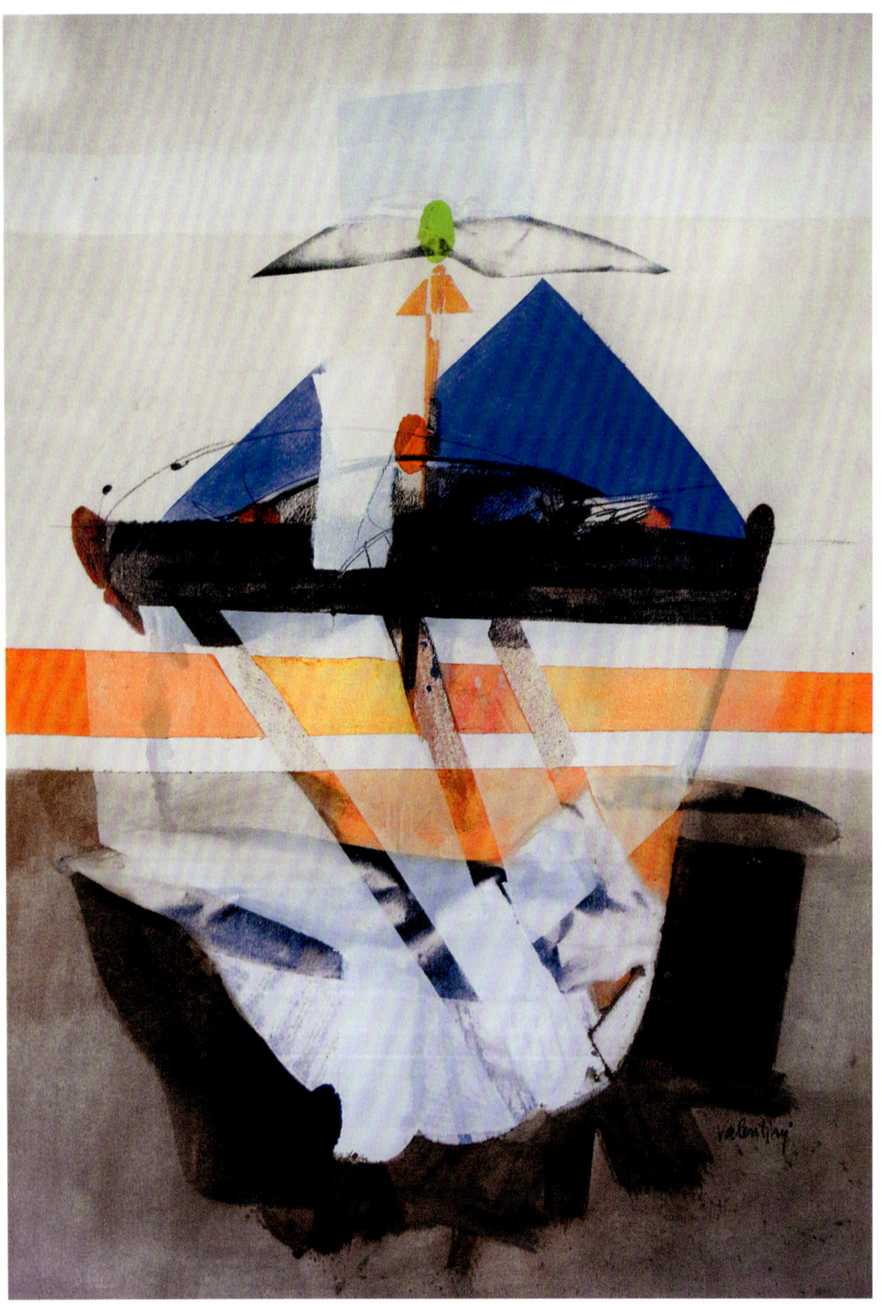

and appreciate the colors he used. The works he produced here and the ones for Charleston's Piccolo Spoleto were very colorful. Those strong colors created a vibration of optimism or happiness.

Silvia believed his works of art "gained more power, more strength through his years in Aiken."

Silvia recalled, "I went to Orvieto frequently after I met him and spent time with his family. I visited his studio and looked at some of his work . . . I will never forget his enthusiasm. He was always looking forward to creating something new on the canvas. He anticipated returning to Aiken every year. He missed Aiken so much. One day he said he had already fulfilled his mission in Orvieto. He thought he was needed more in Aiken; he had found another home and a new set of friends at the university and in the city."[39]

I luoghi dello spirito (The Places of the Spirit), 2004.
Mixed media on lithograph, 96 × 70 cm.
Collection of Jack and Janet Morris.
Photograph by Michael St. John.

CHAPTER SIX

The Story of *Galassia*

LIVIO BELIEVED, AND WE CONCUR, that *Galassia* was the most important contribution to his body of work. In order to appreciate what we experienced with this project, it needs to be seen from at least two points of view: First is the way in which the painting came into existence, its physical dimensions and problems regarding its ultimate placement. Second is the content and the meaning for the artist as he applied paint to canvas and added the separate sculptural elements.

In November of 1999, as Livio concluded his first year in residency, the university invited him to return for a second year and paint a major work for the USCA permanent collection. He was commissioned by the chancellor "to explore the universe of the university." Beyond that he was given free reign to choose the size, style, and medium of the project. He gladly agreed to do so and promised that when he returned in the fall of 2000 he would create his magnum opus and dedicate it to the students. Early in the evolution of the project Livio contemplated a large ceramic sculpture. Professor Al Beyer remembered when Livio decided instead to create a huge painting as an installation piece. The decision of where it would be displayed was driven in large part by the size of the work he proposed. He conceived of eight interconnecting panels to form a canvas approximately twelve feet high and thirty feet wide with a bronze sculptural frieze running horizontally through its center.

In describing his intentions Livio said, "The concept of this galaxy itself is important." When asked why the frieze should be bronze he explained, "Bronze is a good strong significant metal because it is an element found in the stars and moon."[1]

Now that we had commissioned Livio to do what was to become known as *Galassia,* the university was faced with the decision as to where we would display it. Obviously a huge space would be required to show an epic work of art in the most advantageous way. In anticipation of Livio's return to USCA, several colleagues held a series of meetings to determine its placement. Two existing buildings presented some degree of potential. The first was an apparent natural, the Etherredge Center gallery space. We quickly realized the upper wall opposite the balcony gallery was limited by the intrusive configuration of the heating and air conditioning system. The painting could not be placed on this wall because it would hang too low and cover a significant portion of the lower gallery. The second option was the Student Activity Center scheduled for a major renovation at the time. A special space could possibly be created for the painting. Even though a strong case could be made for this location since Livio intended for this work to speak to the students, upon considering the issues of security and the mission of the center, it was agreed this might not be our best choice.

Next the Convocation Center, which was in the design phase, was broached as a possibility. This facility had been planned to serve multiple purposes. The new building would meet the needs of the university and the community, including five thousand seats for large concerts, cultural events, and graduation ceremonies. In addition it would house university athletic events such as basketball and volleyball games.

We asked the architects to meet with Livio and the fine arts committee. Robert Kennedy of GMK Associates, the architectural firm responsible for the final design, met with us to explore the feasibility of having such an exhibit space in the center. Kennedy was a natural because he was both an architect and a painter of regional renown.

Robert Kennedy and Livio connected immediately, using their mutual vocabulary of art and painting. After a great deal of give and take about the best way to show the proposed painting, it was agreed that a large white museum-quality wall at least thirty feet tall and thirty feet wide was necessary. Livio's painting would be the dominant

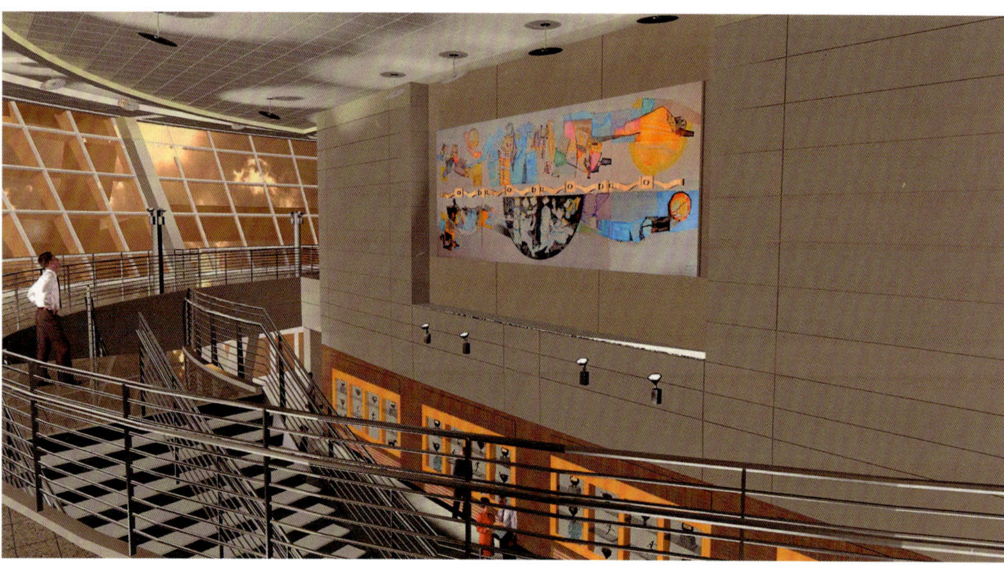

Computer generated view, balcony and *Galassia* in Convocation Center at USCA. Produced by GMK. Collection of USCA.

feature as one entered the Convocation Center. In essence we wanted to create an atrium-like lobby to serve as a gallery and initial gathering place for the two communities. Our vision was to locate the painting in such a way as to allow people to see it as they drove past the center and it would be illuminated at night. Originally the concept included a variety of sculptures, some freestanding on the plaza, others intersecting through the glass into the interior space, and still others throughout the interior of the atrium. A sweeping balcony would give viewers a second level from which to enjoy the painting. Kennedy and his staff proceeded with a magnificent design that inspired excitement and anticipation. The Convocation Center, with *Galassia* in the light-filled atrium, would serve as a dramatic statement of the shared commitment to the arts. Professor Al Beyer commented, "*Galassia* was to be an environment, not just a painting."

With the new commission confirmed and the display area selected, the creation of the epic painting *Galassia* became a huge physical undertaking. Al Beyer worked with Livio to measure the size of each of the eight canvases and plan how the frames would be physically assembled. C. D. Ford, in the USCA physical plant, was responsible for cutting the stretcher boards and designing the joints to hold the entire work together. Professor Beyer stretched the canvases just as he had done for *La Principessa.*

For the making of *La Principessa,* Professor Al Beyer had shared art supplies from his own studio. But now with a huge original commission at hand, it was time to equip Livio with a full palette of colors and art supplies. A trip to Bailie's in Augusta yielded a fine array of acrylic colors. But we also recall Livio saying "big painting, big brush!" For a super size painting we needed masking tape, fresh brushes, etc. With the Lilliputian dictionary in hand, John and Livio set off for Home Depot, securing a shopping cart for what we assumed would be only a few key items. Livio's eyes bulged when he saw the huge aisle dedicated to painting supplies; clearly this was like nothing Orvieto could offer. Finding so many new materials available for such a large project required hours, filling the cart with brushes of every conceivable size, paint rollers and pans, spray paints, yard sticks, and plastic wrap. Our most difficult task became maneuvering Livio through the endless cans and jars, each in need of serious translation. "Is this paint?" No, that's floor adhesive. "Is this paint?" No, that would be wood putty, and on and on. Soon the back seat of John's car was piled high with his merry plunder!

After accumulating a trove of art supplies Livio began to focus on the theme and potential title for the work. John remembers when he arrived in the studio and found Livio surrounded by quick pencil sketches of what appeared to be his own planetarium. Shooting stars and Saturn-ringed planets swam among spiraling astral sprays. Livio was

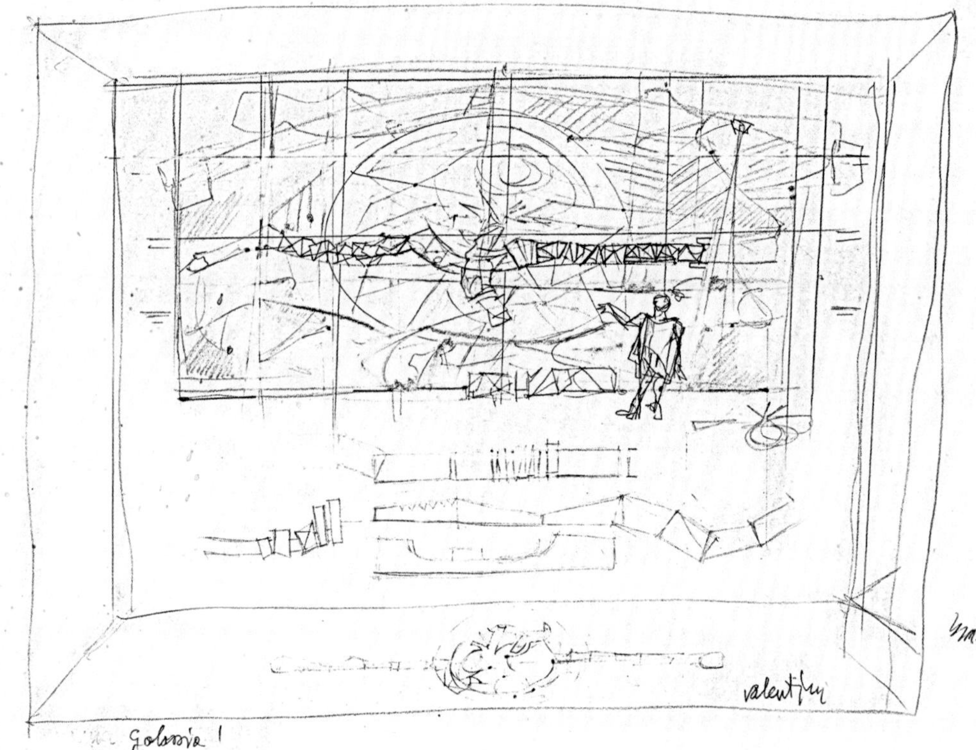

Valentini's original sketch for *Galassia.* Pencil on paper, 46 × 61 cm. Collection of USC Aiken. Photograph by Michael St. John.

clearly ruminating on "the universe of the university." He began to wave sketches about and to say, "*Come si dice*?" ("How do you say this?"). He would show a drawing and John would say in English, "Planet. Asteroid. Star. *Stella*" with his small Italian vocabulary. "And this?" The sketch resembled the Milky Way studded with starbursts and spinning orbs. John said, "Galaxy." Livio repeated, "*Galassia*" and said it a second time. He reached for a pencil and scribbled "*Galassia*" on the page. When next we met it was announced as the official title of the great painting to come.

Continuing our attempt at dietrologia, we sought to explore the origins, influence, and derivations from which Livio's personal galaxy arose. John remembers meeting the Maestro in Orvieto in 1997 when one of the first things Livio said was "*Io sono Etrusco,*" ("I am an Etruscan"). Satolli validated Valentini's Etruscan roots at a seminar held in Orvieto to commemorate Livio's life and work when he called him, "an Etruscan born three thousand years late."[2]

Orvieto was one of the most important cities of Etruria, perhaps the capital city. In Livio's final work for the university he most enthusiastically explored this proud

Etruscan heritage. In the legends of ancient Umbria the relationships between man's present living spirit and his future in the afterlife are well documented. Etruscan mythology introduces us to a frightening bearded male demon named Charu and his winged female comrade, Vanth, who appeared when men were in dire distress. Their responsibility was to accompany the soul to the underworld. We can trace the powerful visual of the spiritual conflict of good and evil all the way back to the pagan Etruscans and their painted tombs at Tarquinia and Chiusi. In the Christian era comparable imagery was introduced. It is believed that the Etruscan frescoes inspired early Christian artists who appropriated the images as angels and demons. It is rather dazzling to consider the artistic syncretism reaching from the pagan afterlife to Signorelli's apocalypse and ultimately to Valentini's *Galassia.*

Maestro Valentini came up with the concept of a galaxy for the new millennium with a long-faceted frieze separating two dueling planes. At the first meeting with the architects Livio described his dream of a huge installation in which sculpture and painting might be combined into one and he acknowledged that his inspiration came from Etruria where tombs sometimes combined two- and three-dimensional features. A well-known example of this art form is the *Tomba dei Relievi* (Tomb of the Reliefs) at Cerveteri.

Before coming to Aiken Livio had experimented with an acrylic work using two colorful panels bisected by a dimensional frieze. We saw the painting, *Colline Umbre* (Umbrian Hills), at the Palazzone Vineyard, owned by Livio's son-in-law, Giovanni

François Tomb. Copy by Augusto Guido Gatti in 1931 of original fresco in Vulci, moved to Villa Albani-Torlonia, Rome. Characters identified as Charu and Vanth. Photograph courtesy of Battlelight, Wikimedia Commons CC-BY-SA 3.0.

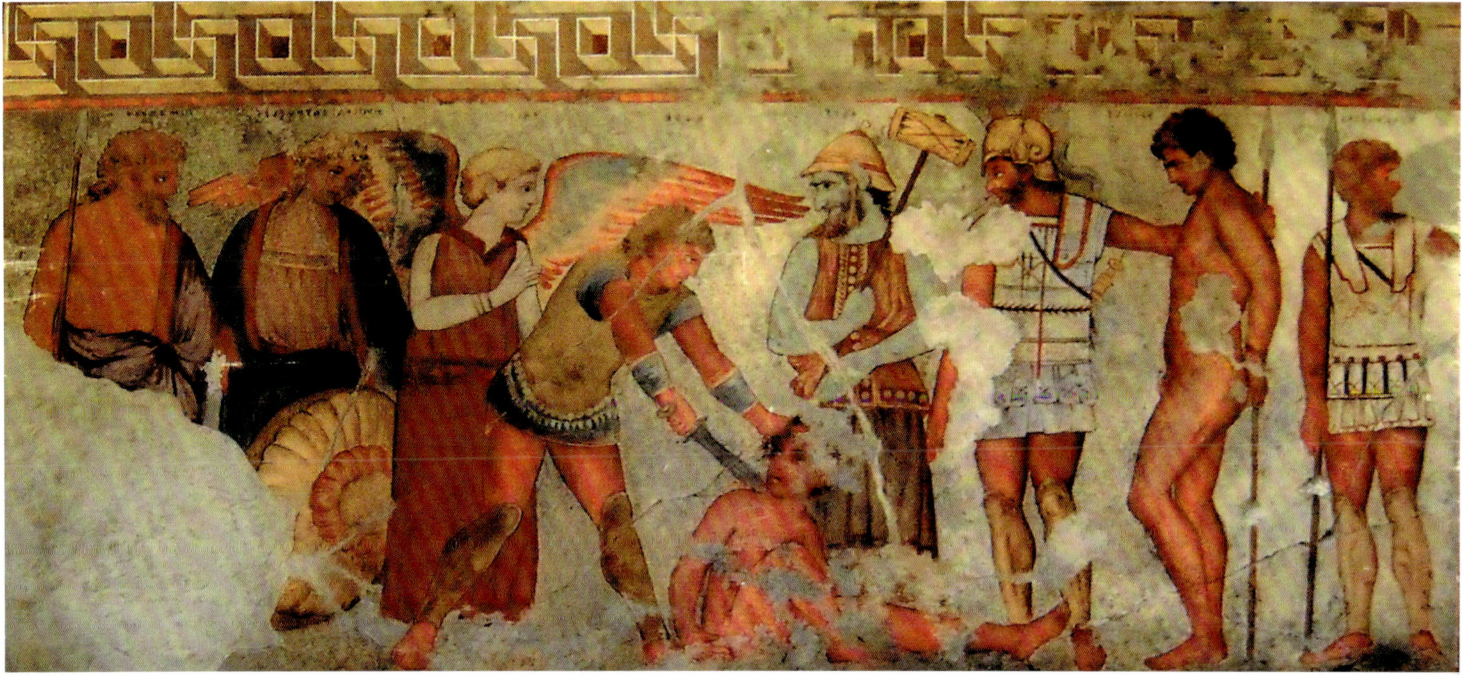

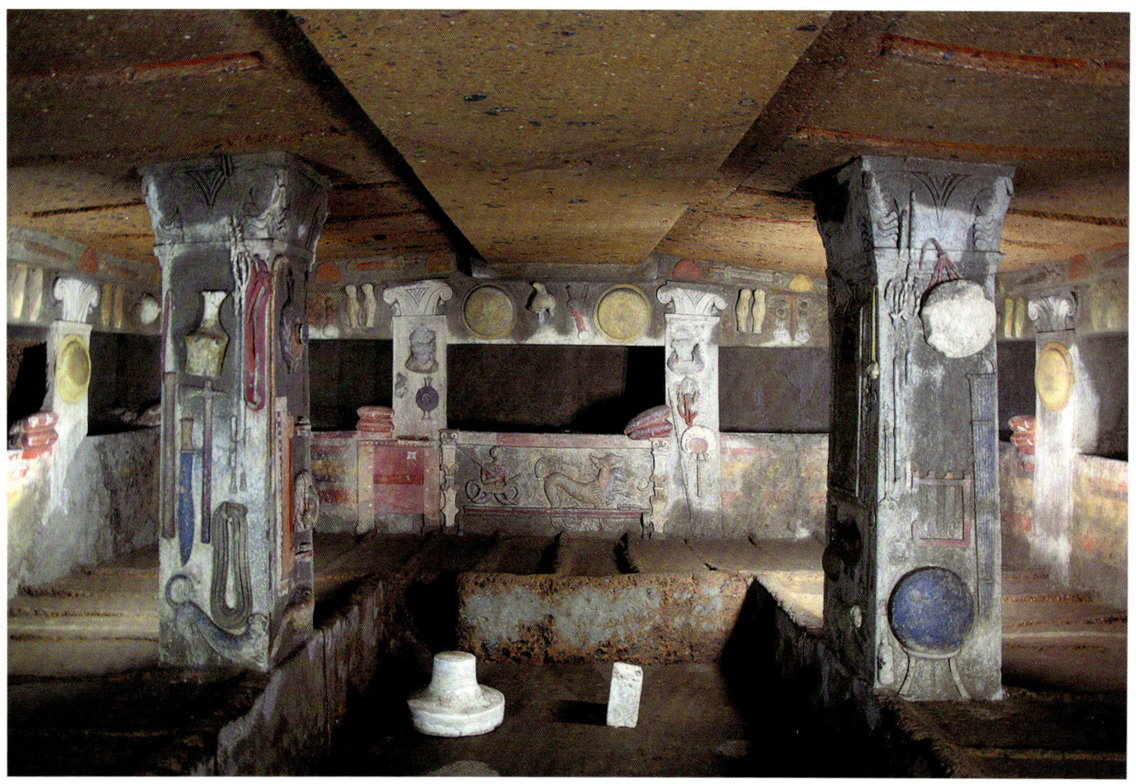

Tomba dei Rilievi (Tomb of the Reliefs) at Cerveteri. Photograph courtesy of Soprintendenza Archeologia del Lazio e del Etruria Meridionale.

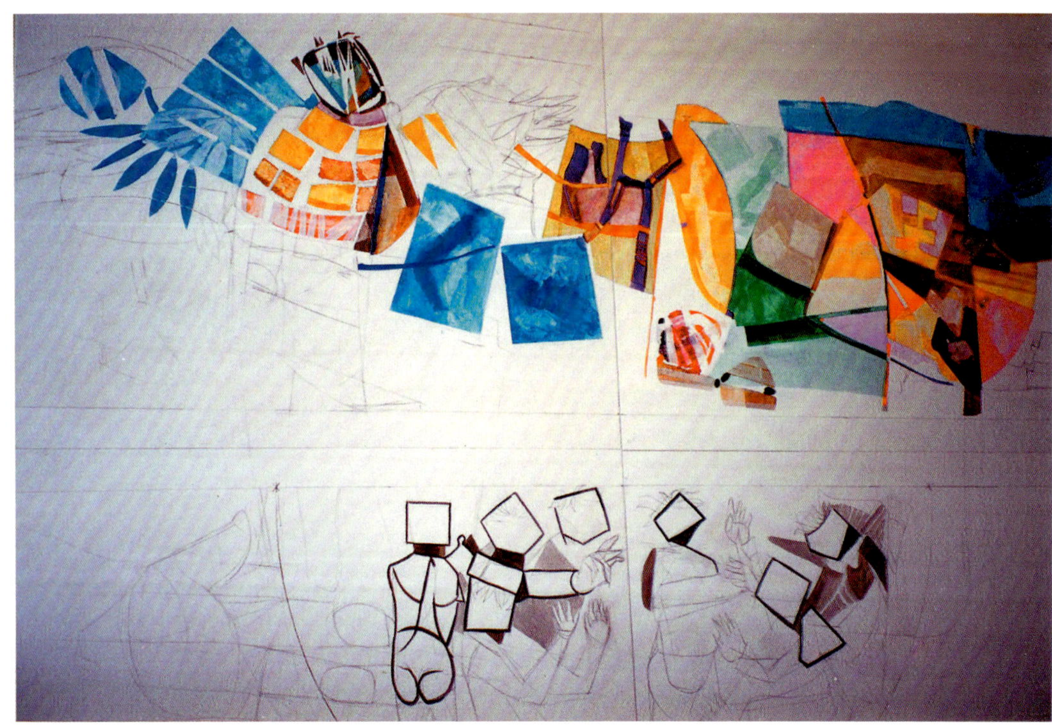

Livio's beginning sketches and color for *Galassia.* Photograph by John Elliott.

Dubini. In this case, the frieze was actually assembled from lengths of grape vine but the upper and lower portions communicated a sense of spirituality, the sacred, and the profane.

In *Galassia* the same dual planes appear, only on a much more majestic scale. In the upper part of the painting the colors are heavenly while those below are earth tones, a sort of contemporary last judgment. At top left is a guardian angel whose face Livio compared to an alien. He said no one today knows what an angel looks like. Later Livio continued, "The angel worried me a lot. Because an angel has many meanings, religious, spiritual and also can refer to human tranquility. In the Catholic religion I always heard people say to me, 'there's an angel who is taking care of you, a guardian angel.' Whenever you are in trouble, you say, dear angel, help me out. We call on the angel in times of suffering, in times of need, in sad or dramatic moments." Livio also admitted his angel was open to interpretation, "a warrior angel, or an evil angel, and it's also a strong angel."[3] As to the question of in what realm this angel exists, one may recall the fierce, armored angels in Signorelli's frescoes. The colors Livio selected for his angel's wings are magnificent. Professor Beyer noted, "The blue pigments showed tremendous variation, from thalo [transparent and almost greenish] to cerulean [more opaque] to ultramarine [transparent and leaning more to purple.]"[4] Close observation of *Galassia* reveals the angel wearing a gown glistening with golden squares like those of the cathedral mosaics. Using black aerosol paint, Valentini produced a trompe l'oeil drop shadow creating an effect like shining armor.

Around the angel, there swirl horizontal areas of color, punctuated by blazing orbs. Here Valentini gives us a remarkable ethereal environment as planets and suns spin through a firmament resplendent with metallic detail. In the lower portion he carved out an earth-toned terrestrial domain, broken by turmoil, eroded by time, and laid waste by war. Perhaps these are references to places of unrest with the angel watching over from above. At one point he described the left portion as the stones of Palestine, where violence has so often broken forth.

What are we to make of the center portion of this earthly plane and its frightening residents? We assert that *Guernica* by Pablo Picasso influenced Valentini's epic vision of the universe. The two artists knew one another in Rome and shared the same intense reactions against war. The paintings are roughly on the same scale and both feature a frenzied figure with upraised palms. One immediately recognizes that the vast center semicircle of *Galassia* mirrors Livio's unforgettable band of imprisonment, the ever-present electrical fences of Buchenwald.

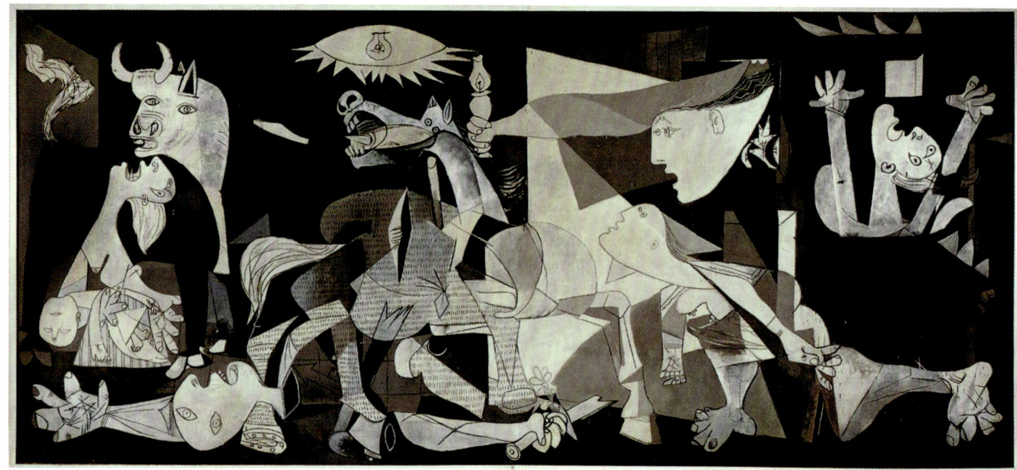

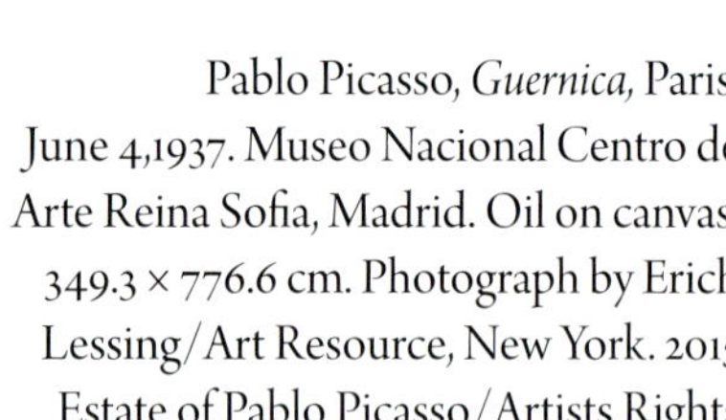

Pablo Picasso, *Guernica,* Paris, June 4,1937. Museo Nacional Centro de Arte Reina Sofia, Madrid. Oil on canvas, 349.3 × 776.6 cm. Photograph by Erich Lessing/Art Resource, New York. 2015 Estate of Pablo Picasso/Artists Rights Society (ARS), New York.

But surely this must also take us, and Livio, back to his Etrusco-Italian roots as well as his immersion in the South Carolina experience. When Valentini attended the football game in Columbia he compared it to both the gladiators of Roman antiquity and saw it as a metaphor for cowboys and American Indians.

Once more Livio explicitly revisited Signorelli using a figure with exposed buttocks and others broadly gesturing to one another. When asked about one of the imprisoned characters who seems to sport an elaborate pair of horns, Livio explained that he might be the king of the underworld!

Next one notices the cubic, mechanized faces of the imprisoned. The reader may remember the astronaut-like helmet on the soldier in *Cain and Abel.* Livio left this frenzied mob open to multiple interpretations. Does this represent man's eternal earthly struggle? Is this an athletic competition, a confrontation on the battlefield, or perhaps

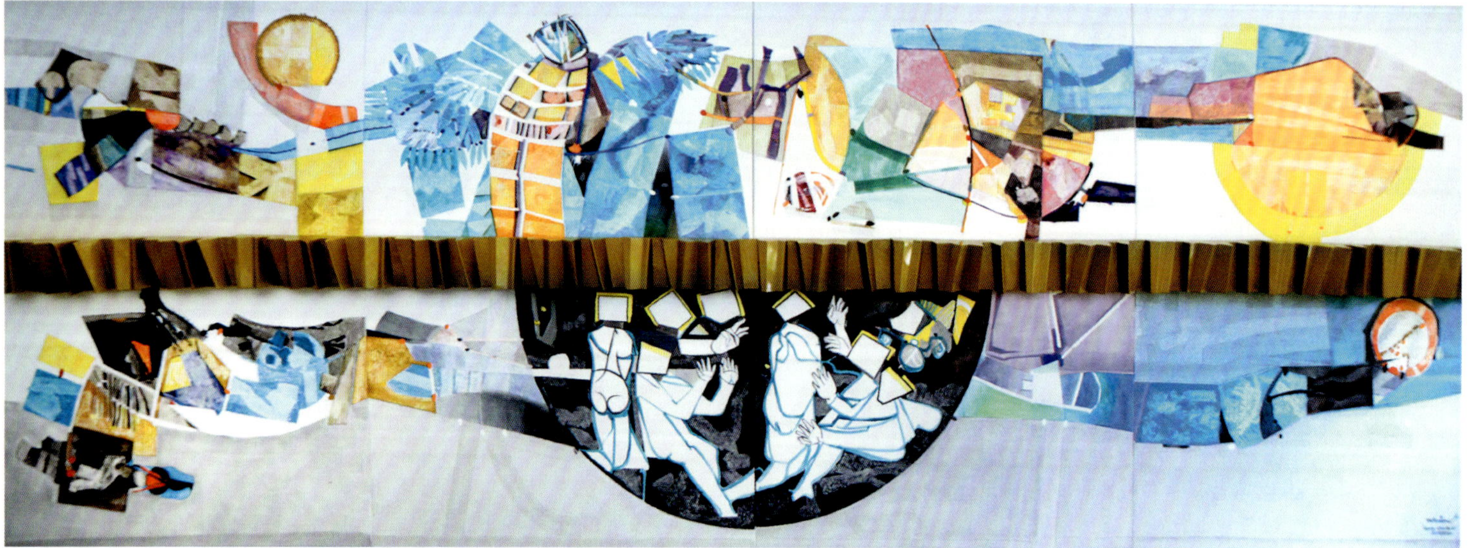

Galassia. Acrylic on canvas, 300 × 803 cm., 2000–2001. Collection of USC Aiken. Photograph by Michael St. John.

university students striving to better themselves through education or technology? One day Valentini expressed his sadness that today's students don't read books, and instead watch monitors. Are these battling robots Livio's comment on our over-wired younger generation?

Livio painted *Galassia* over a two year period punctuated by trips back and forth to Aiken. During his second residency in the year 2000 he painted most of the upper half between August and October. At the end of his stay in Aiken Livio put a temporary signature on the work with a message of promise. "*Livio si riposa per ricominciare l'opera insieme ai grandi amici,*" ("Livio takes a break to rest in order to be able to restart the work with his great friends"). Next to the signature he sketched a sleeping man.

In an interview with Carl Dawson from the USCA development office, Livio expressed his concern about leaving *Galassia* in an unfinished state, saying it was like abandoning his child before it was mature. He explained, "Creativity is like an engine: when it is warmed up, it functions better."[5]

The physical and emotional toll such a project took on Valentini, then in his eighties, must be given consideration. John remembers returning from class and coming to check on Livio. The skeleton of *Galassia* stretched in four-foot sections around Al Beyer's painting studio. John recalls, "I found Livio alone with huge tears rolling down his face. At first I thought I should give him his privacy but I decided to assure myself he was all right. There were so few people on campus with whom he could communicate. 'May I get you something, Maestro," I asked. 'No, I am ok,' he said haltingly. 'I am remembering. So many friends. So many lost. *Capito*?' Do you understand? '*Si, capito,*' I said."

When Livio began the life-sized sketch for this composition the bottom half was quite different from what it is today. There were people stretched all the way across the plane in addition to those now enclosed in the center semicircle. Slowly, as Livio painted over the original charcoal sketches, those other people were eliminated; ironically only those safe in the circle remained. Just as Livio had witnessed the disappearance of his fellow "guests" from the extermination camp one by one, here they were vanishing from *Galassia,* replaced by great gaping, gasping holes, and stony chasms, dark abstractions of the result of war.

No wonder the Maestro's emotions had welled up. None of us would ever quite know what it had been like for him; this struggle to find freedom and then the ultimate goal to get his story told. Now with palette and canvas he was reliving the elimination of his fellow men and moreover, he was in charge of the anguished process. What a dreadful responsibility.

After giving him a brief hug John excused himself and left Livio to his creation, alone with those ghosts. Away from home, away from Flora and his family, the Maestro was remembering the loneliness, the isolation of the Stalag, where day by day his friends had disappeared. If we keep in mind this ultimate dietrologia, what lies underneath the image, the haunting message of *Galassia* becomes profoundly clear.

It seems appropriate to address a question which often came up during Livio's tenure at the university: In what period of art would he place himself and most especially *Galassia*? In 2003, addressing a group of art teachers from the Aiken County high schools, Livio was asked: "If you were going to categorize your work, is it cubism, expressionism, or perhaps post-modern?" He replied, "No, at the beginning, perhaps there was cubism, but *Galassia* is abstract, but real in its concept. The realism is in things themselves. The sun is the sun; it's real, but imagined in an abstract form."[6]

At another discussion John recalls asking Livio directly, "What art period do you belong to?" Livio responded, "At this moment? I have to answer that one correctly. A critic would give you a different answer but I'll say it the way I think. . . . Roughly, my personality is represented in this new figuration, a new way of representing things. Things are represented but in a different way, so a glass is a glass but it's extrapolated. For years I've been doing this, but it has evolved. Even though the art evolves, the concept stays the same."[7]

Years later we asked Professor Al Beyer to analyze *Galassia* with respect to Livio's style and painting techniques. Beyer recognized, above all, the cubist elements in *Galassia* and compared them to Picasso's masterpiece, *Guernica*:

> The artist takes an object and seemingly breaks it into pieces, then partially reassembles it. Boundaries are broken and objects even melt into space. The viewer is left to reconcile inconsistencies and fill in gaps. The cubistic fracturing in *Galassia* is much less violent than in *Guernica.* More of the work is also left to nonobjective shapes in *Galassia.* The issue, however, remains. Much of the answer lies in the simple design principles of symmetry and repetition.
>
> The shapes in *Galassia* are organized into six larger clusters with the most important regions in the middle. The angel dominates the cluster in the top middle with the television people in the semicircular area below. There are two flanking upper clusters and two lower ones. The angel is basically central, but knocked off somewhat to the left to make the work more dynamic. In *Guernica,* you note that the horse's head and the light bulb occupy a similar position. In *Galassia,* the white at the top and the grey at bottom are also roughly symmetrical.

Professor Beyer observed huge technical differences between *Galassia* and *Guernica:*

> Picasso's *Guernica* is the product of numerous sketches and multiple revisions. The paint is mainly opaque and the viewer can see places where the passages have been reworked. This dovetails with the whole concept of cubism where the image is not just a snapshot taken at one time from one angle. For *Galassia,* freshness is at a premium and that freshness comes from the specifics of how Valentini worked. We were able to peek in on Valentini as he painted *La principessa nel sole di Aiken* and *Galassia.* When Valentini began work on *La Principessa,* he filled the room with his own prints and sketches from previous works. He was inspiring himself with combinations of shapes and colors from his own past. For *Galassia,* Valentini started the work by doing several sketches. These were fairly broad and focused on the basic composition. He did not plan out all the shapes in detail. Next, Valentini sketched out the basics on the canvases in charcoal. This was done fairly lightly and is not obvious, except close-up, in most parts of the finished work. There was no general initial toning of the surface and no preliminary washes of paint. A finished area is put down and then the area next to it is tackled. At the most, various areas have one or two layers of paint. Valentini is making at least some of the color choices as he goes. In this sense, the work evolves from the process, rather than having these choices pre-planned in a colored preparatory sketch or in preliminary washes or underpainting on the work itself.
>
> I will mention the obvious: Valentini can compose like this because of the visual repository he has from all his previous works. A work like *Alchimia cosmica* (Cosmic Alchemy), completed in 1990, has much the same design sensibility. Valentini did not have to re-invent the wheel for each painting, just refine it.[8]

Professor Beyer pointed out one relatively small aspect of Livio's design process: the treatment of the seams between adjoining canvases. According to Beyer, "The seams themselves were imposed on Valentini by the sheer size of *Galassia* and the necessity to use multiple panels to produce the broad surface. Seams, in general, can be distracting and an annoyance, but Valentini turned them into a plus."

Livio had encountered this issue before: *La principessa nel sole di Aiken* consists of two panels joined together. Several colors change as they jump the seam. In *Galassia* there is a more nuanced approach. Sometimes when a shape goes across a seam it remains intact: the same color appears on both canvases and there is an unbroken contour of the shape. Elsewhere the color is deliberately different on both sides of the seam. Sometimes the shape is also offset. This became another cubist device that

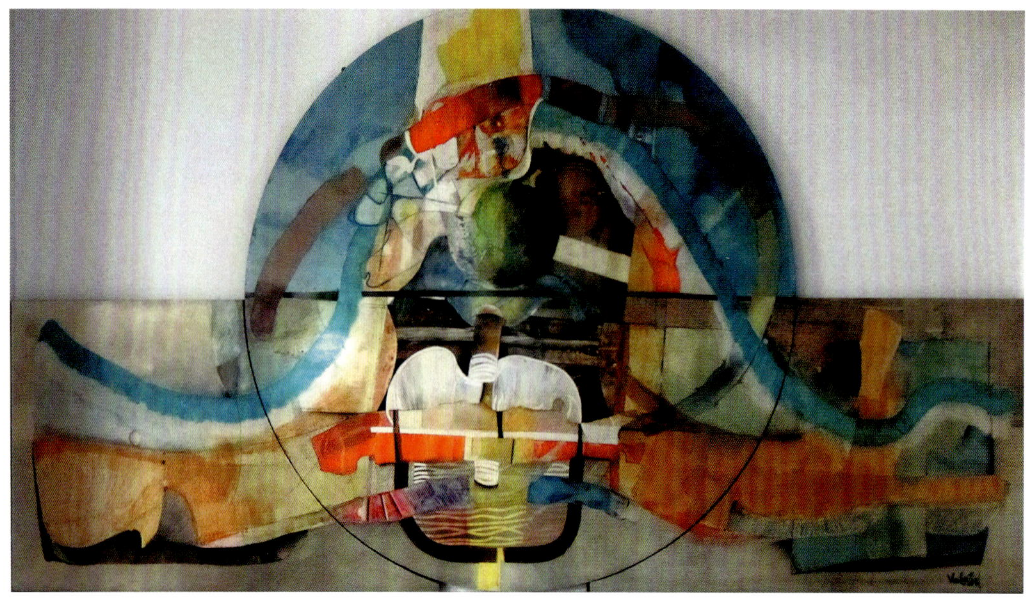

Alchimia cosmica (Cosmic Alchemy), 1990. Mixed media on panel, 200 × 360 cm. Collection of G. Massaccesi.

produces a subtle breaking or fracturing of the shapes. Professor Beyer said, "Stepping back and looking at Valentini as an artist, you see that he took wonderful care with a seemingly minor design aspect of the work."[9]

In May of 2001 Livio returned to Aiken to begin work again on *Galassia*. In particular it was time to decide what form the bronze frieze was to take. One day out of the blue, a wooden crate arrived on campus containing a shining bronze sculpture that combined square sections with lovely curved shapes. Livio had hoped to have the three-foot-tall design repeated end to end in the *Galassia* frieze. However because of the technical difficulties of reproducing this element, Livio, in consultation with the campus committee, suggested a simpler and more geometric design.

So how did Livio's sculpted frieze come to look as it does today? Mike Hosang, the associate chancellor for development at the university, introduced Livio to the craftsmen at United Defense. This company had a major contract to build armored troop carriers and tanks. The Aiken plant was responsible for machining a significant number of the parts for these two military vehicles. Mike convinced Michael Eaton, the plant manager, that United Defense could make an important contribution to the university if the company allowed their engineers and metal craftsmen to help design and construct the *Galassia* sculpture.

In late June of 2001 several people accompanied Livio to the United Defense plant to meet with some of the engineers and metal fabricators who specialized in the use of lasers to cut metal. A key person at the meeting was Silvia Powledge, who used Livio's paper maquette in the difficult task of translating his vision to the engineers and metal specialists. At first Livio was skeptical that men who helped to build military vehicles would understand what he required, much less be willing to execute his vision. It was not long before everyone present realized these men were truly artisans who grasped his concept and were excited about the prospects of being a part of this project. The men, under the leadership of project manager Ben Sandefur, immediately began creating models to demonstrate Livio's idea. The depth of their understanding and their ability to communicate with Livio through their use of models confirmed the special language of the arts that operates on the intuitive level. Nothing specific was settled other than their commitment to help Livio with the project; we all knew the outcome ultimately would be successful.

Al Beyer observed the Maestro's studio techniques and reported:

> *Galassia* is comprised of eight canvases which were bolted together. Valentini worked on individual sections, sometimes placing adjoining ones next to each other so he could see visual relationships. When the work had proceeded to a certain point, the canvases were temporarily assembled so Valentini could see how the work was progressing. When he was actually working on a particular panel, it was placed flat on a table, which kept the fairly fluid paint from running. With the canvas laid flat and the paint thinned down, the surface remained wet for a longer time. Valentini used this to his advantage. With wet paints the colors fused into each other with a soft edge in between. Nice soft gradations played off against the sharper edges of the shapes themselves. On one of the canvases he deliberately tilted it so that some of the wet paint started to run.[10]

Professor Beyer noted Livio's extensive use of transparent paint in the work:

> Some basically opaque pigments, like the cadmiums, are used thinly so they become transparent or translucent. Freshness, however, was at a premium and he avoided overworking areas. Although there are certainly places where Valentini went back to lay down another layer on top of the first, generally he used at the most, two layers of paint. Valentini taped off certain areas with pieces of tracing paper and regular masking tape. In places the paint sneaked under the tape and gave a more ragged edge that plays against some of the sharper ones. In other areas the tape itself was used to

create white lines. He laid it down, painted around it and when it was pulled up, it created a line the width of the tape. Sometimes while the paint was still wet, Valentini layered pieces of *carta culo* (toilet paper) onto the canvas. It soaked up some of the paint and lightened that particular area creating subtle textural effects. Or he applied the paint with a roller, thus varying its consistency and achieving textures ranging from a subtle eggshell to monochromatic striations.[11]

With the painted portion finished and much work remaining to be done on the metallic frieze, Livio signed *Galassia* and with great trust, left it in our hands to await final assembly and installation.

He returned to Italy on July 29, 2001. Periodically he would send a paper model of the evolving design for the sculpture. This design was passed on to Ben Sandefur's staff, the engineers and artisans who experimented with the fabrication, enumerated problems, and then communicated back to Livio. This process continued over an extended period of time and involved several more visits to the plant by John Elliott and Mike Hosang. One of the problems was the tendency of brass to discolor when heat was applied. In addition there was the factor of weight. They experimented with several other lighter metals more easily shaped and molded. Once brass was found impossible to use, everyone at the United Defense plant and the university worried about Livio's reaction. This was particularly true for the artisans who very much wanted to please Livio. They worked diligently with aluminum, which could be more easily manipulated

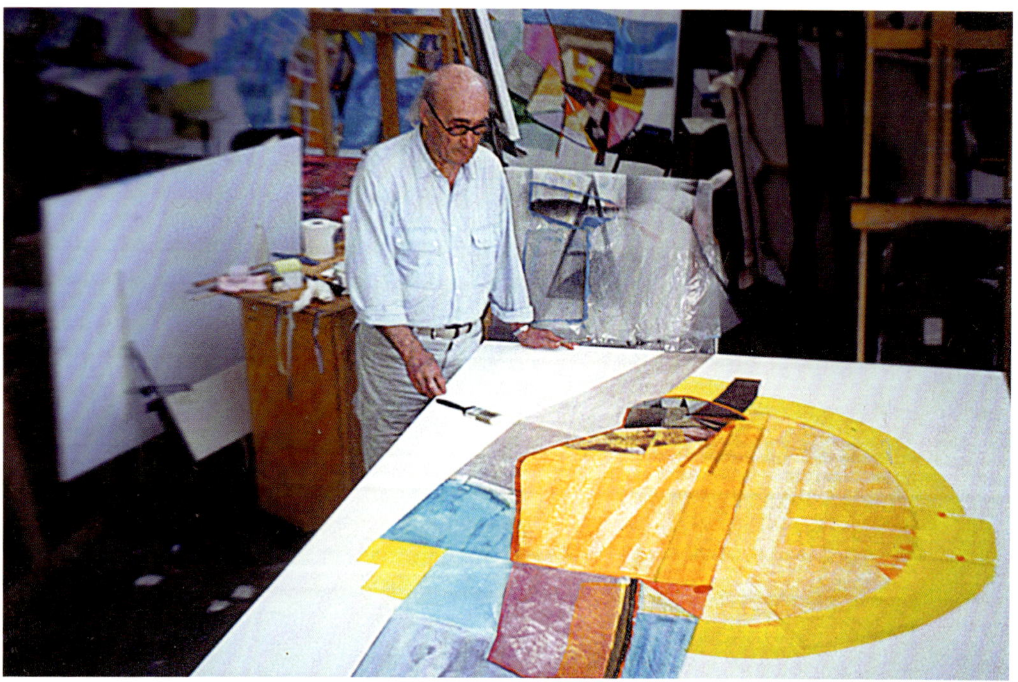

Livio painting *Galassia* and using *carta culo* for texture effects. Photograph by John Elliott.

and painted with a commercial brass-like color applied using a special heating process to ensure a permanent finish.

During Livio's absence the eight painted panels were secured in a storage room awaiting the sculpture and a final determination of how the finished work would be displayed. A palpable level of anxiety permeated the atmosphere as we considered the possibility that the entire project might be put on hold for the second time. There was always the chance something could happen to scuttle our efforts. A lingering concern was that Livio might not be able to visit the university again. The panels themselves were completed but many questions regarding the project remained. The immediate issue was the need for a completed frieze design so the artisans could deliver the final product. Most nagging was the location for display; we were keenly aware it would be temporary.

In the meantime the catastrophic events of 9/11 occurred. The world as we had known it changed immediately. International travel became a significant problem. The manner in which we viewed and were viewed in the world had radically altered. The future of *Galassia* was seriously called into question. New demands by the U.S. defense department raised the concern as to whether United Defense could complete the sculpture. Fortunately the managers at the plant as well as the artisans remained steadfast in their commitment.

Livio's response to 9/11 came to the university in the form of the following letter:

> Dear Friends,
>
> In creating *Galassia*—before the demons were unleashed—I was searching for an alphabet where the reticent delicacy and elegance of certain tones of blue would be something more than a simple translation of a religious wonder. What I wanted was to put across a message, to rescue from the limbo of indifference a language that would help put us in touch with the eternal in our innermost soul. These then were my intentions in this work dedicated to the students. This luminous, joyous, welcoming, mysterious and humanized "Galaxy" takes us back to the great classical concept that man and the universe are in essence one and the same.
>
> I am grateful to those who have helped me in this undertaking with their friendship and trust. I shall always remember you.
>
> Livio

After several months, Livio developed and sent the final paper model, five feet long, undulating with peaks and valleys, and closed on both the top and bottom. He wanted it replicated six times and connected in such a way as to give the sense of a thirty-foot-long solid piece of brass bisecting the entire painting. He left the mechanics of how the sculpture would be attached to the painting and how to connect the six pieces into one for the artisans to determine. They designed and built braces extending from the back of the sculpture to slide between the upper and lower panels. The six pieces were then bolted end to end in an alternating manner to give the patterns continuity and a sense of being one solid piece. The artisans crafted the final sculpture during downtime in the plant, as well as on their own time. It was not finished overnight. Because it was a labor of love for them, and they were determined to achieve perfection, the final project was not completed until April of 2003.

On April 30, Neil Donovan and Hite Bartley, representatives from United Defense, delivered the aluminum sections to the Etherredge Center and very soon after, we began assembling the sculpture in preparation for the grand unveiling. Livio and Flora with their daughter Silvia were arriving in Aiken the next day!

For the very first time *Galassia* was fully assembled by a crew including Bob Alexander, John Cumbee, C. D. Ford, Jane Schumacher, Kojak Martin, Al Beyer, and John Elliott. The staff of the physical plant had crafted a special wooden frame for the painting on which a huge curtain for the special unveiling would hang.

The following day Livio first saw his magnum opus assembled in the gallery and said to himself, "Livio, you're good. Bravo. When I saw it finished, I felt like crying. I was moved. The happiness was very deep." Livio added, "*Galassia* was the result of friendship and courage."[12]

Livio's two- and three-dimensional vision of the universe "happy, welcoming, mysterious and humanized" was now finished. Very early on when he was hard at work on the painting, Livio commented that an artist should not just create a festival of colors but instead begin with a moral intention. He said, "You have to put your work on a moral easel."[13] The critic Dario Micacchi described Livio's technique as playing in "major and minor keys."[14] With the contemporary context of 9/11 coloring our appreciation of the visual symphony that is *Galassia,* it became even clearer why we pursued the dietrologia of Valentini's life work.

An example of this dietrologia would be the extraordinary gleaming frieze, both jarring and jubilant. On one of his last days on campus the Maestro explained his underlying thoughts regarding the addition of this frieze. He said, "Here is something that has never been done before. The painter would paint, the sculptor would make a sculpture, but this crazy artist made a sculpture on a painting! I have taken courage—like going to war. This can be called a *pitto scultura,* a picto-sculpture!"[15]

Livio combined a profoundly modern concept and a throwback to antiquity. He explained, "Plato had said in his time that geometry is what governed everything."[16] Livio envisioned the geometric frieze not only bisecting but also projecting out over the painted surface. We recall Livio's comments that the Etruscans had once employed similar techniques; was this perhaps his reference to the sculpted walls of the *Tomb of the Reliefs*?

Ultimately returning to Livio's Umbrian heritage, perhaps *Galassia* can be interpreted as a revealing self-portrait of a man and his city. Again we are reminded of the dual synthesis usually featured in Valentini's work where violence and peace, the heavenly and the demonic, and ancient and modern exist side by side. If one considers the physical layout of Orvieto, perhaps this is reflected in *Galassia.*

Beneath Orvieto lie tunnels cut into the tufa stone, with Etruscan cisterns and sanctuaries. Above these rose medieval and Renaissance structures. Therefore the modern-day residents of Orvieto live in the knowledge that just below their feet is an ancient underworld, hidden, guarded, slowly being explored and eroded. Orvieto, the dual city, ancient below and modern above, Renaissance somewhere between, coexists in a world of art and spirituality, pagan and Christian, exposed and hidden.

In *Galassia* Valentini unveiled his enigma, dual in nature and dueling in theme: suffering through war, striving for peace. So what is the purpose of the golden frieze? Is it a gleaming thunderbolt or the voice of God, cleaving the space between heaven and earth? Is it a conscious entity like the spirit of Orvieto itself, suspended between celestial clouds and underground earthworks? Or could it be the shining spirit of a transcendent artist, mirroring his artistic journey, an odyssey from Buchenwald's barbed wire to freedom on luminous wings.

Exploring his Etruscan heritage, plumbing the Renaissance age of rediscovery, and using his personal experience with imprisonment as well as his fresh baptism in the new American south, Valentini's art lives in a universe of timeless quest for meaning and freedom. Each person who experiences his work brings his or her own perception of this galaxy sprung from the mind of a modern master.

It should have been a sublime celebration for Livio and the university at the unveiling of *Galassia* in the illuminated atrium of the Convocation Center on May 6, 2003. Unfortunately it was not to be. The building was designed and bids were solicited in accordance with state regulations. The bids came back over budget. This occurred during the time when steel and other building materials were at their peak because of the rapid expansion of the construction industry in China. The local contractor, Reynolds Brothers, had the low bid but it exceeded the budget by two million dollars. Rather than negotiating and increasing the budget to enable the project to proceed, the decision was made to have the building redesigned and rebid the project. The first fatality was the atrium-like lobby. It was reduced to one third of its original size and in the process lost any of the feel embodied in the original concept. Most of the steel was removed from the design and a significant amount of square footage was lost. Tragically when it was rebid the lowest proposal was substantially more than the low bid for the first design. Nevertheless at this point the budget was increased by approximately four million dollars and the university got a much less exciting building and no place to show off the finished work *Galassia.* Ironically the China Construction Company provided the low bid and built the Convocation Center. The result is that the painting continues to be displayed in the Etherredge Center on a temporary rack in the upper gallery. It does not show well because the viewer cannot get enough distance to gain a good perspective. An additional concern is security since there is no barrier between the painting and the general public. Today our best hope is to find new resources to create a permanent home for *Galassia.*

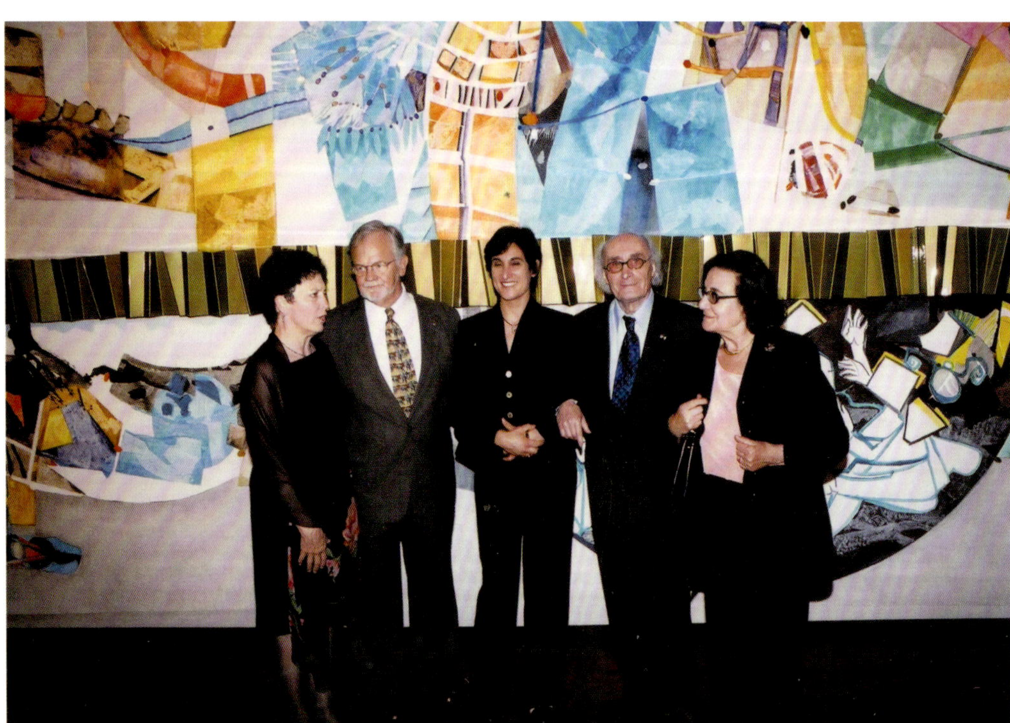

Bob and Leslie Alexander, Livio, Flora, and daughter Silvia at the unveiling of *Galassia.* Photograph by Scott Webster.

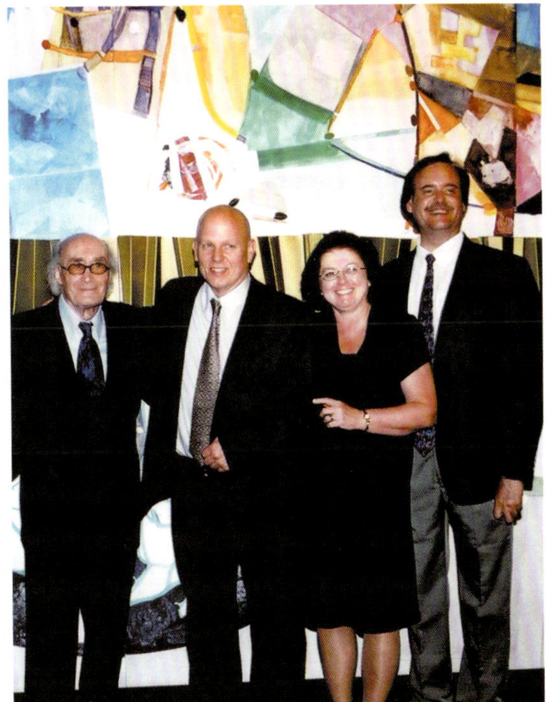

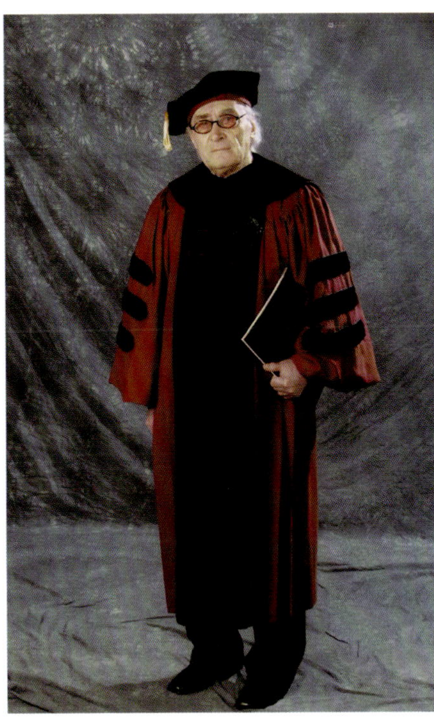

Livio with Al Beyer, Jane Schumacher, and John Elliott at the unveiling of *Galassia*. Photograph by Scott Webster.

Livio receives the honorary doctorate from USC Aiken. Collection of USC Aiken.

When we first undertook this important project, the university had made a commitment to unveil and honor Livio's masterpiece during his lifetime. In addition to the ceremonial unveiling of *Galassia* on May 6th with Livio, Flora, and their daughter Silvia in attendance, the decision was made to recognize Livio at both the university and state level. On May 8, 2003, USCA granted Livio an honorary doctorate of fine arts degree, "for his voyage and friendship and odyssey of artistic exploration." Professor Silvia Powledge recalled Livio's astonishment. Translating for him on the speaker's dais, she remembered him saying, "'Help me. Look at all these people. What am I going to say?' Finally he started talking and the words just flowed from his mouth. Of course, it was wonderful. He was very moved on that occasion."[17]

To celebrate Livio's degree as well as that of the other recipient, Mark B. Templeton, a lovely meal was scheduled at the Green Boundary Club. Both senator John Drummond and senator Tommy Moore attended the evening event. The following day, both senators met at the Pickens Salley House to announce one final surprise for Livio. During the regular legislative session, they had introduced and passed a resolution proclaiming May 12th as Livio Orazio Valentini Day and granting him honorary citizenship from the state of South Carolina, for his "continuous impact and dedication to fine arts education." They presented Livio with the official citation and a South Carolina flag that had flown over the state capitol. Flora spoke up and promised to fly the flag from the balcony of their condominium. As a statement of his appreciation, Livio presented the two senators with a hand-painted revision of *The Places of the Spirit* topped with a stylized South Carolina flag. We all celebrated with a good glass of prosecco. Over the next few years Livio and Senator Drummond exchanged warm correspondence based upon their shared memories.

With the successful completion and unveiling of *Galassia* and the formal honors offered by the university and the state of South Carolina, it was time for Livio, Flora, and daughter Silvia to return to Orvieto. During one of our last trips to Orvieto while Livio was still alive, the entire Valentini family gathered at the Ristorante Maurizio. The date was May 12th and the purpose was to celebrate Livio Orazio Valentini Day in South Carolina. Livio sat at the head of the table, a radiant Cheshire cat smile on his face, with Flora at his right hand. Several of his South Carolina friends and his family joined in celebrating with him; we all gave toasts, ate wonderful food, and told exaggerated stories of our times with "the greatest artist in the world."

Later in the afternoon George and Bob walked through the streets of Orvieto with Livio between them. He shared his great sense of contentment. Livio said, "I have always felt the people around me, even those who love me most, have tried to control and direct me. I have found some of the freedom I have always sought by spending more time in my mind." As he said this he smiled his special smile and tapped his head. In the 2005 documentary Flora observed that she and Livio were entering a third period in their life and Livio was becoming aware the family had grown. He saw it was now a clan. He realized it was worth the sacrifice and recognized a certain order in life was necessary.

As he aged Livio developed a type of Parkinson's disease, which gradually impeded his movement. Over the several preceding days George and Bob had spent with Livio, they noticed he had begun to remove himself from all of his surroundings. It seemed as though Livio had been enveloped by a thick fog or maybe he was escaping into his freedom. Later Silvia and Aldo confirmed our impression, "When we put Livio in the car and took him somewhere for a walk he whispered 'Take me to the airport.'"[18]

CHAPTER SEVEN

The Mostra and the Monuments of Orvieto

BACK IN 1983 Livio had created *Monumento al 3 Reggimento Granatieri,* the monument to the Third Regiment of Grenadiers who died in World War II. Livio's sculpture is located in Piazza Cahen in Orvieto. Erika Bizzarri described it as "another example of a monument in honor of those people who made the ultimate sacrifice."

Monumento al 3 Reggimento Granatieri, 1983. Travertine and copper, 300 × 600 × 80 cm. Courtesy of the city of Orvieto. Photograph by Erika Bizzarri.

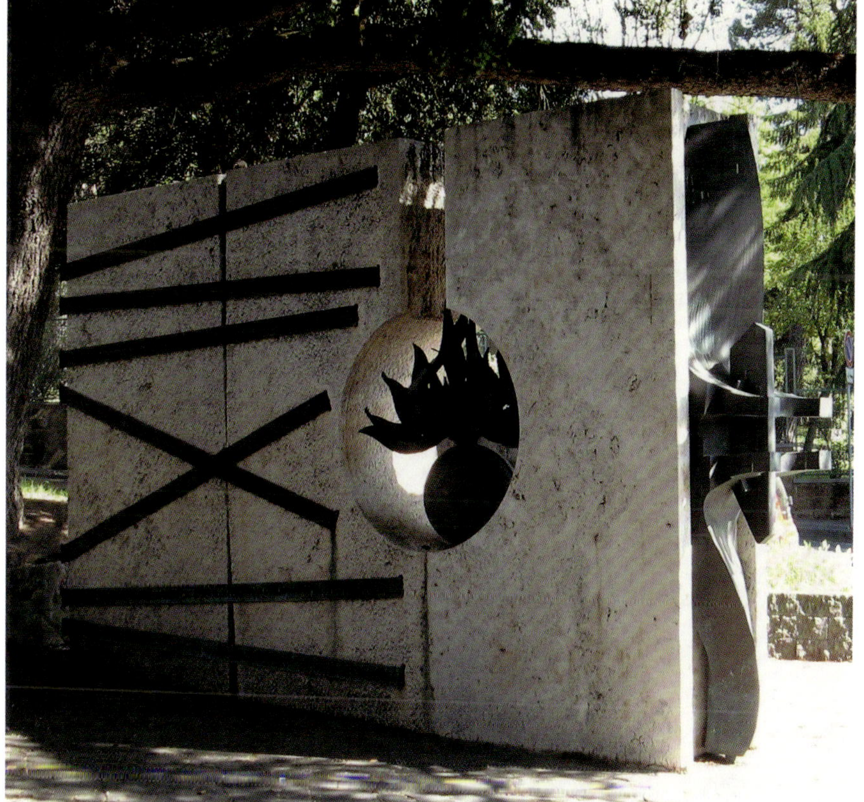

The monument is in travertine and bronze. All the grenadiers' names are written on bronze bars. Livio said, "It was because they gave up their lives, it was their personal involvement. They didn't want to continue killing their fellow men."[1]

In a sphere cut out of the stone, Livio inserted a stylized cast bronze eternal flame. Livio continued, "I don't want to present myself as a pessimist but I am taking the liberty to denounce negativism because I believe strongly in the positive. Somebody has to say that in order to be positive you must denounce the negative. I had to create a monument in memory of soldiers; I believe a memorial will cause people to remember. We need to document a memory and hopefully prevent these things from recurring. So this monument was made not to glorify but to record and remember."

Livio described his technique as "eliminating anything not necessary. Therefore these bars of metal actually hold together the massive slabs of stone and engraved on those bars are the names of 120 soldiers, but we took off their rank

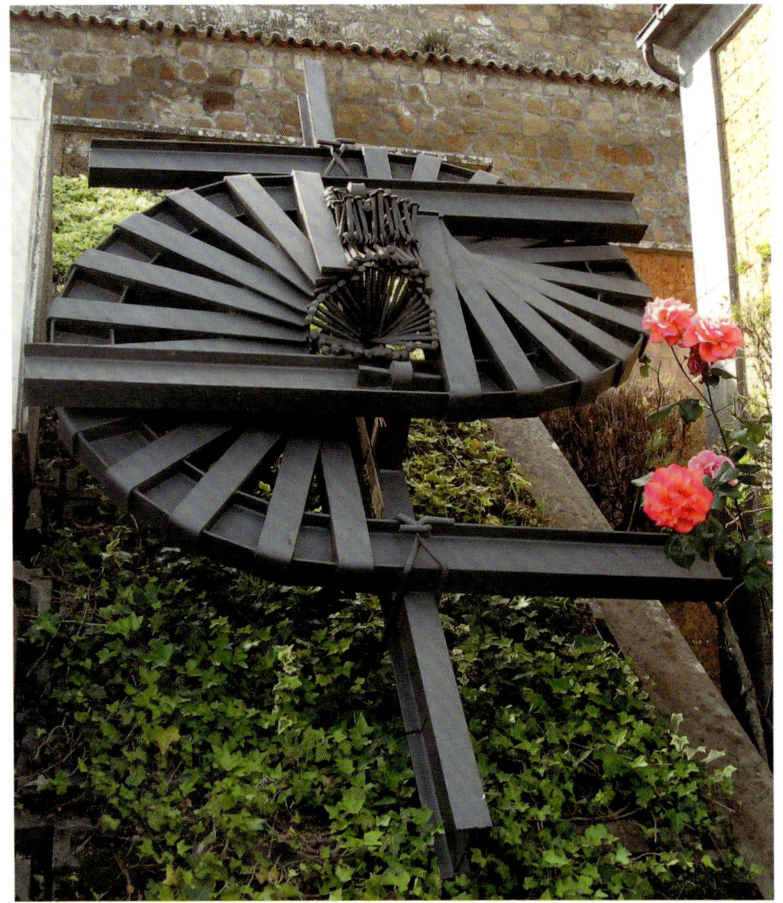

Monumento funebre Famiglia Pecci-Basso (Tomb of the Pecci-Basso family) 1979. Forged iron, 300 × 250 × 40 cm. Photograph by Erika Bizzarri.

and position, leaving only their names. To do this I had to call upon the defense minister because he told me it was not possible to name soldiers and officers without their rank but we argued that these men died as a result of a civil action. They were killed in an extermination camp, which was the result of civil laws and not combat."[2]

During this period, Livio was known to take commissions from private individuals. A unique example is a tomb sculpture requested by the man whose grave it was to mark. *Monumento funebre Famiglia Pecci-Basso* was crafted in 1980 from wrought iron. At first glance one is reminded of a snail shell, created from a heavy I-beam. The curve is overlaid with smaller crosspieces spiraling inward like a lady's fan.

At the very center is a burst of nails opening like the blooms of a flower. As in every Valentini design, one sees his tendency toward self-reference, using now-familiar elements from previous works. Are the nails a remembrance of those used to create his statue of the crucified Christ? Most important on either side of the great spiral is a very clear return to the barbed wire of Buchenwald. This marker for another man's tomb reminds us of the myriad ways in which Livio faced life and death in his years as a soldier.

Livio recalled, "I was commissioned by a person to do this and the man was still alive. I was surprised someone would ask me to make a sculpture for his grave! A little bit before the ten foot tall sculpture was completed, the person who commissioned it asked if he could come see it. I said 'okay,' so he came, accompanied by his son because he wasn't doing very well. He hobbled up to see it, stared at it and was quiet for a long time. Valentini thought, 'Maybe he doesn't like it?' But after a little bit he said, 'I love it. People won't understand the darn thing but I'm going to be famous forever.'"[3]

The year following the unveiling of *Galassia,* Livio expressed his continuing appreciation for the warm hospitality he had received from his friends in Aiken and the university. In reciprocation Livio arranged for the Comune of Orvieto to host an art show including his own paintings, as well as those of Professor Al Beyer and Leslie J. Alexander, who had taken several seminars from Livio during his residency. This Mostra (art display) was seen as part of the larger exchange between Aiken and Orvieto. George Custodi, president of Partners in Friendship, and Massimo Borri,

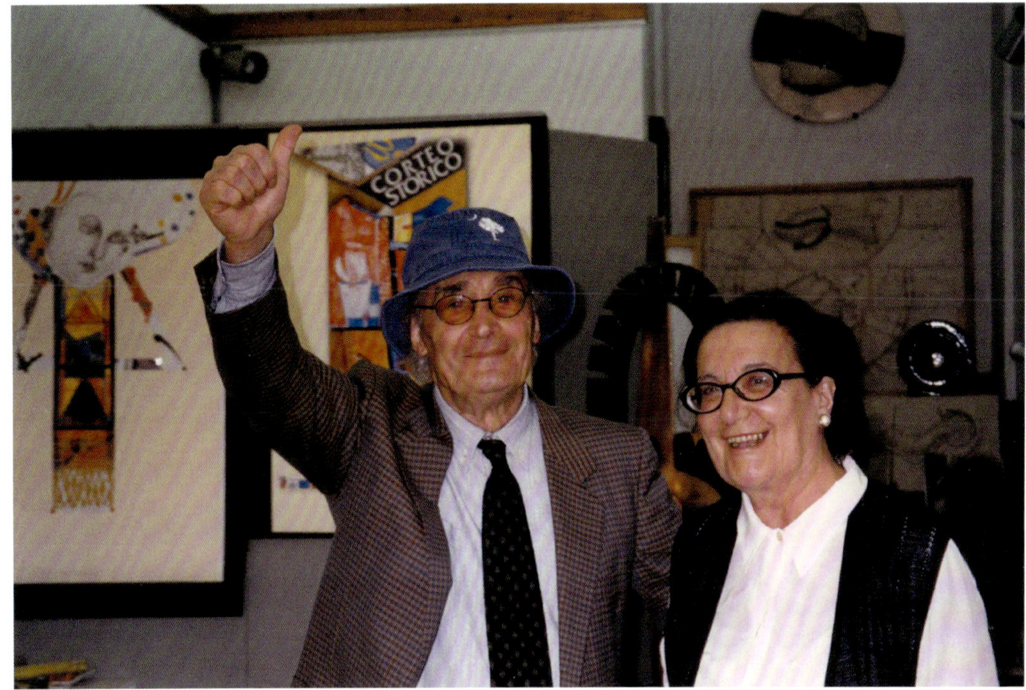

Livio and Flora celebrate with thumbs up. Behind them are two posters Livio designed for the Corteo Storico and the Corteo delle Dame. Livio wears his South Carolina cap. Photograph by Bob Alexander.

coordinator of international affairs for the mayor of Orvieto, negotiated the arrangements. Before the exhibit culminated we experienced both sides of the customs equation, the reality of determining evaluations of paintings, and the implications these decisions had for the Italian customs officials.

The issues of arranging for trans-oceanic shipping included proper crating, insurance, and transportation from customs to Orvieto. None of these matters had simple answers. In fact the closer we got to the Italian bureaucracy, the more unfathomable everything became. Had it not been for George's persistence with Massimo, the entire project would have imploded.

One of the first major decisions was the venue for the exhibit. The first site proposed was the council antechamber in the town hall. With Livio's strong encouragement, Massimo and his staff finally chose the Chiostro di San Giovanni, a cloister dating from the early sixteenth century and originally part of the former convent of San Giovanni. It had been converted into a center for community events. Now called the Palazzo del Gusto, it serves as the headquarters for Orvieto's "Slow Food" movement, which attracts an unusual and interesting group of travelers. Inside its historic courtyard one finds a lovely fountain surrounded by graceful columns. The art gallery is an elongated hall running the entire length of the facility. The space and lighting are very good for displaying paintings. One major shortcoming was its location on the extreme western end of Orvieto, which meant visitors had to think of it as a destination, not a place easily discovered by the average tourist. Its most celebrated feature is the magnificent view it affords of the surrounding valley.

Just as in so many other situations involving Livio, this was the first event of its kind held at the Palazzo del Gusto. The show consisted of thirty paintings. Livio had committed six paintings while Al and Leslie each provided twelve. Initially the Comune agreed to cover the cost of shipping and insurance as well as lodging for the artists. As the time for actually sending the works drew nearer, confusion arose as to what had really been promised. The artists were informed they would have to pay customs charges of more than €4,319 in cash as well as the shipping costs and insurance. It was only after several exchanges between George and Massimo, as well as Erika's intervention with the mayor, that the issue was resolved to a certain degree. The artists paid for shipping and insurance and the Comune assumed responsibility for the customs charges. The customs problem was "handled" by a member of the Comune staff who was known as "Mr. Fixit." According to his recounting he simply drove into the customs area at the Rome airport and told the officials he was from Orvieto and needed to transport the art to the exhibit. They loaded the art on his truck and without further discussion he left for Orvieto. Nothing else was ever said about the requirements of customs, even when the show was returned to Aiken. The lesson for all of us working on this project was that commitments are fluid and ever changing and everything can be negotiated if one is firm and persistent.[4]

Once the art arrived at the cloisters, several days were spent unpacking the crates and determining how the works were to be hung. Silvia Valentini had arranged for her father's glazier to cut the required glass and complete the framing, a two day process.

The exhibit, entitled *Incontro nell'Arte: Aiken in Orvieto* (Meeting in Art: Aiken in Orvieto), opened on March 7, 2004. To the accompaniment of a talented young local violinist, an enthusiastic audience toasted the three featured artists with a local aperitif and fine Orvieto wine, befitting the "Slow Food" culinary theme. Speeches followed acknowledging the city of Orvieto, the province of Terni, the Rotary Clubs of Orvieto and Aiken, and the University of South Carolina Aiken.

Livio said, "This evening I met a lot of people, both Italian and American friends who are following our sistership and therefore this relationship has become even more important. The results can be seen in the people who came here today, the men and

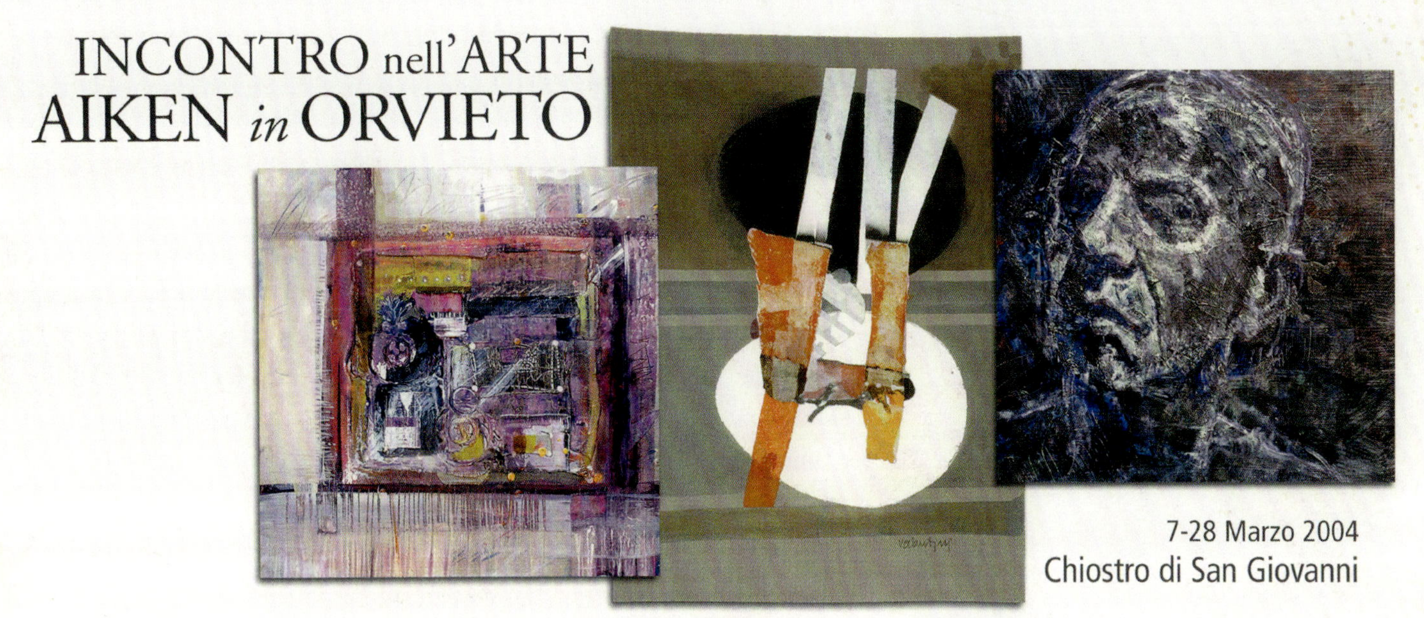

Brochure for *Incontro nell'Arte: Aiken in Orvieto.* Designed by Lamberto Bizzarri.

women who believed. We have much to learn from Aiken and I think Aiken has something that can be learned from Orvieto." Al Beyer said he was "awed by the beauty of the city and by the hospitality of the people." Leslie Alexander spoke in Italian, "*Prego oggi per un supplemento dimensione di umilita' e grazie perche oggi e miracolo! Mio cuore scopplia con amore. Grazie!* (I pray today for an extra measure of humility and thankfulness because today is a miracle! My heart bursts with love. Thank you!)."[5]

Mayor Stefano Cimicchi said, "The seed of friendship between Orvieto and Aiken has matured with time and yielded marvelous fruits. . . . Ever since Fred Cavanaugh and I, together with our wives, planted the partnership tree, no more than a sapling, not a year has passed without important initiatives in one or the other city. . . . We hope this flourishing tree of friendship will continue to bear fruits."[6]

Of the pieces Livio submitted for the Mostra, probably the most unique was *Marte, pianeta immaginato* (Mars, Imagined Planet) dated 2004. Painted in acrylic on canvas, the large-scale painting was splashed with vibrant Martian-red shades. In an interview conducted by local art students, Livio explained that this painting was his "attempt to paint Mars, a heavenly body we're trying to understand." The recent spacecraft sent to explore the surface of this mysterious planet had inspired Livio.

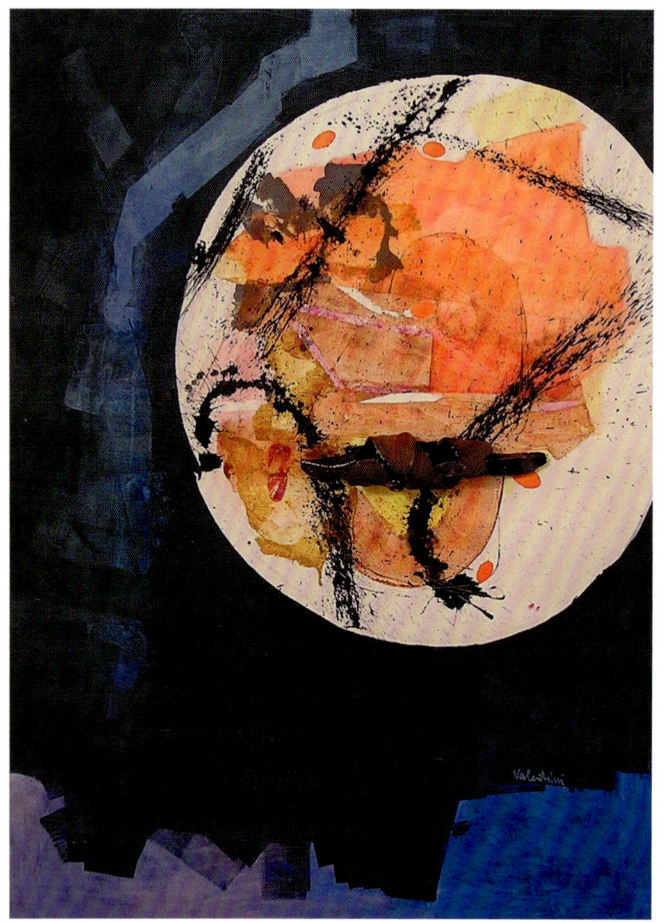

Marte, pianeta immaginato (Mars, Imagined Planet). Acrylic on canvas with ceramic addition, approximately 2 × 1.3 m. Photograph by John Elliott.

Rising out of the upper portion of the painted surface was a glazed ceramic shape. Critic Massimo Duranti described it as "a tribute to the conquest of Mars by the robot, translated into paint in the form of a great luminous sphere on which an elegant Raku ceramic has just landed."[7] So why did Livio choose to represent the planet in such terms? He explained, "It's a new world that has to be discovered. So I decided to try and paint it. . . . This piece of ceramic, which is very highly fired, could really exist on Mars. Ceramics are made of oxides, metal materials, which Mars might very well contain."[8]

Perhaps what is most exciting is that, now returned to his native city, the Maestro had created another one of a kind picto-sculpture in the tradition of *Galassia.* In this very permanent way he continued the ties that memorialized his time spent in Aiken and Orvieto. The same concept would be true of his next and final design.

The last important commission of Livio's career took him out of his *bottega* on the Via Maitani and into an allegiance with a group of young artisans in nearby Deruta. Over a two-year period Livio designed and executed a large ceramic sculpture in league with Nicola Boccini and his comrades at the Scuola d'Arte Romano Ranieri, a private ceramic school in operation since 2001. The result of this alliance is *Orvieto Città Unita* (City United), which was dedicated on June 9, 2004. The roughly thirty-foot-tall installation stands at the center of the rotunda entrance to Orvieto Scalo, the portion of the city around the train station. It was Mayor Cimicchi who helped Livio locate an urban space where this work dedicated to the city could be placed. The mayor also helped settle the debate regarding the feasibility of incorporating such an important work of art into the complexity of modern day traffic.[9]

Livio began the project with the working title *Orvieto Alta e Strana,* literally high and strange. The inspiration for that unusual phrase came from a fourteenth-century poem by Fazio degli Uberti. The poem, "Il Dittamondo," saluted the artists who had "labored with great professionalism and passion at Orvieto."[10] Livio later explained his sculpture "honored the Orvieto ceramicists, the potters who have been working in Orvieto ever since Etruscan times."[11]

So why did Livio originally choose the phrase "high and strange?" Livio appreciated how accurately this described his famed city. "High" because of the way Orvieto stands on its tufa cliff, and "strange" because of the historic accretions of construction giving the city its famously irregular profile.

So did Livio choose a historic technique for the manufacturing of his masterpiece that welcomes the visitor to his city? No, he relied upon contemporary technology. At first glance *Orvieto Città Unita* resembles some ancient Egyptian obelisk smothered with unreadable hieroglyphs. For a little while Livio considered an ancient style stonework, relating to Orvieto's relationship with the Rupe, the rock cliff. He commented on how Orvietani constantly monitor the internal life of the tufa, those Etruscan cavities splitting off like veins through its body.[12]

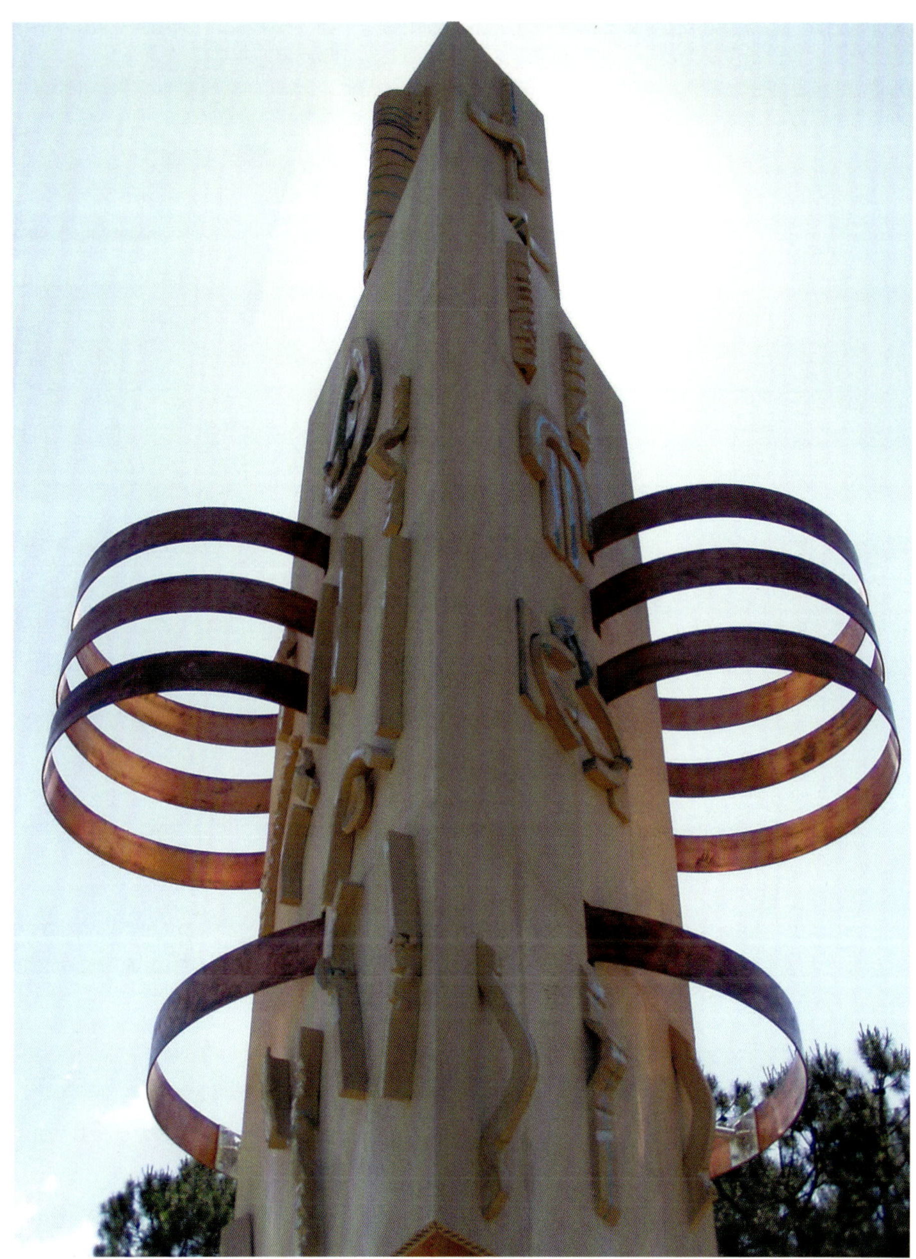

Orvieto Città Unita, 2004, created with Nicola Boccini. Refractory clay over steel armature, decorated with copper rings, 9.6 m. tall, 3 m. diagonal at base. Photograph courtesy of Nicola Boccini.

But instead of a fragile tufa sculpture, he elected to erect a uniquely high tech ceramic totem pole upon which to display some of his now very familiar symbols. Livio designed his sculpture in the shape of three parallelepipeds, three-dimensional figures each formed by six parallelograms. Each side was formed of refractory clay, hand modeled, and then hand decorated by Livio in Deruta. The elaborate ornamentation that appears rather randomly across the surface is covered with a Raku glaze, a traditional Japanese technique, chosen because with it he could simulate the colors and textures of the tufa of Orvieto. Livio, acknowledging the young artists who assisted him, stated that this project expressed in a symbolic manner what it feels to be Orvietani, "our membership with the place."[13] A total of 1700 pounds of clay was required for the work, all of it supported by an astonishing steel armature, built by the Ficola group. Wonderful photographs capture the skeleton rising, the ceramic panels being securely bolted into place, and then a very enthusiastic Livio joining his young crew and riding the cherry picker up to inspect their progress.

Livio chose to embellish the columnar shape with curving bands of copper, three on each side. According to him the bands symbolize the three ancient gates to the city. In the same way their shape mirrors the famous *Pozzo di San Patrizio,* designed by

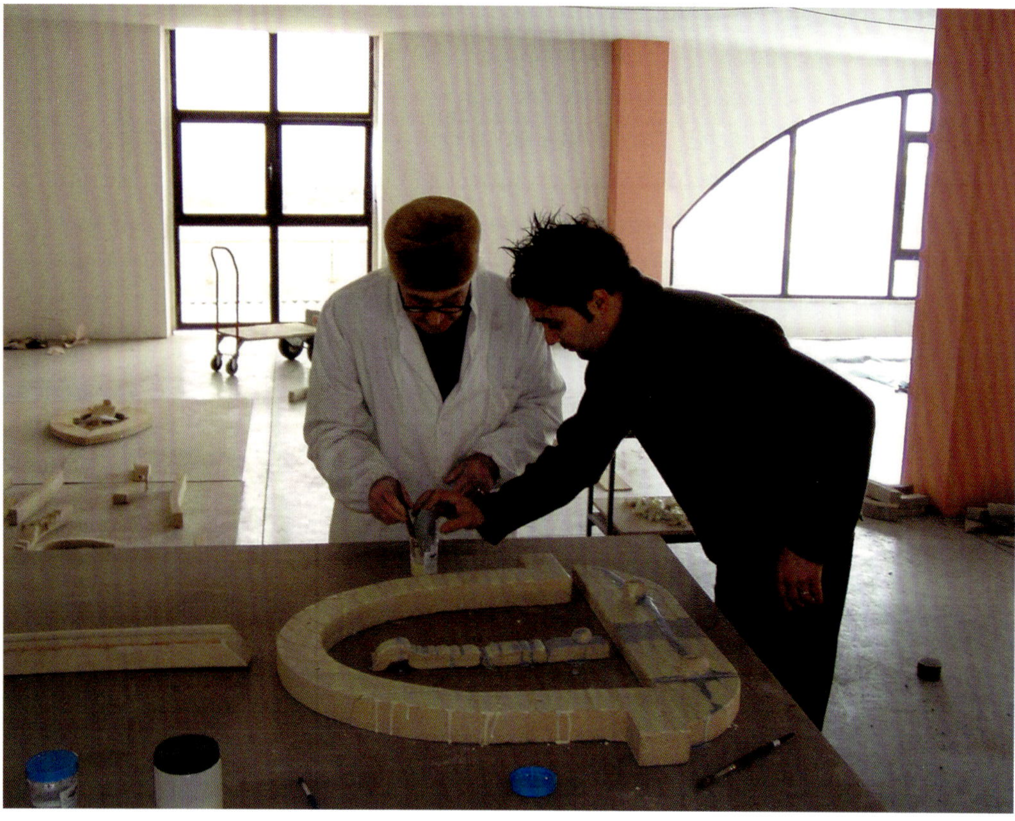

Livio Valentini and Nicola Boccini glaze ceramic symbols for *Orvieto Città Unita,* in Deruta, 2004. Photograph courtesy of Nicola Boccini.

Antonio da Sangallo the Younger. Next Livio wrapped a thick parallel band traversing side to side around the, if you will, second story of the statue. Livio explained that the band was like a barricade protecting the doors and windows of the citadel.

The silhouette of the monument changes greatly when seen from one angle or another. From one central view the column rises straight as a rod, with the copper rings acting like symmetrical wings. Each cubic story sits askance from the next, projecting here, twisting catty-corner there. In this way the seemingly tottering tower brings to mind the postcard illustrated by Livio back in 1950. In both works of art no side quite matches the other, as if under the effects of a bit too much Orvieto Classico.

It makes perfect sense that Livio would use the earth itself to mold a portrait of his city. In describing the circumstances of this commission he said, "From the Etruscan period to the Middle Ages, the Renaissance and up to modern times, pots and potters tell the story of our city better than any books because they speak the language of form and color."[14]

In an interview in Orvieto, Fabrizio Trequattrini explained, "Livio saw ceramics as a material that moved from one state to another until it was fired. He put it in spiritual terms. The raw clay is malleable allowing the artist to tear and knead and pull and shape it with the intent to transform it. The malleable material goes through a violent transformation as it is fired. The artist does not know if it will be broken. It is like the human experience where one is either broken or tempered. The artist is not in complete control. It is easy to change a painting but not so with ceramics."[15] According to Giorgio Di Genova, Livio "achieves a kind of 'sacred marriage' between color signs on the one hand and earthenware forms on the other; the abstract and the concrete."[16]

Writing of Livio's organic style, Alessandro Bosi observed, "Livio was a country boy, out of his element. . . . Valentini came straight out of the Neolithic age. . . . He understands the stones, the winds, the sea and its waves. Faced with the elements, he is full of resources."[17] One does feel as though the ceramic symbols on the column should be legible, perhaps with traces from some lost Etruscan text. Of this quality Massimo Duranti wrote, "Livio created chromatic volumes that spring from his mature experience in inventing palimpsests of highly original primordial concretions."[18]

Although these symbols don't appear to be taken from any known language, many of the forms are recognizable to anyone who has studied Livio's earlier works. Livio compared the shapes in his *La principessa nel sole di Aiken* to emblems on a knight's shield and said that Aiken's trees were her sculptures. Similarly in *Orvieto Città Unita* Livio crafts an epic rising trunk of rhomboidal shapes, adorned with ceramic insignia. Some merely rise and fall like huge clay door handles while others twist in seashell fashion reminiscent of the organic elements in Livio's *Germination* series. Some figures appear as heraldic, symmetrical structures borrowed from his own vocabulary of shape and color. One recognizes the mirrored curve Livio used unconsciously in *Formella*. We instantly recall the Buchenwald fence form and detect the now-famous use of the thumbprint-like spheres. Many times in our on campus seminars we witnessed Livio forming these iconic clay balls pierced by a wooden dowel. Now they serve as huge punctuation points pinning the dimensional bands into place.

Livio glazed only some of the shapes in no apparent order. He chose dusty sky blues, marine greens, and in one case a striking metallic bronze that creates an astonishing illusion of the real copper used elsewhere. Erika Bizzarri reports that the copper rings which once gleamed brilliantly in the sun have now darkened, taking on the patina so common in outdoor sculptures. Livio's friend Fabrizio compared the dark colors to those on Etruscan bucchero pottery.

In this case Livio took yet another opportunity to meld his sculptural and painterly skills into one entity. Like *Galassia* this final Italian masterwork acts as a picto-sculpture, marking the entrance into the beloved city with colorful painted glazes intertwined with dimensional shape. *Orvieto Città Unita* offers another striking example of Livio's ability to reinvent himself, to elevate the status of arts in his community. Livio said, "Art is not exhibited to leave us passive, but art makes us argue, makes us think, whether we like it or not."[19]

The reaction in town to Livio's sculpture was very enthusiastic. Giorgio Di Genova said, "*Orvieto Città Unita,* was a gift, not only for Orvieto, but for humanity." In a similar view, mayor Stefano Cimicchi said, "it marked the end of the twentieth century and the beginning of the third millennium, a journey into the new Renaissance, the new humanism."[20]

There is one more metaphor this sculpture brings to mind. Consider the theme we have been pursuing: analyzing the ellipses of Livio's life experiences and his ever-changing periods of art. Perhaps *Orvieto Città Unita,* with its majestic wingspan, can remind us of Livio's personal quest: always rising progressively higher, reaching farther outward toward freedom only to find himself bound by one more ring of responsibility. However at the narrowest pinnacle, literally "high and strange," the rings have vanished and the Rupe, the rock, stands alone.

In March 2004 Bob Alexander, in Orvieto for his wife Leslie's exhibit at the Palazzo del Gusto, joined Livio on a visit to the ceramic studio in Deruta. Bob observed, "It was clear to me that *Galassia* had been a statement of summation of his career in painting and *Orvieto Città Unita* was to be a summation of his work in sculpture. In a sense, they speak in a metaphorical way of the great bridge of friendship between Aiken and Orvieto. Because one is in Orvieto, the other in Aiken, and yet they reach out spiritually to one another, as his spiritual contribution to both places."

He continued, "I believe we were experiencing Livio the man and Livio the artist. We were exploring in more depth his family, the people who influenced him, all the elements of his personal life. Not to be intrusive, but rather comprehensive. We sought to understand the man, his art and his message."[21] In the 2005 documentary Livio reiterated what he had said to John and Bob on several previous occasions when asked if he was afraid of death. His response was, "No!"

On July 23, 2008, Livio died in his sleep next to Flora. She woke at her regular time and reached over to rouse him only to find that his body was warm but his spirit had departed to its ultimate freedom. The next day, the *Aiken Standard* featured the headline, "Orvieto artist Valentini dies at eighty-seven."[22] The article explained that "the renowned artist had been ill for some time."

When we learned that our beloved friend had passed, we immediately began to think of ways we could commemorate the Maestro and our time together. Our memories swept us back to our last interview with him. On May 12, 2003, at the time of the unveiling of *Galassia* and his being given an honorary doctoral degree and citizenship in South Carolina, Livio joined us for a discussion of his life and art. Keith Pierce filmed while Bob Alexander guided the interview and Silvia Powledge translated. Today those comments have a very special meaning to those of us fortunate enough to have counted Livio as our friend.

Livio explained how he viewed his purpose in the many visits he made to Aiken and how important it was that our citizens had come to know him as an individual. We recall Livio saying, "An artist is known by what he represents in his work. He's known for his honesty; he's known for his wisdom."

As we came to know Livio it was his spontaneous affection and caring ways that shone through. In the final interview he called himself a "spiritual, simple, humble man who was made to choose between peace and war." It must be remembered that our encounters with Livio pre-dated the horrors of 9-11. For many of us, most especially the USCA students, the stories he shared were our most immediate contact with the world of such brutal conflict.

Livio said, "I said no to war. I said I didn't want any guns. I didn't want anything that has to do with the war." If one considers the horrors of his wartime imprisonment, deprived of sustenance and human respect, we might expect to find an overwhelming severity in Livio's work or in his relationships. Instead all of us who knew him were met with kindness every day, reminded by his example of the positive way that one can deal with this harsh and often violent world.[23]

From the Italian Renaissance comes a tale of the choices such an artist can be forced to make. We are told that Lorenzo Ghiberti (c.1378–1455) was chosen over Filippo Brunelleschi (1377–1446) to design the *Gates of Paradise* for the Baptistery of San Giovanni. Why was the one artist preferred over the other? The competition judges recognized that Ghiberti had emphasized the spiritual rather than the physical in his interpretation of Abraham's sacrifice of Isaac. By following our accounts of Livio's relationship with Aiken and USCA, we hope the reader has come to recognize the same quality in our comrade. Livio always chose to direct our eyes towards the ethereal and healing in art. His visions spoke not of doom but of rebirth, not of bitterness but of calm and hope.

On several occasions Livio expressed abundant gratitude for the generous hospitality with which he was welcomed to Aiken. He recognized that his time spent here had changed him and especially the manner of his art. Livio said, "I realized I was becoming a normal man. I needed strongly this human reality. I needed to be a man who serves other men. And here I lived this experience in an extraordinary way."

At the final interview Bob said to Livio, "The people of Aiken took you in, loved you, and the students and the faculty of the university had the great pleasure of being with you." Livio spoke so warmly of his friendship with Bob. "You, my dear friend, you keep speaking of your friendship and of the clear culture of the body, the culture of the soul, the wine which feeds the pure imagination of honesty, of the work you do. . . . It's the union of different historic times, the responsibilities of artistic representation. It's important that each artistic work represent its time, the time in which it is created. It represents history. So you and I formed an extraordinary union, which produced all this. And I will finish my life with this hope in my heart."[24]

In cultural history one defines a Renaissance man as one who has mastered multiple fields of arts or crafts. The legendary Michelangelo Buonarroti, for example, was a painter, sculptor, architect, and poet. His work was documented and celebrated in both Florence and Rome. One might use the same glowing term to discuss our friend Livio's accomplishments in so many fields. Our chapters have traced Livio's mastery of painting and printmaking as well as sculpture in both ceramic and metalwork. In the same manner, we recall that Livio shepherded cultural revolutions in two regions—the provinces of Umbria, Italy, and the southern United States. One might say that the places where Livio lived and worked often experienced a miraculous rebirth.

We often read of our great southern heritage. This idea was significantly expanded when Livio arrived in our neighborhood, both on campus and throughout the city. It is our hope that future visitors to Aiken will undertake a pilgrimage to the Etherredge Center, to pursue this newly important part of any southern heritage tour. May they pause to contemplate Livio's American arrival in *Odissea,* understand his long-term appreciation of our city in *La Principessa,* and perhaps come to share his world view, his universal spirituality, in *Galassia.* These works of art have become a permanent, priceless part of the legacy of one gentle man and have helped change forever the way our civic and educational institutions now view the concepts of war and peace, humanity and courage, spirituality and freedom.

Accompanying the authorship of this book, the university committed to install a video kiosk in the Etherredge Center to help guests and especially students come to understand Valentini's remarkable life and artistic legacy. The sources for this video include the sixty-seven DVDs of interviews and art demonstrations conducted by the Maestro both in Orvieto and in Aiken.

Giorgio Vasari, the renowned biographer of the greatest artists of the Italian Renaissance, tells us that on February 18, 1564, the divine Michelangelo died. In his extant will, "the artist left his soul to God, his body to the earth, and his goods to his nearest relatives." Michelangelo also struggled to complete a sculpture intended to mark his own grave.[25]

In remembering our Livio, one more element of dietrologia awaits us, one final puzzle to unravel. Livio, working with Alberto Satolli, designed the tombstone marking his grave. Livio was buried in the cemetery of Rocca Ripesena, since there was no ground plot available in the Orvieto cemetery. Satolli supervised the carving of an eight-inch-high travertine monument, at the center of which appears a great ceramic disk, *Magia del mare* (Magic of the Sea), glazed by Livio himself. The monument is divided into four sections. On the upper right and lower left corners, a curved wall rises above and around the ceramic circle. Are these the barriers that were so often a part of Livio's life experience? The opposite corners however, upper left and lower right, offer open access—no walls and a level plane suitable for exploration and freedom for any

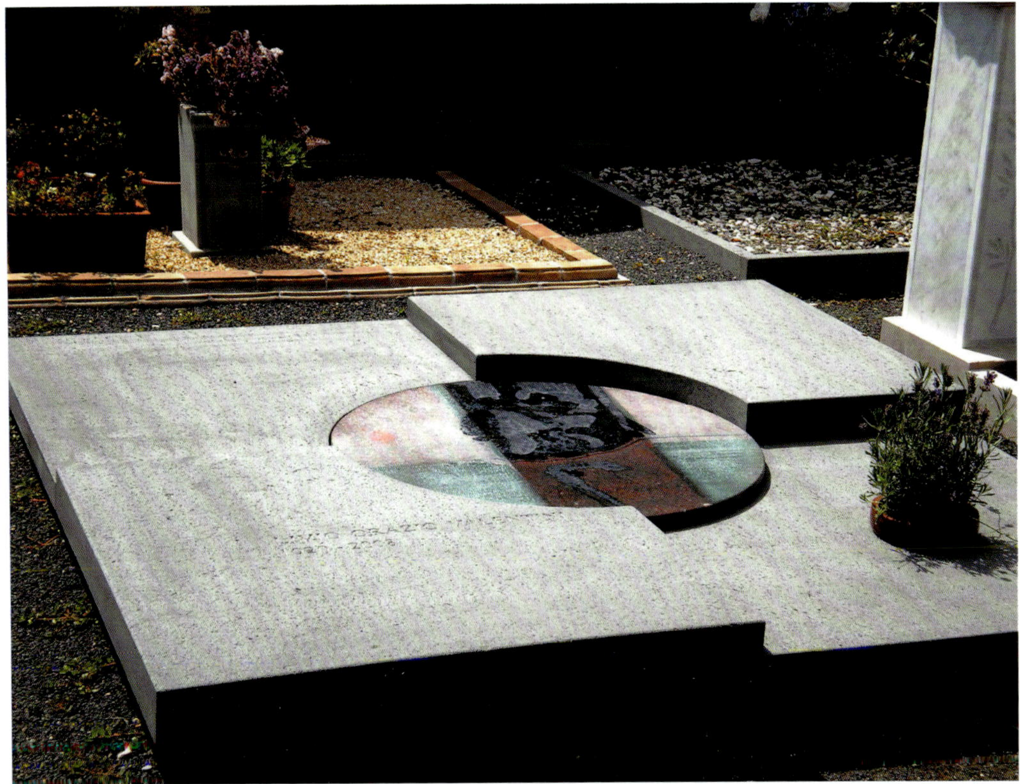

Tomb of Livio Orazio Valentini. *Magia del mare* tondo was glazed by the Maestro himself. Photograph by George Custodi.

quest. A Raku glaze punctuates the center ceramic in colors of light and shadow, washed with hues of grey, olive, and rose. These color schemes remind us of the ones he began in his *Fuga nel Quaternario* series and continued through *Orvieto Città Unita.*

This tondo, so precious because it was crafted by the Maestro himself, is reminiscent of so many other circular designs by Livio: the egg, the bird's nest, the cage of *La Palombella,* both the wretched encampment of Buchenwald and the magnificent rose window of the Duomo. Are we pursuing his symbolism too imaginatively when we notice the ceramic disk seems bisected into two distinct regions? Below on what could be a blood-soaked field, one recognizes one final time the rising arc of the electrical fence. And above in a darkened field a pale cloud of abstraction stretches forth. Surely we are not imagining within that cloud the fluttering of wings. We are inclined to remember his guardian angel, or is it simply a transcendent spirit rising in the form of a dove?

Our friend's tomb is inscribed simply, "Livio Orazio Valentini, 1920–2008." With all of life's barriers broken, Livio had ultimately, both symbolically and physically, escaped, slipped beyond that final ellipse. No longer tethered, bound to place or people or responsibility, Livio's spirit achieved the state of freedom he had so long sought, for which he had sacrificed so much.

We are so grateful to have known him and we came to view him like a member of our family. At a final gathering in Orvieto to remember Livio's career, Carlo Ponti acknowledged "dear Flora, Cristiana, Francesca, and Silvia, Livio Orazio's women who for decades surrounded him with warmth and love."[26] In the same way, we extend our great thanks to Flora and her daughters for their generous support of this project and for sharing their loving memories with us towards this research.

In an interview marking Livio's passing, former mayor Stefano Cimicchi remembered Livio as "the ambassador of art and creativity."[27] In that regard the Valentini daughters, having studied with him as young girls and found their own significant roles in the fabric of Orvieto, have established the Associazione Livio Orazio Valentini, to continue and commemorate their father's important work. When the logo for the new organization was revealed, it seemed a most appropriate choice. Borrowed from one of his paintings, the logo features the symbolic curve of the Buchenwald fence bound up to, and no doubt straining against, other forces that would serve to limit freedom.

Conclusion

In these pages we have introduced you to our great friend, Livio Orazio Valentini. Embarking on this extended dietrologia, exploring the complex challenges of his personal life and extraordinary career, we have journeyed through the elliptical dimensions of a life filled with magnanimous human spirit. We recognized that Livio spent his life reaching for, and coming to know, the divine.

As we first came to know him, Maestro Valentini was a concentration camp survivor and an active participant in Amnesty International. Carlo Ponti observed that when Livio described his captivity at Buchenwald he never called himself a "deportee or prisoner" but instead considered himself to be a "guest" in the Stalag, because he always viewed the situation as strictly temporary.[1]

To experience such a positive outlook coming from a man who had endured long hardship was a wondrous surprise, a revelation of his depth of spirit and reverent dedication to the miracle of peace. When Livio brought his vision to the Etherredge Center, none of us could have dreamt that the result would be *Galassia* in which he set out to explore "the universe of the university" as we entered the new millennium. The unexpected result features a magnificent duality of forms: both painting and sculpture; a last judgment, heavenly and terrestrial, sacred and profane. Most significantly Valentini revealed that center arena where contemporary men reside in conflict, but overhead hovers the celestial angel, herald of hope and friendship among nations.

For those who had grown up with Livio, who had matured at his side in Orvieto, the scope and depth of such an epic project should not come as a surprise. At a gathering to commemorate Livio's passing and announce the formation of the Livio Orazio Valentini Association, Ponti proclaimed, "After all, we are a stone's throw from the site of the Miracle of Bolsena, in the city of the Corpus Domini and the doves that challenge the aerial abyss of the skies. Livio knew this, in the sense that he participated emotionally, as a visionary and man of fantasy, constructor of allegories and signs, in the Babel of stigmas, in this forest of symbols that is history."[2]

Alan Graham-Collier once described Livio as "an Italian master, in the Italian tradition. . . . . 'A man for all seasons.' He restored hope to jaded souls like ourselves through his creative genius in revealing all manners of truth, all manner of beauty."[3]

We shall be forever thankful that Livio brought his same earnest emotion, his confident belief in Providence, to the university and the grateful community of Aiken. All who came to know him, care for him, and most especially learn from him recognize that his Aiken period formed a most significant spiral in his eternal search for freedom. Livio's quest for the sacred in this world went beyond what many only paid lip service to, what they did not have the courage to pursue. The unique longing for connection, for revelation, for divine inspiration, separated the Maestro from his peers. With great respect, sincere admiration, and warmest affection, we acknowledge dear Livio's humanity and the miracle of spiritual aspiration he shared with us all.

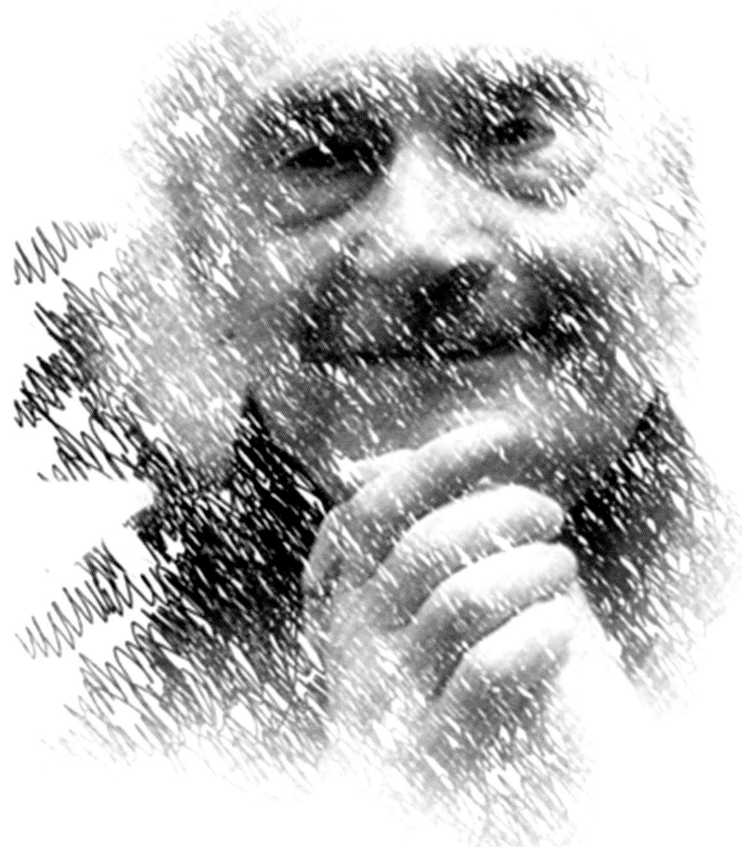

Drawing by Al Beyer after original photograph by Shelly Marshall Schmidt.

Notes

Preface

1. Robert Alexander, unpublished interview with Valeriano Venturi, 12 April 2005, Orvieto, Italy.

2. Robert Alexander, unpublished interview with Fabrizzio Trequattrini, 12 April 2005, Orvieto, Italy.

3. Arendt, *Human Condition.*

Introduction

1. Robert Alexander, unpublished interview with mayor Fred Cavanaugh, 31 July 2012, Aiken, SC.

2. Robert Alexander, unpublished interview with George Custodi, 11 September 2012, Aiken, SC.

3. Ibid.

4. Ibid.

5. Robert Alexander, unpublished interview with Livio O. Valentini, 13 May 2003, Aiken, SC, DVD.

6. Ibid.

7. Alan Graham-Collier, "Lecture on Livio Valentini's Art." 14 September 2000, Aiken, SC, DVD.

8. Livio O. Valentini, "Lecture on Printmaking," 22 October 1999, Aiken, SC, DVD.

9. Robert Alexander, unpublished interview with Livio O. Valentini, 13 May 2003, Aiken, SC, DVD.

10. Ibid.

11. "Orvieto: The City on a Plateau. http://www.famouswonders.com/orvieto-the-city-on-a-plateau (accessed 8 February 2016). Here and throughout, please be aware that Internet links in endnotes may not work correctly in all browsers.

12. Ibid.

13. Fabrizzio Galeazzi, "From Palombella to Corpus Christi," http://www.bellaumbria.net/en/events/2013-from-the-palombella-to-corpus-christi-orvieto/.html (accessed 8 February 2016).

14. "Orvieto—Brief History." http://www.mmdtkw.org/VOrvieto1.html (accessed 8 February 2016).

15. Ibid.

16. http://www.frommer's.com/destinations/orvieto/attractions/overview (accessed 8 February 2016).

17. http://www.mmdtkw.org/VOrvieto1.html (accessed 8 February 2016).

18. Ibid.

19. Smith, *Modern Italy*, 3.

20. Mammarella, *Italy after Fascism*, vi.

21. John Hooper, "In Orvieto," *The Guardian,* 28 April 2004, 1–3.

22. "Albert Kesselring," *Wikipedia: The Free Encyclopedia*, Wikimedia Foundation, Inc., (3 February 2016), 14.

23. John Hooper, "In Orvieto," *The Guardian*, 28 April 2004, 1–3.

24. Livio O. Valentini, "Ceramic Demonstrations for Lynn Pope's Art Class," 11 and 12 October 1999, Aiken, SC, DVD.

Chapter One: Livio's Early Life

1. Smith, *Modern Italy*, 271–82.

2. Livio O. Valentini, "Lecture about His Childhood," 7 November 1997, North Aiken Elementary School, SC, DVD.

3. Ibid.

4. Robert Alexander, unpublished interview with Livio and Flora Valentini, 18 May 2006, Orvieto, Italy.

5. Lo Presti, *Livio Orazio Valentini,* 99.

6. Livio O. Valentini, "Lecture on the Egg," 12 November 1997, lecture in professor Al Beyer's class, Aiken, SC, DVD.

7. Ibid.

8. Smith, *Modern Italy,* 387–97.

9. "Albert Kesselring," *Wikipedia: The Free Encyclopedia.*

10. Lo Presti, *Livio Orazio Valentini,* 6.

11. Livio O. Valentini, "Lecture on Use of Birds as Metaphor of Man's Violence against Man," 28 October 1999, Aiken, SC, DVD.

Chapter Three: Livio's Life as Seen by Others

1. Lo Presti, *Livio Orazio Valentini,* 7.

2. Robert Alexander, unpublished interview with Livio O. Valentini, 13 April 2005, Orvieto, Italy.

3. Robert Alexander, unpublished interview with Pia Custodi, 10 April 2005, Orvieto, Italy.

4. Robert Alexander, unpublished interview with Torquato Terracina, 13 April 2005, Orvieto, Italy.

5. Ibid.

6. Silvia Valentini, e-mail message to authors, 7 January 2012.

7. Robert Alexander, unpublished interview with Livio and Flora Valentini, 18 May 2006.

8. Robert Alexander and John Elliott, unpublished interview with Livio and Flora Valentini, 8 March 2004, Orvieto, Italy, DVD.

9. Maurizio Parrini, e-mail message to authors, 19 June 2006.

10. Robert Alexander, unpublished interview with Torquato Terracina, 13 April 2005, Orvieto, Italy.

11. Robert Alexander and John Elliott, unpublished interview with Livio and Flora Valentini, 8 March 2004, Orvieto, Italy, DVD.

12. Silvia Valentini and Flora Valentini, e-mail message to authors 16 February 2012.

13. Robert Alexander, unpublished interview with Laura Boletta, 6 April 2005, Orvieto, Italy.

14. Robert Alexander and John Elliott, unpublished interview with Livio and Flora Valentini, 8 March 2004, Orvieto, Italy, DVD.

15. Ibid.

16. Robert Alexander, unpublished interview with Giulio Montanucci, 7 April 2005, Orvieto, Italy.

17. Robert Alexander, unpublished interview with Vladimiro Giulietti, 16 May 2006, Orvieto, Italy.

18. Bosi, "Interview with Valentini," 83–84.

19. Robert Alexander, unpublished interview with Vladimiro Giulietti, 16 May 2006, Orvieto, Italy.

20. Robert Alexander, unpublished interview with Donato Catamo, 16 May 2006, Orvieto, Italy.

21. Robert Alexander, unpublished interview with Vladimiro Giulietti, 16 May 2006, Orvieto, Italy.

22. Robert Alexander and John Elliott, unpublished interview with Livio and Flora Valentini, 8 March 2004, Orvieto, Italy, DVD.

23. Robert Alexander, unpublished interview with Donato Catamo, 16 May 2006, Orvieto, Italy.

24. Ibid.

25. Robert Alexander and John Elliott, unpublished interview with Livio and Flora Valentini, 6 March 2004, Orvieto, Italy, DVD.

26. Robert Alexander, unpublished interview with Donato Catamo, 16 May 2006, Orvieto, Italy.

27. Robert Alexander, unpublished interview with Alberto Satolli, 5 April 2005, Orvieto, Italy.

28. Robert Alexander, unpublished interview with Donato Catamo, 16 May 2006, Orvieto, Italy.

29. Robert Alexander, unpublished interview with Marino Moretti, 18 April 2005, Viceno, Italy.

30. Livio O. Valentini, "Lecture on Use of Birds as a Metaphor of Man's Violence against Man," 28 October 1999, Aiken, SC, DVD.

31. Ibid.

32. Robert Alexander, unpublished interview with Marino Moretti, 18 April 2005, Viceno, Italy.

33. Robert Alexander, unpublished interview with Don Marcello Pettinelli, 12 April 2005, Orvieto, Italy.

34. Livio O. Valentini, "Lecture on Use of Birds as Metaphor of Man's Violence against Man," 28 October 1999, Aiken, SC, DVD.

35. Ibid.

36. Robert Alexander, unpublished interview with Flora Valentini, 5 April 2005, Orvieto, Italy.

37. Livio O. Valentini, "Lecture on Use of Birds as Metaphor of Man's Violence against Man," 28 October 1999, Aiken, SC, DVD.

38. Dates of visits: Giulia, June 2004; and Raffaele, June 2006.

39. Robert Alexander, unpublished interview with Silvia Valentini family, 13 April 2005, Orvieto, Italy.

40. *L' Alfiere del Vento: ritratto di Livio Orazio Valentini.* Directed and screenplay by Giovanni Bufalini. Parteuile, 2005. Film.

41. Cathy Marreno and Frances Causey, personal conversation with Livio and Flora Valentini, 7 March 2004, Orvieto, Italy.

Chapter Four: Periods of Valentini's Art

1. Livio O. Valentini, "Lecture on Signorelli," 19 October 1999, Aiken, SC, DVD.

2. Ibid.

3. Duranti, "Livio Orazio Valentini. An Introduction," 128.

4. Livio O. Valentini, "Lecture on Significance of Color in the Evolution of his Paintings," 14 October 1999, Aiken, SC, DVD.

5. Lo Presti, *Livio Orazio Valentini,* 8.

6. "Scuola Romana," *Wikipedia: The Free Encyclopedia.* Wikimedia Foundation, Inc., (accessed 14 April 2014) 3.

7. Livio O. Valentini, "Lecture on Significance of Color in the Evolution of his Paintings," 14 October 1999, Aiken, SC, DVD.

8. Lo Presti, *Livio Orazio Valentini,* 7.

9. "Contemporary Art in Umbria." Claudio Lattanzi, ed. http://www.umbriaonline.com/english/contemporary-art-umbria.phtml (accessed 10 March 2015).

10. Soby and Barr, *Twentieth-Century Italian Art,* 16.

11. Lo Presti, *Miscellanea,* 95.

12. Erika Bizzarri, e-mail message to authors, 24 February 2015.

13. Ibid.

14. Micacchi, Toesca, and Barlozzetti, *Valentini e il Finimondo,* 4.

15. Soby and Barr, *Twentieth-Century Italian Art,* 30.

16. Micacchi, Toesca, and Barlozzetti. *Valentini e il Finimondo,* 5.

17. "Lauda Sion." http://www.umbriaonline.com/english/contemporary-art-umbria.phtml. (accessed 8 February 2016).

18. Lo Presti, *Livio Orazio Valentini,* 36.

19. Donati, *Orvieto,* 56.

20. Butler, *Lives of the Saints,* vol. 7, 1866.

21. Toesca, "Dovuto a Valentini," 134.

22. Lo Presti, *Livio Orazio Valentini,* 60.

23. "Art Gallery: The Master Livio Orazio Valentini." http://www.orvietohotelduomo.com/en/art_gallery.html (accessed 8 February 2016).

24. Duranti and Ponti, "Livio Orazio Valentini," 128.

25. "Renato Guttuso," *Wikipedia: The Free Encyclopedia.* Wikimedia Foundation, Inc. (accessed 21 January 2016).

26. Livio O. Valentini, "Lecture on Significance of Color in the Evolution of His Paintings," 14 October 1999, Aiken, SC, DVD.

27. Ibid.

28. Silvia Valentini, e-mail message to authors, 25 March 2015.

29. Maurizio Parrini, e-mail message to authors 19 June 2006.

30. Lo Presti, *Livio Orazio Valentini,* 20.

31. Soby and Barr, *Twentieth-Century Italian Art,* 30.

32. Livio O. Valentini, "Lecture on Significance of Color in the Evolution of His Paintings," 14 October 1999, Aiken, SC, DVD.

33. David Cohen, "Alberto Burri," http://www.artcritical.com/DavidCohen/SUN-2008/0110.htm (accessed 9 February 2016).

34. Lo Presti, *Livio Orazio Valentini,* 22.

35. Robert Alexander, unpublished interview with Don Marcello Pettinelli, 12 April 2005, Orvieto, Italy.

36. "Renato Guttuso," *Wikipedia: The Free Encyclopedia.* Wikimedia Foundation, Inc. (accessed 21 January 2016).

37. "Art Gallery: The Master Livio Orazio Valentini." http://www.orvietohotelduomo.com/en/art_gallery.html (accessed 8 February 2016).

38. Robert Alexander and John Elliott, unpublished interview with Livio O. Valentini, 8 March 2004, Orvieto, Italy, DVD.

39. Ibid.

40. Livio O. Valentini, "Lecture on Significance of Color in the Evolution of His Paintings," 14 October 1999, Aiken, SC, DVD.

41. Robert Alexander and John Elliott, unpublished interview with Livio O. Valentini, 8 March 2004, Orvieto, Italy, DVD.

42. Livio O. Valentini, "Lecture on Works of Artists Including Picasso, Signorelli, and Several of His Own Works," 14 October 1999, Aiken, SC, DVD.

43. Ricordi, p. 44.

44. Livio O. Valentini, "Lecture on Works of Artists Including Picasso, Signorelli, and Several of His Own Works," 14 October 1999, Aiken, SC, DVD.

45. Lo Presti, *Livio Orazio Valentini,* 25.

46. Livio O. Valentini, "Lecture on Works of Artists Including Picasso, Signorelli, and Several of His Own Works," 14 October 1999, Aiken, SC, DVD.

47. Ibid.

48. "Art Gallery: The Master Livio Orazio Valentini." http://www.orvietohotelduomo.com/en/art_gallery.html (accessed 8 February 2016).

49. Lo Presti, *Miscellanea,* 101.

50. Lo Presti, *Livio Orazio Valentini,* 24–25.

51. Di Genova, "Livio Orazio Valentini Joie de Vivre Regained," 9.

52. Livio O. Valentini, "Lecture on Ceramic Works by Picasso and Valentini," 11 October 1999, Aiken, SC, DVD.

53. Livio O. Valentini, "Lecture on *The Massacre of Camorena* and Commission for a Grave Monument," 14 November 1997, Aiken, SC, DVD.

54. Livio O. Valentini, "Lecture on Etruscan Tomb Paintings," 14 October 1999, Aiken, SC, DVD.

55. Ibid.

56. Livio O. Valentini, "Lecture on Works of Artists Including Picasso, Signorelli, and Several of His Own Works," 14 October 1999, Aiken, SC, DVD.

57. Livio O. Valentini, "Lecture on the Birds and Experiences in Buchenwald," 28 October 1999, Aiken, SC, DVD.

58. Acts 2:1–41; Fabrizio Galeazzi, "From the Palombella to Corpus Christi," http://bellaumbria.net/en/events/2013-from-the-palombella-to-corpus-christi-orvieto/ (accessed 20 September 2017).

59. Livio O. Valentini, "Lecture to the International Club and Commission for a Grave Monument," 5 November 1997, Aiken, SC, DVD.

60. Livio O. Valentini, "Lecture on *The Massacre of Camorena* and Commission for a Grave Monument," 14 November 1997, Aiken, SC, DVD.

61. Duranti and Ponti, "Livio Orazio Valentini," 130.

62. Livio O. Valentini, "Lecture on His Art Periods: The Tonal to the Flight of the Quaternary," 1 November 1997, Aiken, SC, DVD.

63. Duranti and Ponti, "Livio Orazio Valentini," 117.

64. Livio O. Valentini, "Conducts Walkthrough Lecture on the *Odissea* Exhibit," 12 November 1997, Aiken, SC, DVD.

65. Livio O. Valentini, "Lecture on His Art Periods: The Tonal to the Flight of the Quaternary," 1 November 1997, Aiken, SC, DVD.

66. Ibid.

67. Livio O. Valentini, "Conducts Walkthrough Lecture on the *Odissea* Exhibit," 12 November 1997, Aiken, SC, DVD.

68. Graham-Collier, *Odissea Exhibit 1997–98*.

69. Livio O. Valentini, "Lecture on Works of Artists including Picasso, Signorelli, and Several of His Own Works," 14 October 1999, Aiken, SC, DVD.

70. Di Genova, *Odissea: Livio Orazio Valentini*, 10.

71. Livio O. Valentini, "Lecture Continues on Nigeria, the Signorelli series, the Etruscans, Barilla Pasta, and Germination," 14 November 1997, Aiken, SC, DVD.

72. Livio O. Valentini, "Conducts Walkthrough Lecture on the *Odissea* Exhibit," 12 November 1997, Aiken, SC, DVD.

Chapter Five: Livio and Aiken

1. Celestiel East, "Benvenuto Signore Valentini," *Pacer Times*, 5 November 1997, 4.

2. Robert Alexander, unpublished interview with Livio O. Valentini, 13 May 2003, Aiken, SC, DVD.

3. Livio O. Valentini, "Address to Town and Country," 7 October 1999, Etherredge Center, Aiken, SC, DVD.

4. Ibid.

5. Livio O. Valentini, "Lecture at Elementary School," 7 November 1997, Aiken, SC, DVD.

6. Livio O. Valentini, "Description of Periods of Art: Tonal to Flight of the Quaternary," 1 November 1997, Aiken, SC, DVD.

7. Livio O. Valentini, "The Mystery of the Bird's Imprint on the Window," 16 November 1997, Aiken, SC, DVD.

8. Livio O. Valentini, "Conducts Walkthrough Lecture on the *Odissea* Exhibit," 12 November 1997, Etherredge Center, Aiken, SC, DVD.

9. Livio O. Valentini, "Opening Remarks at *Odissea* Gala," 13 November 1997, Aiken, SC, DVD.

10. Robert Alexander, unpublished interview with Elizabeth and Rick Benton, 22 June 2012, Aiken, SC.

11. Robert Alexander, unpublished interview with Silvia Powledge, 6 November 2012, Aiken, SC.

12. Livio O. Valentini, "Address to Town and Country," 7 October 1999, Etherredge Center, Aiken, SC, DVD.

13. Ibid.

14. Ibid.

15. Personal conversation with John Elliott and Calvin Smith, 25 October 1999, Aiken, SC.

16. Personal conversation with John Elliott and Stanley Rich, 1999.

17. Personal conversation with Bob Alexander, John Elliott, and Professor Al Beyer, 27 October 1999, Aiken, SC.

18. Personal conversation with the Alexander family, 1999.

19. Robert Alexander, unpublished interview with Dorothy Ridley, 31 July 2012, Aiken, SC.

20. Personal conversation with Brad and Barbara Sue Brodie, 1999, Aiken, SC. Robert Alexander, unpublished interview with Barbara Sue Brodie, 3 October 2012, Aiken, SC.

21. Personal conversation with Sandra Field, George and Sandi Custodi, Bob and Leslie Alexander, and Livio Valentini, 2 October 1999, Columbia, SC.

22. Robert Alexander, unpublished interview with Sandy and Tony Harris, 18 September 2012, Aiken, SC.

23. Robert Alexander, unpublished interview with Joan Bondor, 24 October 2012, Aiken, SC.

24. Bosi, "Interview with Valentini," 83.

25. Livio O. Valentini, "Painting Seminar in Etherredge Center Studio," 22 October 1999, Aiken, SC, DVD.

26. Ibid.

27. Dottie Ashley, "Old Country to Low Country," *Post and Courier*, 5 June 2001, 5A, 8A.

28. Robert Alexander, unpublished interview with Joan Bondor, 24 October 2012, Aiken, SC.

29. Robert Alexander, unpublished interview with Silvia Powledge, 6 November 2012, Aiken, SC.

30. Personal conversation with Benjamin and Jerry Dell Gimarc, 7 June 2001, Spoleto Festival, Charleston, SC.

31. Robert Alexander, unpublished interview with Sandy and Tony Harris, 18 September 2012, Aiken, SC.

32. Personal conversation with Barbara Morgan, June 2001, Charleston, SC.

33. Personal conversation with Livio Valentini, Bob and Leslie Alexander, and a translator from the College of Charleston, June 2001, Fish restaurant, Charleston, SC.

34. Robert Alexander, unpublished interview with Silvia Powledge, 6 November 2012, Aiken, SC.

35. Livio O. Valentini, "Lecture on Art and Politics," 18 October 1999, Girma Negash's political science class, Aiken, SC, DVD.

36. Robert Alexander, unpublished interview with Livio O. Valentini, 14 September 2000, Aiken, SC, DVD.

37. Personal conversation with Rob Alexander, Jimmy Hartley, Thomas Coleman, George Custodi, and Livio O. Valentini, June 5, 2013.

38. Robert Alexander, unpublished interview with Joan Bondor, 24 October 2012, Aiken, SC.

39. Robert Alexander, unpublished interview with Silvia Powledge, 6 November 2012, Aiken, SC.

Chapter Six: The Story of *Galassia*

1. Livio O. Valentini, "Lecture To Aiken County High School Art Teachers," 5 May 2003, Aiken, SC, DVD.

2. Alberto Satolli, *Commemoration of Valentini's Life and Art.* Orvieto, Italy, 14 January 2012.

3. Livio O. Valentini, "Lecture to Aiken County High School Art Teachers," 5 May 2003, Aiken, SC, DVD.

4. John Elliott, unpublished interview with Professor Al Beyer, 18 January 2013, Aiken, SC.

5. Carl Dawson, personal interview with Livio O. Valentini, 19 September 2000, Aiken, SC, DVD.

6. Livio O. Valentini, "Lecture to Aiken County High School Art Teachers," 5 May 2003, Aiken, SC, DVD.

7. John Elliott, unpublished interview with Livio O. Valentini, 7 October 2000, Aiken, SC.

8. John Elliott, unpublished interview with professor Al Beyer, 18 January 2013, Aiken, SC.

9. Ibid.

10. Ibid.

11. Ibid.

12. Livio O. Valentini, "Assembling *Galassia,*" 30 April 2003, Etherredge Center Gallery, Aiken, SC, DVD.

13. Livio O. Valentini, "Conversation with Students about *Galassia,*" 30 September 2000, Aiken, SC, DVD.

14. Micacchi, Toesca, and Barlozzetti, *Valentini e il Finimondo,* 4.

15. Livio O. Valentini, "Lecture To Aiken County High School Art Teachers," 5 May 2003, Aiken, SC, DVD.

16. Livio O. Valentini, "Conversations with the Architects," 25 September 2000, Aiken, SC, DVD.

17. Robert Alexander, unpublished personal interview with Silvia Powledge, 6 November 2012, Aiken, SC.

18. Silvia Valentini, e-mail message to authors, 10 February 2014.

Chapter Seven: The Mostra and the Monuments of Orvieto

1. Livio O. Valentini, "Address to International Club," 5 November 1997, Aiken, SC, DVD.

2. Livio O. Valentini, "Lecture to Professor Al Beyer's Class," 14 November 1997, Aiken, SC, DVD.

3. Livio O. Valentini, "Lecture on the Commission for the Funeral Monument," 7 November 1997, Aiken, SC, DVD.

4. Robert Alexander, unpublished interview with Massimo Borri, 5 March 2004, Orvieto, Italy; E-mails exchanged between George Custodi and Massimo Borri concerning the exhibit.

5. Livio O. Valentini, Leslie Alexander, Al Beyer, former mayor Cimicchi, and Mayor Stefano Mocio, "Remarks at the Mostra Exhibit," 7 March 2004, Orvieto, Italy, DVD.

6. Stefano Cimicchi, *Incontro nell' arte: Aiken in Orvieto,* March 2004.

7. Massimo Duranti, "Artist in USA with Livio Orazio Valentini," *Corriere dell' Umbria.* 6 March 2004, 53.

8. Livio O. Valentini, "Meeting the Press at the Mostra," 5 March 2004. Orvieto, Italy, DVD.

9. Alessandra Cannistra, "La scultura 'alta e strana.' Valentini legge Valentini," *Lettera Orvietana* N.12, May–August 2004, 7.

10. Ibid.

11. Robert Alexander and John Elliott, unpublished interview with Livio O. Valentini, 8 March 2004, Orvieto, Italy, DVD.

12. Alessandra Cannistra, "La scultura 'alta e strana.' Valentini legge Valentini," *Lettera Orvietana*. N.12, May–August 2004, 7.

13. Ibid.

14. Ibid.

15. Robert Alexander, unpublished interview with Fabrizzio Trequattrini, 12 April 2005, Orvieto, Italy.

16. Di Genova, *Odissea: Livio Orazio Valentini,* 10.

17. Bosi, "Interview with Valentini," 79.

18. Massimo Duranti, "The Sign that Joins, *Corriere dell' Umbria,* 13 March 2004, 42.

19. Cannistra, "La scultura 'alta e strana,' Valentini legge Valentini," 7.

20. Stefano Cimicchi, "Livio Orazio Valentini and the City of Orvieto," *Orvietonews.it.* http://www.orvietonews.it/politica/2004/06/10/l-ultimo-discorso-di-cimicchi-da-sindaco-6683.html (accessed 22 March 2017).

21. Robert Alexander, unpublished interview with Livio O. Valentini, 8 March 2004, Orvieto, Italy, DVD.

22. Haley Hughes, "Orvieto Artist Valentini dies at 87," *Aiken Standard,* 24 July 2008, 1A, 10A.

23. Robert Alexander and John Elliott, unpublished interview with Livio O. Valentini, 8 March 2004, Orvieto, Italy, DVD.

24. Robert Alexander, unpublished interview with Livio O. Valentini, 13 May 2003, Aiken, SC, DVD.

25. Coughlan, *World of Michelangelo,* 179.

26. Ponti, *Commemoration of Valentini's Life and Art.* Orvieto, Italy, 14 January 2012. Erika Bizzarri, e-mail message to the authors.

27. Stefano Cimicchi, "Livio Orazio Valentini and the City of Orvieto," *Orvietonews.it.,* 2, http://www.orvietonews.it/politica/2004/06/10/l-ultimo-discorso-di-cimicchi-da-sindaco-6683.html (accessed 22 March 2017).

Conclusion

1. Ponti, *Commemoration of Valentini's Life and Art.* Orvieto, Italy, 14 January 2012. Erika Bizzarri, e-mail message to the authors.

2. Ibid.

3. Alan Graham-Collier, "Lecture on Livio Valentini's Art," 14 September 2000, Aiken, SC, DVD.

Bibliography

Books

Arendt, Hannah. *The Human Condition.* Chicago: University of Chicago Press, 1958.

Bassetti, Sandro. *Orvieto città aperta.* Milan: Lampi di stampa, 2009.

Bosi, Alessandro. "Interview with Valentini: The Philosophy of Good Sense of Valentini." In *Livio Orazio Valentini Pittore.* Pietro M. Toesca, ed. 79–91.Parma: La Nazionale, 1971.

Butler, Rev. Alban. *The Lives of the Saints.* Vol. 7. Brewster, MA: Paraclete Press, 2005.

Coughlan, Robert. *The World of Michelangelo.* Alexandria, VA: Time-Life Books, 1966.

de Blasi, Marena. *The Lady in the Palazzo: At Home in Umbria.* Chapel Hill, NC: Algonquin Books, 2001.

Donati, Roberto. *Orvieto.* Narni, Italy: Plurigraf Books, 1994.

Di Genova, Giorgio. "Livio Orazio Valentini Joie de Vivre Regained." In *Odissea: Livio Orazio Valentini.* Fabbrizio Fabbri, ed. 9–11. Perugia, Italy: EFFE Press, 1997.

Duranti, Massimo and Antonio Carlo Ponti. "Livio Orazio Valentini: An Introduction." In *Livio Orazio Valentini Opere 1970–1993.* Massimo Duranti and Antonio Carlo Ponti, eds. 11–22. Perugia: Guerra Edizioni, 1994.

Lo Presti, Aldo. *Livio Orazio Valentini, il pittore di Orvieto.* Orvieto, Italy: INTERMEDIA Edizioni, 2011.

———. *Miscellanea Orvietana 10/2014.* Orvieto, Italy: INTERMEDIA Edizioni, 2014.

Mammarella, Giuseppe. *Italy after Fascism: A Political History 1943–1965.* Notre Dame, IN: University of Notre Dame Press, 1966.

Micacchi, Dario, Pietro Toesca, and Guido Barlozzetti. *Valentini e il Finimondo di Signorelli.* Rome: Cassa di Risparmio di Orvieto, 1986.

Origo, Iris. *War in Val d'Orcia: An Italian War Diary, 1943–1944.* Boston: David R. Godine, 2010.

Satolli, Alberto. *Orvieto: New Illustrated Guide.* Translated by Graham Cotter. Città di Castello: Edimond SRL, 2001.

Smith, Denis Mack. *Modern Italy: A Political History.* Ann Arbor: University of Michigan Press, 1969.

Soby, James T., and Alfred H. Barr, Jr. *Twentieth Century Italian Art.* New York: Museum of Modern Art, 1949.

Toesca, Pietro. "Dovuto a Valentini." In *Orvieto: progetto per una città utopica.* Pietro M. Toesca, ed. 133–34. Siena: Cooperativa Nuovi Quaderni, 1985.

Valentini, Livio Orazio. *Un muro, l'eccidio degli Uccelli.* Rome: Il Punto Editrice, 1980.

Brochures

Bizzarri, Lamberto, ed. *Incontro nell'Arte: Aiken in Orvieto.* 2004.

Graham-Collier, Alan. *Odissea Exhibit 1997–98.* 1999.

Index